Gay, Lesbian, Bisexual, and Transgendered Literature

Genreflecting Advisory Series

Diana Tixier Herald, Series Editor

Gay, Lesbian, Bisexual, and Transgendered Literature

A Genre Guide

Ellen Bosman and John P. Bradford

Edited by Robert B. Ridinger

Genreflecting Advisory Series
Diana Tixier Herald, Series Editor

LIBRARIES
UNLIMITED
A Member of the Greenwood Publishing Group
Westport, Connecticut • London

Library of Congress Cataloging-in-Publication Data

Bosman, Ellen.
  Gay, lesbian, bisexual, and transgendered literature : a genre guide / Ellen Bosman
and John P. Bradford ; edited by Robert B. Marks Ridinger.
      p. cm. — (Genreflecting advisory series)
  Includes bibliographical references and indexes.
  ISBN 978-1-59158-194-9 (alk. paper)
  1. Gays' writings, American—Bibliography. 2. Gays' writings—Bibliography.
3. American fiction—20th century—Bibliography. 4. Homosexuals—Fiction—Bibliography.
5. Homosexuality and literature—History—20th century. 6. Sexual minorities in literature.
7. Gays in literature. 8. Readers' advisory services—United States. 9. Libraries and sexual
minorities—United States. 10. Fiction in libraries—United States. I. Bradford, John P. II.
Ridinger, Robert B. Marks, 1951- III. Title.
  Z1229.G25B67   2008
  [PS153.G38]
  016.8108'0920664—dc22   2007049022

British Library Cataloguing in Publication Data is available.

Library of Congress Catalog Card Number: 2007049022
ISBN: 978-1-59158-194-9

First published in 2008

Libraries Unlimited, 88 Post Road West, Westport, CT 06881
A Member of the Greenwood Publishing Group, Inc.
www.lu.com

Printed in the United States of America

The paper used in this book complies with the
Permanent Paper Standard issued by the National
Information Standards Organization (Z39.48–1984).

10 9 8 7 6 5 4 3 2 1

In memory of

Barbara Gittings (1932–2007)
and
Israel Fishman (1938–2006)

for their unparalleled courage and commitment to gay and
lesbian readers and literature

Contents

Acknowledgments

Many thanks to my coauthors and editor, Barbara Ittner, for their commitment, persistence, valuable contributions, and suggestions throughout this project, and to Louis Lang for his hard work on the database; to mom for taking me to the library as a child and setting me on a career path; and to Teresa for her unfailing patience, love, and support.—Ellen Bosman

To Louis Lang, for creating, maintaining, and troubleshooting the database we used to hold all this together, and Barbara Ittner, for her editorial midwifery.—John P. Bradford

I would like to acknowledge the advice and support of Michael Cienfuegos of the Chicago Public Library for his help in navigating the sea of popular GLBT literature in the preparation of this book . . . and to thank John Bradford for the invitation to participate in this project.—Robert B. Ridinger

Part 1

Introduction to GLBT Readers' Advisory Service

Chapter 1

Introduction

Perhaps the most significant feature of the existing gay, lesbian, bisexual, and transgender (GLBT) reference and bibliographical works is their intended audience —young persons. There is no reference work geared toward the adult GLBT reader. Of course, there are a few topical publications that may be of interest to adults, but only if those adults are interested in the designated topics, for example, science fiction, periodical articles, or pulp fiction. The adult GLBT reader simply looking for "something good to read," or the librarian trying to assist such a reader, has no readers' advisory tool. By providing guidance to adult GLBT literature, this volume completes a gap in general reference literature, as well as in GLBT adult literature.

This volume aims to provide the reader and librarian with an introduction to twentieth-century GLBT literature. For the purposes of this volume, GLBT literature is defined as that written by GLBT authors, or with GLBT protagonists or themes. GLBT literature is often published by a GLBT press or imprint.

The forms of literature examined include fiction, biography, and drama. General nonfiction titles and scholarly works are not included. Simply by the sheer number of titles available, fiction dominates. The book is further divided into chapters based on popular genres, such as mystery, romance, and historical novel, as well as overriding themes (e.g., coming out and AIDs) and literary forms and formats (e.g., drama and graphic novels). This categorization is meant to help readers and readers' advisors find recreational reading suggestions and to help collection development specialists balance and grow their collections.

Selection Criteria

Because the number of titles in this area is vast, the guide focuses on the best and most popular literature available in each genre, theme, and format. The majority of the works cited are GLBT literary award winners. In many cases, the best literature may not be the most popular among readers, so the authors utilized several additional resources to identify non-award-winning titles with demonstrated reader popularity. The results include titles by major publishers/imprints, small presses, and those specializing in GLBT literature. With these principles in mind, the following criteria were applied, in order of importance:

- **Award status:** The first criterion for inclusion is quality, as determined by an award committee. With few exceptions, notably in the classics and biography chapters, all entries have either won or been shortlisted for one of the following American GLBT book awards: Ferro-Grumley Award, Firecracker Alternative Book Award, *Foreward Magazine* Book Award, Gaylactic Spectrum Award, Goldie Award, IPPY Award, Lambda Literary Award, Publishing Triangle Book Award, Stonewall Book Award, and James Tiptree, Jr. Award. The emphasis on GLBT book awards rather than other awards, such as the National Book Award or the Pulitzer Prize, is deliberate. Although many GLBT authors or works with GLBT content have won prestigious national and international awards, our emphasis is on titles contributing to the GLBT literary canon.

- **GLBT content:** All entries have GLBT themes, characters, or settings. Novels with incidental and minor GLBT characters or themes are for the most part not covered by this guide, unless they have received one of the GLBT awards.

- **Availability:** Although titles that have received awards are included without having to meet any other criteria, the titles selected for inclusion in the classic fiction and biography chapters must be in print according to *Books in Print* or be held by at least thirty libraries according to OCLC's WorldCat.

- **Publishing date:** Most works have imprint dates after 1969, although in the classic fiction chapter the works may predate the nineteenth century. Because more GLBT titles have been published in recent decades, newer publications outweigh older works. The most recent American hardcover is used for the publisher and publication date citation, unless a hardcover was never published or is out-of-print, in which case the paperback is used. Titles in the classic fiction chapter also include the first date of American publication in parentheses.

- **Language:** Only English-language publications are included. Some works written in foreign languages and translated into English are covered.

- **Age appropriateness:** The titles selected are appropriate for adult readers. However, titles of interest to young adults, either because of subject matter or reading level, are indicated with the symbol **Teen** for "Teen."

- **Diversity:** Every attempt has been made to balance GLBT content and include works reflecting cultural and racial diversity.

Compilation Procedure

Following the selection criteria listed above, several search strategies were employed. First, lists of award winners were consulted to identify the best titles within genres. These lists were readily available via the Internet, and gaps in the information were filled by consulting *Books in Print* for information about awards.

Because the purpose of this work is to provide a general reading guide to adult GLBT fiction and assist librarians in providing readers advisory services, nonfiction award winners and scholarly works of biography, autobiography, and memoir were excluded even if they had received one of the GLBT awards. In addition, a small number of titles were disqualified because they lacked clear GLBT content, characters, or plot. Readers and librarians wishing to find complete lists of award winners should consult the Web sites cited in the bibliography.

After titles were selected for inclusion, a database was developed to include pertinent bibliographic data. The authors read or examined the books. If a book was not available for examination, at least two book reviews were consulted to verify the presence of GLBT content. A short descriptive summary was then prepared for each title. Included for each title are

- a bibliographic citation (author, title, publisher, year of publication);
- an annotation (a brief plot summary);
- interest indicators—
    - **G** = gay
    - **L** = lesbian
    - **B** = bisexual
    - **T** = transgendered, transsexual, transvestite, hermaphrodite, inter-sexed
    - **Teen**
- awards received (🏵 at the beginning of an entry indicates that the title is an award winner);
- subject headings (including series notations where applicable); and
- read-alikes.

An analysis of GLBT literature involves examining a broad range of literature directed at a specific population. Every genre represented in the larger world of literature is mirrored in GLBT literature. However, GLBT literature differs because it is often developed for and marketed to a specific subset of the larger population, namely gay, lesbian, bisexual, or transgendered readers. Although it may seem adequate to apply the term "GLBT literature" to these works, it is important to remember that the GLBT population is as diverse as any other segment of the population, and such a simplistic approach would be insufficient to assist readers who may be seeking only a specific subset of the genre, such as lesbian mysteries or biographies of transgendered persons. Recognizing the unique subsets in GLBT literature (e.g., genres, themes, and formats) and acknowledging that readers may elect to read within a narrowly defined area, the authors have provided interest indicators. The interest indicator allows users to identify the potential audience for a given work. The indicator is based on the sexual or gender orientation or identity of the main characters of each title, rather than upon that of the author. Titles with multiple representations of sexual or gender orientation or identity have more than one indicator.

The assignment of an interest indicator is admittedly based on subjective interpretations; however, in the larger context, the distinction between sexual orientation and gender identity is also subject to individual interpretation, as well as laden with sociocultural, linguistic, and political meaning. It is beyond the scope of this work to address these issues, but for the purpose of this book and the convenience of readers, the authors opted to collapse the distinctions among gender identity, gender orientation, sexual orientation, and sexual identity. This decision is particularly evident in relation to titles with an interest level indicator of **T**, which groups transgendered, transsexual, transvestites, hermaphrodites, and the intersexed into a single indicator.

The **Teen** indicator permits users to locate titles appealing to younger audiences. Determining teen interest involved consulting review sources and assessing reading level, characterization, and plot.

Subject headings provide greater access to the material than could be adequately conveyed in a brief summary. Each title features a minimum of one subject, although three to five headings are more common. The subjects are represented in the subject index, along with logically related cross references. Assigning subject categories was based on reading the titles and sometimes consulting reviews. Occasionally the authors also consulted outside sources, such as OCLC's WorldCat, for subject heading suggestions.

Works similar in appeal, theme, subject matter, or writing style are designated as "read-alikes." In the chapters dealing with genres, such as mystery, the entries serve as read-alikes to each other, and thus the authors have not repeated an entry as a read-alike within the same chapter. Occasionally GLBT-friendly titles, or those titles with not enough GLBT content to qualify as main entries, are listed as read-alikes. This is particularly the case in a series where only one or two books have appreciable GLBT content. When corresponding read-alikes were not known, no entry is provided. The authors did not necessarily read the titles suggested as read-alikes, nor are they necessarily covered in this volume; however, they generally do qualify as GLBT literature.

GLBT-related titles in a series are listed under that series title. A separate entry for the series title appears in the title index. Titles in a series that did not contain GLBT content are excluded from this book.

Organization

Chapters are organized according to popular genres, formats, and reading interests, including "General Fiction," "Drama," and "Life Stories," and further arranged by subgenre and theme. This approach groups titles with similar appeal together, which assists with the location of "read-alikes." Two chapters, "Coming Out" and "HIV/AIDS and Other Health Issues," represent two significant themes in GLBT literature that warrant their own chapters, although most titles therein qualify as "general fiction."

Is This a Genre?

Much debate surrounds the question of what constitutes GLBT literature. Is a work considered GLBT literature simply because the author identifies as a member of the GLBT community? Are there definable characteristics that make it qualify as a genre? Or is it simply a theme or reading interest?

Many theorists argue that readers bring personal experiences, beliefs, and perceptions to the act of reading. As a result, reading is a very individualized act, subject to personal interpretations. What one reader sees as GLBT literature, another may not. This principle certainly applies to GLBT literature, because for decades homosexual themes and characters were denigrated, parodied, or portrayed in a subtle, socially acceptable manner, forcing GLBT readers to read between the lines.

GLBT literature exhibits the same characteristics that all other literature does, but what distinguishes it are sexual and gender orientation or identity and voice. The authors assert that this identity is so central to the literature that it qualifies these works as a genre. But whether you consider it a genre, a reading interest, or a theme, it is a body of literature well worth consideration. Chapter 2, a brief history of GLBT literature, provides context for this body of literature. Chapter 3 is devoted to addressing the needs of GLBT readers.

1

2

3

4

5

6

7

8

Chapter 2

History of Gay and Lesbian Literature

Introduction

Though often overlooked, condemned, or hidden, literature with same-sex themes has been available for many centuries. Early Greek myths contain references to gender morphing gods, and the surviving fragments of Sappho's poetry are considered the first written evidence of same-sex literature.

In the centuries since then, same-sex literature was stigmatized as the "love that dare not speak its name." Likewise, the literature dared not exist and resorted to coded inferences of desire and attraction. Intense friendships and "Boston marriages," defined as "romantic unions between women that were usually monogamous but not necessarily sexual,"[1] are inferred examples of same-sex love.

The first contemporary novel with homosexual content marketed to the general population appeared in 1889, when Alfred J. Cohen published *A Marriage Below Zero* as a warning to young women who might unwittingly marry a homosexual. Although representing a negative motivation for publishing GLBT literature, Cohen's work is significant as the first fictional treatment of homosexuality, as well as the first purely American gay novel in terms of setting, characters, and publication.

The Turning Point

Until the end of the Second World War, medical books and journals remained the primary venue for information about homosexuality. The wall of silence surrounding homosexuality began to crumble with the changing moral values and gender roles brought about by two world conflicts. Prior to that war, many Americans possessed a superficial knowledge of homosexuality, but one book, published three years after the war, greatly enhanced the public's awareness of homosexuality.

Alfred Kinsey's 1948 publication *Sexual Behavior in the Human Male* was devoured by the public, even achieving best-seller status. No doubt the public approached *Sexual Behavior* unaware of its homosexual content, but soon found a scientific reference point to replace haphazardly acquired homosexual stereotypes. Kinsey's work initiated a public dialogue about sex and sexuality, and publishers realized a market for sexually themed materials.

Although Kinsey's work became a foundation for the future sexual revolution, the hysteria of the McCarthy era quickly silenced homosexual writers. Homosexual novels were produced during the 1950s, but these were mainly poor-quality, dime store novels. Popular among the dime store crowd were Ann Bannon, Vin Packer (nom de plume of M. E. Kerr), Claire Morgan (pseudonym for Patricia Highsmith), Valerie Taylor, Tereska Torres, Gale Wilhelm, and Miriam Gardner (aka Marion Zimmer Bradley). Serious efforts, such as James Baldwin's *Giovanni's Room*, faced a mixed reception. The publication of nonfiction works with GLBT themes also suffered during this period. For example, librarian Jeannette H. Foster self-published her exploration of lesbian literature, *Sex Variant Women in Literature*, because no publisher in 1956 was willing to take the risk.

Periodicals were the one bright spot for GLBT literature during the McCarthy era. An unknown lesbian writing under a pseudonym began *Vice Versa* in 1947. This early effort was narrow in scope; distributed locally; and limited in content to unsigned articles, short stories, and review items. Nevertheless, as Roger Streitmatter noted in *Unspeakable: The Rise of the Gay and Lesbian Press in America*, the publication represented a new venue.[2]

The early success of GLBT literature is directly related to the formation of "homophile" organizations. Derived from Latin, *homophile*, meaning love of the same, was adopted by early GLBT civil rights organizations because the term seemed more palatable to society than "homosexual." Homophile groups, such as the Mattachine Society and the Daughters of Bilitis, served dual functions, acting as a social venue and advocate for GLBT rights. A group called ONE Incorporated, a subset of the Mattachine Society, published the journal *ONE* from 1953 to 1968, and the Daughters of Bilitis launched *The Ladder* in October 1956. *ONE* adopted an outspoken style and highlighted the various injustices and civil rights violations suffered by the GLBT community. In contrast, *The Ladder* summarized lesbian-related literature and became a vehicle for original poetry, short stories, and fiction. According to Streitmatter, the importance of these publications cannot be overestimated because they "advanced beyond *Vice Versa* in several crucial respects. They were distributed nationally. They withstood attacks by the U.S. Senate, postal officials, and the FBI to win the legal right for gay-oriented materials to be sent through the mail. They also achieved longevity: each of the three journals published for more than a dozen years."[3] These publications established the template for future magazines and ensured the continuation of GLBT magazines and newspapers as vital information resources for the increasingly visible community.

The 1960s–1970s

The social unrest of the 1960s and the subsequent Stonewall Riots, a series of violent confrontations between New York City police and GLBT bar patrons in June 1969, began a transitional period for GLBT literature in all formats. The GLBT literature produced during this decade was characterized by improved quality and increased production, visibility, and availability. Although the proliferation of lurid dime store novels persisted, serious literature, such as the novels of Christopher Isherwood and

Jane Rule, began painting a positive, unapologetic view of homosexuals. Three Isherwood novels of the period feature homosexual characters and equate homosexuals to heterosexuals. This period also saw the dawning of GLBT literature targeted to a young adult audience, with the publication of *I'll Get There It Better Be Worth the Trip,* by John Donovan (1969).

In addition to the changing scope of the genre, production of GLBT-themed literature increased. Consulting the OCLC bibliographic database for English-language GLBT fiction published between 1950 and 1959 results in 72 titles, but the same search for 1960–1969 results in 259 titles (excluding erotica), nearly a fivefold increase. Although an imperfect measure because it relies on libraries' reported ownership of items, such a search provides some indication of the growing production of the genre.

By the 1970s, approximately 255 English-language GLBT fiction titles were available, excluding erotica. Now that GLBT literature was out of the closet, reprints of classics such as E. M. Forster's *Maurice,* André Gide's *The Counterfeiters,* and Genet's *Querelle* proliferated. The first decade in which authors could openly publish GLBT-themed works without fear of reprisals saw the authorial debuts of many writers of enduring popularity, including Felice Picano, Edmund White, Larry Kramer, Armistead Maupin, Patricia Nell Warren, and Rita Mae Brown. The growth in young adult literature was slower, with only a handful of titles published during the decade, but this period saw the emergence of Isabelle Holland's *The Man without a Face* (1970), Sandra Scoppettone's *Trying Hard to Hear You* (1974) and *Happy Endings Are All Alike* (1978), Rosa Guy's *Ruby* (1976), and Mary W. Sullivan's *What's This About, Pete?* (1976)

It was also during this period that the first scholarly periodicals began to appear. *The Journal of Homosexuality,* founded in 1974, was the first to focus on homosexuality and the first periodical solely devoted to reviewing GLBT books. *Gay Books Bulletin/Cabirion* was established in 1979. The launching of both titles is indicative of changing attitudes toward homosexuality. That both titles began under the auspices of the Scholarship Committee of the New York Chapter of the Gay Academic Union indicates that academia saw homosexuality as a legitimate research area, and a book review periodical signaled the growing availability of GLBT publications.

The Dark Years

During the 1980s GLBT fiction became far more available. An analysis of titles utilizing the *Books in Print* (BIP) database reveals 206 unique titles published between 1980 and 1989. Several classics were reprinted, including Radclyffe Hall's *Well of Loneliness,* Ann Bannon's Beebo Brinker series, and John Rechy's *City of Night.* The Dave Brandstetter mysteries by Joseph Hansen proved popular, with nine titles in the series issued, while Katherine V. Forrest produced six new titles, including three titles for the Kate Delafield mystery series. Bursting onto the GLBT literary scene during this period were Dorothy Allison, Christopher Bram, David Leavitt, Michael Nava, and Sarah Schulman.

The AIDS epidemic emerged in the 1980s, and the subject dominated the literature for the next decade, proving a double-edged sword for the literary arts. Although AIDS simultaneously robbed the community of beloved writers, such as Reinaldo Arenas, Melvin Dixon, Robert Ferro, David B. Feinberg, Essex Hemphill, Paul Monette, and Randy Shilts, these same writers produced some of their best works in their last years: Monette's *Borrowed Time, Halfway Home,* and *Becoming a Man;* Feinberg's *Eighty-Sixed;* and Hemphill's *Gay Men's Anthologies* and *Ceremonies* were all award winners.

The preferred literary form for GLBT writers during this dark period was biography and personal narrative as a means to memorialize the self and loved ones. Returning to OCLC to ascertain the availability of literature reveals 168 uniquely titled AIDS narratives published between 1984 and 1999, or an average of approximately one title per month. Production of AIDS memoirs peaked in 1997, with the appearance of twenty-six titles in a twelve-month period.

Fictionalizing and dramatizing the AIDS crisis was equally popular during the same period. A search of *Books in Print* for 1984–1999 reveals approximately 100 unique fiction titles concerning AIDS. The number of plays on the subject is more difficult to gauge because many plays are not released as monographs. Notable dramatic pieces about AIDS include Terrence McNally's *Lips Together, Teeth Apart* (1991), William Finn's *Falsettoland* (1990), and Larry Kramer's *The Normal Heart* (1985) and *The Destiny of Me* (1992). Other plays are more recognizable in their cinematic form, such as McNally's *Love! Valour! Compassion!,* Jonathan Larson's *Rent,* Paul Rudnick's *Jeffrey,* and Tony Kushner's epic *Angels in America,* originally a seven-hour stage production.

Political polemics against ineffectual government management of the disease and society's rejection of the gay population were also common and include Dennis Altman's groundbreaking *AIDS in the Mind of America* (1986), Randy Shilts's award-winning *And the Band Played On* (1987), Douglas Crimp's *AIDS: Cultural Analysis/Cultural Activism* (1988), and Larry Kramer's *Reports from the Holocaust* (1989).

AIDS literature for young adults developed slowly. The relatively early appearance of M. E. Kerr's *Night Kites* (1986) signaled the first attempt to openly address AIDS for a juvenile audience. Over the next decade, fewer than one AIDS-themed book per year appeared for this audience. Although AIDS literature for the young adult audience was uncommon throughout much of the 1980s, the availability of GLBT literature for young people was expanding and attracting unwelcome attention in the form of frequent censorship challenges. Nancy Garden's *Annie on My Mind* (1982) and Lesléa Newman's *Heather Has Two Mommies* (1989) are the decade's most recognizable victims of attempted book banning.

Contemporary Literature

As the AIDS crisis dissipated in the United States due to the development of new treatments and medications, the GLBT community turned its attention to securing equal political rights and protections. Andrew Sullivan, Urvashi Vaid, and Michelangelo Signorile published passionate discourses arguing for equal civil rights for homosexuals. On the cusp of the twenty-first century, well-established novelists such as Edmund White, Michael Cunningham, Christopher Bram, Dorothy Allison, Andrew Holleran, Armistead Maupin, Sarah Schulman, Katherine V. Forrest, and Felice Picano continued to be popular. Leading GLBT authors in the new millennium include newcomers such as Christopher Rice, Sarah Waters, Lucy Jane Bledsoe, Emma Donoghue, Brian Malloy, Eileen Myles, Amber Hollibaugh, Michelle Tea, Ivan E. Coyote, Stacey D'Erasmo, and Mack Friedman.

It is impossible in a work such as this to explore the history of GLBT literature in depth. Fortunately, this history is well documented in other sources, two of which have been mentioned here (Foster, Streitmatter), as well as Roger Austen's *Playing the Game: The Homosexual Novel in America* (Bobbs-Merrill, 1977), Terry Castle's *The Literature of Lesbianism: A Historical Anthology from Ariosto to Stonewall* (Columbia University, 2003), and Claude J. Summers's *The Gay and Lesbian Literary Heritage: A Reader's Companion to the Writers and Their Works, from Antiquity to the Present* (Routledge, 2002). Consult the bibliography for additional recommendations.

Availability

In the United States prior to 1969 the availability of GLBT literature was severely limited. Readers seeking nonscientific books with unambiguous homosexual content would be fortunate to discover a self-published volume or to stumble upon an imprint from one of the few private publishers catering to GLBT audiences. Materials were not advertised through standard means and were usually only available via subscription and were subsequently passed around among friends, or as David Leavitt and Mark Mitchell note, as "pages passed from hand to hand."[4]

Today as in the past, determining the exact availability of GLBT titles is difficult. Bibliographies are one possible source for locating the early literature. The production of a bibliography assumes that enough literature exists on a topic to warrant gathering the material together.

In Europe, particularly Germany and the Netherlands, bibliographies of gay literature were published in the early twentieth century; however, the earliest English-language, American bibliographies appeared in the 1950s. The first list was compiled by famed science fiction writer Marion Zimmer Bradley in 1958 and continued through 1962.

Such lists were underground publications, often typewritten and mimeographed, and were not widely available. Notable exceptions include Jeannette H. Foster's aforementioned work and the 1959 publication *The Homosexual in Literature: A Chronological Bibliography, circa 700 B.C.–1958*, by Noel I Garde, reputedly a pseudonym for Edgar Leoni. By the mid-1960s GLBT authors were still utilizing pen names to hide their identities, but it was safe to use the words *lesbian, gay,* and *homosexual* in print. Such was the case in 1967, when Gene Damon, an alias for Barbara Grier, published "The Lesbian in Literature" in the Daughters of Bilitis newsletter *The Ladder*. Although the situation had generally improved for GLBT publications, the continued use of pseudonyms and the limited availability of such bibliographies are clear evidence of society's continued marginalization of GLBT persons and literature.

Consulting bibliographic databases such as OCLC is another approach to identifying the availability of GLBT literature. Unfortunately, this method relies on reported library ownership and the consistent use of subject headings. Duplication of cataloging records may inflate availability, further demonstrating the difficulty of relying on bibliographic utilities for genre analysis. For example, a search of OCLC's WorldCat using the keywords lesbian, gay, and homosexual confined to the subject field was undertaken. Identifying fiction works published between 1900 and 1969 resulted in 414 hits. The dates of several novels were not noted, but the earliest definitively dated work was Rosamond Lehmann's 1927 novel of unrequited teenage love, *Dusty Answer*.

Measures of Success

The rise of GLBT literature in such a remarkably short period of time (from 1969 to the present) deserves a brief analysis. What contributed to the rise of the genre? What benchmarks are useful to establish the history of the genre and demonstrate its success? What measures predict its future? The primary factor contributing to the rise of the genre was the increasing visibility of GLBT persons, coupled with society's changing attitudes toward sexuality. As a historical development and social trend, GLBT literature can be measured by the rise and fall of publishing houses, book and reading clubs, and bookstores; the development of professional organizations related to reading and publishing; and literary awards and conferences.

Advent of GLBT publishers

Early publishing efforts in the form of periodicals produced by private individuals and early homophile groups have already been discussed. The emergence of GLBT presses can be attributed to GLBT novelists, such as June Arnold, Bertha Harris, and Felice Picano, looking for avenues through which to publish their own works. Lesbians led the effort; in 1973, Arnold, Harris, Parke Bowman, and Charlotte Bunch established Daughters Inc. In addition to issuing works by the founding partners, the press published Rita Mae Brown's now-classic *Rubyfruit Jungle* (1973); Blanche McCrary Boyd's first novel, *Nerves* (1973); and Elana Nachman's *Riverfinger Women* (1974). The press closed in 1978.

Naiad Press represents sustained success among women-led presses. Life partners Barbara Grier and Donna McBride established the press in 1973 with financial support from Sarah Aldridge. Intended "to free lesbian literature from the monopoly of the large publishers," Naiad issued fiction and nonfiction "to make sure that someday, any woman, any place, can recognize her lesbianism and be able to walk into a bookstore and pick up a book that says to her: 'Yes, you are a lesbian and you are wonderful'."[5]

Naiad's first publication was Aldridge's *Latecomer*. Its long list of significant publications includes Ann Allen Shockley's *The Black and White of It* (1980), J. R. Robert's award-winning *Black Lesbians: An Annotated Bibliography* (1981), *Curious Wine* by Katherine V. Forrest (1983), and *Lesbian Nuns Breaking Silence* (1985). Reviving interest in long-lost lesbian classics expanded Naiad's title list with Jeannette H. Foster's *Sex Variant Women in Literature*, Gale Wilhelm's *Torchlight to Valhalla* and *We Too Are Drifting*, Claire Morgan's *The Price of Salt*, and Jane Rule's *Desert of the Heart*. Naiad's success continued for thirty-one years, until Grier and McBride retired and turned over their title list to Bella Books in 2004.

Gay Sunshine Press, based in San Francisco since the mid-1970s, was an outgrowth of the newspaper of the same name and focused mainly on locating and translating gay and lesbian writings from Latin America under the direction of Winston Leyland. This foreshadowed the development of Latino GLBT literature, with the notable collections *Now the Volcano: An Anthology of Latin American Gay Literature* (1979) and *My Deep Dark Pain Is Love* (1983.)

On the East Coast, author Felice Picano is credited with founding New York's first gay publishing house, SeaHorse Press, in 1977. SeaHorse did not enjoy long-term success, but merged with other small presses to form Gay Presses of New York, which went on to publish Dennis Cooper, Martin Duberman, Harvey Fierstein, Brad Gooch, and Doric Wilson.

A more enduring venture, Alyson Publications, was founded in 1980 by Sasha Alyson, who also authored the press's first book, *Young, Gay and Proud!* Early in the company's history, Alyson became the North American distributor for British-based Gay Men's Press (GMP), a successful partnership that brought otherwise overlooked European GLBT books, such as Heinz Heger's *Men with the Pink Triangle*, to American readers. The establishment of the Alyson Wonderland imprint in 1990 marked a revolutionary moment in GLBT publishing—the first GLBT imprint specifically aimed at the juvenile market. Alyson is responsible for producing groundbreaking works such as Lesléa Newman's *Heather Has Two Mommies* (1989) and Michael Willhoite's *Daddy's Roommate* (1990).

In 1995 Alyson Publications was sold to Liberation Publications Inc., which owns the *Advocate* magazine, and two new imprints were created: Alyson Books and Advocate Books. The partnership appears healthy, with approximately 20 new releases each year and 200 books in print.[6]

Following in the tradition established by Naiad Press, more publishing houses appeared in the latter half of the twentieth century, devoting their attention to lesbian writers and their works and feminist publishing in general. Among these are Spinsters Ink, Cleis Press, Firebrand Books (publisher of Alison Bechdel's immensely popular Dykes to Watch Out For series); New Victoria Publishers, based in Norwich, Vermont; and most recently Washington D.C.'s Redbone, which specializes in works dealing with lesbians of color. Rising Tide Press, an independent publishing house in Huntington Station, New York, also issued lesbian mysteries and fiction between 1992 and 2002.

Also important in the emergence of twenty-first-century queer writing is Soft Skull Press, an independent house created in 1992 and based in Brooklyn, which has produced an impressive line of cutting-edge novels, poetry, criticism, and commentary. Another New York-based press, Kensington Books, publishes works featuring gay men (the New Orleans–based Scott Bradley mystery series by Greg Herren is an example) and some lesbian titles, although male-oriented titles predominate. GLB Publishing, founded in 1990 by Bill Warner, has been a pioneer in electronic publishing, making titles available for download in up to eight different formats.

The development of GLBT imprints by mainstream American presses signals the growing assimilation of the genre. Among the mainstream houses that have developed GLBT lines is Haworth Press, which has the Harrington Park Press imprint. For a time Crossing Press carried a notable gay and lesbian series of works, and beginning in 1986 New York's St. Martin's Press produced forty-eight titles, both fiction and nonfiction, in its Stonewall Inn Editions series (discontinued in 2002).

Some university presses have developed gay and lesbian book series, notably the University of Wisconsin's Living Out series and the University of Chicago's Worlds of Desire Series on sexuality, gender, and culture. The Feminist Press at The City University of New York has reissued some classic lesbian novels, such as Ann Aldrich's *We Too Must Love,* while New York University Press sponsored the Cutting Edge: Lesbian Life and Literature Series from 1992 to 2001.

Outside the United States, the Gay Men's Press (GMP) ceased operations in 2006, but other notable sources of gay and lesbian books are the British house Millivres Prowler Group (a blending of the older Millivres Limited and Prowler Press in 1999) and Wayward Books (also British), which publishes gay fiction from new authors. Absolute Press (Bath, England) published the Outlines Series from 1997 to 2002. The series focused on famous people in the arts, including Benjamin Britten, David Bowie, k.d. lang, Somerset Maugham, and Armistead Maupin.

Book and Reading Clubs

Book and reading clubs are often connected to bookstores, but prior to the rise of GLBT bookstores, private individuals attempted to connect the GLBT community to relevant reading material. One of the earliest commercial book clubs for a GLBT audience was the Cory Book Service, a subscription service created in 1952 by Edward Sagarin, whose pen name was Donald Webster Cory. The Service was small and short-lived, but it proved there was an audience for gay-themed books.

The imprimatur of a book club no longer carries the cachet enjoyed in the past, yet the demand for GLBT book clubs and reading groups persists. GLBT reading groups are often sponsored by bookstores, including commercial bookstores such as Borders™ and Barnes and Noble™, and by GLBT libraries, such as the Gerber/Hart.

The advent of the Internet allows readers in remote areas to share the reading experience with others via online reading groups and clubs, such as Lavender Salon Reader Online and the InsightOut Book Club™, which also facilitates the purchase of GLBT literature.

Rise of GLBT Bookstores

The rise of GLBT bookstores is further evidence of the success of GLBT literature. The first GLBT bookstore, the Oscar Wilde Bookstore, opened in 1967 under the proprietorship of Craig Rodwell. A small stock of books and periodicals, including a new periodical entitled *The Advocate,* filled the New York City–based store. The *Advocate* originally highlighted local events in the Los Angeles area and evolved over time into a reputable national publication with a circulation of nearly 100,000, making the *Advocate* the oldest continuously published GLBT periodical. Patrons were as likely to find James Baldwin, Djuna Barnes, Thom Gunn, Christopher Isherwood, Audre Lorde, John Rechy, Jane Rule, May Sarton, Gertrude Stein, and Gore Vidal among the shelves, as they were to find Kinsey and Freud. Rodwell's vision and courage in founding the store two years before Stonewall were complemented by a stock of approximately twenty-five titles and the intention to make serious (i.e., not pornographic) GLBT literature available.[7]

Rodwell's success spawned GLBT bookstores throughout the country. Deacon Maccubbin, founder of Lambda Rising, recalls his reaction to visiting the Wilde shop: "If you told me you could make money selling gay and lesbian books, I would have laughed because I didn't think it was possible. There just wasn't that much out there. I remember our first advertisement bragged that we had over 250 titles, which was pretty much everything. It was really hard to find 250 titles."[8]

The growth of GLBT bookstores was both a measure of success for the community and a lightning rod for community development. The establishment of stores signaled the end of the underground era, of GLBT literature being "pages passed from hand to hand." The literature acquired a public presence devoid of luridness and the legal association with obscenity; for the first time in history, the power to disseminate GLBT literature was openly and legally in the hands of the gay and lesbian community.

In the 1990s the nearly simultaneous rise of the Internet and mega-bookstores resulted in the mainstreaming of GLBT publications to a far larger audience than could be reached via independently owned GLBT bookstores, which were predominantly located in urban areas. The increased competition resulted in declining sales for GLBT bookstores and, in turn, the closing of many stores. The Oscar Wilde Bookstore was saved by Maccubbin one day before it was to close. Although there are no concrete statistics to document the decline in GLBT bookstores, it is telling that bookstores in major metropolitan areas such as Chicago, Los Angles, and Seattle have closed. Although the demise of GLBT bookstores is disconcerting, other avenues of promotion for GLBT literature include professional organizations, literary conferences, and book awards.

Development of Professional Organizations

The increasing interest in GLBT literature led to the creation of the earliest GLBT professional organizations in the United States. Appropriately leading the way was the American Library Association (ALA). In 1969, ALA established the Social Responsibilities Round Table to address neglected issues in librarianship, and two members, Janet Cooper and Israel Fishman, proposed The Task Force on Gay Liberation, with the intention of advocating for GLBT literature in libraries. Under Fishman's guidance, the task force met the following year during the ALA Conference and sponsored several professional programs, began compiling an extensive bibliography, and established a book award.

Over the decades the task force has changed its name, expanded the book awards, and grown from a handful of members to nearly 600. The Gay, Lesbian, Bisexual, and Transgendered Round Table remains the oldest GLBT professional association in the United States and parent to the Stonewall Book Awards, the oldest GLBT book awards.

Another literature-related professional organization did not appear until twelve years later. The Gay and Lesbian Press Association (GLPA), founded in 1981, represented the unification of several periodical publishers. The GLPA published a newsletter, began a wire service, created a media training program for nonprofit community organizations, presented awards, and sponsored conventions. Unfortunately, the organization collapsed in the mid-1990s due to declining membership and income.

The founding of the Publishing Triangle in 1988 offered the GLPA some competition. The Triangle was established to "further the publication of books and other materials written by lesbian and gay authors or with lesbian and gay themes."[9] The group sponsors a variety of book awards, a book expo, and other programs. The organization has approximately 150 members and is open to anyone who loves books.

In 1991 the National Lesbian & Gay Journalists Association (NLGJA) was founded. The 1,300 members "work within the news industry to foster fair and accurate coverage of lesbian, gay, bisexual and transgender issues" in all forms of media.[10] The organization has twenty-four state chapters and affiliates in Germany and Canada. It sponsors programs, conferences, and awards, and publishes various reports.

Literary Festivals and Writers' Conferences

Professional organizations may promote GLBT literature through a number of efforts, including literary festivals, writers' conferences, and book awards. Each effort draws attention to particular genres, authors, and works and allows readers to get up-close and personal with writers.

The growth of GLBT publishing and the mainstream availability of the genre gave rise to GLBT literary festivals and writers' conferences. Although this is not surprising, the phenomenon is relatively recent. OutWrite, a national lesbian and gay writers' conference, was founded in 1990 and routinely attracted several hundred writers, editors, and publishers. The first two conferences were sponsored by the San Francisco–based magazine *OUT/LOOK*; beginning in 1993 Bromfield Street Educational Foundation assumed sole sponsorship. The conference featured publishers' exhibits, panel discussions, "caucuses and readings spanning all written genres and media from paper to stage to film to video to electronic publishing."[11] The list of participants read like a writers' "who's who" list: Edward Albee, Dorthoy Allison, Essex Hemphill, Minnie Bruce Pratt, Edmund White, and Mark Doty are just a few of the luminaries the conference attracted before its demise in 1999.

Beginning in 1997, literature lovers had the additional opportunity to attend the weekend-long Behind Our Masks Literary Festival. Bearing the cachet of the Lambda Literary Foundation, creator of the well-known Lambda Book Awards, this event routinely attracted 200 to 300 attendees, who took part in programs; enjoyed GLBT-themed performances; and mingled with authors such as Andrew Holleran, Jewelle Gomez, Christopher Bram, Felice Picano, and Karla Jay. Eventually the somewhat depressing mask moniker was replaced by the more recognizable

Lambda Literary Festival, but financial difficulties forced the discontinuance of the conference in 2004.

The Association of Lesbians and Gay Men in Publishing, inspired by the Harlem Book Fair, organized the annual Pink Ink book exposition. Since 2002, Pink Ink has immersed approximately 100 attendees in three days of GLBT literature with author readings, book signings, and practical programming aimed at aspiring authors. The exposition was temporarily suspended in 2004.

The annual Saints and Sinners Literary Festival in New Orleans, Louisiana, founded in 2002, is the most recent successor to the defunct OutWrite and Lambda festivals. Participants are drawn to the occasion to hear well-known authors such as Jim Grimsley, Sarah Schulman, Patricia Nell Warren, and Christopher Rice read from and autograph their books. Corporate sponsorships help fund the event, and monies raised are donated to GLBT charitable causes.

The Fire & Ink Writers Festival is a grassroots effort organized by Lisa C. Moore of Redbone Press. First held in Chicago during 2002, the festival "is devoted to increasing the understanding, visibility and awareness of the works of [GLBT] writers of African descent and heritage."[12] Among the many writers and performance artists in attendance in previous years were poet Marvin K. White and authors James Earl Hardy and Cheryl Clarke. Workshops about how to get published, how to find an agent, basic screenwriting, and magazine publishing are offered. An attempted follow-up conference in 2005 failed, and the future of the event is uncertain.

Collectively these festivals and workshops parallel the growth and acceptance of GLBT literature while simultaneously demonstrating the difficult nature of maintaining such an event. Book awards are a more common and less expensive method for promoting literature.

Book Awards

Methods of literary acclaim include book reviews, best-seller list placement, book club designation, and book awards, but receiving a book award is the penultimate achievement for authors. The internationally recognized Nobel Prize for Literature, established in 1901, is the oldest and most prestigious award. Thomas Mann (1929), André Gide (1947), and T. S. Eliot (1948) are some of the GLBT authors this crowning achievement has been bestowed upon.

In the United States, the oldest continuously awarded book prize is the prestigious Pulitzer Prize (founded in 1917). Prizes are given in several categories, such as literature, poetry, and drama. Notable gay and lesbian Pulitzer recipients include Willa Cather (literature, 1923), Edna St. Vincent Millay (poetry, 1923), W. H. Auden (poetry, 1948), Tennessee Williams (drama, 1948, 1956), John Cheever (literature, 1979), Alice Walker (literature, 1983), and Michael Cunningham (literature, 1999.)

Although GLBT authors have been recognized with these prestigious awards, prior to the Second World War "few [GLBT novels] . . . garnered acclaim as masterworks"[13] because the genre was forced to hide and cryptically code themes and characters. The emergence of GLBT book awards is largely an American phenomenon, rooted in the late twentieth century and closely paralleling publishing patterns and society's changing perceptions.

GLBT Book Awards*

The Task Force on Gay Liberation of the American Library Association created the first award for GLBT literature in 1971. The Gay Book Award, as it was known, represents "exceptional merit relating to the gay, lesbian, bisexual, transgendered experience" and was a grassroots effort involving the cooperation of librarians and nonlibrarians, including the renowned Barbara Gittings. Initially, literature and nonfiction competed equally for the prize, and decisions regarding winners were made by consensus. Such was the nature of this homegrown initiative that early award recipients might receive anything from a hand-lettered scroll to a commencement cap, a lavender cape, or even a kite.

By 1981, the availability of GLBT literature had increased to the point that it was impossible to make decisions by consensus, so an awards committee with formal guidelines and procedures was begun. The following year the Gay Task Force petitioned the American Library Association's award committee for official recognition for the Gay Book Award; the request was granted in 1986. Other significant developments related to ALA's Gay Book Award include cash awards for winners (1986), separate awards for literature and nonfiction (1990), designation of "Honor Book" status for runners-up (2001), and renaming the awards the Stonewall Book Awards (2002).

The narrowness of Stonewall's categories of literature and nonfiction guarantees tough competition, lending some prestige to the award. The first winner was Isabel Miller's *Patience and Sarah*. A selective list of winning authors includes life partners Del Martin and Phyllis Lyon, Joan Nestle, Jim Grimsley, Randy Shilts, Edmund White, and Leslie Feinberg. Lillian Faderman was the first author to triumph twice in the same category, and Sarah Schulman was the first to earn Stonewalls in different categories. Other milestones include the first African American awardees, Essex Hemphill (1993) and Marci Blackman (2000); the earliest Asian winners, Urvashi Vaid (1996) and Noel Alumit (2003); and the first person of Hispanic origin to acquire the award, Moisés Kaufman, a native of Venezuela (2002).

Like the Stonewall Awards, the Lambda Literary Awards are landmarks in the world of GLBT literature. Founded in 1988, the Lammys are presented annually by the Lambda Literary Foundation (LLF) for the purpose of "recogniz[ing] excellence in gay, lesbian, bisexual, and transgender literature and publishing." The categories in which Lammys are given have varied greatly over the years. Initially Lambda awards were given for fiction, nonfiction, poetry, first novel, and science fiction/fantasy/horror. The explosion of GLBT literature necessitated the creation of new categories: children's/young adult, humor, mystery, and anthologies were all added in 1989, the latter further divided into fiction/nonfiction in 1994. Other added categories are queer studies and biography/autobiography (1993), photography/visual arts and drama (1994), spirituality/religion (1995), transgender/bisexual (1996), and erotica and romance (2001). AIDS books were included as a special category between 1988 and 1990. Categories were readjusted in 2004, with several categories eliminated and previous categories, such as debut fiction, resurrected.

The sheer quantity of awards presented by LLF guarantees a long and diverse list of winning authors. For example, thirteenth-century Arab scholar Ahmad al-Tifashi tied with Hispanic American Michael Nava for the first Lammy in the Gay Men's Small Press category, making al-Tifashi the first posthumously awarded author and Nava the first Hispanic winner. The unusual rule that allows for consideration in more than one category has led to the same title winning more than once in the same year, such as Martin Duberman's *Hidden from History* and Paul Monette's *Borrowed Time*. The expansion of categories and a rule change permitting male and female authors to compete equally within selected genres reduces the likelihood of repeat winners in a given year.

There is substantial overlap between Lammy and Stonewall honorees. Andrew Hollinghurst, winner of the first Lammy for gay male fiction, also won the Stonewall the same year. Other authors to appear on both lists include but are not limited to Dorothy Allison, Alison Bechdel, Christopher Bram, Michael Cunningham, Nancy Garden, David Leavitt, and Achy Obejas.

The Publishing Triangle Awards (PTA) and the Ruth Benedict Prize are examples of awards originating with a group of GLBT professionals. Founded in 1989 by the Association of Lesbians and Gay Men in Publishing, the PTAs intend to "further the publication of books . . . written by lesbian and gay authors or with lesbian and gay themes." All awards are presented annually to the best female and male author in each category and carry a cash prize.

The Bill Whitehead Award, the oldest PTA, honors lifetime achievement and is presented to a male in odd-numbered years and to a female in even-numbered years. Whitehead winners have included Audre Lorde, Armistead Maupin, John Rechy, and M. E. Kerr. The playwriting award, established in 1994, also alternates between males and females and has acknowledged Lisa Kron, Doric Wilson, Paula Vogel, Chay Yew, and Christopher Shinn.

Nonfiction and poetry PTAs were added in 1997 and 2001, respectively. David Sedaris, Amber Hollibaugh, Terry Wolverton, Neil Miller, and John D'Emilio are just a few of the nonfiction awardees; Mark Doty and Marilyn Hacker are representative of the poetry winners circle.

To signal the new millennium, the PTA sponsored two lists of the 100 best lesbian and gay novels. The Triangle List was selected by a panel of judges, all notable authors in their own right. The second list was created based on the recommendations of visitors to the PTA Web site and resulted in slightly fewer than 100 books. Somewhat surprisingly, there was little overlap between the award lists. Of the 187 titles, only four appear on both the judges' and the readers' lists, or approximately a 4 percent overlap. Clearly there is a considerable difference between what a panel of experts considers quality literature and reader popularity.

The Ferro-Grumley Awards (FGAs) collaborated with the Publishing Triangle Awards in 1994. Originally established in 1990, the FGAs are awarded for literary fiction and have paid tribute to Felice Picano, Michael Cunningham, Jeanette Winterson, and Carol Anshaw.

The Society of Lesbian and Gay Anthropologists, a division of the American Anthropological Association, have presented the Ruth Benedict Prize annually since 1986. Two prizes, one for a single-authored monograph and another for an edited volume, recognize excellence in scholarly anthropological works about lesbian, gay, bisexual, or transgendered topics. As this award recognizes scholarly achievement and scholars tend to have a narrow research focus, it is common to see repeat winners such as Esther Newton, Ellen Lewin, and William Leap.

The 1990s were a watershed period for GLBT book awards, with the creation of five new prizes. Kicking off the decade was the James Tiptree, Jr. Memorial Award. Loosely associated with WisCon, a feminist science fiction convention, this award is independently operated and financed. Although not specifically GLBT in scope, the Tiptree honors science fiction or fantasy daring to bend traditional gender concepts. The nomination process is open, and five judges determine the winners, who receive a cash award. A retrospective award was presented on the Tiptree's fifth anniversary to pay tribute to titles whose publication predated the award. Ursula Le Guin has won several Tiptrees, including the retrospective award. Many titles with GLBT themes, including works by Nicola Griffith, have received the award since 1991.

Between 1996 and 2000, at least one new GLBT award was established each year, with 1996 witnessing two new awards, the Arch and Bruce Brown Foundation Awards and the Firecracker Alternative Book Awards. The Arch and Bruce Brown Foundation Awards are given in categories that rotate annually among three disciplines: theater, full-length fiction, and short story. Submissions must present GLBT life in a positive manner and have some historical connection, either "based on or inspired by a historic person, culture, event, or work of art." More than one winner per year is permitted, and a cash prize granted. Lesléa Newman, author of *Heather Has Two Mommies* and several volumes of lesbian short stories, is the best-known winner of this narrowly defined award.

Book industry professionals are responsible for producing the Firecracker Alternative Book Awards (FAB). Not specifically GLBT, Firecrackers honor works that other award juries might consider too wild or insurrectionary. In keeping with this revolutionary attitude, the ten categories include awards for the best books dealing with sex and drugs. Traditional genres are also included: fiction, nonfiction, poetry, art/photography, children's, music, and politics, as well as erratic recognition for zines. Several books with GLBT content have won FABs. Unfortunately, the FABs ceased in 2002.

The entry-fee-based Independent Publisher Book Awards, or "IPPY" awards, began in 1997. The awards recognize the best independently published titles in fifty-five categories, including GLBT titles. GLBT works had their own category from the beginning, although fiction and nonfiction works compete equally for the award. One winner and multiple finalists are awarded each year. The IPPY is the first awards program open exclusively to independently published books; therefore, the winners are lesser-known authors, such as two-time honoree Perry Brass, author of *Warlock, a Novel of Possession*.

Unique among GLBT awards are the genre-specific Gaylactic Spectrum Awards, which began in 1998 under the auspices of the Gaylactic Network, an organization for gay and lesbian fandom, and became independent of the Network in 2002. The awards honor "works in science fiction, fantasy and horror which include positive explorations of gay, lesbian, bisexual or transgendered characters, themes, or issues."

The annually juried awards have an open nomination process within three permanent categories: novel, short fiction, and other work. Hall of Fame inductees are selected yearly in tribute to works originally released prior to 1998. Winners and Hall of Fame inductees read like a "who's who" of science fiction: Madeline L'Engle, Marion Zimmer Bradley, Mercedes Lackey, Arthur C. Clarke, and Clive Barker.

ForeWord Magazine, a trade magazine for independent publishers, established the Book of the Year Awards in 1999. A work must originate with an independent or university press and submit the entry fee for consideration in one of the forty-nine categories. Originally, GLBT fiction and nonfiction vied against one another; however, this practice was quickly replaced with separate classes for the genres. Like the IPPYs, many of the winners lack notoriety; however, the well-read will undoubtedly recognize some of the names, such as Minne Bruce Pratt, Patricia Nell Warren, Michelle Tea, and Lawrence Schimel.

Two awards, the Alice B. and the Goldie, are devoted to fostering lesbian authors and literature. The Alice B. Reader's Appreciation Award, named after Alice B. Toklas, began in 2000 as an effort to promote manuscript submissions to Rising Tide Press. With the demise of Rising Tide, the Alice metamorphosed into a reader's appreciation award recognizing lesbian writers for a body of work. Winners, including Gerri Hill, Nancy Sanra, Aya tsi scuceblu Walksfar, and Radclyffe, receive a monetary prize and commemorative medallion.

In 2005 the Golden Crown Literary Society formed a network of authors, readers, and volunteers from the publishing industry to promote lesbian fiction. The society's first effort was the formation of a book award, the Goldie. Focusing on three categories—romance/erotica, science fiction/fantasy, and mystery/action/adventure/thriller—judges select three winners. Karin Kallmaker is perhaps the most recognizable name among the first honorees, which also included Radclyffe (who won two awards in different categories), Ellen Hart, Jessica Thomas Jean Stewart, Cate Culpepper, and Judy MacLean

The Violet Quill is an award about which little information is available. Named in honor of a writing group that included Edmund White, Felice Picano, and Andrew Holleran, the award is presented annually to an emerging GLBT writer whose work is offered by the InsightOut Book Club. Further information regarding this award is unavailable.

At the beginning of the twenty-first century, electronic books are touted as a replacement for print. GLBT literature will persist and adapt to the e-book environment. It is only a matter of time before one of the established award juries recognizes an e-book, or perhaps a new award will be created. Whatever the future, the existence of GLBT literature awards are testament to the determination of GLBT writers and readers everywhere.

Conclusion

Taken as a group, the trends discussed here reflect the rapid rise and rich history of GLBT literature. However, they also speak of an uncertain future.

Society's changing attitudes toward reading as a form of entertainment and enlightenment are colliding with market factors to create unfavorable conditions for GLBT literature. Competition with movies, television, and the Internet, coupled with higher book prices, have had a cascading negative effect on publishing and related industries that does not bode well for the future of the printed word. The future of GLBT publishing may depend on the ability of small, independent business operations to thrive in a global marketplace. If these operations are successful, the development of GLBT writing and the emergence of new authors are guaranteed.

Bibliography

Publishers

Absolute Press: http://www.absolutepress.co.uk/

Alyson: http://www.alyson.com

Bella Books: http://www.bellabooks.com/

Cleis Press: http://www.cleispress.com/

Crossing Press: http://www.tenspeed.com/aboutus/crossing.htm

Feminist Press: http://www.feministpress.org/

Firebrand: http://www.firebrandbooks.com/

GLB Publishers: http://www.glbpubs.com/

Haworth Press: http://www.haworthpress.com

Kensington Books: http://www.kensingtonbooks.com/

Millivres Prowler Press: http://www.millivres.co.uk/mpg/

New Victoria Publishers: http://www.newvictoria.com

New York University Press: http://www.nyupress.org/

Redbone: http://www.redbonepress.com/

Romentics: http://www.romentics.com

Soft Skull: http://www.softskull.com/

Spinster's Ink: http://www.spinsters-ink.com/

St. Martin's Press: http://www.stmartins.com/

University of Chicago Press Worlds of Desire Series: http://www.press.uchicago.edu/ Complete/Series/WD-CSSGC.html

University of Wisconsin Press Living Out Series: http://www.wisc.edu/wisconsinpress/ books/livingout.htm

Wayward Books: http://waywardbooks.com

Professional Associations

American Library Association Gay, Lesbian, Bisexual, and Transgendered Round Table: http://www.ala.org/template.cfm?Section=glbtrt

National Lesbian & Gay Journalists Association: http://www.nlgja.org/

Publishing Triangle: http://publishingtriangle.org/

Literary Festivals

Fire and Ink: http://www.fireandink.org

Pink Ink: http://publishingtriangle.org/pinkink.asp

Saints and Sinners: http://sasfest.org/index.php

Book Awards

Alice B. Reader's Appreciation Award: http://www.alicebawards.org/

Arch and Bruce Brown Foundation Awards: http://www.aabbfoundation.org/

ForeWord Magazine Book of the Year Awards: http://www.forewordmagazine.com/awards/

Gaylactic Spectrum Awards: http://www.spectrumawards.org/

Goldie Awards: http://www.goldencrown.org/awards.html

Independent Publisher Book Awards: http://www.independentpublisher.com/awardwinners.php

Lambda Literary Awards: http://www.lambdaliterary.org/index.html

Publishing Triangle Awards: http://publishingtriangle.org/awards.asp

Ruth Benedict Prize: http://www.uvm.edu/~dlrh/solga/prizes/Benedict/BenMain.html

Stonewall Awards: http://www.ala.org/ala/glbtrt/stonewall/stonewallbook.htm

Tiptree Awards: http://www.tiptree.org/

Notes

*This section is reprinted with permission of www.glbtq.com, the world's largest encyclopedia of gay, lesbian, bisexual, transgender, and queer culture.

1. Teresa Theophano, "Boston Marriages," in *glbtq: An Encyclopedia of Gay, Lesbian, Bisexual, Transgender, and Queer Culture,* ed. Claude J. Summers (2004). Available at www.glbtq.com/social-sciences/boston_marriages.html (accessed October 15, 2007).

2. Roger Streitmatter, *Unspeakable: The Rise of the Gay and Lesbian Press in America* (Boston: Faber and Faber, 1995), 2.

3. Streitmatter, *Unspeakable,* 18.

4. David Leavitt and Mark Mitchell, *Pages Passed from Hand to Hand: The Hidden Tradition of Homosexual Literature in English from 1748 to 1914* (Boston: Houghton Mifflin, 1998).

5. Bonnie Ruth Beebe, "Happy Birthday, Naiad!" *Lambda Book Report* 6, no. 7 (February 1998): 23.

6. Lisa C. Moore, "A History of Publishing Pride," *Lambda Book Report* 11, no. 91 (April–July 2003): 38–40.

7. L. Cuffie, "Oscar Wilde Memorial Bookstore," *Gay Community News,* December 18, 1976, 11.

8. Michael Archer, "Gospel According to Deacon: Lambda Rising and Oscar Wilde Bookstore Owner Maccubbin Reflects on His Mission," *Publishers Weekly* 250, no. 34 (August 25, 2003): 20–22.

9. http://publishingtriangle.org/ourmission.asp (accessed February 11, 2008).

10. http://www.nlgja.org/about/history.html (accessed February 11, 2008).

11. Shelley Bindon, "Politics and Poetry Converge at OutWrite 8," *Lambda Book Report* 7, no. 18 (March 1999): 10–12.

12. http://www.fireandink.org/aboutus.html (accessed February 11, 2008).

13. Wayne Dynes, ed. *Encyclopedia of Homosexuality* (New York: Garland Publishing, 1990), 901.

Chapter 3

Collection Development and Readers' Advisory

Introduction

In contrast to other topical areas of literature, the librarian faced with demands from patrons for specific titles or authors of GLBT literature needs to be especially aware of the myths and potential controversy associated with this type of writing and the variety of issues involved. These can range from misunderstandings about the need for GLBT literature to demands for the censorship of this class of book and its complete banning or elimination from the library collection. This chapter reviews some of the issues related to GLBT library service, particularly readers' advisory service, and contains information about where to locate other GLBT materials for reading, reviewing, or purchasing.

Appeal of the Genre

T. S. Eliot named three reasons to read: the pleasure of entertainment, the enjoyment of art, and the acquisition of wisdom. Although these reasons are appropriate to all types of literature, perhaps they resonate more strongly with the GLBT community because GLBT readers were invisible to the larger population as well as to publishers for many generations. Just as laws and social standards prevented individuals from expressing their true identity, authors and publishers risked censorship and monetary penalties for issuing publications testing the limits of those laws and of social expectations. Consequently, GLBT readers rarely saw themselves portrayed in literature. How very satisfying, then, for the contemporary reader to finally see stories that reflect the entire spectrum of the GLBT community.

The positive portrayal of the GLBT community in literature is another reason for reading; readers may look to such literature to find acceptance and hope. Personal narratives may prove especially powerful in the quest for affirmation, signaling both experiences common to all humanity (such as growing up, developing relationships, marriage and parenting, and seeking philosophical or spirituality enlightenment), and the unique perspective being homosexual brings to these experiences. For example, same-sex love, marriage, and parenting are humorously addressed in Dan Savage's

The Commitment (Dutton, 2005), and *Amazing Grace,* by Malcolm Boyd and Nancy L. Wilson (Crossing Press, 1991), chronicles ten average individuals seeking the spiritual realm. Fictional depictions may prove equally affirming, such as Rochelle H. Schwab's *Departure from the Script* (Orlando Place, 2002), which features a young woman telling her parents she desires a traditional Jewish wedding—to a woman—and her family's gradual redefinition of love, marriage, and faith.

Coming out literature is a unique and usually affirming subset of the GLBT genre. The very personal nature of coming out lends itself well to autobiographical renderings, such as Karla Jay's and Allen Young's anthology *After You're Out: Personal Experiences of Gay Men and Lesbian Women* (Link Books, 1975) and Nancy Adair's and Casey Adair's *Word Is Out: Stories of Some of Our Lives* (Dell, 1978), two early examples. Coming out memoirs of highly visible individuals, such as athletes, politicians, and Hollywood stars, often attract considerable attention, perhaps because the revelation is a surprise or confirms rumors. The coming out stories of individuals such as Olympic gold-medal swimmer Greg Louganis in *Breaking the Surface* (Random House, 1995) and rock musician Melissa Etheridge's *The Truth Is: My Life in Love and Music* (Villard, 2001) confirm the possibility of being both out and successful.

Readers will find a cacophony of affirming coming out fiction directed at both adult and young adult audiences. Adult readers may enjoy Edmund White's *The Beautiful Room Is Empty* (Knopf, 1988), featuring a nameless narrator arriving at self-acceptance on the eve of the Stonewall Riots (1969), or Jane Rule's classic *Desert of the Heart*, in which an older divorcée struggles with her attraction to a younger woman. Classic coming out tales for young adults are rare, but include John Donovan's *I'll Get There*, Nancy Garden's *Annie on My Mind*, and Patricia Nell Warren's *The Front Runner*. Author Alex Sanchez recently burst upon the young adult literature scene with several stories about discovering one's sexual orientation, most notably *So Hard to Say* and the Rainbow Boys series. Young lesbians can look to Lauren Myracle's *Kissing Kate*, Julie Ann Peters's *Keeping You a Secret*, and Sara Ryan's *Empress of the World* for contemporary coming out stories.

In addition to providing an affirming context, GLBT fiction also provides a means to learn about the history of the community. For example, Ethan Mordden uses the history of the gay and lesbian movement from World War II through the AIDS crisis as a setting for *How Long Has This Been Going On*; *Franny Queen of Provincetown*, by John Preston, features a fictional drag queen's monologues spanning 1950–1990. *Mrs. Stevens Hears the Mermaids Singing* is a novelized account of author May Sarton's life; Collette's scandalous 1941 novel of lesbian love, *The Pure and the Impure*, is considered a fictional account of her affairs; and *Rubyfruit Jungle*, by Rita Mae Brown, is perhaps the most widely read example of this type. Fictionalized accounts of prominent events or individuals may attract readers otherwise reluctant to read about gays and lesbians. Finally, fictionalized histories and personal accounts allow readers to acquire bits of knowledge about GLBT history and hopefully engender a greater understanding of and appreciation for the community.

Gaining an appreciation of GLBT literature requires understanding a variety of myths and problems associated with the genre. Librarians in particular must cultivate familiarity with these issues in order to alleviate user anxiety, better serve users, battle stereotypes, and resist censorship.

Myths about GLBT Literature

The most persistent and damaging myth is the assumption that GLBT literature is pornographic. Because homosexuality historically was associated with deviant, criminal behavior, homosexual literature was similarly branded and demonized as obscene. For example, all references to Oscar Wilde's relationship with Alfred Douglas were removed from the 1905 publication *De Profundis*, but by 1962 society's attitudes about homosexuality had evolved enough to restore the text to its original form. Sexual contact in Radclyffe Hall's *The Well of Loneliness* is merely inferred by the statement "and that night, they were not divided," yet the publisher was convicted of obscenity in 1928, and James Baldwin's *Another Country*, also devoid of explicit sex, was removed from libraries as recently as 1962.

Unfortunately the myth that gay or lesbian content renders a work obscene persists. Books with homosexual content consistently top the American Library Association's (ALA) list of most challenged works. Among the ten most challenged books of 2006 tracked by the ALA, 40 percent were attacked based on homosexual content, including a children's book, based on a true story, about gay penguins—clearly neither obscene nor pornographic.

GLBT literature, like any form of literature, consists of various genres, such as mystery, horror, science fiction, and romance, which may or may not contain sexually explicit material. The idea that any type of literature is inherently pornographic is at best a subjective judgment, changing over time based on society's shifting attitudes about sexuality.

Another common misconception concerns the sexual orientation of writers, namely the idea that only a lesbian could write a convincing lesbian story and only a gay man could produce a realistic gay novel. Readers assume that authors write primarily from personal experience. This is particularly true regarding GLBT literature, because authors were forced to hide their sexual orientation, opting in many cases to transpose their stories into characters with different sexual orientations. Walt Whitman successfully changed the gender of his male lover to female in much of his poetry, and Mary Renault, a lesbian, authored the classic tale of male–male attraction *The Charioteer*. Clearly, an author's sexual orientation does not necessarily correlate with a work's subject matter.

Just as an author's sexual orientation does not predict his or her subject matter, the subject matter does not predict its audience. The idea that GLBT literature is confined to GLBT characters and therefore of limited audience interest represents interconnected misconceptions. Works with exclusively GLBT content, whether in the form of characters or subjects, certainly exist, particularly in the science fiction genre; however, most works represent a spectrum of characters, subject matters, and sexual orientations. Heterosexual characters may appear in GLBT novels as friends, family, coworkers, neighbors, or service personnel. Steven McCauly's *The Object of My Affection*, for example, features a straight woman trying to convince her gay friend to function as a father figure for her child. Books featuring ensemble casts often include both gay and straight characters, examples being Christopher Rice's college drama *The Snow Garden* and Alan Hollinghurst's political novel *The Line of Beauty*. The representation of all types of characters and sexual orientations support readership beyond the GLBT community.

Readers may seek out GLBT-themed literature for a variety of reasons, including school or research assignments, to understand themselves or family members, or to learn more about the gay/lesbian community. Although many GLBT books are marketed exclusively to gay/lesbian audiences, certain types of stories have demonstrated crossover appeal to heterosexual audiences. Coming-of-age stories and books in which GLBT characters are central to a non-gay plot, such as Michael Cunningham's Pulitzer Prize winner *The Hours*, are examples of literature that gains wide readership and commercial success. Non-gay audiences may also encounter GLBT literature in the classroom through the works of Genet, Gide, Capote, Gertrude Stein, Audre Lorde, Evelyn Waugh, and many other authors. The various examples of the crossover appeal of GLBT literature easily dispel the myth that it is only of interest to the GLBT population.

Unhappy endings are the final myth associated with GLBT literature, although there is evidence that at one time this may have been more than a myth. Prior to the American medical establishment's declassification of homosexuality as a mental illness in 1973, the American population believed homosexuals were evil, prone to pedophilia and substance abuse, and generally unable to lead productive lives. Naturally, the literature of the period reflected these concepts, and even Norman Mailer admitted, " I have been as guilty as any contemporary novelist in attributing unpleasant, ridiculous, or sinister connotations to the homosexual . . . characters in my novels."[1]

As a result of this formulaic and widespread vilification, GLBT characters were frequently killed off, imprisoned, or institutionalized, or the victims of unrequited love. Consider Gore Vidal's *The City and the Pillar* (Dutton, 1948), in which Jim's unrequited love for Bob leads to murder; Lillian Hellman's play *The Children's Hour* (Knopf, 1934), in which Martha commits suicide because of a rumored lesbian affair; or the heroine of Rosamund Lehmann's *Dusty Answer*, who suffers a nervous breakdown and is exiled to Scotland.

The unhappy ending syndrome began to thaw in the 1950s. Author Marijane Meaker, who wrote as Vin Packer and Ann Aldrich, recalls that during this period her publisher required happy endings in order to avoid censorship from postal officials. Ironically, her publisher's idea of a happy conclusion involved restoring characters to heterosexuality, a convoluted approach, but an improvement over victimization and vilification. Nevertheless, mid-twentieth-century works such as Claire Morgan's (aka Patricia Highsmith) 1952 novel *The Price of Salt*, wherein the characters neither die nor resort to heterosexuality, began to counter the unhappy ending trend in GLBT literature.

In young adult literature, unhappy endings persisted into the 1970s. Michael Cart documents several instances in his article "Honoring Their Stories." Cart notes that in Judy Blume's 1975 novel *Forever*, Artie's confusion about his sexuality leads to a failed suicide attempt. Cart continues, "consider that in . . . John Donovan's *I'll Get There It Better Be Worth the Trip*, Isabelle Holland's *The Man Without a Face*, *Trying Hard to Hear You* by Sandra Scoppettone; and Lynn Hall's *Sticks and Stones*—either the gay character or someone (or something in the case of poor Fred) close to the gay character dies, usually in a car crash."[2]

Problems with GLBT Literature

The Problem of Controversy and Censorship

GLBT literature has long been a target of community opposition, book challenges, and attempted censorship. An examination of the American Library Association's list of most challenged books between 1990 and 2000 reveals 515 challenges based on homosexuality, ranking sixth among reasons cited for a challenge. This pattern continues into the twenty-first century; in the three-year period beginning in 2000, eighty-four items were challenged. Despite various attempts to suppress GLBT literature, these statistics are evidence of society's improving attitude toward GLBT literature; a 2004 survey by the National Opinion Research Center demonstrated that only 27 percent of the population thought GLBT books should be removed from libraries, a decrease from 45 percent in previous surveys.[3]

Lest readers and librarians find comfort in these statistics or believe challenges are isolated incidents without long-term effects, consider how *King & King* by Linda de Haan and Stern Nijland sparked a firestorm of outrage and political action in 2005. This simple, thirty-two-page children's picture book tells the story of a young prince forced by his mother to marry. After meeting several prospective princesses, the young prince falls for Prince Lee, and in typical fairy tale fashion everyone lives happily ever after. Originally published in the Netherlands, where same-sex marriage is legal, in the United States this book was singled out by readers who demanded its removal from libraries in Oklahoma, Louisiana, and Alabama. Spurred by the book's "controversial" subject matter, the legislatures of these states took up the issue of homosexual-themed library books, but only Oklahoma passed legislation calling for the relocation of homosexually themed materials to a special area in public libraries. Oklahoma further threatened to back up the legislation by withholding funding from noncompliant public libraries. The issue moved to the national level when Rep. Walter Jones, (D-NC), after hearing complaints about *King & King*, introduced federal legislation that would require school districts to create parent councils to review acquisitions of materials for classrooms and libraries.

The consequences of censorship challenges may be mitigated by a clearly defined collection development policy. Such a policy should be rooted in the principles of intellectual freedom as expressed in various ALA policies, particularly Policy 53.1.15, *Access to Library Resources and Services Regardless of Sex, Gender Identity, or Sexual Orientation* and the *Resolution on Threats to Library Materials Related to Sex, Gender Identity, or Sexual Orientation*. Examples of collection development policies specifically designed for GLBT collections can be found at http://www.cervone.com/html/glbt_collection_development.html.

When a collection development policy does not thwart a challenge, library staff may turn to a number of resources for information and support. Two organizations exist in conjunction with ALA. The Freedom to Read Foundation (http://www.ala.org/ala/ourassociation/othergroups/ftrf/freedomreadfou ndation.htm) was established in 1969 "to support and defend librarians whose positions are jeopardized because of their resistance to abridgments of the First Amendment; and to set legal precedent for the freedom to read on behalf of all the people." The foundation provides financial support to assist groups and individuals with censorship-related litigation and may directly participate in legal actions in support of freedom of speech and of the press. Working in concert with the foundation is ALA's Office of Intellectual Freedom (http://www.ala.org/template.cfm?Section=oif), which aims to educate both librarians and their patrons about the importance of intellectual freedom in libraries and to assist librarians facing challenges to individual books.

The local GLBT community may also be a source of support during book challenges. Forging a relationship with this community may produce allies willing to stand up to challenges, start or support petition drives, or speak to the personal importance or relevance of GLBT literature to the larger community.

The Problem of Discomfort and Unfamiliarity

Opposition to the inclusion of GLBT materials in the collection may also come from members of the library staff, often rooted in personal discomfort with sexuality, unfamiliarity with the genre, and a reluctance to suggest books on topics that may be perceived as socially sensitive or locally unacceptable. Recent research on librarian discomfort with GLBT issues revealed that 30 percent of librarians seemed "cold, reserved or neutral" and 15 percent were "clueless" and "frightened."[4]

Librarians should work to overcome their own discomfort and speak openly and frankly with patrons about GLBT materials. Overcoming personal discomfort or unfamiliarity with GLBT literature and issues may be accomplished by attending conference presentations, actively monitoring GLBT electronic lists, and visiting GLBT literature Web sites for book reviews and recommendations. Developing a readers' advisory checklist for GLBT literature would be useful to librarians and readers alike. Consider the following when developing a readers' advisory checklist, or during a reference interview:

- Ask what books the reader has previously enjoyed and then explore what he or she enjoyed about that book.
- Determine if the reader enjoys a particular genre—e.g., mystery, historical.
- What level of sex is acceptable? How does the reader feel about graphic language or violence?

Discomfort with GLBT material is present among patrons as well, many of whom may be afraid to ask for books or authors for fear of being labeled. Many readers are unwilling to raise personal subjects with the librarian, particularly those they believe might cause a hostile or unfriendly response. Other readers may simply be unaware of the existence of this kind of literature. Easing patron discomfort and unfamiliarity can be as simple as ensuring that GLBT material is in the collection and adequately cataloged to facilitate self-discovery; just knowing GLBT literature is in the local library may encourage a reader to continue to search for additional materials or consult a librarian. Librarians encountering an uneasy reader may wish to provide a list that includes both GLBT and non-GLBT materials. Other approaches to enhance awareness and access while preserving patron anonymity include compiling recommended reading lists for distribution and posting them on the library's Web site, creating book displays, and utilizing special spine labels or shelving areas to make GLBT materials readily identifiable when browsing.

The Problem of Access

Accessing GLBT literature has been complicated by inaccurate and misleading subject headings, inadequate cataloging, and broad classification schema in libraries and elsewhere; as well as by a lack of readily available, reliable reviews. These factors in combination make it difficult for both readers and collection development librarians and readers' advisors to find the material they seek.

The Problem of Subject Headings

Subject headings for GLBT literature can create complications for both librarians and readers, whether in an online catalog or at the Web sites of major bookstore chains. If specific subject headings exist for the topics addressed in a particular book, they may not be included in the information supplied by the publisher, or local library processing may omit them in the catalog. Sometimes the subject of homosexuality and same-sex relationships is avoided, and at other times it is used to the exclusion of other important subject headings. An example of omitted or insufficient subject headings is those used for the autobiography of the Rev. Troy Perry, founder of the Metropolitan Community Church and author of *The Lord Is My Shepherd and He Knows I'm Gay* (1972). The Library of Congress (LC) subject headings provided for this book are *Homosexuality—Personal narratives* and *Gay men—United States—Biography*. No subject heading for religion is given. Although the name of the church is included as a heading, this will not help anyone who is not already familiar with the book's title or the name of this specific church. Adding a subject heading for religion would greatly improve access to this title.

The problem lingers, as evidenced by the cataloging for the 2003 memoir by New York novelist and gay man Augusten Burroughs about his alcoholism, *Dry*. In this case, Library of Congress headings are provided for geographical location, the author's profession, and alcoholism, but there is no mention of his sexual orientation. GLBT persons struggling with alcoholism or seeking information related to homosexuality and alcoholism would never find this book.

The larger book retailers with a Web presence, such as Barnes & Noble and Amazon.com, include subject headings for GLBT materials, although their sources and standards of application are unclear. The struggle to provide effective and useful subject access in this context can be easily illustrated. For the aforementioned autobiography by Troy Perry, Amazon.com provides only one subject heading, *Religion*, and the title is not even carried on the Barnes & Noble site. Consulting Amazon.com for the Burroughs memoir is equally disappointing in terms of subject access, with patrons offered a lengthy list of headings beginning with *twentieth century* and *Advertising agencies*, and including highly repetitive and confusing references to *Biography & Autobiography*. Burroughs's career is referenced multiple times, but gay aspects of the book are ignored. Barnes & Noble's treatment of the title is less complicated in the application of subject headings: the biographical aspect is subsumed under *Adult child abuse victims*. Burroughs's career is represented by the heading *Advertising* and his addiction by *Alcoholics*. Finally, the aspect of the author's sexual orientation is represented.

Subject headings and changing cataloging practices present a major challenge to genre analysis. Early nonfiction authors used several terms to describe individuals that today would be called gay, lesbian, bisexual, transgendered, transsexual, or homosexual. The term *homosexual* appeared in 1868, coined by Karl Maria Kertbeny in a letter to pioneering German sexologist Karl Heinrich Ulrichs. Ulrichs, in conjuction with coauthor Magnus Hirschfeld, utilized the terms *third sex* and *Uranian*. Havelock Ellis's 1897 book *Sexual Inversion* established *inversion* as an acceptable term for homosexuality. The proliferation of terminology associated with GLBT literature was clearly an impediment to researchers and readers.

Subject headings also reflected the stigmatization associated with homosexuality. The Library of Congress's decision not to use Kertbeny's, Ulrich's, and Ellis's terms contributed to the confusion. In the earliest printed editions of the *Library of Congress Subject Headings* (1910–1914), LC opted to describe nonheterosexual acts under the derogatory phrase "sexual perversion." Despite the fact that LC cataloged the first English-language book with "homosexuality" in the title as early as 1923, the term did not become an official subject heading until 1945. Four years later, *lesbianism* was added; by 1955 *homosexuality, bisexuality,* and *sodomy* were added as "see" references. Unfortunately, the phrase "sexual perversion" remained in use and was applied to GLBT works until 1969, when it was replaced with the equally inflammatory phrase "sexual deviation". To this day, it is possible to find records with the subject headings "sexual perversion," "sexual deviation," and "sexual inversion."

Professional and novice librarians have devised several solutions to subject headings problems. Several subject classification systems were created to address the weaknesses in the LC system. The earliest system was developed in 1980 by the Library Committee of the National Gay Archives. The thirty-one-page document *National Gay Archives Library Classification System* included nine major classes, with geographic, religious, and form subdivisions. Other systems include the *GDC: Gay Decimal Classification, A Classification Scheme Designed for Use in a Gay Studies Library*, by Phil Parkinson (1984); *International Gay and Lesbian Archives Classification System*, by David Moore, Walter Williams, and Jim Kepner (1985); and the *Michel/Moore Classification Scheme*, by Dee Michel (1988, 1990).

Repeated petitioning of the Library of Congress has expanded subject access and removed derogatory terms. The result has been the addition of nearly 500 GLBT-related subject headings. Clearly LC's expanded terminology is useful for librarians performing readers' advisory service, yet there remains room for improvement.

The readers' advisor should begin by becoming acquainted in further detail with the development and impact of subject headings on GLBT materials. Readings to consult include Ellen Greenblatt's "Homosexuality: The Evolution of a Concept in the Library of Congress Subject Headings" in *Gay and Lesbian Library Service* (MacFarland, 1990) and James V. Carmichaels's "Effects of the Gay Publishing Boom on Classes of Titles Retrieved under the Subject Headings 'Homosexuality,' 'Gay Men,' and 'Gays' in the WorldCat OCLC Database" in the *Journal of Homosexuality*. Where application of alternative classification schemes is impossible, a conscientious effort to discern GLBT content and supply locally created subject headings is strongly recommended.

Recent enhancements to online catalogs may also improve subject access via user-created "tags." Tagging defies traditional cataloging on a number of levels—anyone can create a tag, there are no rules, and tags can be inconsistent (e.g., GLBT versus LGBT)—but the advantage of tagging is obvious: It puts subject classification in the hands of those most familiar with an item—the readers.

The Problem with Book Reviews

The challenge of keeping up with the volume of writing for the GLBT market is best addressed through journals, both print and electronic, and Web sites; yet even in these sources, book reviews are less available for the majority of GLBT titles than for their mainstream counterparts. Although standard sources such as *Library Journal* and *Publishers Weekly* continue to provide reliable reviews of the genre, print reviewing resources devoted to GLBT books, such as *Lambda Book Report*, *Women's Review of Books*, *Gay and Lesbian Review Worldwide*, and the *Journal of Homosexuality*, are more comprehensive in their coverage.

Valuable Web sites offering reviews of GLBT books of all types include *Books to Watch Out For* (http://btwof.com) and the online journals *Blithe House Quarterly* and *The Lavender Salon Reader* (http://www.focol.org/lsr/). More specialized information on the genres of horror, science fiction, and fantasy can be found at *Queer Horror* (http://www.queerhorror.com/), *GLBT Fantasy Fiction Resources* (http://www.glbtfantasy.com), and *Lambda Sci-Fi* (http://www.lambdasf.org/fsf/books/recommend.html).

Although online reviewing sources are convenient, several problems are inherent in them. The primary problem is that reviews are not usually available for works published prior to the construction of the Internet in the 1990s, so readers may find themselves relying on the opinions of others who have read these books. These reviews—which are sometimes the only critical data accessible on a GLBT book—often vary greatly in length, ranging from a single line to several pages. Consequently the reader is unable to evaluate quality, although colorful language often conveys a good sense of the original.

From the reader's point of view, there are numerous advantages to the Internet as a source of book information. The Internet knows virtually no boundaries. Constrained by neither geography nor time of day, users no longer need to live in a large population center or have direct access to a GLBT bookstore. The Internet is also an efficient one-stop shopping experience for both patrons and acquisitions librarians, providing data on title availability along with bibliographic records and reviewing data in one location. Retailers' invitations to readers to personalize their online interaction by creating annotated reading lists, rating their enjoyment of each item, and contributing book reviews also generate suggestions for further reading. Finally, and perhaps most important, readers seeking GLBT literature online are reasonably anonymous in an online environment and can safely explore genres that may or may not be represented adequately or at all in their local library's holdings. For the readers' advisor, this holds the promise and challenge of dealing with a public potentially more knowledgeable about the GLBT literary landscape than the librarian.

Ultimately what any reader wants is a good story. GLBT readers and the collection development or readers' advisory librarian will find the tools discussed in the next section useful in locating good stories. Additional resources are included in the bibliography at the end of the book.

GLBT RA Resources

There are professional guides that can serve as handbooks for readers' advisors venturing into the field of GLBT literature. *Gay and Lesbian Library Service*, by Cal Gough and Ellen Greenblatt (McFarland, 1990), was the first attempt to present background and advice for librarians on building collections and providing outreach to their GLBT patrons.

In 1990, the same year that *Gay and Lesbian Library Service* appeared, a second edition of Eric Garber's *Uranian Worlds: A Guide to Sexuality in Science Fiction, Fantasy and Horror* was issued by G. K. Hall, followed more recently by Wayne Gunn's *Gay Male Sleuth in Print and Film: A History and Annotated Bibliography* (Scarecrow Press, 2005) and Judith A. Markowitz's *Gay Detective Novel: Lesbian and Gay Main Characters and Themes in Mystery* (McFarland, 2004).

Chronological and historical surveys of GLBT literature are common and include Noel I. Garde's *Homosexual in Literature: A Chronological Bibliography, Circa 700 B.C.–1958* and Claude J. Summers's *Gay Fictions: Wilde to Stonewall: Studies in a Male Homosexual Literary Tradition* (Continuum, 1990). Several works assume a scholarly approach to the genre, including Bonnie Zimmerman's *Safe Sea of Women: Lesbian Fiction, 1969–1989* (Beacon Press, 1990) and Georges-Michel Sarotte's *Like a Brother, Like a Lover: Male Homosexuality in the American Novel and Theatre from Herman Melville to James Baldwin* (Anchor/Doubleday, 1978).

Librarians and readers seeking an overview of the significant writers, works, and themes can consult several definitive encyclopedic works. Emmanuel S. Nelson's *Contemporary Gay American Novelists: A Bio-bibliographical Critical Sourcebook* (Greenwood, 1992) and Sandra Pollack's and Denise D. Knight's *Contemporary Lesbian Writers of the United States: A Bio-bibliographical Critical Sourcebook* (Greenwood, 1993) provide biographical information on selected authors, analyze reception of authors' works, and provide sources for additional discovery. Claude J. Summers's *Gay and Lesbian Literary Heritage: A Reader's Companion to the Writers and Their Works, from Antiquity to the Present* (Holt, 1995) was revised in 2002 and remains the hallmark, single-volume reference work on GLBT literature. Broader in scope, but lacking in critical analysis, is Gabriele Griffin's *Who's Who in Lesbian and Gay Writing* (Routledge, 2002). Finally, *Gay Histories and Cultures: An Encyclopedia*, by George E Haggerty (Garland, 2000), and *Lesbian Histories and Cultures: An Encyclopedia*, by Bonnie Zimmerman (Garland, 2000), contain extensive articles about literature and are essential to any reference collection.

Michael Cart, Christine A. Jenkins, and Frances Ann Day are a few of the authors responsible for creating useful readers' advisory tools for young audiences. Small presses have issued bibliographies, including Jenkins's *Look at Gayness: An Annotated Bibliography of Gay Materials for Young People* (Kindred Spirit Press, 1982) and Anna B. Friedler's *Guide to the 400 Best Children's and Adult's Multicultural Books about Lesbian and Gay People* (Lift Every Voice, 1997). Subsequent efforts received wider critical acclaim, such as Day's *Lesbian and Gay Voices: An Annotated Bibliography and Guide to Literature for Children and Young Adults* (Greenwood Press, 2000), recipient of the Stonewall Honor Book from the American Library Association, and Michael Cart's and Christine A. Jenkins's *Heart Has Its Reasons: Young Adult Literature with Gay/Lesbian/Queer Content, 1969–2004* (Scarecrow, 2006), which provides an excellent historical overview.

Collection development and readers' advisory for GLBT materials have become easier with the rise of publishers specializing in such literature, as well as a willingness of mainstream houses to include titles for the gay market as part of their catalogs. Library staff serving as readers' advisors have an unusual opportunity for professional growth. Identifying the diverse and widely dispersed sources of information on book production, evaluation, and selection in the field of GLBT literature can be time consuming and challenging. The question of the degree to which GLBT fiction will be represented in the electronic world of online resources such as *Ebrary* is only one example of the emerging issues that will challenge both readers and librarians in the years to come in the search for new voices and views in the world of GLBT literature.

Bibliography

Books

Cart, Michael, and Christine A. Jenkins. *Heart Has Its Reasons: Young Adult Literature with Gay/Lesbian/Queer Content, 1969–2004.* Lanham, MD: Scarecrow Press, 2006.

Day, Frances Ann. *Lesbian and Gay Voices: An Annotated Bibliography and Guide to Literature for Children and Young Adults.* Westport, CT: Greenwood Press, 2000.

Friedler, Anna B. *Guide to the 400 Best Children's and Adult's Multicultural Books about Lesbian and Gay People.* Centre, MA: Lift Every Voice, 1997.

Garber, Eric, and Lyn Paleo. *Uranian Worlds: A Guide to Sexuality in Science Fiction, Fantasy and Horror.* 2nd ed. Boston: G. K. Hall, 1990.

Garde, Noel I. *Homosexual in Literature: A Chronological Bibliography, Circa 700 B.C.–1958.* New York: Village Press, 1959.

Gough, Cal, and Ellen Greenblatt. *Gay and Lesbian Library Service.* Jefferson, NC: McFarland, 1990.

1

2

3

4

5

6

7

8

Griffin, Gabriele. *Who's Who in Lesbian and Gay Writing*. New York: Routledge, 2002.

Gunn, Drewey Wayne. *Gay Male Sleuth in Print and Film: A History and Annotated Bibliography*. Lanham, MD: Scarecrow Press, 2005.

Haggerty, George E. *Gay Histories and Cultures: An Encyclopedia*. New York: Garland, 2000.

Jenkins, Christine. *Look at Gayness: An Annotated Bibliography of Gay Materials for Young People*. Ann Arbor, MI: Kindred Spirit Press, 1982.

Markowitz, Judith A. *Gay Detective Novel: Lesbian and Gay Main Characters and Themes in Mystery*. Jefferson, NC: McFarland, 2004.

Nelson, Emmanuel S. *Contemporary Gay American Novelists: A Bio-bibliographical Critical Sourcebook*. Westport, CT: Greenwood, 1992.

Pollack, Sandra, and Denise D. Knight. *Contemporary Lesbian Writers of the United States: A Bio-bibliographical Critical Sourcebook*. Westport, CT: Greenwood, 1993.

Sarotte, Georges-Michel. *Like a Brother, Like a Lover: Male Homosexuality in the American Novel and Theatre from Herman Melville to James Baldwin*. Garden City, NY: Anchor/Doubleday, 1978.

Summers, Claude J. *Gay and Lesbian Literary Heritage: A Reader's Companion to the Writers and Their Works, from Antiquity to the Present*. New York: Routledge, 2002.

———. *Gay Fictions: Wilde to Stonewall: Studies in a Male Homosexual Literary Tradition*. New York: Continuum, 1990.

Zimmerman, Bonnie. *Lesbian Histories and Cultures: An Encyclopedia*. New York: Garland, 2000.

———. *The Safe Sea of Women: Lesbian Fiction, 1969–1989*. Boston: Beacon Press, 1990.

Journals

Gay and Lesbian Review Worldwide: http://glreview.com/index.html

Journal of Homosexuality: http://www.haworthpress.com/store/product. asp? sku=J082

Lambda Book Report: http://www.lambdaliterary.org/lambda_book_report/lbr.html

Women's Review of Books: http://www.wcwonline.org/womensreview

Journal Articles

Carmichaels, James V. "Effects of the Gay Publishing Boom on Classes of Titles Retrieved under the Subject Headings 'Homosexuality,' 'Gay Men,' and 'Gays' in the WorldCat OCLC Database." *Journal of Homosexuality* 42, no. 3 (2002): 65–88.

Web Sites

Books to Watch Out For: http://btwof.com

Blithe House Quarterly: http://www.blithe.com/

GLBT Fantasy Fiction Resources: http://www.glbtfantasy.com

Lambda Sci-Fi: http://www.lambdasf.org/fsf/books/recommend.html

The Lavender Salon Reader: http://www.focol.org/lsr/

Queer Horror: http://www.queerhorror.com/

Notes

1. Norman Mailer, "The Homosexual Villain," *One* 3 (1955): 8–12, reprinted in *Advertisements for Myself* (New York: Putnam, 1959).

2. Michael Cart, "Honoring Their Stories, Too: Literature for Gay and Lesbian Teens," *The Allan Review* 25, no. 1 (Fall 1997). Available at http://scholar.lib.vt.edu/ejournals/ALAN/fall97/cart.html (accessed February 11, 2008).

3. http://tinyurl.com/47943 (accessed February 11, 2008).

4. Ann Curry, *If I Ask, Will They Answer? Evaluating Public Library Reference Service to Gay/Lesbian Youth.* Available at http://www.slais.ubc.ca/PEOPLE/faculty/curry-p/pdf/GLBT.pdf (accessed February 11, 2008).

Part 2

The Literature

Chapter 4

Classics

Definition

To qualify as a classic, a work must be (or have been) widely read and have significant cultural impact by serving as a model for later writers (through structure, plot themes, or purpose of creation) of proper literary technique and creative possibility. The term itself also carries the implication of a work being established for some time as a part of the literary world, an aspect reflected in the inclusion here of the first-century Roman work *The Satyricon* as a beginning point. The majority of the titles included here come from Western European and American literature published in the nineteenth and twentieth centuries, with the Stonewall Riots of June 1969 serving as an end date.

Description and Characteristics

Readers may be surprised at the inclusion of such familiar standard fiction titles as Melville's *Moby Dick* in this section. The intention has been to illustrate the texts and subtexts within these novels that may appeal to a GLBT audience, rather than attempting to reclassify these works' basic character in any way. In considering GLBT literature, the term *classic* describes works that present gay, lesbian, bisexual, or transgender characters as recognizable human beings, also preserving—and often successfully challenging—the attitudes of the eras in which they were written. The orientation of the author is also considered. Many of these works were not originally written for the communities that would later adopt them into an emerging canon of representation, or were written by individuals who would not be considered members of those populations. The relatively small number of literary works worldwide written prior to the nineteenth century makes describing the beginnings of this genre relatively easy, although as queer theory is applied to the analysis of more and more novels, the pool of possible titles can be expected to grow.

The history of GLBT-related publication during the twentieth century can be divided into two eras. The first covers the period from 1900 to 1950, a time when homosexuality was only mentioned in medical and psychological periodicals, and works of literature portrayed gay men or lesbians by either depicting them as pathological (and usually killed them off in some fashion by story's end) or showing them as exceptions to the common rules of society. A well-known example of the latter is Radclyffe Hall's 1929 novel *The Well of Loneliness*.

The second era begins with the founding of the Mattachine Society in 1950 in Los Angeles, which marked the birth of what was termed by the activists of the day the "homophile" movement, whose aim was to effect improvement of social and legal conditions for homosexuals through education. It was during this period that many of the pulp paperbacks that would influence the writers of the gay liberation era—in some cases by stimulating reactions to their plot lines—were published, among them the lesbian novels of Ann Bannon. Its end came in June 1969 with the Stonewall Riots in New York City.

The unprecedented resistance to police harassment offered by the patrons of the Stonewall Inn sparked a new approach to the struggle for gay and lesbian civil rights in the United States, abandoning the slower homophile process for direct public confrontations and emphasizing the separate and distinct nature of the gay community as a revolutionary population, both politically and culturally. The literature of the post-Stonewall era , which can be said to have ended at least in part with the beginnings of the AIDS pandemic in 1981, was marked by an unabashed celebration of same-gender sexuality. A difficulty with some of this material is that it was written for a contemporary audience and often makes reference to events and cultural practices current at the time within the lesbian and gay community, but which have faded from popular memory, if they were ever in fact there, an issue which readers of works deemed " classic " may encounter as well.

Issues for the Readers' Advisor

The chief problem with choosing titles for this category is that these decisions are highly subjective. Because there was no formal way to canonize GLBT literature until publication and reviews increased and various awards were established, lists vary according to personal tastes; experiences; and referrals from sources as varied as friends, reading lists put out by gay and lesbian organizations, professional associations, and Web sites of every description. Thus, when working with readers who express an interest in classics, the best approach is to ask patrons about areas of interest or what they have previously read, then to point out some older titles that have dealt with similar subject matter. If a patron has no clear idea or has no background in gay and lesbian literature of any kind, it may be useful to begin with American writers and provide the patron with some information that will assist them in placing a work in the context of gay activism and its issues.

Chapter Organization

To demonstrate the development of the literature over time, this chapter arranges titles chronologically by the period in which they were published, beginning with the classical Roman era and proceeding through the nineteenth and mid-twentieth centuries. Readers will note the cultural variance in the entries, ranging from works originally published in Brazil and China to those rooted in the Anglo-Saxon tradition. Nevertheless, the entries within each timeframe may be considered read-alikes for one another, or readers may consult chapter 8 on historical fiction for additional works with historical settings, characters, or themes.

Resources

Bergman, David. "American Literature, Gay Male, Post-Stonewall." In *Gay and Lesbian Literary Heritage,* edited by Claude J. Summers, 42–47. New York: Holt, 1995.

Cady, Joseph. "American Literature, Gay Male, 1900–1969." In *Gay and Lesbian Literary Heritage,* edited by Claude J. Summers, 30–39. New York: Holt, 1995.

Smith, Martha Nell. "American Literature, Lesbian, 1900–1969." In *Gay and Lesbian Literary Heritage,* edited by Claude J. Summers, 39–42. New York: Holt, 1995.

Wadsworth, Ann. "American Literature, Lesbian, Post-Stonewall." In *Gay and Lesbian Literary Heritage,* edited by Claude J. Summers, 47–53. New York: Holt, 1995.

Pre-nineteenth Century

Petronius Arbiter. Translated by P. G. Walsh.

🎗 *The Satyricon.* New York: Oxford University Press, 1999. G B
Only fragments of this first-century story from classical Rome survive, painting a portrait of Encolpius, whose obsessive love for the slave boy Giton leaves him brokenhearted. He desires revenge, commits murder, and is cursed with impotence. A debauched satire first translated into English in the seventeenth century.

Awards: Publishing Triangle's 100 Best Lesbian and Gay Novels

Subjects: Antiquity • Books to film • Murder

Nineteenth Century

Alcott, Louisa May.

🎗 *Little Women.* New York: Random House, 2005 (1868). L
The popularity of Alcott's classic story of the March sisters, Amy, Beth, Meg, and Jo, practically defies the need for description. The young girls grow into women, fighting and loving each other as fiercely as only sisters could. Readers often interpret the tomboy Jo as being a lesbian.

Awards: Publishing Triangle's 100 Best Lesbian and Gay Novels

Subjects: Books to film • Relationships, parent–child • Siblings

Balzac, Honoré de.

🎗 *Lost Illusions.* New York: Random House, 2001 (1844). **G**

Craving fame and fortune, the young poet Lucien relocates to Paris and obtains the patronage of Madame de Bargeton and Marquise d'Espard. His meteoric rise is tainted by increasingly amoral behavior. Lucien's acquaintance, Vautrin, is clearly homosexual.

Awards: Publishing Triangle's 100 Best Lesbian and Gay Novels

Subjects: Authors • Crime • France

Caminha, Adolfo. Translated by E. A. Lacey.

🎗 *Bom-Crioulo: The Black Man and the Cabin Boy.* New York: Penguin, 1982 (1895). **G** **B**

A runaway slave finds freedom in naval service and love with a young cabin boy. The affair, marked by age and racial differences, is one-sided and obsessive for the former slave, and the story's arc becomes a slow, repetitive spiral into tragedy. Noteworthy for its nonjudgmental portrayal of homosexuality. Originally published in Brazil.

Awards: Publishing Triangle's 100 Best Lesbian and Gay Novels, Reader's Choice

Subjects: Age differences • Brazil • Interracial relationships • Love triangles • Slavery • Soldiers and sailors

Read-Alikes: For a lesbian-themed novel of the same period and locale, readers should try Aluisio Azevedo's *Slum*, sometimes entitled *Brazilian Tenement*.

Fu, Shen.

🎗 *Six Chapters of a Floating Life.* New York: Penguin Group, 1983 (1805). **L** **B**

Based on a true story. The eighteenth-century author relates his wife Shen Yun's attraction to a female singer. Shen Yun attempts to integrate the singer into the family as her husband's concubine. The unsuccessful effort leads to a sad ending. The first publication date is unknown, although the earliest copyrighted English-language edition is 1805. An alternative title is *Six Records of a Floating Life*.

Awards: Publishing Triangle's 100 Best Lesbian and Gay Novels, Reader's Choice

Subjects: China • Love triangles

James, Henry.

🎗 *The Bostonians.* New York: Modern Library, 2003 (1896). **L**

A spinster grooms a young woman for oratorical success in the suffrage movement. Their intense emotional bond is challenged by a Southern gentlemen wishing to marry the young woman and end her suffragist career.

Awards: Publishing Triangle's 100 Best Lesbian and Gay Novels

Subjects: Books to film • Feminism • Love triangles • Politics

Read-Alikes: James may have patterned his book after English author Eliza Lynn Linton's *Rebel of the Family*.

Melville, Herman.

🎗 *Billy Budd.* New York: Pocket Books, 1999 (1924). **G**

Pressed into naval service, the handsome, congenial Billy draws the wrath of a corrupt officer, Claggart. Billy and Claggart's interactions can be interpreted as those of unrequited lovers. Their conflict is resolved in opposition to their personalities. Written in 1891 but not published until 1924.

Awards: Publishing Triangle's 100 Best Lesbian and Gay Novels

Subjects: Books to film • England • Soldiers and sailors • War

🎗 *Moby Dick.* New York: Modern Library, 2003 (1851). **G**

Although not considered GLBT literature by contemporary standards, Captain Ahab's quest for revenge has numerous homoerotic elements. Ishmael and Queequeg's bed sharing becomes romance, and the "Squeeze of Hand" sequence represents masturbation. Frequent textual references to sperm and the title's sexually suggestive slang add credibility to a queer reading.

Awards: Publishing Triangle's 100 Best Lesbian and Gay Novels

Subjects: Boating • Books to film • Revenge • Soldiers and sailors

Wilde, Oscar.

🎗 *The Picture of Dorian Gray.* New York: St. Martin's Press, 2000 (1891). **G**

During a portrait session, Dorian Gray's wish for eternal youth is granted. Forever young, his thrill seeking leads to debauchery. Eventually, his desire for a normal life is trumped by fate. Basil and Lord Henry's attraction to Dorian is implied, although Dorian's sexual proclivities are unclear.

Awards: Publishing Triangle's 100 Best Lesbian and Gay Novels

Subjects: Art and artists • Books to film

Read-Alikes: Will Self's *Dorian: An Imitation* successfully re-creates Wilde's classic in the AIDS-ridden twentieth century.

1900–1950

Barnes, Djuna.

Ladies Almanack. New York: Penguin Group, 1993 (1928). **L**

Using the almanac as a literary device, complete with illustrations, Barnes satirizes Natalie Barney and members of her French literary salon. The erratic, archaic, and allegorical style camouflages a diversity of lesbian identities and celebrates lesbian sexuality. Originally privately published in France under the pseudonym "A Lady of Fashion."

Subjects: Authors • Autobiographical fiction • France • Humor

🎗 *Nightwood.* New York: Modern Library, 2000 (1937). **L** **T**

The lives of five pathological and pathetic characters are intertwined in this stylistic novel, which is driven by descriptive detail rather than plot or characterization. The codependent love affair between Robin and Nora is tested by infidelities and love triangles, in a decadent Parisian setting. A demanding work requiring the reader's commitment and attentiveness.

Awards: Publishing Triangle's 100 Best Lesbian and Gay Novels

Subjects: Autobiographical fiction • France • Love triangles • Sexual abuse

Read-Alikes: *Lover,* by Bertha Harris, is frequently compared to Djuna Barnes's *Nightwood*.

Bowles, Jane.

🌿 *Two Serious Ladies.* London: Peter Owen, 2003 (1943). **L B**

This psychological, semiautobiographical novel concerns the relationships of the spinster Christina and Frieda, a married woman. As Frieda falls in love with a Panamanian prostitute, Christina attempts to achieve moral correctness through personal debasement and prostitution. Darkly comedic subversion of gender roles.

Awards: Publishing Triangle's 100 Best Lesbian and Gay Novels

Subjects: Autobiographical fiction • Gender roles • Infidelity • Love triangles • Sex workers

Read-Alikes: Angela Carter subverts gender roles and gender identity in *Passion of New Eve*.

Burns, John Horne.

🌿 *The Gallery.* New York: New York Review of Books, 2004 (1947). **G B**

A bombed-out shopping area in occupied Italy serves as the backdrop for these vignettes. American soldiers mingle with locals and transact every type of business, from selling food to selling flesh. One story revolves around male homosexuality. Based on the author's war experiences.

Awards: Publishing Triangle's 100 Best Lesbian and Gay Novels

Subjects: Autobiographical fiction • Italy • Soldiers and sailors • War • World War II

Bussy, Dorothy.

🌿 *Olivia.* London: Virago, 1987 (1949). **L**

Young Olivia's year at finishing school features a crush on a teacher and observation of her beloved's affair with another teacher.

Awards: Publishing Triangle's 100 Best Lesbian and Gay Novels

Subjects: France • Students

Read-Alikes: Boarding school homosexuality is a common literary device, as illustrated in Antonia White's *Frost in May*.

Capote, Truman.

🌿 *Other Voices, Other Rooms.* New York: Random House, 2004 (1949). **G**

Ornate prose and southern gothicism infuse the tale of Joel, a young boy forced to live with family members who are both strange and strangers. The effeminate, motherless Joel struggles to grow up and find love.

Awards: Publishing Triangle's 100 Best Lesbian and Gay Novels

Subjects: Books to film • Coming-of-age • Families • Louisiana

Read-Alikes: Although stylistically different, Jackson Tippett McCrae's *Bark of the Dogwood* reconstructs elements of Capote's work, including life in a nontraditional, multiracial household and struggles with sexual orientation. In an obvious connection, Mc-Crae's main character uses Capote's real-life middle name.

Cather, Willa.

🏆 *Death Comes for the Archbishop.* Lincoln: University of Nebraska Press, 1999 (1927). **G**

Cather celebrates the male pioneering spirit and spiritual bonds as two Catholic clergymen, Latour and Vaillant, travel across the American Southwest during the nineteenth century. The bond experienced by the two eclipses earthly relationships, and after Vaillant's death Latour imagines their reunion in heaven.

Awards: Publishing Triangle's 100 Best Lesbian and Gay Novels

Subjects: Native Americans • New Mexico • Religion

Cocteau, Jean.

🏆 *Holy Terrors.* Norfolk, CT: New Directions Publishing, 1966. **G B**

Gerard has a crush on Paul, who has a crush on another boy and is in an emotionally incestuous relationship with his sister, Elizabeth. The three live together in lazy squalor until Elizabeth's friend Agatha appears and shifts alliances into a love triangle, with Elizabeth as master manipulator. Slim GLBT content. Originally published in France (1929) as *Les Enfants Terribles*.

Awards: Publishing Triangle's 100 Best Lesbian and Gay Novels

Subjects: Books to film • France • Love triangles • Siblings

🏆 *Livre Blanc.* San Francisco: City Lights Books, 1989. **G L B**

After the sight of a naked man awakens the narrator's sexuality, he attempts to direct his feelings toward women. When that fails he embraces religion, but still cannot escape his homosexuality. Feeling outcast, he enters self-imposed exile, leaving behind a diary condemning society's intolerance. Loosely autobiographical. Originally published anonymously in France (1928); the English title translates as *White Book* or *White Paper*.

Awards: Publishing Triangle's 100 Best Lesbian and Gay Novels, Reader's Choice

Subjects: Homophobia • Homophobia, self-directed • Religion

Read-Alikes: Critics interpret this work as a response to André Gide's *Croydon*.

Firbank, Ronald.

🏆 *Concerning the Eccentricities of Cardinal Pirelli.* London: Duckworth, 1977 (1926). **G T**

A Spanish cardinal, well versed in wicked worldly ways, enjoys dressing as a woman, sneaking into taverns, and fawning over the altar boys. To make matters worse, the cardinal's housekeeper is a spy. A hilarious examination of hypocrisy.

Awards: Publishing Triangle's 100 Best Lesbian and Gay Novels

Subjects: Cross-dressing • Humor • Religion • Secrets

Read-Alikes: Brigid Brophy employs a similar campy style in *Finishing Touch*.

Ford, Charles Henri, and Parker Tyler.

🏵 *Young and Evil.* Salem, NH: Ayer, 1975. **G**

A fictional exploration following Karel and Julian through the gay New York sub-culture of bars and drag shows between the world wars. Stylistically convoluted and therefore difficult to read, this vivid, gritty book is considered the first un-apologetic work of gay fiction, written by a gay author for a gay audience. Origi-nally published in France in 1933 and banned in America until 1975.

Awards: Publishing Triangle's 100 Best Lesbian and Gay Novels

Subjects: Art and artists • Autobiographical fiction • New York City • Race relations • Re-lationships

Forster, E. M.

🏵 *Maurice.* New York: W. W. Norton, 1993 (1971). **G**

In this story of class conflict and societal constraints, Maurice and Clive repress their mutual attraction in favor of a platonic friendship. Horrified at their feelings, Clive retreats into marriage, while Maurice seeks therapy. After years of self-loathing, Maurice accepts himself and finds love. Written in 1913–1914, *Maurice* was not published until 1971 because Forster feared the topic would repulse readers.

Awards: Publishing Triangle's 100 Best Lesbian and Gay Novels

Subjects: Books to film • Class conflict • England • Homophobia • Homophobia, self-di-rected

Fuller, H. B. (Henry Blake).

🏵 *Bertram Cope's Year.* New York: Penguin, 1998 (1919). **G**

Set in a fictitious Midwestern town. Cope, a handsome, unmarried university in-structor, is pursued by the town's single women, who mistake his politeness for romantic interest. A comedy of manners and misunderstandings ensues, particu-larly since a few men are interested in Cope as well. A rare, positive portrayal of daily gay domestic life.

Awards: Publishing Triangle's 100 Best Lesbian and Gay Novels, Reader's Choice

Subjects: Students, college • Teachers

Genet, Jean.

🏵 *Funeral Rites.* New York: Grove/Atlantic, 1987 (1969). **G** **B**

The death of Jean's lover at the hands of the Nazis and his subsequent period of grief and recovery mirror France's defeat during World War II. A complex work with a multiplicity of interlinked characters, time distortions, and cruelty. Origi-nally published in France in 1949.

Awards: Publishing Triangle's 100 Best Lesbian and Gay Novels, Reader's Choice

Subjects: France • Love triangles • Nazis

🏵 *Our Lady of the Flowers.* New York: Grove Press, 1987 (1955). **G**

Jean is an imprisoned thief and male prostitute with a vivid fantasy life. Fantasies and prison life are recounted in a dreamlike, explicit narrative complete with re-ligious imagery, which blurs reality and fantasy. Probably autobiographical and intentionally provocative. Originally published in France in 1942. First published in the United States as *Gutter in the Sky*.

Awards: Publishing Triangle's 100 Best Lesbian and Gay Novels

Subjects: Autobiographical fiction • Crime • Cross-dressing • Sex workers

Read-Alikes: Predating Genet's masterpiece is African American author and former prisoner Chester Himes's *Yesterday Will Make You Cry*, a frank exploration of race and homosexuality.

Querelle. New York: Grove/Atlantic, 1994. **G**

A French sailor explores same-sex attraction through deliberate gambling losses, which allow him to sleep with men. A beautifully fatalistic, character-driven novel about the duality of human nature. Originally published in France in 1947.

Awards: Publishing Triangle's 100 Best Lesbian and Gay Novels, Reader's Choice

Subjects: Books to film • Murder • Sex workers

The Thief's Journal. New York: Grove • Atlantic, 1987 (1964). **G**

Gentle prose is a sharp contrast to the harshness suffered by Jean, the protagonist in this fictionalized autobiography. From a lonely existence in reform school to a life of petty crime, imprisonment, and squalor, betrayal, abjection, and rejection are commonplace. The first American edition was released fifteen years after the work's appearance in France (1949.)

Awards: Publishing Triangle's 100 Best Lesbian and Gay Novels, Reader's Choice

Subjects: Autobiographical fiction • Crime • Sex workers

Gide, André.

The Counterfeiters. New York: Knopf, 1973. **G**

In a complex plot about Edouard and his nephews, Edouard accidentally flirts with his youngest nephew; the middle boy has a crush on his uncle, and the oldest is involved with a married woman who is also Edouard's friend. Read between the lines for the homoerotic content. Originally appeared in French under the title *Les faux-monnayeurs* in 1925.

Awards: Publishing Triangle's 100 Best Lesbian and Gay Novels

Subjects: Families • France • Friendship

The Immoralist. New York: Penguin, 2001 (1948). **G B**

Recovering from serious illness, Michel resolves to live a full life. He rejects societal constraints, travels, and pursues every possible experience, including relationships with young men. The stress of his double life takes a tragic toll, in this readable yet morally complex tale.

Awards: Publishing Triangle's 100 Best Lesbian and Gay Novels

Subjects: Africa • France • Teachers

Hall, Radclyffe.

The Unlit Lamp. St. Clair Shores, MI: Scholarly Press, 1972 (1924). **L**

Follow Joan, an intelligent tomboy, as she struggles from adolescence to adulthood in early twentieth-century England. Railing against society's gender roles, torn between her teacher and her codependent mother, Joan slowly deteriorates into madness.

Awards: Publishing Triangle's 100 Best Lesbian and Gay Novels, Reader's Choice

Subjects: England • Families • Mental health • Relationships, parent–child

🏶 *The Well of Loneliness.* New York: Anchor Books, 1990 (1928). **L**

Her parents named her Stephen. Afflicted with intense attractions to women, Stephen is unable to name her disease. Appalled and emotionally dead, Stephen is eventually consumed by a love so intense that she will do anything for her lover, including give up on their love. Melodramatic by today's standards, *The Well* remains required reading.

Awards: Publishing Triangle's 100 Best Lesbian and Gay Novels

Subjects: England • Families • Homophobia, self-directed • Love

Read-Alikes: Readers may want to try Rosamond Lehmann's boarding school love story, *Dusty Answer.*

Isherwood, Christopher.

🏶 *Berlin Stories.* Norfolk, CT: New Directions, 1963 (1945). **G**

Blackmail, espionage, political intrigue, communism, fascism, and nightclubs figure prominently in these two novellas based on Isherwood's real-life experiences. This text forms the basis for the popular 1972 film *Cabaret.*

Awards: Publishing Triangle's 100 Best Lesbian and Gay Novels

Subjects: Autobiographical fiction • Books to film • Germany • Politics

Lawrence, D. H.

🏶 *Women in Love.* New York: Modern Library, 2002 (1920). **G** **B**

In postwar England, Ursula is attracted to Rupert, and her sister Gudrun is longing for Gerald. The women struggle with love versus the constraints of marriage, while the men resist homosexual urges. A character-driven story abundant in personal reflection.

Awards: Publishing Triangle's 100 Best Lesbian and Gay Novels

Subjects: Books to film • Dating • England • Siblings

Read-Alikes: Lawrence's *Rainbow* is considered a prequel to this book.

Mann, Thomas.

🏶 *Death in Venice.* New York: Ecco, 2004 (1925). **G**

A middle-aged writer, Gustav von Aschenbach, vacations in Venice where his long-suppressed homosexual yearnings are ignited by the sight of a beautiful young boy. Believing beauty fuels artistic creation, Gustav follows the boy to the point of deadly obsession. Richly evocative writing. First published in 1911 in German under the title *Der Tod in Venedig.*

Awards: Publishing Triangle's 100 Best Lesbian and Gay Novels

Subjects: Authors • Books to film • Italy

Read-Alikes: In *Hotel,* by Elizabeth Bowen, the vacationing Mrs. Kerr is attracted to Sydney.

Maxwell, William.

🎗 *The Folded Leaf.* New York: Knopf, 1996 (1945). **G**

Circa 1920, Spud and Lymie strike up a high school friendship and continue on to become college roommates. Spud's move to a fraternity house and his love for Sally test the relationship and push Lymie over the edge. Beautifully captures time and place.

Awards: Publishing Triangle's 100 Best Lesbian and Gay Novels, Reader's Choice

Subjects: Coming-of-age • Students, college

Mayne, Xavier.

Imre: A Memorandum. Peterborough, ON: Broadview Press, 2003 (1908). **G**

Oswald, a British citizen vacationing in nineteenth-century Hungary, sends a "memorandum" to a friend describing his love of Imre, a soldier. Fearing rejection, Oswald nevertheless admits his love for Imre, with surprisingly positive results. Xavier Mayne is a pen name used by Edward Prime-Stevenson.

Subjects: Hungary • Soldiers and sailors

Read-Alikes: John Osburn's *A Patriot for Me* is another Austro-Hungarian love story with a military theme.

Meeker, Richard.

🎗 *Better Angel.* Los Angeles: Alyson Books, 2000 (1933). **G**

Teenager Kurt Gray senses his difference from other children. Puberty results in fear and attempted redemption through religion; college culminates in a one-sided relationship. Graduate studies and a European vacation yield experience and idolized love in this mature, balanced narrative. Richard Meeker was the pen name used by Forman Brown.

Awards: Publishing Triangle's 100 Best Lesbian and Gay Novels, Reader's Choice

Subjects: Coming out • Families • Friendship • Love triangles • Music

Mishima, Yukio.

🎗 *Confessions of a Mask.* Norfolk, CT: New Directions Publishing, 1968 (1958). **G** **B**

Kochan attempts to fit into a society devoted to conformity. By dating a woman, he hopes to distract himself from attractive men. Internal conflicts parallel external experiences during World War II in Tokyo. Universal themes with a Japanese setting and writing style characterize this 1949 publication, which appeared in the United States in 1958.

Awards: Publishing Triangle's 100 Best Lesbian and Gay Novels

Subjects: Homophobia, self-directed • Japan • Sadomasochism

Musil, Robert.

🎗 *Young Torless.* New York: Pantheon, 1982 (1955). **G**

Thomas Torless, a boarding school student, discovers his best friends are extorting, torturing, and sexually abusing a classmate to whom he is attracted. Thomas must choose between loyalty to friends or personal feelings and moral beliefs. Originally published in Germany as *Confusions of Young Törless* in 1906.

Awards: Publishing Triangle's 100 Best Lesbian and Gay Novels

Subjects: Abuse • Books to film • Students

Read-Alikes: Complicity in evil is the theme of Gunter Grass's *Tin Drum*.

Proust, Marcel.

🌶 *Remembrance of Things Past.* New York: Knopf, 1982 (1934). G L B

Inspired by people and events in the author's life. The narrator delves into minutiae, detailing every expression and feeling with a complexly beautiful sentence structure. Homosexuality is presented within the class structures of numerous characters, but the most obvious is Baron de Charlus. A long, challenging read alternatively entitled *In Search of Lost Time*. Volumes are often individually titled: *Swann's Way, Within a Budding Grove, Guermantes' Way, Cities of the Plain, Captive, Sweet Cheat Gone,* and *Past Recaptured*.

Awards: Publishing Triangle's 100 Best Lesbian and Gay Novels

Subjects: Class conflict • France

Read-Alikes: André Aciman's sensual style in *Call Me by Your Name,* which tells the story of young Oliver and Elio's romance, recalls Proust's style.

Renault, Mary.

🌶 *Friendly Young Ladies.* New York: Knopf, 2003 (1945). L B

In this 1944 novel, multiple love triangles feature prominently. Helen loves Leo. Leo's sister Elsie desires Peter, who in turn desires Leo. Leo falls for Joe and "recovers" her sexual identity, in this contradictory story of mistaken sexual identity. Originally published in the United States as *Middle Mist*.

Awards: Publishing Triangle's 100 Best Lesbian and Gay Novels

Subjects: England • Love triangles • Sexual identity

Read-Alikes: In Compton Mackenzie's *Extraordinary Women,* Rosalba sleeps with both men and women, much to the chagrin of her lover.

Sinclair, Jo.

🌶 *Wasteland.* Philadelphia: Jewish Publication Society, 1987 (1946). L

Jake's visits to a psychiatrist are the medium for revealing his intense shame about his lesbian sister Debbie and his Jewish immigrant parents. Debbie's self-acceptance allows her to become the family's psychological salvation. Her character is the first well-rounded Jewish lesbian in American literature, and the story serves as a semiautobiographical representation of the author. Jo Sinclair is the pen name used by Ruth Seid.

Awards: Publishing Triangle's 100 Best Lesbian and Gay Novels

Subjects: Autobiographical fiction • Families • Jews • Mental health • Photography

Read-Alikes: Readers should try Paul Goodman's *Making Do* and *Parent's Day*.

Stein, Gertrude.

🎗 *The Autobiography of Alice B. Toklas.* New York: Modern Library, 1993 (1933). **L**

A self-professed genius, Stein pretends to be Alice writing about Gertrude, but in reality, Stein is writing about herself. Glimpses of the legendary couple's life are possible, but the book mainly works as a portrait of Paris, particularly the art and literary scene, before, during, and after World War I.

Awards: Publishing Triangle's 100 Best Lesbian and Gay Novels

Subjects: Autobiographical fiction • France • Stein, Gertrude • Toklas, Alice B.

Read-Alikes: The Stein–Tolkas love letters can be found in *Baby Precious Always Shines*. For another lesbian's perspective on Paris during the same period, readers may want to check out Janet Flanner's *Paris Was Yesterday, 1925–1939*.

🎗 *Three Lives.* Boston: Bedford/St. Martin's, 2000 (1909). **G L B**

Three women, three lives, three stories, each with characters that can be interpreted as gay or lesbian. Anna forms a romance with a widow. Melanctha, a black woman, learns about life from Jane, and Lena marries a suspiciously gay man. Stein's unconventional prose makes these stories challenging reading.

Awards: Publishing Triangle's 100 Best Lesbian and Gay Novels

Subjects: African Americans • Race relations • Relationships

Vidal, Gore.

🎗 *The City and the Pillar.* New York: Vintage, 2003 (1948). **G**

Jim wanders around the world engaging in unsatisfactory love affairs while looking for his first lover, Bob. When Jim finally finds Bob and attempts to rekindle their affair, the harsh reality of idolized love proves disastrous. Originally published in 1948 and republished in 1965 with an alternative ending.

Awards: Publishing Triangle's 100 Best Lesbian and Gay Novels

Subjects: Coming out • Love • Murder • Sexual abuse

Waugh, Evelyn.

🎗 *Brideshead Revisited.* New York: Knopf, 1993 (1945). **G**

Sebastian, a wealthy, Catholic Englishman, befriends Charles, a middle-class Protestant, at Oxford University. Religion, politics, class struggles, and the decline of the aristocracy are played out against Charles's recollections of his strangely intense relationship with Sebastian and his family. A story of faith and sorrow.

Awards: Publishing Triangle's 100 Best Lesbian and Gay Novels; Publishing Triangle's 100 Best Lesbian and Gay Novels, Reader's Choice

Subjects: Books to film • Class conflict • England • Religion

Wescott, Glenway.

🏃 *The Grandmothers.* Madison: University of Wisconsin Press, 1996 (1927). **G**

Alwyn, an American Midwesterner living in Europe, searches for his identity by reconstructing family history through memories and trinkets. The process delineates the differences between the continental nature of his life and the frontier suffering of his ancestors. A sweeping, lavishly descriptive historical novel.

Awards: Publishing Triangle's 100 Best Lesbian and Gay Novels, Reader's Choice

Subjects: Families • Wisconsin

Winsloe, Christa.

🏃 *The Child Manuela.* Salem, NH: Ayer, 1975. **L**

After her mother's death, Manuela forms a bond with a friend's mother. At boarding school, her attraction to older women continues with a crush on a teacher. Manuela openly proclaims her affections and suffers the consequences. Simple, clear writing with strong female characters. Originally a play entitled *Ritter Nérestan (Knight Nérestan)* and retitled *Gestern und heute (Yesterday and Today)*, this 1933 work forms the basis for the classic German film *Mäedchen in Uniform*.

Awards: Publishing Triangle's 100 Best Lesbian and Gay Novels

Subjects: Books to film • Students, high school

Read-Alikes: Clemence Dane's *Regiment of Women* may have influenced Winsloe. Dorothy Baker's *Trio* also began as a dramatic play about an evil lesbian seductress.

Woolf, Virginia.

🏃 *Mrs. Dalloway.* New York: Harcourt, 2002 (1925). **L**

Fretting over the success of a party, Clarissa reflects upon her relationships with the guests and her life choices. Contrasting with Clarissa's angst is Septimus, a shell-shocked veteran. Although the two never meet, their lives are linked via a party guest.

Awards: Publishing Triangle's 100 Best Lesbian and Gay Novels

Subjects: Books to film • England • Love triangles • Parties

Read-Alikes: Michael Cunningham takes his title for *The Hours* directly from Woolf's early drafts of *Mrs. Dalloway*. For a male twist on the story, readers may want to try Robin Lippincott's *Mr. Dalloway*.

🏃 *Orlando.* London: Vintage, 2004 (1928). **T**

Orlando, a young seventeenth-century English aristocrat, mysteriously acquires immortality. As befits a man of noble position, he pursues politics, poetry, and love, until he is suddenly transmogrified into a woman. The pursuit of love and other ideals is severely altered and curtailed based on society's gender expectations.

Awards: Publishing Triangle's 100 Best Lesbian and Gay Novels

Subjects: Books to film • Gender identity Time travel

Read-Alikes: Jeanette Winterson's *Powerbook* is a virtual reality version of *Orlando*.

1950–1969

Baldwin, James.

🏃 *Another Country.* New York: Vintage, 1993 (1962). **B**

Rufus Scott, a black musician, feels racially oppressed, yet is drawn into intimate relations with white lovers. Subconsciously Rufus detests himself for being attracted to lovers whose race represents oppression. He acts out his frustrations by destroying relationships and, eventually, destroying himself. A complexly plotted examination of race and sexuality.

Awards: Publishing Triangle's 100 Best Lesbian and Gay Novels

Subjects: African Americans • Interracial relationships • Music • Race relations

Read-Alikes: Baldwin plumbs the depths of interracial same-sex relationships in *Just Above My Head,* and his *Tell Me How Long the Train's Been Gone* contrasts a heterosexual interracial liaison with a homosexual affair within an ethnic group.

🏃 *Giovanni's Room.* New York: Modern Library, 2001 (1956). **G** **B**

As a boy, David had a sexual encounter with his best friend; but he ignored the memory and denied the feelings until, as an adult living in Paris, he meets Giovanni. With David's girlfriend out of the country, he and Giovanni embark on a disastrous affair mixed with love and self-loathing.

Awards: Publishing Triangle's 100 Best Lesbian and Gay Novels

Subjects: France • Homophobia, self-directed

Read-Alikes: Kate sabotages her relationship with Esther and admits her love too late, in Jane Rule's *This Is Not For You.*

Bannon, Ann.

Beebo Brinker Chronicles. **L** **B**

A classic "big girl in the city" tale featuring Betty Jean "Beebo" Brinker and the cast of characters she encounters.

Subjects: 1950s • Abuse • Butches • Dating • Friendship • Homophobia, self-directed • Love • New York City

Read-Alikes: *Spring Fire,* by Vin Packer, is considered the forerunner of the Brinker series. In Monica Nolan's *Lois Lenz, Lesbian Secretary,* a former cheerleader enters the work world and finds herself surrounded by women in the typing pool and her all-girl boarding house.

Odd Girl Out. San Francisco: Cleis, 2001 (1957).

Laura Landon is eased into 1950s sorority life with the assistance of popular and vivacious Beth. Her attraction to Beth evolves slowly and becomes painfully obviously to Beth, who takes advantage of the situation. Light reading romance novel notable for the survival of its protagonist.

I Am a Woman. San Francisco: Cleis, 2002 (1959).

Laura Landon has signed all the yearbooks, attended her college graduation, and left behind heartbreak to find a lesbian life in

Manhattan. Through her divorcée roommate, Laura meets Jack, a campy, closeted gay man who introduces her to a bevy of beautiful butches and Beebo Brinker.

Women in the Shadows. San Francisco: Cleis, 2002 (1959).

Beebo's obsessive and controlling love for Laura turns violent, driving Laura into Jack's arms. Striving to be normal, Jack and Laura take the socially acceptable route by marrying and having a child, but Laura cannot shake her same-sex feelings. A violent, depressing turn of events in the series.

Journey to a Woman. San Francisco: Cleis, 2003 (1960).

Beth is a married mom but is still dreaming of Laura and becoming friends with lesbian model Vega. As a result of reading a few lesbian books, Beth ends up writing the author, visiting New York, and trying to find Laura.

Beebo Brinker. San Francisco: Cleis, 2001 (1962).

Here is Beebo before she meets Laura. Ejected from her Midwestern home, Beebo travels to New York City circa 1950, finds the lesbian neighborhood, and promptly sets the femme community aquiver. This last volume in the series presents Beebo at her youngest and can be read as the first volume in the series.

Barr, James.

🖋 *Quatrefoil.* Boston: Alyson Publications, 1991 (1950). **G**

Personal choices, familial expectations, and the need for self-acceptance collide in this story of a love affair between two naval officers. In 1946, Phillip Froelich, facing a court martial for insubordination, meets the older officer Tim Danelaw, who guides Phillip toward self-awareness and acceptance.

Awards: Publishing Triangle's 100 Best Lesbian and Gay Novels, Reader's Choice

Subjects: Love • Soldiers and sailors

Burroughs, William S.

🖋 *Naked Lunch.* New York: Grove, 2003 (1962). **G**

A narcotic-addicted exterminator kills his wife and begins a drug-induced descent into madness in this semiautobiographical, science fiction work that is totally lacking in structure and linear plot. References to "fags" and "fruits" demonstrate Burroughs's conflicted feelings about his sexual orientation. The U.S. publication resulted in an obscenity trial.

Awards: Publishing Triangle's 100 Best Lesbian and Gay Novels

Subjects: Autobiographical fiction • Books to film • Mental health • Science fiction • Sex • Substance abuse

🖋 *Queer.* New York: Viking, 1985 (1951). **G**

William Lee tries to kick a guilt-induced drug habit while pursuing Eugene. Lee's obsession with Eugene is like his lust for drugs—destructive and difficult to quit. Burroughs's forthright and satirical style makes this an easier read than his later work.

Awards: Publishing Triangle's 100 Best Lesbian and Gay Novels, Reader's Choice

Subjects: Mexico • Substance abuse • Travel

Chester, Alfred.

🎗 *The Exquisite Corpse.* Santa Rosa, CA: Black Sparrow Press, 2000 (1967). **G** **L** **B** **T**

In a series of interconnected stories in which time and reality are irrelevant, pained characters shift names and personalities with no apparent purpose other than to demonstrate life's cruel beauty.

Awards: Publishing Triangle's 100 Best Lesbian and Gay Novels

Subjects: Class conflict • Gender identity • Race relations

Donovan, John.

I'll Get There, It Better Be Worth the Trip. New York: Dell, 1971 (1969). **G** **Teen**

After his grandmother's death, Davy is sent to live with his mother. A new school brings a new and confusing type of friendship with Altschuler. Through these radical changes Davy's dog Fred is a constant companion and comfort.

Subjects: Coming-of-age • Death and dying • Families • Pets

Read-Alikes: The title character in Rosa Guy's *Ruby* is involved in a love affair that she and Daphne are prepared to forget in favor of male friends.

Durrell, Lawrence.

🎗 *Alexandria Quartet.* Boston: Faber and Faber, 1968.

A complex, multipart story within a story, featuring an aspiring writer fearful of failure in love and career. Throughout the lushly descriptive tale runs the subtle implication that male bonding causes impotence in love and writing. Originally published as four separate novels, entitled *Justine* (1957), *Balthazar* (1958), *Mountolive* (1958), and *Clea* (1960)

Awards: Publishing Triangle's 100 Best Lesbian and Gay Novels

Subjects: Authors • Egypt • Relationships

Friedman, Sanford.

🎗 *Totempole.* San Francisco: North Point Press, 1984 (1965). **G**

Follow Stephen Wolfe from childhood through army service in the Korean War as he struggles to conform to heterosexual society and resolve his sexuality in relation to his Judaism. Stephen eventually finds peace through friendship with a Korean prisoner of war.

Awards: Publishing Triangle's 100 Best Lesbian and Gay Novels, Reader's Choice

Subjects: Jews • Korea • War

Hansen, Joseph.

🎗 *Known Homosexual.* Canoga Park, CA: Major Books, 1977 (1968). **G**

Steve is a married, black man involved with Coy, a white male. When Coy ends up murdered, Steve is the prime suspect. Interracial tensions and society norms in the mid-twentieth century lend credence to Steve's presumed guilt. James Colton, sometimes spelled Coulton, was a pseudonym

used by Hansen. Alternative titles for this work are *Stranger to Himself* and *Pretty Boy Dead*.

Awards: Publishing Triangle's 100 Best Lesbian and Gay Novels, Reader's Choice

Subjects: African Americans • Interracial relationships • Intrigue • Murder

Highsmith, Patricia.

🏵 *The Price of Salt.* New York: W. W. Norton, 1990 (1952). **L**

Nearly divorced Carol is a refined, financially secure mother; the younger, orphaned Therese struggles to make ends meet and hopes for a career break as a stage designer. Despite obvious differences, they are inexplicably attracted to one another and pursue a relationship set against the mores of 1950s America. Originally published under the pseudonym Claire Morgan and sometimes entitled *Carol*.

Awards: Publishing Triangle's 100 Best Lesbian and Gay Novels; Publishing Triangle's 100 Best Lesbian and Gay Novels, Reader's Choice

Subjects: 1950s • Coming out • Homophobia • Love

Isherwood, Christopher.

🏵 *A Single Man.* Minneapolis: University of Minnesota Press, 2001 (1964). **G**

Presents one day in the life of George, a British professor mourning the death of his American lover. George suffers alone, because it would be socially unacceptable to acknowledge the source of his grief.

Awards: Publishing Triangle's 100 Best Lesbian and Gay Novels

Subjects: California • Couples • Death and dying • Grief

Read-Alikes: In *Hood*, by Emma Donoghue, Pen silently mourns Cara's death.

Knowles, John.

🏵 *A Separate Peace.* New York: Simon & Schuster, 2003 (1960). **G**

The athletic Finny and studious Gene are roommates at a private boy's boarding school during World War II. Idealized male bonding implies a same-sex attraction, until Gene's resentments and jealousies jeopardize Finny's life.

Awards: Publishing Triangle's 100 Best Lesbian and Gay Novels, Reader's Choice

Subjects: Books to film • Coming-of-age • Friendship • Students, high school

Read-Alikes: Knowles's *Peace Breaks Out* is the sequel to this work.

Leduc, Violette.

🏵 *La Bâtarde.* Normal, IL: Dalkey Archive Press, 2003 (1964). **L** **B**

Violet is shipped off to boarding school, where she explores her sexuality through a romance with fellow student Isabella. Violet's unrequited love for both women and men, a failed marriage, war-induced deprivation, and general self-loathing are poetically rendered in this beautifully tragic work of autobiographical fiction.

Awards: Publishing Triangle's 100 Best Lesbian and Gay Novels

Subjects: Autobiographical fiction • Coming-of-age • France

Read-Alikes: *Intimate Memories*, by Mabel Dodge Luhan, is a frank fictionalization of her boarding school passions.

♥ *Therese and Isabella.* New York: Farrar, Straus & Giroux, 1967. **L**

Therese narrates this short, sensual love story of her relationship with fellow boarding school student Isabella. Originally written as a chapter in Leduc's *La Bâtarde*, it was excised by the publisher as a condition of publication.

Awards: Publishing Triangle's 100 Best Lesbian and Gay Novels

Subjects: Books to film • France • Students

Read-Alikes: Ivy Compton-Burnett's *More Women Than Men* features a cast of homosexual staff at a boarding school.

Lezama Lima, José. Translated by Gregory Rabassa.

♥ *Paradiso.* Normal, IL: Dalkey Archive Press, 2000 (1974). **G**

Cemi's childhood centers on family and the death of his father. Entering adolescence, he begins looking for his father in each experience and, through an all-male love triangle, emerges ready for adulthood. A lengthy, prose-heavy work of autobiographical fiction for readers who like a challenge. First published in Cuba in 1966.

Awards: Publishing Triangle's 100 Best Lesbian and Gay Novels

Subjects: Autobiographical fiction • Coming-of-age • Cuba • Hispanics • Love triangles

Read-Alikes: Reinaldo Arenas's *Farewell to the Sea* exhibits the same sweeping scope and beauty, minus the florid style.

Mann, Thomas.

♥ *Confessions of Felix Krull.* New York: Signet Classics, 1957. **G** **B**

In Mann's comic masterpiece, the narcissistic con man Felix Krull successfully charms, tricks, and seduces everyone he meets, male and female. In episodic fashion, the amoral Felix manipulates his way up the social ladder, building a fortune through theft.

Awards: Publishing Triangle's 100 Best Lesbian and Gay Novels, Reader's Choice

Subjects: Books to film • Crime

Miller, Isabel.

♥ *Patience and Sarah.* Vancouver, BC: Arsenal Pulp Press, 2005 (1969). **L**

This beloved classic features Patience, a financially comfortable unmarried woman, and Sarah, a free-spirited young woman dressing as a man for practical reasons. Longing for a place to be together, the two devise a means to spend their lives together. A touching story based on historical characters. Originally self-published under the title *A Place for Us* by Isabel Miller.

Awards: Publishing Triangle's 100 Best Lesbian and Gay Novels; Stonewall Book Award, 1971

Subjects: Cross-dressing • Gender identity • Love

Read-Alikes: In Miller's *Side by Side,* Patience and Sarah are reimagined as Patricia and Sharon. *Ladies,* by Doris Grumbach, is also based on real women who lived together, in eighteenth-century Wales.

Mishima, Yukio.

🏵 *Forbidden Colors.* New York: Knopf, 1999 (1968). **G**

Women are the focal point for Shunsuke's worldly disappointments; and he extracts revenge through the beautiful, emotionally shallow Yuichi. Through Yuichi, a marriage is destroyed, a woman reduced to a state of shock, and another woman tricked into Shunsuke's bed. A dark tale set in post–World War II Tokyo. The author's real name was Hiraoka Kimitake.

Awards: Publishing Triangle's 100 Best Lesbian and Gay Novels, Reader's Choice

Subjects: Japan • Lust • Revenge

Read-Alikes: Lovers of Japanese literature may find Stephen D. Miller's anthology *Partings at Dawn* of interest.

Nabokov, Vladimir.

🏵 *Pale Fire.* New York: Knopf, 1992 (1962). **G**

A 999-line poem by fictional poet John Shade opens the story and is followed by the commentary of deranged homosexual Kinbote. Throw a murder plot into this multilayered novel, and the average reader can read as much into the work as the confused Kinbote.

Awards: Publishing Triangle's 100 Best Lesbian and Gay Novels

Subjects: Authors • Mental health • Murder • Poetry

Peyrefitte, Roger.

🏵 *Special Friendships.* New York: Vanguard Press, 1950. **G**

The tensions at a Catholic boys' boarding school mount as strict teachers stifle every manifestation of male bonding, while secretly harboring their own desires. Georges, lusting after the attractive Lucien, stops at nothing to obtain his heart's desire, destroying priests and students alike. Shades of autobiography. Originally entitled *Amitiés particulières* and published in France in 1945.

Awards: Publishing Triangle's 100 Best Lesbian and Gay Novels

Subjects: Autobiographical fiction • Books to film • Lust • Religion • Students, high school

Read-Alikes: Peyrefitte's friend Henry de Montherlant also penned a boy's boarding school love story, entitled *Boys*.

Purdy, James.

🏵 *Eustace Chisholm and the Works.* London: Gay Men's Press, 1984 (1967). **G** **B**

Eustace and his friends need to survive depression, both physically and emotionally. Eustace suffers from marital problems and writer's block. Dan's rejection of Amos drives Amos into another's arms. Guilt ridden, Dan believes he's unlovable and submits to a cruel relationship. Slowly, each character becomes a ghost of his former self.

Awards: Publishing Triangle's 100 Best Lesbian and Gay Novels

Subjects: Friendship • Sadomasochism

Rechy, John.

🏵 *City of Night.* New York: Grove Press, 1988 (1963). **G**

In this character-driven story, an unnamed male hustler wanders across America. Afraid to form intimate attachments, denying his sexual orientation, and racked with lifestyle-inflicted guilt, he runs from city to city searching for life's meaning. Poetic prose offsets this long, rambling look at society's underworld.

Awards: Publishing Triangle's 100 Best Lesbian and Gay Novels

Subjects: Sex workers

Read-Alikes: Luis Zapata's *Adonis Garcia* follows a gay hustler through Mexico's gritty nightlife. Paul T. Rogers's Pushcart prize–winning novel *Saul's Book* tells the story of a hustler and his criminal lover.

Renault, Mary.

🏵 *The Charioteer.* New York: Vintage, 2003 (1959). **G**

Wounded World War II veteran Laurie must choose between his openly gay school chum Ralph, also maimed in the war, and Andrew, a sexual innocent and conscientious objector. Renault's frequent use of metaphors, similes, and quotations from classical literature creates a subtle, poetic style. Published in England in 1953.

Awards: Publishing Triangle's 100 Best Lesbian and Gay Novels, Reader's Choice

Subjects: England • World War II

Read-Alikes: Nearly an homage to Renault, *God in Flight,* by Laura Argiri, is more overtly romantic.

Rosenthal, Irving.

🏵 *Sheeper.* New York: Grove Press, 1968. **G**

Arranged in a series of short chapters and lacking a linear story arc, this forgotten work of autobiographical fiction featuring drugs, prostitution, and insects at times borders on erotica.

Awards: Publishing Triangle's 100 Best Lesbian and Gay Novels

Subjects: Sex workers • Substance abuse

Read-Alikes: *Just Like Beauty,* by Lisa Lerner, is a lighthearted examination of society's commercialization, complete with mutant grasshoppers and twisted beauty contests.

Rule, Jane.

Desert of the Heart. Vancouver, BC: Talonbooks, 1991 (1964). **L**

Evelyn, a refined professor, travels to 1950s era Nevada for a quick divorce. During her stay she befriends a much younger woman, the ranch hand Ann, and a romance ensues between these two seemingly opposite women. As the divorce date and the possibility of separation looms on the horizon, the women struggle with their differences of class, education, and expectations.

Subjects: 1950s • Books to film • Love • Nevada • Teachers

Read-Alikes: In the contemporary tale *The White Palazzo,* by Ellen Cooney, age differences are overcome by Tara and Guida.

Salinger, J. D.

🦋 *The Catcher in the Rye.* Harlow: Longman, 2003 (1951). **G**

One gay scene stands out in this classic coming-of-age drama. Holden Caulfield spends the night at a teacher's house and is shocked and repulsed when the teacher touches him. When the book was published, gay readers probably perceived the scene as a signal of Holden's homosexuality, although Salinger never revealed how it should be interpreted.

Awards: Publishing Triangle's 100 Best Lesbian and Gay Novels, Reader's Choice

Subjects: Coming-of-age • New York City • Students, high school

Sarton, May.

🦋 *Mrs. Stevens Hears the Mermaids Singing.* New York: W. W. Norton, 1993 (1965). **L B**

This unconventional novel lacking a traditionally linear plot concerns fictional poet and novelist Hillary Stevens. During the course of an interview, Stevens reflects on the relationship between art and artist and recalls that her muses were often women.

Awards: Publishing Triangle's 100 Best Lesbian and Gay Novels; Publishing Triangle's 100 Best Lesbian and Gay Novels, Reader's Choice

Subjects: Authors • Books to film

Talsman, William.

🦋 *Gaudy Image.* New York: Masquerade Books, 1995 (1958). **G T**

An obscure book featuring Tatiana and her drag queen friends, snipping at each other while competing for good-looking hunks and hustlers in 1940s New Orleans. First published in 1958 and seized by the U.S. Customs Service as pornography, this overly long story seems mild by contemporary standards.

Awards: Publishing Triangle's 100 Best Lesbian and Gay Novels

Subjects: 1940s • Cross-dressing • Louisiana

Read-Alikes: Also set in New Orleans is Jim Grimsley's *Boulevard,* a shorter but equally rambling, character-driven story.

Vidal, Gore.

Myra Breckinridge Series. **T**

These satirical novels poke fun at Hollywood and society's sexual mores. Myra, a transsexual formerly known as Myron, asserts personality elements stereotypically associated with both genders.

Subjects: Actors and actresses • Books to film • Humor • Sex change

🦋 *Myra Breckinridge.* New York: Penguin, 1997 (1969).

Ultra-feminist Myra wants to collect her inheritance, which is a piece of property currently serving as an acting school. Duping the school's owner into giving her a teaching job, Myra sets about her second goal—righting all the wrongs done to women throughout history. A campy story told with biting humor.

Awards: Publishing Triangle's 100 Best Lesbian and Gay Novels

Myron. New York: Random House, 1974.

Myra, who is now living as her castrated male alter ego Myron, is transported via a television into a movie set. Trapped inside the endlessly running, second-rate movie, Myron and Myra's personalities battle for supremacy and possess the bodies of fellow actors.

Wilson, Angus.

🎗 *Hemlock and After.* London: House of Stratus, 2001 (1952). **G** **B**

Despite his wife's illness and his secret homosexual affairs, Bernard Sands is at the pinnacle of success, until a disturbing encounter shakes him both mentally and physically. Questions of personal motivation and the capacity for self-delusion lurk beneath the surface in this first British novel to depict homosexuality openly.

Awards: Publishing Triangle's 100 Best Lesbian and Gay Novels, Reader's Choice

Subjects: Authors • England

Wittig, Monique.

🎗 *Guerilleres.* New York: Viking Adult, 1971 (1969). **L**

Inspired by the myth of the Amazonian, Wittig utilizes a stream-of-consciousness, poetical style to paint a story about a tribe of women overthrowing the patriarchy.

Awards: Publishing Triangle's 100 Best Lesbian and Gay Novels

Subjects: Feminism • Gender roles • Politics • Utopias

Read-Alikes: Women with supernatural skills populate Sally Gearheart's female utopia, in *Wanderground.*

Yourcenar, Marguerite.

🎗 *Memoirs of Hadrian.* New York: Farrar, Straus & Giroux, 2005 (1951). **G**
B

Emperor Hadrian enlightens his successor on all things worldly. His ruminations on conquest, both in the political and romantic arenas, reveal his intense love for the former slave boy Antinous. Yourcenar's lyrical style enhances this excellently researched novel.

Awards: Publishing Triangle's 100 Best Lesbian and Gay Novels

Subjects: Age differences • Antiquity • Hadrian

Read-Alikes: In *Julian,* Gore Vidal copied Yourcenar's style.

Chapter 5

General Fiction

Definition

General fiction is a catchall category and can also be considered "mainstream" or "literary" fiction.

Description and Characteristics

In addition to winning or being nominated for an award, works in this category frequently feature gay and straight characters, but emphasize neither sexual orientation nor dominant GLBT themes. The appeal of this type of literature has been discussed by Joyce Saricks and Nancy Pearl in *Now Read This*, who classify appeals into categories: character, story, setting, and language.

History and Development

Historically, all fiction books were considered general fiction, and therefore a history of this category would be akin to a history of literature in general, which is beyond the scope of this book, or a history of GLBT literature, which is covered in chapter 2.

Issues for Readers' Advisors

A primary difficulty is recognizing or deciding what constitutes GLBT fiction. Some books lend themselves to easy categorization, such as coming out stories, but the majority of the works contain varying degrees of GLBT characterization and themes. For example, in *The Shipping News* by Annie Proulx, the character Angis is lesbian, but her sexual orientation is not relevant to the plot. Nevertheless, this book was selected by readers for a place on the Publishing Triangle's 100 Best Books list, which would seem to indicate that the limited GLBT content was enough for readers to perceive the book as GLBT. From this example, as well as many other titles with limited or inferred GLBT content, just how much of a book must contain GLBT content to "qualify" as GLBT fiction varies according to a reader's tastes and is not something easily measured.

Librarians seeking to identify GLBT general fiction face a challenge. Familiarity with the genre and relevant readers' advisory tools is critical to compensate for poor or absent subject and genre headings. Content summaries could enhance OPAC searching, as well as implementation of Web 2.0 techniques such as reader reviews and tagging.

Chapter Organization

This chapter is divided into three sections—novels, short story collections by a single author, and short story anthologies by multiple authors—and then arranged by author name.

Sources

Pearl, Nancy, et al. *Now Read This: A Guide to Mainstream Fiction, 1978–1998.* Englewood, CO: Libraries Unlimited, 1999.

Novels

Allison, Dorothy.

🐾 *Bastard Out of Carolina.* New York: Dutton, 1992. **L**

Stereotypical rednecks pervade the story of Ruth Anne, alias Bone, the bastard child of Annie. Desperate to legitimize Bone, Annie marries Glen, whose initial doting on Bone turns abusive. An intensely raw story packaged in lyrical prose.

Awards: Publishing Triangle's 100 Best Lesbian and Gay Novels; Publishing Triangle Award, 1993

Subjects: Books to film • Relationships, parent–child • Sexual abuse, child • South Carolina

🐾 *Cavedweller.* New York: Dutton, 1998. **L**

After a wild life on the road, Delia returns to Georgia with a daughter. The object of scorn because she abandoned her children, she is determined to improve her life and correct past mistakes. Delia begins by caring for her ailing ex-husband in exchange for reuniting with her estranged daughters. A meandering tale.

Awards: Lambda Literary Award, 1998

Subjects: Books to film • Death and dying • Georgia • Relationships, parent–child

Anshaw, Carol.

🐾 *Aquamarine.* Boston: Houghton Mifflin, 1992. **L**

Seduced to distraction by fellow female swimmer Marty Finch, Jesse loses the Olympic medal of her dreams. The loss forms a pivotal point in Jesse's life, which Anshaw uses to spin three allegorical tales about choices and consequences.

Awards: Publishing Triangle's 100 Best Lesbian and Gay Novels

Subjects: Swimming

Read-Alikes: Rather than three alternative realities, Jenifer Levin's *Sea of Light* focuses on the lives and self-discoveries of three female swimmers.

🎗 *Lucky in the Corner.* Boston: Houghton Mifflin, 2002. **L**

A plethora of characters populates this sweet, slice-of-life story about Fern and her eccentric family and friends. Fern's difficulty adjusting to her mother's coming out put a dent in their mother–daughter relationship, but through it all Lucky, Fern's dog, has remained a constant source of love and support.

Awards: Ferro-Grumley Award, 2003

Subjects: Coming out • Pets • Relationships, parent–child

Read-Alikes: Readers of all ages who enjoyed *Lucky in the Corner* may also enjoy *Dive,* by Stacy Donovan, which features a young girl's relationship with her dog.

Arnold, June.

🎗 *Sister Gin.* New York: Feminist Press, 1989 (1975). **L**

Arnold's insightful exploration of a lesbian couple and their friends searching for a lesbian identity while dealing with aging and menopause is set during the height of the women's movement. The experimental style and tone make this a challenging read.

Awards: Publishing Triangle's 100 Best Lesbian and Gay Novels

Subjects: Age differences • Couples • Substance abuse

Read-Alikes: For an equally challenging read, readers may want to try Djuna Barnes's *Nightwood*.

Baldwin, James.

🎗 *Just Above My Head.* New York Delta, 2000 (1979). **G** **B**

Narrated by Hall, the story concerns his brother Arthur, a gay black gospel singer. By casting the brothers' stories among historical events, the conflicts and convergences of Arthur's sexuality, career, and racial identity are explored.

Awards: Publishing Triangle's 100 Best Lesbian and Gay Novels, Reader's Choice

Subjects: African Americans • Grief • Interracial relationships • Siblings

Bartlett, Neil.

The House on Brooke Street. New York: Dutton Adult, 1997. **G**

A haunting and disturbing novel of the relationship between a shop clerk and an aristocrat, set in the mannered world of London during the 1920s.

Subjects: Class conflict • England • Homophobia

Read-Alikes: Interracial class conflict in contemporary America is the theme of Timothy Murphy's *Getting off Clean*.

Bechard, Margaret.

If It Doesn't Kill You. New York: Viking, 1999. **G** **Teen**

High school freshman Ben has enough to deal with—his football team is a disaster, his teammates mock gay people, his neighbor drags him on outrageous adventures, and his dad moves in with a boyfriend—in this tale of believable teenage angst.

Subjects: Coming out • Football • Relationships, parent–child • Students, high school

Read-Alikes: A parallel story is told in Sarah Withrow's *Box Girl,* in which Gwen's dad is gay.

Berlin, Adam.

🎗 *Belmondo Style.* New York: St. Martin's Press, 2004. **G** **Teen**

With movie-style pacing, a petty criminal father turns to revenge after his son is the victim of a gay bashing. The escalating violence leads to larger crimes and a life on the run. Although this is a wordy novel, it is readable enough to be enjoyed by a young adult audience.

Awards: Ferro-Grumley Award, 2005

Subjects: Crime • Hate crimes • Relationships, parent–child • Students, high school

Read-Alikes: Pat Jordan's *A. K. A. Sheila Weinstein* is a Florida-based mystery complete with stereotypical GLBT characters.

Blackbridge, Persimmon.

Prozac Highway. Vancouver, BC: Press Gang Publishers, 1997. **L**

Jam is more comfortable in the virtual world than in reality. So what if she has trouble getting out bed, maintaining basic personal hygiene, and leaving the house? On the Internet Jam finds escape, a lifeline. Or is it? The story alternates between narration and e-mail exchanges.

Subjects: Computers • Mental health

Read-Alikes: In an early Net-based novel, *Metaphysical Touch,* Sylvia Brownrigg writes about the online relationship between Emily and the mysterious JD.

🎗 *Sunnybrook.* Vancouver, BC: Press Gang, 1996. **L**

Diane lies about her employment history to secure a job at Sunnybrook, a psychiatric hospital, where she finds the patients far more interesting than the staff. This illustrated, creative book buzzes with the energy of the sometimes-frenetic experiences of the mentally ill.

Awards: Ferro-Grumley Award, 1997

Subjects: Mental health

Read-Alikes: In *Bogeywoman,* by Jaimy Gordon, Ursula Koderer's knack for getting into trouble and crushing on older women lands her in the "bughouse."

Blackman, Marci.

🎗 *Po' Man's Child.* San Francisco: Manic D Press, 1999. **L**

After a rough sexual encounter (and not her first), Po checks herself into a mental hospital. Believing herself and her family cursed, Po reflects on thirty years of dysfunctional family life and the methods she and her family have used to ignore issues and numb personal pain. Taut and realistically written.

Awards: Firecracker Alternative Book Award, 2000; Stonewall Book Award, 2000

Subjects: African Americans • Families • Sadomasochism

Read-Alikes: *Leash,* by Jane Delynn, is a funnier though no less graphic exploration of sadomasochism.

Bledsoe, Lucy Jane.

This Wild Silence. Los Angeles: Alyson Books, 2003. **L**

Thirty-something sisters Liz and Christine are complete opposites, bound together by the loss of their brother and a terrible family secret. A fierce storm and exposure to nature's elements in California's Sierra Nevada Mountains slowly force rivalries and jealousies to the surface, culminating in the revelation of their disturbing secret.

Subjects: Secrets • Siblings • Skiing

Read-Alikes: In Joan M. Drury's *Silent Words,* Tyler Jones uncovers deeply buried family secrets.

🏵 *Working Parts.* Seattle: Seal Press 1997. **L** **Teen**

Lori has a way with bicycles—she loves to ride them and fix them. She even dreams of owning a bike shop, but when the opportunity arises, Lori must overcome personal obstacles to realize her dream. This smooth riding story is appropriate for all reading levels.

Awards: Stonewall Book Award, 1998

Subjects: Bicycles • Disability • Literacy

Blum, Louise A.

🏵 *Amnesty.* Boston: Alyson Publications, 1995. **L** **Teen**

Shamed by a draft-dodging brother, Maura's family copes in different ways until pain drives the family apart. Death prompts a reunion and forces family members to decide if forgiveness is warranted. Told in flashbacks, this short novel is suitable for advanced young adult readers.

Awards: Publishing Triangle's 100 Best Lesbian and Gay Novels, Reader's Choice

Subjects: Families • Vietnam War

Read-Alikes: In Teresa Stores's *Getting to the Point,* Dixie left her family years ago, but returns to care for her ailing grandmother.

Boyd, Randy.

Bridge Across the Ocean. Indianapolis, IN: West Beach Books, 2001. **G**

HIV-positive, African American Derek vacations in Mexico and falls hopelessly in love with teenage Rob. Derek befriends Rob and his family, with promising results.

Subjects: African Americans • Age differences • Interracial relationships

Read-Alikes: In Philippe Besson's *In the Absence of Men,* Vincent is torn between the love of a man his age and a much older, fictional Marcel Proust.

Bram, Christopher.

🌺 *Lives of the Circus Animals.* New York: Perennial, 2004. **G**

A week in the lives of a six-pack ensemble cast of theater wonks with intertwined destinies. Angst over success and failure onstage, off stage, in life, and in love is all covered in this novel look at the New York theater world and its gay subculture. The ending is a bit predictable.

Awards: Lambda Literary Award, 2003

Subjects: Actors and actresses • Authors • Theater

Read-Alikes: For a dose of real-life theater antics, readers should check out David Kaufman's *Ridiculous*.

Breedlove, Lynn.

Godspeed. New York: St. Martin's Press, 2002. **L** **T**

Jim is a foul-mouthed, wisecracking street kid, a butch lesbian with addictions to heroin, bicycles, punk rock, and Ally, a go-go dancer. Ally refuses to see Jim until he gets clean. Speeding aimlessly through life, dreaming of Ally and the next high, Jim struggles to meet Ally's demands, only to find the situation turned against him.

Subjects: Bicycles • Butches • Music • Substance abuse

Read-Alikes: Michelle Tea's fictionalized versions of her life as an ex-goth girl are recounted in *Passionate Mistakes and Intricate Corruption of One Girl in America* and *Valencia*.

Brockton, Joseph.

Queer as Folk Series. **G**

Fans of the wildly successful television show can get an extra dose of the characters.

Subjects: Coming-of-age • Friendship • Students, high school

Every Nine Seconds. New York: Pocket Books, 2003.

Meet Michael and Brian during their last year in high school, attend their prom, as well as Babylon's grand opening, and watch a graduation day prank.

Brockton, Quinn.

Queer as Folk Series. **G** **L**

The friends from Liberty Avenue laugh, love, and live together in this series based on the television series.

Subjects: Friendship • Students, college

Read-Alikes: Ben Tyler's *Hunk House* and *Tricks of the Trade* feature a cache of superficial characters living soap-opera lives centered around dancing, drinking, and dating.

Never Tear Us Apart. New York: Pocket Books, 2003.

Best friends Michael and Brian have completed high school and moved on to different colleges, where they make new friends and deal with a variety of typical adolescent experiences. Brian meets Lindsey and Michael meets Emmett.

Always Have, Always Will. New York: Pocket Books, 2004.

> Follow the friends after college. Brian brings his larger-than-life attitude and sex drive to the corporate world, while love forlorn Michael toils away at a discount store. Lindsey struggles as an artist, but finds true love for the first time.

Brown, Rita Mae.

🏵 *Rubyfruit Jungle.* London: Penguin, 2001 (1973). **L**

> Tomboy Molly Bolt roughs up the local boys while breaking the hearts of female classmates, in this raucous read, which is somewhat reminiscent of a twentieth-century lesbian version of *Huckleberry Finn* and *Tom Sawyer*. A contemporary classic.

Awards: Publishing Triangle's 100 Best Lesbian and Gay Novels

Subjects: Adoption • Coming-of-age • Coming out

Read-Alikes: In Fannie Flagg's *Fried Green Tomatoes at the Whistle Stop Café*, Idgie shares Molly Bolt's Southern spunk.

Hunsenmeir Sisters Series. **L** **B** **T**

> The Hunsenmeir sisters, Louise (Wheezie) and Julia (Juts), serve as a focal point for weekly card games and gossip in these humorous stories.

Subjects: Families • Humor • Siblings

🏵 *Six of One.* New York: Bantam, 1999 (1978).

> An eccentric cast of family and friends, including the lesbian aristocrat Celeste, enlivens this character-driven story about the love–hate relationship between sisters Wheezie and Juts. A humorous, loosely historical novel with something for everyone: prohibition, murder, and lesbian parents.

Awards: Publishing Triangle's 100 Best Lesbian and Gay Novels, Reader's Choice

Bingo. New York: Bantam Books, 1999 (1988).

> The octogenarian sisters battle for the affection of a new man in town, while Julia's lesbian daughter Nickel finds her job and love life falling apart.

Loose Lips. New York: Bantam Books, 1999.

> This installment covers the World War II years, when the sisters were middle aged women. Nickel is seen growing up, while Celeste and her lover only appear briefly. This installment has the least GLBT content in the series.

Chabon, Michael.

🏵 *The Mysteries of Pittsburgh.* New York: Perennial, 2005. **G** **B**

> Follow Art Bechstein through his first year after college, as he explores various facets of his life—career, friendship, and sexuality. Concerning the latter, Art experiences all of life's possibilities and sleeps with both men and women,

eventually entering a love triangle. A humorous and poignant tale, with lushly descriptive prose.

Awards: Publishing Triangle's 100 Best Lesbian and Gay Novels, Reader's Choice

Subjects: Books to film • Love triangles • Pennsylvania

Read-Alikes: Greg Hrbek's *The Hindenburg Crashes Nightly* is a provocatively written tale featuring a love quadrangle.

Chee, Alexander.

🎗 *Edinburgh.* New York: Welcome Rain Publishers, 2001. **G**

Fee, sexually abused by his choir director, is unable to prevent his best friend and secret crush from experiencing similar abuse. Haunted by the past, the adult Fee confronts a similar situation and must either face or flee his demons. Myth, shifting viewpoints, and stark imagery converge.

Awards: Lambda Literary Award, 2001

Subjects: Asians • Music • Sexual abuse, child

Read-Alikes: A teacher–student affair is the cornerstone of Paul Elliott Russell's *Coming Storm.*

Cheever, John.

🎗 *Falconer.* New York: Vintage, 1992 (1977). **G** **B**

Ezekiel Farragut, imprisoned for murder, is a postmodern man, completely alienated from society, lacking a sense of personal morality, and thoroughly addicted to searching for pleasure, no matter where it is found. Through flashbacks, the reader learns of Farragut's fall from grace.

Awards: Publishing Triangle's 100 Best Lesbian and Gay Novels, Reader's Choice

Subjects: Crime • Murder • Substance abuse • Teachers

Cooper, Dennis.

🎗 *Closer.* London: Serpent's Tail, 1994. **G**

A group of aimless high school students trudges through life, expecting nothing but pain. Sex and violence are a means to escape the daily feelings of despair and alienation. Punk rock motifs abound.

Awards: Publishing Triangle's 100 Best Lesbian and Gay Novels; Ferro-Grumley Award, 1990

Subjects: Music • Sadomasochism • Students, high school

Cooper, T.

Some of the Parts. New York: Penguin Group, 2002. **G** **L** **B** **T**

Lacking a central plot, this slice-of-life story alternates between the first- and third-person narration of four family members. HIV-positive Charlie moves in with his pill-popping sister Arlene, much to the consternation of Charlie's hustler-boyfriend, the transgendered Isak, who reacts by leaving for Los Angeles. Eventually, Arlene's gorgeous daughter sleeps her way to LA, where she finds Isak and the two begin a cross-country trip to reconcile with Charlie and Arlene.

Subjects: Cross-dressing • Families • Sex workers

Read-Alikes: Jonathan Strong's *Circle Around Her* also centers on the dysfunctions of a New England family.

Cunningham, Michael.

🎗 *Flesh and Blood.* New York: Farrar, Straus & Giroux, 1995. **G**

Con, obsessed with money and machismo, works hard to realize the American dream and raise his family from poverty, but his mistakes, including infidelity, violence, and inappropriate attention toward his children, resound for generations.

Awards: Lambda Literary Award, 1995; Publishing Triangle's 100 Best Lesbian and Gay Novels, Reader's Choice

Subjects: Immigrants

Read-Alikes: Patrick Gale's *Facts of Life* is similar in scope.

🎗 *A Home at the End of the World.* New York: Farrar, Straus & Giroux. 1990. **G**

Lifelong friends Bobby and Jonnie share an apartment and form a love triangle with roommate Clare, ultimately deciding to start a unique family. An emotional search for home, family, and a place in the world.

Awards: Publishing Triangle's 100 Best Lesbian and Gay Novels, Reader's Choice

Subjects: Books to film • Death and dying • Families • Love triangles

Read-Alikes: *Fall Love*, by Anne Whitehouse, features a love triangle between two women and a bisexual man.

D'Erasmo, Stacey.

🎗 *A Seahorse Year.* Boston: Houghton Mifflin, 2004. **L**

Christopher has a great life with his two moms and gay dad, until his diagnosis as schizophrenic upsets everything and forces family members to renegotiate their relationships to one another. The story unfolds slowly, much like a mental illness, and tests the bounds of love.

Awards: Lambda Literary Award, 2004; Ferro-Grumley Award, 2005

Subjects: California • Families • Mental health • Students, high school

🎗 *Tea.* Chapel Hill, NC: Algonquin Books of Chapel Hill, 2000. **L**

Isabel, the introspective child of an unhappy and emotionally withdrawn mother, narrates this character-driven, three-part story. As a child Isabel makes tea for her mother; as a young adult, Isabel sips tea while recalling the impact of her mother's death on her formative years.

Awards: *ForeWord Magazine's* Book of the Year Award, 2000

Subjects: Death and dying • Relationships, parent–child

Read-Alikes: Michael Cunningham uses a book as a device to weave together three stories in *The Hours*.

D'Haene, Elise.

🕈 *Licking Our Wounds.* Sag Harbor, NY: Permanent Press, 1997. **G** **L**

Grief permeates Maria's life. Her failed relationship seems to have zapped her sexuality, two best friends are suffering from AIDS-related complications, and family bonds are fragile. Ribald recollections of sex stand side-by-side with moving memories of deceased friends, but Maria manages to find meaning.

Awards: Independent Publisher Book Award, 1998

Subjects: AIDS • Friendship • Grief

Dixon, Melvin.

🕈 *Vanishing Rooms.* New York: Penguin Group, 2001. **G**

Jesse, reeling from the death of his lover Metro, seeks solace from his female friend Ruella, who begins falling in love with Jesse, giving rise to conflicting feelings for Jesse. Lonny is also confused about his sexuality, when he accidentally becomes involved in Metro's murder. An exploration of the interconnected lives of three individuals marginalized because of sexual orientation and race. Dance serves as a metaphor for human interaction in this perfectly pitched emotional tale set in the 1970s.

Awards: Ferro-Grumley Award, 1992

Subjects: African Americans • Dancing • Grief • Hate crimes • Murder • Race relations

Read-Alikes: Dixon's work is frequently compared to James Baldwin's.

Donoghue, Emma.

Stir-Fry. New York: HarperCollins 1994. **L**

Maria (rhymes with pariah), a young Irish girl, leaves her small town for college life in Dublin, where she takes up residence with Ruth and Jael. Much to Maria's surprise, she discovers her roommates are lovers; and she consequently learns about her own sexuality.

Subjects: Coming out • Ireland • Students, college

Read-Alikes: Love among college girls is the subject of Rita Mae Brown's *Alma Mater*.

Donoso, José. Translated by Suzanne Jill Levine.

🕈 *Hell Has No Limits.* Copenhagen: Green Integer, 1999. **T**

The social conditions, mores, and human interactions of a Chilean town are explored through the character of La Manuela, a transsexual whorehouse owner. Detailed descriptions and flashbacks reveal the shattering effects of lust and violence.

Awards: Publishing Triangle's 100 Best Lesbian and Gay Novels

Subjects: Chile • Sex workers

Flesh, Henry.

🕈 *Massage.* New York: Penguin Group 1999. **G**

Randy, abused as a child, escapes to New York to pursue a career as a masseur cum prostitute. One particular business relationship develops into something more personal and intimate. This is a brutal and sexually explicit story.

Awards: Lambda Literary Award, 1999

Subjects: AIDS • Sadomasochism • Sex workers

Read-Alikes: A cast of conflicted characters populates John Rechy's *Coming of the Night*.

Frank, Judith.

🎗 *Crybaby Butch.* Ithaca, NY: Firebrand, 2004. **L**

Generations clash when a butch literacy instructor, Anna, works with Chris, an older butch client. The self-loathing, recently dumped by her girlfriend Anna struggles to find common ground with Chris, the victim of an abusive relationship. Their passive-aggressive relationship culminates in a redeeming shared experience.

Awards: Lambda Literary Award, 2004

Subjects: Age differences • Butches • Literacy • Students • Teachers

Gambone, Philip.

Beijing. Madison: University of Wisconsin Press, 2004. **G B**

As a way of drowning grief, David, an American doctor, accepts a one-year contract to practice in China. There he begins an affair with a man trapped in a prearranged marriage. When the contract is up, David must decide whether to stay on or attempt a long-distance relationship.

Subjects: China • Healthcare workers

Garden, Nancy.

Holly's Secret. New York: Farrar, Straus & Giroux, 2000. **L** **Teen**

When Holly and her family move to the suburbs, she decides to assume an alternate identity and hide the fact that her parents are lesbians. Her shame begets lying, until the charade can no longer be maintained.

Subjects: Families • Homophobia • Secrets

Read-Alikes: Younger readers may want to try Lesléa Newman's *Heather Has Two Mommies, Daddy's Roommate* by Michael Willhoite, and Nancy Garden's *Molly's Family*.

Gerrold, David.

The Martian Child. New York: Forge, 2002. **G**

A humorous and touching story of a gay man pursuing the adoption of a troubled boy. Life and art intersect when the new dad, a science fiction writer, is informed that the child believes he is a Martian. Based on a true story.

Subjects: Adoption • Books to film • Parenting • Relationships, parent–child

Read-Alikes: In Michael Downing's *Breakfast with Scot*, family dysfunction leads Ed to take custody of his cross-dressing nephew Scot.

Gladstone, Jim.

The Big Book of Misunderstanding. New York: Harrington Park Press, 2002. **G**
Josh Royalton, who reflects on his childhood and realizes that sometimes people even misunderstand themselves, replays misunderstandings common to family life.

Subjects: Coming out • Families

Read-Alikes: In K. M. Soehnlein's *World of Normal Boys,* the protagonist, Robin's father, is abusive, his mom is an alcoholic, and his brother has serious medical problems.

Grimsley, Jim.

🎗 *Dream Boy.* Chapel Hill: Algonquin Books of Chapel Hill, 1995. **G**
In this atmospheric Southern gothic love story, Nathan, stinging from his abusive home life, begins an unexpected relationship with Roy, until peer pressure results in violence. A tender love story appropriate for older, emotionally mature young adults.

Awards: Stonewall Book Award, 1996; Publishing Triangle's 100 Best Lesbian and Gay Novels, Reader's Choice

Subjects: Families • Love • North Carolina • Sexual abuse • Students, high school

Read-Alikes: In *Tramps Like Us,* by Joe Westmoreland, Joe drifts about the country in search of himself and love.

Guess, Carol.

Switch. Corvallis, OR: Calyx Books, 1998. **L B T**
Searching for love amid the secrets of a rural Indiana town is central to this mystical tale featuring a cast of characters whose lives intertwine through the local diner. Alternating narrators reveal vulnerabilities and love's protective impulse.

Subjects: Butches • Love • Magic • Pets • Secrets

Read-Alikes: A small town on the cusp of the twentieth century is the setting for Paulette Callen's murder mystery-love story, *Charity.*

Gurganus, Allan.

🎗 *The Practical Heart: Four Novellas.* New York: Vintage, 2002. **G**
Gurganus's four novellas center on the citizens of Falls, North Carolina. The two with gay themes, *Preservation News* and *He's One, Too,* feature a eulogy to a historic home preservationist and the reflections of a gay man on the arrest in the 1950s of a neighbor for public indecency.

Awards: Lambda Literary Award, 2001

Subjects: Friendship • North Carolina

Harris, Bertha.

🎗 *Lover.* New York: New York University, 1993 (1976). **L T**
An experimental novel featuring a sometimes cross-dressing artist-novelist participating in dramatic productions. The cast of characters includes Veronica, a forger; Flynn; Samaria, whose mother is a prostitute; the twins Rose and Rose-lima; Bertha, who may represent the author; and many others. Lacking a

clearly defined linear plot and drawing on historical personas, myth, and fantasy, *Lover* is best described as a "family history."

Awards: Publishing Triangle's 100 Best Lesbian and Gay Novels

Subjects: Art and artists • Cross-dressing • Feminism • Relationships

Read-Alikes: Harris emulates the style of Yvonne Rainier in *Mind Is a Muscle*.

Harris, E. Lynn.

Invisible Life Trilogy. G B

Long before television viewers had the African American GLBT characters of *Noah's Arc*, Harris provided readers with positive images in the form of Raymond and his friends, coping with everyday life, homophobia, and the additional challenges of race and cultural restraint.

Subjects: African Americans • AIDS • Coming out • Homophobia, self-directed • Race relations

Read-Alikes: Some of the same characters appear in Lynn's other novels. Readers should try James Earl Hardy's B-Boy Blues series.

Invisible Life: A Novel. Atlanta, GA: Continuum, 1991.

> Raymond leads a double life, engaged to a woman but attracted to men. Afraid, he flees to New York, where he pursues relationships with both sexes.

Just as I Am. New York: Doubleday, 1994.

> Ray and his constellation of friends and lovers are back. Ray and Nicole alternate as narrators in a dialogue-driven story. Ray remains closeted and attracted to a football player. Kyle is ill and requires tending, reuniting Ray and Nicole in caregiver roles.

Abide with Me. Waterville, ME: Thorndike Press, 2003 (1999).

> Raymond and Trent are happily partnered, although a career opportunity presents a challenging obstacle. Nicole's acting success may come at a price, and Basil is in therapy. The loose ending leaves readers awaiting a sequel.

Harvey, Andrew.

🔥 *Burning Houses.* Boston: Houghton Mifflin, 1986. G

Young Charles reads his novel *Burning House*, about his failed love affair with a married man, to senior citizen Adolphe. In this dialogue-driven novel within a novel, the lines between life and art are intentionally blurred.

Awards: Publishing Triangle's 100 Best Lesbian and Gay Novels, Reader's Choice

Subjects: Age differences • Authors • France

Read-Alikes: Alan Hollinghurst's *The Spell* contains four interlocking stories about the search for love.

Healey, Trebor.

� *Through It Came Bright Color*s. Binghamton, NY: Haworth, 2003. G

Alternates among the stories of three men whose lives converge during a clinic visit. Neil cares for his ailing brother Peter; but he also begins a relationship with Vince, a manipulative lover. The decaying relationships mirror the declining physical and mental health of each man.

Awards: Publishing Triangle Award, 2004

Subjects: Illness • Siblings

Read-Alikes: In a subplot of Renee Manfredi's *Above the Thunder,* Anna, a straight, middle-aged woman, becomes enmeshed in the life of HIV-positive Jack.

Heim, Scott.

🌲 *In Awe.* New York: HarperCollins, 1997. G

Teenage Boris, senior citizen Harriet, and promiscuous Sarah have an unlikely friendship forged around Marshall, Harriet's AIDS-stricken son. The trio copes with homophobic attacks, stalking, and unrequited love. Heim's poetic language describes three characters longing for the unobtainable.

Awards: Firecracker Alternative Book Award, 1998

Subjects: Friendship • Hate crimes • Homophobia • Kansas

Read-Alikes: In Dale Peck's *Now It's Time to Say Goodbye,* homophobia, hate crimes, murder, and AIDS converge in racially divided Kansas.

🌲 *Mysterious Skin.* New York: HarperCollins, 1995. G

Brian believes he and a Little League teammate were victims of alien abduction, but he can remember neither the event nor the teammate's name. Unable to move forward in life, his pursuit of the truth has startling revelations. Various characters share the narration.

Awards: Publishing Triangle's 100 Best Lesbian and Gay Novels, Reader's Choice

Subjects: Aliens • Baseball • Books to film • Kansas • Secrets • Sexual abuse, child

Read-Alikes: William J. Mann's *All American Boy* unearths Wally Day's family secrets.

Hensley, Dennis.

Misadventures in the (213). New York: Rob Weisbach Books, 1998. G

Tales of the City meets *Beverly Hills 90210* in this story set in contemporary Los Angeles, where "213" is the area code. Pop culture references, name-dropping, and bumping into starlets are part of the everyday life of friends Dandy and Craig. Wacky, over-the-top characters make for light reading.

Subjects: Actors and actresses • California

Read-Alikes: In *California Screaming,* by Doug Guinan, Kevin is a kept man.

Holland, Isabelle.

The Man without a Face. New York: HarperTrophy, 1987 (1972). G **Teen**

Charles finds both a father figure and a friend in severely scarred neighbor Justin McLeod. The single homosexual incident in the book was significant at the time of the book's publication and remains noteworthy because the film excised the incident.

Subjects: Books to film • Friendship • Pets

Holleran, Andrew.

🔖 *The Beauty of Men.* New York: Morrow, 1996. **G**

Mr. Lark is as lonely as the fleetingness of his name implies. Closeted, middle-aged, and the lone survivor among his group of friends, Lark has only his memories of a life wasted in pursuit of fantasy lovers and temporary relationships.

Awards: Ferro-Grumley Award, 1997; Publishing Triangle's 100 Best Lesbian and Gay Novels, Reader's Choice

Subjects: Aging • Florida • Friendship • Relationships, parent–child

Read-Alikes: In *A Single Man,* by Christopher Isherwood, the closeted protagonist, George, silently suffers the death of his partner.

Hollinghurst, Alan.

The Line of Beauty. New York: Bloomsbury Publishing, 2004. **G**

Nick house sits for a wealthy, politically connected family and becomes a permanent boarder. Set amid the early days of AIDS and Thatcherism, when being gay was okay if it was never discussed, Nick unearths family secrets while personal and political shenanigans threaten to topple everyone.

Subjects: Books to film • England • Politics

Read-Alikes: Class conflicts and conflicting passions in 1920s Ceylon are central to Shyam Selvadurai's *Cinnamon Gardens.*

🔖 *The Swimming-Pool Library.* London: Vintage, 1998. **G**

Elderly Lord Natwich employs the young aristocrat William Beckwith to write his biography. The diaries and photographs underpinning the biography, as well as William's perceptions and experiences, drive this story of England's hidden gay world from World War I to the cusp of the AIDS crisis. A novel of manners wrapped in an unapologetically carnal package.

Awards: Lambda Literary Award, 1988; Publishing Triangle's 100 Best Lesbian and Gay Novels; Stonewall Book Award, 1989

Subjects: England • Lust • Sex

Read Alikes: In Joseph Olshan's *Vanitas,* a dying art dealer hires a biographer.

Homes, A. M.

Jack. New York: Macmillan, 1989. **G** **Teen**

Forced to deal with normal teenage troubles, Jack thinks of his parents only as parents, not as people, until Jack's dad announces he is gay. Now Jack must decide if there is room in his life for a gay father.

Subjects: Books to film • Relationships, parent–child • Students, high school

Read-Alikes: In Ron Koertge's *Arizona Kid,* Billy lives with his gay uncle.

House, Tom.

The Beginning of Calamities. Bridgehampton, NY: Bridge Works Publishing, 2003. **G**

An illustrated Bible storybook inspires Danny to create an imaginary friend and write a passion play. As the play plods toward disaster, Danny's imaginary friend encourages mischief and sexual awakening.

Subjects: Religion • Students, elementary school

Read-Alikes: *Tragedy of Miss Geneva Flowers,* by Joe Babcock, also features a Catholic school student with a dramatic flair.

Jackson, Shelley.

The Melancholy of Anatomy. New York: Anchor Books, 2002. **G L B**

Drawing inspiration from a seventeenth-century medical essay, Jackson creates a series of anatomically odd stories about various body functions. Disturbing and intriguing, with some GLBT content.

Subjects: Medicine

Jenkins, A. M.

Breaking Boxes. New York: Dell, 2000. **G Teen**

Normally a loner, Charlie takes a chance on friendship with Brandon, trusting him with a family secret. Will Brandon prove himself a worthy friend, or betray Charlie's secret?

Subjects: Friendship • Homophobia • Secrets • Siblings

Johnson, Greg.

Sticky Kisses. Los Angeles: Alyson Books, 2001. **G**

Alienated from his family because of his homosexuality, Thom contacts his sister and suggests visiting for the Christmas holiday.

Subjects: Christmas • Siblings

Read-Alikes: In Jim Grimsley's *Comfort and Joy,* Dan takes home his lover at Christmas.

Jolley, Elizabeth.

🌂 *Miss Peabody's Inheritance.* New York: Viking, 1984. **L**

Miss Peabody drips with domesticity. Raised to care for home and hearth, she lives with an ailing mother, her only happiness the occasional letters from an Australian novelist-pen pal, Diana Hopewell. Wrapped in the letters is the story of an English schoolmarm traveling with her lesbian lover. A story within a story.

Awards: Publishing Triangle's 100 Best Lesbian and Gay Novels

Subjects: Australia • Authors • England • Friendship

Katz, Judith.

🎗 *Running Fiercely Toward a High Thin Sound.* Ithaca, NY: Firebrand Books, 1992. **L**

Sisters Nadine and Jane, the former mentally ill and the latter a lesbian, are family outcasts whose reunion in a local college town sets the stage for family reconciliation. Various family members narrate this tale.

Awards: Lambda Literary Award, 1993

Subjects: Coming-of-age • Coming out • Families • Jews • Mental health

Kay, Jackie.

🎗 *Trumpet.* New York: Pantheon, 1998. **T**

Jazz musician Joss Moody and his wife kept a secret from everyone, even their own son, until Joss's death reveals the startling truth. Now each person in Joss's life struggles with the truth and must decide between honoring Joss's memory and feeling deceived by a loved one.

Awards: Lambda Literary Award, 1999

Subjects: Cross-dressing • Families • Music • Scotland

Read-Alikes: Chris Bohjalian's *Trans-Sister Radio* is stylistically similar, alternating narrators to tell the story of a male college professor transitioning to life as a female.

Keenan, Joe.

Blue Heaven. New York: Penguin, 1993. **G**

Before he worked on the television shows *Frasier* and *Desperate Housewives*, Joe Keenan put his comic touch to work in this debut novel about shallow, social climbing friends Gil and Moira, who plan a sham marriage just to get the gifts. Gil's ex-boyfriend Phil and his straight friend Claire are dragged into the plan, along with the Mafia, and the story takes a wild turn. Sitcom-like pacing and humor.

Subjects: Crime • Friendship • Humor

Read-Alikes: *Putting on the Ritz* continues the story, with Phil and Claire composing music while spying on a socialite for Gil.

Kerr, M. E.

Deliver Us From Evie. New York: HarperCollins, 1994. **L** **Teen**

Evie's brothers hate farming and are glad she wants to take over the family business; however, Evie's sudden relationship with the banker's daughter threatens the boys' plans. Betrayed by her brothers, eighteen-year-old Evie and her girlfriend run away.

Subjects: Coming out • Families • Farmers • Students, high school

Read-Alikes: *Sugar Rush,* by Julie Burchill, features two young women from completely different backgrounds who fall in love.

Klein, Norma.

Breaking Up. New York: Pantheonn, 1980. **L** **Teen**

After her parents' divorce, Ali must cope with her father's relocation and remarriage, as well as discovering that her mother is a lesbian. This is one of the earliest books to deal with homosexual parents from the child's perspective.

Subjects: Relationships, parent–child

Koja, Kathe.

Skin. New York: Delacorte, 1993. **L** **B**

Tess creates menacing metal sculptures that are seen by performance artist Bibi. The two form a partnership of love and art, designing a show combining dangerous dance with mobile, bladed sculptures. However, Bibi's increasingly extreme acts of self-mutilation finally force Tess to break the partnership.

Subjects: Art and artists • Body modification • Dancing

Strange Angels. New York: Delacorte Press, 1994. **B**

A photographer with a creative block, Grant finds Robin, an artistic genius, among the patients his psychologist girlfriend is treating. Obsessed with the need to help him fulfill his potential, Grant becomes his confidant and custodian, with results disastrous to them both.

Subjects: Art and artists • Mental health

Konecky, Edith.

Place at the Table. New York: Random House, 1989. **L** **B**

Jennifer, an aging novelist, has a chaotic emotional life as she struggles with ending her relationship with a much younger woman, counseling a divorcing friend, becoming a grandmother, and surviving cancer.

Subjects: Aging • Authors • Friendship • Illness • Jews • Mental health

Kramer, Larry.

🎗 *Faggots.* New York: Grove, 2000 (1978). **G**

Emotionally shallow fellows indulge in every imaginable drug and sexual escapade while searching for Mr. Right and bemoaning a culture that emphasizes form over substance. Stylistically complex writing and a cast of thousands make this a challenging read.

Awards: Publishing Triangle's 100 Best Lesbian and Gay Novels, Reader's Choice

Subjects: Dating • New York City • Sadomasochism

Read-Alikes: Andrew Holleran's protagonist *in Dancer from the Dance* looks for love in all the wrong places.

Kwa, Lydia.

This Place Called Absence. New York: Kensington, 2002. **L**

Two interconnected stories spanning the twentieth century from beginning to end are told by four narrators in diary-like entries. Wu Lan, a Canadian psychologist, is haunted by her father's death and the dissolution of her relationship. She stumbles upon the story of two Chinese prostitutes, and from their story learns about love, letting go, and family secrets.

Subjects: Asians • Relationships, parent–child • Secrets • Sex workers

Read-Alikes: In a more violent vein, Poppy Z. Brite uses different eras to tell the story of three Asian boys in *Triads*.

Lamb, Wally.

🏵 *She's Come Undone.* Boston: Compass Press, 1997. **G** **L** **B**

Product of a broken home, Delores feels responsible for everything: her father's departure, mom's nervous breakdown, a stillborn sibling, and even being raped. She seeks solace in food and inappropriate relationships. A college kiss and same-sex experience are part of adolescent experiences, as well as encounters with various GLBT secondary characters.

Awards: Publishing Triangle's 100 Best Lesbian and Gay Novels, Reader's Choice

Subjects: Sexual abuse, child • Substance abuse

Leonardi, Susan J.

And Then They Were Nuns. Ithaca, NY: Firebrand Books, 2003. **L**

Julian Pines Abbey is like no other convent in history. God might be a woman, nuns serve as priests, and celibacy is optional, in this parody of religious life.

Subjects: Humor • Religion

Read-Alikes: There are several mystery novels set in convents, but *The Case of the Not So Nice Nurse,* by Mabel Maney, parodies the lesbian sleuth genre and features a convent full of nuns.

LeRoy, J. T.

The Heart Is Deceitful Above All Things. New York: Bloomsbury, 2001. **G** **T**

Ten interconnected stories follow Jeremiah as he attempts to gain his neglectful mother's attention by imitating her self-destructive behaviors and pleasing her abusive boyfriends. These raw, almost horrific stories are not for the faint of heart.

Subjects: Books to film • Families • Sex workers • Sexual abuse, child • Substance abuse

Read-Alikes: LeRoy's tender depictions of damaged characters have been compared to Jean Genet and André Gide.

Lewis, Heather.

🏵 *House Rules.* New York: Serpent's Tail, 1995. **L**

Kicked out of boarding school and unwilling to face an abusive father at home, fifteen-year-old Lee returns to the horse show circuit. Her crush on another rider, Tory, leads to a passionate affair, but then takes her into a maelstrom of drug use, violence, and domination.

Awards: Ferro-Grumley Award, 1995

Subjects: Sadomasochism • Substance abuse

Read-Alikes: Gary Indiana's *Gone Tomorrow* is a similarly brutal exploration of gay male life.

Livia, Anna.

Bruised Fruit. Ithaca, NY: Firebrand Books, 1999. **G L B T**

There's something for every reader in this story about a circle of acquaintances. Caroline escapes an abusive relationship and falls in love with hermaphrodite Sydney, while the abused Patti seeks revenge on her lovers. Not for the faint of heart.

Subjects: Abuse • Murder • Sadomasochism

Read-Alikes: David L. Lindsey's *Mercy* features a sadistic murderer targeting lesbians.

Lopez, Erika.

They Call Me Mad Dog. New York: Simon & Schuster, 2001. **L B**

Tomato "Mad Dog" Rodriguez is a bad ass, bisexual, motorcycle girl whose impulsiveness and taste for revenge land her in prison. A funny, comic-book style novel.

Subjects: Hispanics • Humor • Motorcycles • Murder

Read-Alikes: *Flaming Iguanas* is the prequel to this book.

Lorde, Audre.

🎖 *Zami: A New Spelling of My Name.* Freedom, CA: Crossing Press, 2001 (1982). **L**

Elements of autobiography, fiction, and personal mythology blend into what Lorde called a "biomythography." Beginning in her Depression era childhood and progressing through early adulthood, Lorde expresses an outsider's loneliness, from being the only black girl in school to being a black lesbian circa 1950.

Awards: Publishing Triangle's 100 Best Lesbian and Gay Novels

Subjects: African Americans • Authors • Lorde, Audre • Relationships, parent–child

Read-Alikes: In *Soldier*, June Jordan shares her story of growing up in New York City as the child of Caribbean immigrants.

Lowenthal, Michael.

Avoidance. Saint Paul, MN: Graywolf, 2002. **G**

A scholarly camp counselor with an interest in the Amish and an urbane camper, both feeling the void of their father's deaths, form a friendship. The relationship is tested by adversity, in this idealized northwoods exploration of the complexity of desire.

Subjects: Grief • Religion • Sexual abuse • Students, college • Students, high school

Read-Alikes: For a darker tale of the relationship between abuser and victim, readers should check out Dennis Cooper's *Try*.

Mann, William J.

Jeff and Lloyd Series. **G**

Jeff and Lloyd serve as models for exploring how boys turn into gay men.

Subjects: Couples • Friendship • Love • Lust

The Men from the Boys. New York: Dutton, 1997.

> Meet Jeff O'Brian as he begins a midlife crisis at the tender age of thirty-three. His family life is upset by death, and his love life becomes tumultuous when lover Lloyd announces the flame in their relationship has burned out.

Where the Boys Are. New York: Kensington Books, 2003.

> Jeff and Lloyd deal with a friend's death by withdrawing from each other and pursuing different pastimes. Family, in the form of old friends and new lovers, stand in the way of a potential reunion. Campy dialogue and a variety of perspectives.

Men Who Love Men. New York: Kensington, 2007.

> A reunited Jeff and Lloyd contemplate marriage and operate a guesthouse in Provincetown. Henry, manager of the guesthouse, is the focus of the story, using his job to pursue handsome young lovers.

Manrique, Jaime.

🎗 *Latin Moon in Manhattan.* Madison: University of Wisconsin Press, 2003. **G**

> This is a fast-paced, character driven, pop-culture-infused and entertaining story about a gay, Colombian immigrant, Sammy, simultaneously dealing with work, an overbearing mom, a dying pet, and various colorful individuals.

> **Awards:** Publishing Triangle's 100 Best Lesbian and Gay Novels, Reader's Choice

> **Subjects:** Families • Hispanics • Immigrants • New York City

Martin, Douglas A.

Outline of My Lover. New York: Soft Skull, 2000. **G**

> A sensitive, spare story of a young man's desire for a neighbor, a famous rock star. The two become lovers, but as is frequently the case, the reality of a dream come true is disappointing. A thinly veiled roman à clef about musician Michael Stipe.

> **Subjects:** Autobiographical fiction • Georgia • Love • Music

> **Read-Alikes:** Felice Picano's *The Book of Lies* is part mystery, part roman à clef about the Violet Quill literary salon.

Mastbaum, Blair.

🎗 *Clay's Way.* Los Angeles: Alyson Books, 2004. **G**

> Disaffected skateboarder Sam is on his way out of the closet when he meets hunky surfer Clay. Every day the passion between them heightens, along with questions about their relationship and motives. Does Sam love Clay, or is it lust, or maybe obsession? Even the ending will leave readers guessing.

> **Awards:** Lambda Literary Award, 2004

> **Subjects:** Hawaii • Music • Students, high school • Substance abuse

Maupin, Armistead.

The Night Listener. New York: HarperCollins, 2000. **G**

Via the telephone, Gabriel Noone develops a father and son-like bond with Pete, a sexually abused, physically ill boy. Unexpectedly, Noone finds himself confiding in the boy, until questions about Pete's identity provoke a quest to prove his existence. A story within a story.

Subjects: Books to film • Intrigue • Relationships, parent–child

Read-Alikes: The protagonist of Louise Welsh's *Cutting Room* embarks on a mysterious search for truth.

Tales of the City Series. **G L B T**

The lives of a large ensemble cast intertwine at Mrs. Madrigal's San Francisco apartment house. <u>Tales</u> is a microcosm of life, dripping with soap opera drama.

Subjects: Books to film • California • Friendship • Intrigue • Love • Lust • Secrets

Read-Alikes: In Nisa Donnelly's *Love Songs of Phoenix Bay*, Phoenix creates a family from friends.

Tales of the City. New York: HarperPerennial, 1989 (1978).

This groundbreaking, satirical novel began as a series of newspaper stories about the residents of a San Francisco apartment house circa 1970. As the residents interact, personal stories and persons become entwined, until the characters share more than an address.

Awards: Publishing Triangle's 100 Best Lesbian and Gay Novels, Reader's Choice

More Tales of the City. New York: HarperPerennial, 1994 (1980).

Mystery and suspense form the crux of this volume, with evil persons plotting against Mrs. Madrigal, whose secrets are slowly and shockingly revealed. Parts of Mona's past are discovered during a vacation, and Michael comes out and goes on vacation with best friend Mary Ann.

Further Tales of the City. New York: HarperPerennial, 1994 (1982).

The somewhat over-the-top main plot centers on DeDe and her children, who are fleeing a Jim Jones cultlike figure. Mary Ann solidifies a relationship with Brian, and Mona escapes to Seattle.

Babycakes. New York: HarperPerennial, 1994 (1984).

The carefree days of the 1970s are over, the beloved characters are older, and AIDS is on the prowl. Michael, mourning the death of lovers and friends, runs off to England, where he crosses paths with Mona. Mary Ann and husband Brian try unsuccessfully to have a child, until help arrives in a most unlikely form.

Significant Others. New York: HarperPerennial, 1994 (1987).

Coinciding vacations have Michael and Brian staying at a gay resort near a women's music festival attended by DeDe, providing Maupin the perfect setting to skewer the sometimes exclusive GLBT community. Michael develops a love interest in Thack; Brian awaits the results of his AIDS test.

Sure of You. New York: HarperPerennial, 1994 (1989).

Career-minded Mary Ann leaves her family for New York, and Brian attempts to be a single father and get back into the dating game. Through Thack's influence, Michael begins to shed the Mouse persona and develop moral outrage at the AIDS crisis. Mrs. Madrigal and Mona engage in holiday flings, forcing Mrs. M. to choose between love and the chosen family of Barbary Lane.

Michael Tolliver Lives. New York: HarperCollins, 2007.

Maupin insists this is not a new volume in the series, although after an eighteen-year hiatus, some Barbary Lane inhabitants are back. Although they no longer share the storied address, many remain interconnected through children or lovers. The primary focus is on Michael, who has miraculously survived his HIV positive status and finds new life with a much younger boyfriend.

McCabe, Patrick.

Breakfast on Pluto. New York: HarperFlamingo, 1998. **T**

Taking a page from the Neil Jordan film *Crying Game*, McCabe's story centers on Patrick "Pussy" Brady, a cross-dressing sometime prostitute-performance artist recruited to work for the Irish Republican Army. Pussy's preoccupation with music and film are the backdrop in her search for love and acceptance. The 2005 film, also directed by Neil Jordan, received one Golden Globe nomination.

Subjects: Books to film • Cross-dressing • Humor • Ireland

Read-Alikes: Chilean politics and love collide in *My Tender Matador,* by Pedro Lemebel.

McCauley, Stephen.

🌹 *The Object of My Affection.* New York: Simon & Schuster, 1987. **G**

A zany cast of secondary characters complements the relationship between heterosexual Nina and George, her gay roommate. When Nina becomes pregnant, she asks George to assume a parental role, in this heartfelt story of friendship and creating family.

Awards: Publishing Triangle's 100 Best Lesbian and Gay Novels, Reader's Choice

Subjects: Books to film • Friendship • Love triangles • Parenting

Read-Alikes: *Leaps of Faith,* by Rachel Kranz, features Flip and Warren's dealings with a niece.

McClain, Ellen Jaffe.

No Big Deal. New York: Puffin Books, 1997. **G** **Teen**

Narrated by an overweight junior high student, Janice, who unravels the tale of class bully Kevin and his homophobic reaction to popular teacher Mr. Padovano. Through vandalism observed by Janice, Kevin exposes Mr. P.'s secret and sparks a parent-student movement to remove the teacher. Janice opposes the movement and in the process discovers Kevin's hate is motivated by something much more personal.

Subjects: Homophobia • Students, elementary school • Teachers

McGehee, Peter, and Doug Wilson.

Boys Like Us Series. [G]

This series of novels introduces readers to Zero and his gang of friends at the height of the AIDS crisis. As a result of the setting, the various characters cope with life in serious and satirical ways, while facing the specter of illness.

Subjects: AIDS • Canada and Canadians • Couples • Death and dying • Friendship • Humor • Love

Read-Alikes: Follow the adventures of Leonard and Larry in Tim Barela's series of graphic novels.

Boys Like Us. New York: St. Martin's Press, 1991.

On the rebound from his failed relationship with David, Zero takes up with Clay, but finds himself attracted to his HIV-positive best friend, Randy. Will a trip back to Arkansas and his Southern roots help him sort out his emotional life? Simply written and plotted.

Sweetheart. New York: St. Martin's Press, 1992.

Zero is back in Canada, making new friends through his work as an AIDS volunteer and determined to live every day to its fullest in the face of tragedy.

Labour of Love. New York: St. Martin's Press, 1993.

Zero becomes the focal point as his health begins to fail. David, Zero's HIV-positive lover, narrates the story of Zero's battle to live and the zany antics of their network of friends.

Millett, Kate.

🌳 *Sita.* Champaign-Urbana: University of Illinois Press, 2000 (1977). [L]

A painfully sad, depressing story of the end of an obsessive love affair between Kate and Sita. A semiautobiographical story in which the stream of consciousness style mimics the frantic directions the mind can take when pondering the unbelievable.

Awards: Publishing Triangle's 100 Best Lesbian and Gay Novels

Subjects: Anger • Autobiographical fiction • Couples • Infidelity • Love

Mootoo, Shani.

Cereus Blooms at Night. New York: Grove Press, 1996. [G] [T]

The imaginary island of Lantanacamara provides the backdrop for this colorful exploration of the definitions and limits of gender, both societal and self-applied. The main character is Mala Ramchandin, an aging woman who, years before, suffered abuse at the hands of her father and whose multiple connections with her male nurse, Tyler, and his secret lover, Otoh, weave a thoughtful mystery. A sharply drawn portrait of immigrant and island life.

Subjects: Canada and Canadians • Caribbean • Gender identity

Mowry, Jess.

Babylon Boyz. New York: Simon & Schuster, 1997. **G**

Three friends—overweight Wyatt, health-compromised Dante, and gay Pook—live in the ghetto and dream of escape. When they cross paths with a local gangster, a tempting opportunity for a better life evolves. Gritty, realistic language and adult situations appropriate for older YA readers.

Subjects: African Americans • Crime

Read-Alikes: *Sunday You Learn to Box,* by Bil Wright, also concerns the life of a young African American gay boy trapped in the inner city.

Murr, Naeem.

🎗 *The Boy.* Boston: Houghton Mifflin, 1998. **G B**

A nameless boy adopts multiple personalities and, with ruthless charm, seduces and manipulates all those around him; yet this same child may hold the key to one family's suffering, in this dark, disturbing novel.

Awards: Lambda Literary Award, 1998

Subjects: England • Intrigue

Obejas, Achy.

🎗 *Days of Awe.* New York: Ballantine, 2002. **L B**

While growing up in Chicago, Cuban-born exile Alejandra always felt a curious affinity with her Jewish neighbors. Upon learning the reason for this kinship, Ale embarks on a journey of self-discovery by returning to Cuba.

Awards: Lambda Literary Award, 2001

Subjects: Cuba • Hispanics • Immigrants • Jews • Religion

🎗 *Memory Mambo.* New York: Penguin Group, 2001. **L**

Cuban-born Juani Casas walks the thin line between fact and fiction. She hides the fact of her lesbianism behind fictional stories to avoid culturally induced homophobia, until a situation forces her to create a web of lies so complex she can no longer separate the truth from the lies.

Awards: Lambda Literary Award, 1996

Subjects: Families • Hispanics • Immigrants

Orleans, Ellen.

🎗 *The Butches of Madison County.* Bala Cynwyd, PA: Laugh Lines Press, 1995. **L B**

Billie, a promiscuous butch, visits rural Iowa and finds love and passion with an otherwise straight, married farm wife. A parody of the movie *The Bridges of Madison County.*

Awards: Lambda Literary Award, 1995

Subjects: Butches • Humor • Iowa • Lust

Peters, Julie Anne.

Luna. New York: Little, Brown. 2004. **T**

Liam, a boy by day, transforms into Luna at night, with the help of sister Regan and her wardrobe. Regan's unfaltering support wavers when she starts dating, and family members must decide how Liam's cross-dressing affects their lives. A unique perspective on a tricky subject, handled with style.

Subjects: Cross-dressing • Sex change • Siblings • Students, high school

Picano, Felice.

The Book of Lies. Los Angeles: Alyson Books, 2000. **G**

With a touch of mystery and strong connections to the author's real life, this is the story of a professor in search of a research topic, who discovers an odd manuscript and begins a quest for answers that leads to a surprise ending.

Subjects: Authors • Intrigue • Teachers

Pinera, Virgilio.

🏅 *Rene's Flesh.* New York: Marsilio Publishers, 1992. **B**

The family and friends of Rene, heir to a messianic/political movement devoted to the cult of the flesh, try to secure him to this world with the blandishments of the body, while Rene tries to escape his doom.

Awards: Publishing Triangle's 100 Best Lesbian and Gay Novels

Subjects: Politics • Sadomasochism • Sex

Read-Alikes: Yukio Mishima's semiautobiographical *Confessions of a Mask* is similarly disturbing.

Plum-Ucci, Carol.

What Happened to Lani Garver? San Diego: Harcourt, 2002. **G L B T Teen**

Lani Garver arrives at school just in time to help recovering cancer patient Claire readjust, but Lani is unlike anyone Claire and her friends have ever seen. Is Lani a boy? A girl? An angel? Lani's ambiguity leads to trouble and additional unanswered questions, in this suspenseful novel.

Subjects: Illness • Friendship • Intrigue • Students, high school

Proulx, Annie.

🏅 *The Shipping News.* New York: Scribner, 1993. **L**

A widowed, middle-aged man moves with his daughters and lesbian aunt to the ancestral home in Newfoundland. Among the harsh yet beautiful landscape, the family heals and learns that love does not have to hurt. Slim GLBT content.

Awards: Publishing Triangle's 100 Best Lesbian and Gay Novels, Reader's Choice

Subjects: Books to film • Canada and Canadians • Families

Read-Alikes: Proulx is also responsible for "Brokeback Mountain," the story of gay cowboys found in *Close Range: Wyoming Stories.*

Puig, Manuel.

🏵 *Kiss of the Spider Woman.* New York: Vintage, 1991. **G** **T**

The paths of two men, a political prisoner and a gay man, collide in an Argentinean prison. Initially indifferent to each other, the two develop a friendship. A highly descriptive, dialogue-driven novel in which not everything is as it appears. Originally titled *El beso de la mujer arena* and published in Argentina in 1976.

Awards: Publishing Triangle's 100 Best Lesbian and Gay Novels

Subjects: Argentina • Books to film • Crime

Read-Alikes: Colm Tóibín's historical novel *Story of the Night* is also set in Argentina.

Purdy, James.

🏵 *In a Shallow Grave.* San Francisco: City Lights Books, 1988. **G**

Garnet Montrose, a war veteran, attempts to woo back his wife's affection through notes authored by Daventry. Over time, it becomes clear that Daventry's prose is inspired by his affection for Garnet. The simple narrative style and dialogue of the characters creates a believable story.

Awards: Publishing Triangle's 100 Best Lesbian and Gay Novels, Reader's Choice

Subjects: Books to film • Love letters • Love triangles • Race relations

Reading, J. P.

Bouquets for Brimbal. New York: HarperCollins, 1980. **L** **Teen**

Anne Brimbal is an aspiring young actress who joins the local theater troupe with tagalong friend Macy. Both girls develop relationships, but Macy questions Anne's interactions with Lola. Does Anne love Lola? What should Macy feel about her friendship if Anne is a homosexual?

Subjects: Friendship • Theater

Ridgway, Keith.

The Long Falling. Boston: Houghton Mifflin, 1999. **G**

Fleeing her abusive husband, Grace relocates near her son. Through proximity, each rediscovers the other, as well as secrets that force them to reevaluate everything. Moral and relationship complexities converge in this finely rendered debut novel.

Subjects: Abuse • Ireland • Relationships, parent–child • Secrets

Robbins, Tom.

🏵 *Even Cowgirls Get the Blues.* Boston: Houghton Mifflin, 1976. **L**

Sissy's freakishly oversized thumbs are a gift from the gods destining her for life as a hitchhiker. Arriving at the Rubber Rose Ranch, Sissy meets a group of cowgirls and a philosophical mountain man who alter the course of her life. A quirky, humorous story.

Awards: Publishing Triangle's 100 Best Lesbian and Gay Novels, Reader's Choice

Subjects: Books to film • Feminism • Humor • Travel

Robson, Ruthann.

A/K/A. New York: St. Martin's Press, 1997. **L**

Two women, one a popular soap opera actress, the other paying for law school with the money she makes as a professional escort, play so many roles that they start to lose sight of who they really are. As their lives implode, the women pull together and find in each other salvation and love.

Subjects: Actors and actresses • New York City • Sex workers

Rodi, Robert.

Bitch Goddess. New York: Plume, 2002. **G**

Hollywood is the setting for this campy tale about the reinvigorated career of a forgotten actress who hires a gay ghostwriter to prepare her memoirs. Told in the form of interviews, articles, and e-mails in which blackmail, secrets, and affairs abound. Be on the lookout for a surprise ending.

Subjects: Actors and actresses • Secrets

Salvatore, Diane.

🎗 *Paxton Court.* Tallahassee, FL: Bella Books, 2003. **L**

Four lesbian couples purchase adjoining retirement properties in sunny Florida and are received by their new neighbors with varying degrees of acceptance and hostility. Disturbed by neighbors, the couples' friendships are tested, with some interesting results.

Awards: Publishing Triangle's 100 Best Lesbian and Gay Novels, Reader's Choice

Subjects: Aging • Florida • Friendship

Sanchez, Alex.

🎗 *So Hard to Say.* New York: Simon & Schuster, 2004. **G** **Teen**

On the cusp of high school, Xio and her friends are hip, calling themselves "sexies." Attracted to the new boy, Xio sets about wooing Frederick as a friend. Once the friendship is established, Xio schemes to turn Frederick into her boyfriend, but his attraction to Victor brings on a full-scale identity crisis. Funny and touching.

Awards: Lambda Literary Award, 2004

Subjects: Hispanics • Students, elementary school

Read-Alikes: In Kathe Koja's *Talk,* Lindsay falls for a closeted costar.

Schulman, Sarah.

🎗 *Rat Bohemia.* New York: Dutton, 1995. **L**

A trio of friends—David, Rita, and Killer—are disenfranchised from their families because of their homosexuality. Each character takes a turn narrating this slice-of-life tale, in which the dirt and grit of urban life are metaphors for death, decay, and rejection.

Awards: Publishing Triangle's 100 Best Lesbian and Gay Novels; Ferro-Grumley Award, 1996

Subjects: AIDS • Families • Homophobia • New York City

Scoppettone, Sandra.

Trying Hard to Hear You. Boston: Alyson Books, 1996 (1974). **G** **Teen**

This early classic concerns a group of friends in a drama club who become cruel when one of their own admits to being a homosexual attracted to another member of the group.

Subjects: Friendship • Homophobia • Students, high school • Theater

Shannon, George.

Unlived Affections. New York: HarperCollins, 1989. **G** **Teen**

Upon the death of his grandmother, Willie discovers a cache of letters exchanged between his parents and unearths a long-hidden secret linking the past to the present.

Subjects: Relationships, parent–child • Secrets • Students, high school

Shimko, Bonnie.

🎗 *Letters in the Attic.* Chicago: Academy Chicago, 2002. **L** **Teen**

Almost thirteen, Lizzy is wise beyond her years from tending her mom's emotionally fragile heart. After another heartbreak, they move in with Lizzy's grandparents, whom she has never met. A cache of old letters contains family secrets, and self-discovery leads to more secrets.

Awards: Lambda Literary Award, 2002

Subjects: Love letters • Relationships, parent–child • Secrets

Read-Alikes: Lissa, the protagonist in *Kissing Kate* by Lauren Myracle, is a motherless sixteen-year-old with feelings for her best friend.

Scott, D. Travers.

Execution, Texas: 1987. New York: St. Martin's Press, 1997. **B**

While high school senior Seeger King counts down the days to graduation, he relies on friends to relieve the tedium with trips, intense confessionals, and young bi love. His family—a deluded mother, an egotistical father, and a religious stepmother—are outside Seeger's life when tragedy strikes.

Subjects: Families • Religion • Students, high school

Sibley, William Jack.

Any Kind of Luck. New York: Kensington Books, 2001. **G**

To care for an ailing parent, boyfriends Clu and Chris move from Manhattan to rural Texas. A cast of stereotypical redneck characters interferes with the men's relationship. The comic book style cover is a good indication of the campy style and story.

Subjects: Couples • Humor • Relationships, parent–child • Texas

Read-Alikes: In Orland Outland's *Different People,* two boyhood friends are reunited by a father's illness.

Springer, Nancy.

Looking for Jamie Bridger. New York: Dial Books for Young Readers, 1995. **G** **Teen**

Raised by her unloving grandparents, Jamie has no idea what happened to her parents. Upon grandpa's death, Jamie launches an unplanned expedition to find her family. Ultimately, she discovers a gay brother and a bittersweet ending.

Subjects: Families • Homophobia • Secrets • Siblings

Storandt, William.

The Summer They Came. New York: Villard, 2002. **G**

What happens when a group of gay real estate developers decides to create a new gay summer mecca? Readers get a funny, slightly stereotypical look at how a cast of characters with different political, personal, and economic agendas reacts to the dilemma of new neighbors.

Subjects: Friendship • Humor • Stereotypes

Read-Alikes: *Cathedral City,* by Gregory Hinton, also turns on small-town real estate development, but with negative overtones.

Swados, Elizabeth.

Flamboyant. New York: Picador, 1999. **G** **L** **Teen**

Chana, an Orthodox Jew, accepts a position teaching at an alternative school for gay and lesbian students. Her work experiences clash with her religious beliefs about homosexuality, as she finds herself sympathetic to the students' plight, particularly that of a young prostitute, Flamboyant.

Subjects: Jews • Race relations • Students, high school • Teachers

Read-Alikes: *Push,* by Sapphire, is a graphic story about an incest survivor redeemed by a student–teacher relationship.

Taylor, Robert.

🌟 *Whose Eye Is on Which Sparrow?* New York: Haworth Press, 2005. **G**

A married doctor finds himself unexpectedly attracted to a patient. Multidimensional conflicts arise regarding professional ethics, adultery, race relations, and career choice. This is good beach reading.

Awards: IPPY Award, 2005

Subjects: African Americans • Healthcare workers • Infidelity • Interracial relationships

Read-Alikes: *Scrub Match,* by Bill Eisele, uses basketball to relate the story of a mixed-race man looking for love.

Tóibín, Colm.

🌟 *The Master.* New York: Simon & Schuster, 2004. **G**

An excellent fictionalized account of the life of author and critic Henry James, often dubbed "master of the psychological novel," including James's interior conflicts about his sexuality, which provided frequent fodder for his novels. James watches the trial of Oscar Wilde with mixed sympathy and horror even as he hides an attraction to a manservant, spends a chaste night in bed with Oliver Wendell Holmes, and later finds love with an Italian sculptor.

Awards: Lambda Literary Award, 2004; Stonewall Book Award, 2005

Subjects: Authors • James, Henry

Read-Alikes: David Lodge presents his fictionalized version of James's life in *Author, Author*.

Tondelli, Pier Vittorio.

🎗 *Separate Rooms.* New York: Serpent's Tail, 1992. **G**

In an attempt to deal with his grief, Leo reminisces about his intense and volatile relationship with Thomas. This evocative book packs a heart-breaking punch.

Awards: Publishing Triangle's 100 Best Lesbian and Gay Novels, Reader's Choice

Subjects: Death and dying • Grief • Travel

Read-Alikes: Martin Hyatt's *Scarecrow's Bible* concerns a Mississippi man in love with someone much younger.

Torres, Laura.

November Ever After. New York: Holiday House, 1999. **L**

Grieving for her mother, Amy turns to Sara for support, but becomes upset when Sara spends more time with Anita. Upon learning Sara is romantically attracted to Anita, Amy reassesses the friendship in light of her religious beliefs and worries about being considered gay by association. A "love the sinner, hate the sin" approach.

Subjects: Friendship • Grief • Religion • Students

Tournier, Michel.

🎗 *Gemini.* Baltimore: Johns Hopkins University Press, 1998 (1981). **G**

Spans the mid-twentieth century. Twins Jean and Paul are so alike they are referred to collectively as Jean-Paul, and the intimacy of their interdependent relationship is like that of lovers. As they grow older, the men create separate identities and their lives serve as a vehicle for exploring human nature, including homosexuality. Originally published in France in 1975 as *Les Météores*, this is a book of ideas for readers who like a challenge.

Awards: Publishing Triangle's 100 Best Lesbian and Gay Novels

Subjects: France • Siblings

Trujillo, Carla.

What Night Brings. Willimantic, CT: Curbstone Press, 2003. **L**

Marci is an unconventional preteen, asking too many questions, being kicked out of catechism class, wishing her abusive father would disappear, spying on her father's infidelities, and praying that she can become a boy. Marci knows that as a boy, she could stand up to her father and capture the girl of her dreams.

Subjects: Abuse • Coming-of-age • Families • Hispanics

Read-Alikes: Readers may want to try Terri de la Peña's *Margins,* in which a twenty-something woman finds the courage to confront familial and cultural homophobia.

Tulchinsky, Karen X.

Love Ruins Everything. Vancouver, BC: Raincoast Book, 1998. **G** **L** **B**

Ride the rollercoaster of Naomi Rabinovitch's life, from the depths of break-up despair to the heights of unexpected reunion with an old flame. Throw in a possible government conspiracy, and the plot becomes a stew of emotional and political intrigue.

Subjects: Butches • Intrigue • Jews

Read-Alikes: Anne Azel's *Seasons* finds Robbie Williams unexpectedly in love with her sister-in-law.

Tyler, Ben.

Gay Blades. New York: Kensington, 2004. **G**

Look out Tonya Harding: here comes Tag Tempkin, who will stop at nothing to get ahead in the prima donna world of figure skating. A wicked skewering of this insular sporting community.

Subjects: Humor • Skating

Read-Alikes: David Leavitt skewers the literary world in *Martin Bauman.*

Van Arsdale, Sarah.

Toward Amnesia. New York: Riverhead Books, 1995. **L**

Reeling from the dissolution of her relationship, the unnamed narrator decides to check out of life by consciously invoking amnesia and taking a road trip. Escapism becomes a way of finding one's self.

Subjects: Travel

Weltner, Peter.

How the Body Prays. Saint Paul, MN: Graywolf Press, 1999. **G**

Two brothers from a family of war heroes, Andy and Aaron, take different paths during the Vietnam War. One dies, while the other, seeking to heal emotional scars, discovers hidden family secrets. Shifting narrators, time frames, and a large cast of characters add challenging elements to the story.

Subjects: Secrets • Siblings • Vietnam War

White, Edmund.

The Farewell Symphony. New York: Knopf, 1997. **G**

An unnamed narrator's yearning for fame and love are counterpoised in his failed publishing attempts and endless sexual contacts. The highly stylized, sketchlike rendering of episodes closely parallels the author's early to middle adulthood.

Subjects: Authors • Autobiographical fiction

Read-Alikes: For a different perspective on White's life, readers may want to try Keith Fleming's *Boy with the Thorn in His Side*.

Womack, Craig S.

Drowning in Fire. Tucson: University of Arizona Press, 2001. **G**

All of the other boys except Jimmy ridicule Josh Henneha, a Muskogee Creek Indian growing up in Oklahoma. Confused by the mores of a strict upbringing and his attraction to Jimmy, Josh finds solace in the stories and beliefs of his Creek heritage.

Subjects: Magic • Native Americans

Read-Alikes: For another tale featuring a Native American protagonist, readers should try Cynthia Thayer's *Strong for Potatoes,* in which Blue finds strength and wisdom with the encouragement of her grandfather. Will Roscoe edited *Living the Spirit,* a collective approach to Native American GLBT lives.

Woodson, Jacqueline.

🏵 *Autobiography of a Family Photo.* New York: Dutton, 1995. **L** **Teen**

An unnamed African American girl narrates this slim volume of diarylike chapters. The heroine's conflicting sexual experiences and feelings run concurrently with her family's disintegration amid the turmoil of the Vietnam War, sexual abuse, and poverty.

Awards: Lambda Literary Award, 1995; Publishing Triangle's 100 Best Lesbian and Gay Novels

Subjects: African Americans • Families • Sexual abuse

Read-Alikes: In Madelyn Arnold's *Year of Full Moons,* Jos deals with a disintegrating family, mounting national events, and her secret attraction to women.

🏵 *From the Notebooks of Melanin Sun.* New York: Scholastic, 1995. **L** **Teen**

As the only child of a single mom, Mel has a great relationship with his mom, until she announces that she loves a woman. Appalled, Mel retreats to his diary to work out his fears and decide whether he will reject or accept his mother.

Awards: Lambda Literary Award, 1995

Subjects: African Americans • Relationships, parent–child

🏵 *The House You Pass on the Way.* Waterville, ME: Thorndike Press, 2004. **L** **Teen**

Staggerlee, treated as an outsider because of her mom's mixed racial identity, feels different because she kissed a girl, until cousin Trout admits similar feelings. Woodson tackles racial and gender issues with grace and poise.

Awards: Lambda Literary Award, 1997

Subjects: Adoption • African Americans • Coming-of-age • Race relations

Xavier, Emanuel.

Christ-Like. New York: Painted Leaf Press, 1999. **G**

> Abused as a toddler, Mikey, a softhearted fellow, masks his pain with a tough exterior characterized by prostitution and drug abuse.
>
> **Subjects:** Hispanics • Religion • Sex workers • Substance abuse

Youngblood, Shay.

Black Girl in Paris. New York: Riverhead Books, 2000. **L B**

> Eden, an aspiring writer, is searching for the secret to successful writing. Disillusioned by the daily struggle to survive, Eden discovers her muse cannot be found in the experience of others. Resembles a travel diary, with tucked-in bits of illustration.
>
> **Subjects:** African Americans • Authors • France
>
> **Read-Alikes:** Wayne Koestenbaum's musical protagonist in *Moira Orfei in Aigues-Mortes* ponders his performance ability.

Soul Kiss. New York: Riverhead, 1998. **L Teen**

> Tomboy Mariah, raised by two aunts, is keenly aware of her attraction to other girls, but it competes with the emotional hole left by her mother's abandonment. As she grows up, Mariah searches for her family. Poetic, with a real-world ending. Suitable for upper-level high school readers.
>
> **Subjects:** African Americans • Coming-of-age • Families

Short Story Collections (Single Author)

Allison, Dorothy.

🎖 *Trash.* New York: Plume, 2002. **L**

> With a Southern sensibility and a writing style as smooth as sipping whiskey, these gritty stories offer vivid scenes of growing up poor white trash, being the victim of multiple types of abuse, and surviving against all odds.
>
> **Awards:** Lambda Literary Award, 1988
>
> **Subjects:** Anthologies • Families • Sexual abuse • Southern states • Substance abuse
>
> **Read-Alikes:** Mary Potter Engel's interconnected short stories in *Strangers and Sojourners* feature a homeless transgendered person, a HIV-positive husband, and a gay African American drummer.

Cooper, Bernard.

Guess Again: Short Stories. New York: Simon & Schuster, 2006. **G B**

> First loves, couples struggling with illness, and Mormons hosting dinner parties for gay friends are the subjects of a few of the stories in this excellent collection.
>
> **Subjects:** Anthologies • Coming-of-age • Friendship • Relationships
>
> **Read-Alikes:** Smooth prose characterizes the interconnected stories in Richard McCann's *Mother of Sorrows*.

Doenges, Judy.

🎗 *What She Left Me.* Hanover, NH: University Press of New England, 1999. **G** **L**

Thematically similar short stories and a novella concerning the gritty side of blue-collar gay and lesbian life. In the titular story, a waitress obsesses over her deceased mother's possessions; the novella features a butcher's attraction to a coworker.

Awards: Ferro-Grumley Award, 2000

Subjects: Anthologies • Class conflict • Coming out • Crime • Dating • Grief

Donnelly, Nisa.

🎗 *Bar Stories.* New York: St Martin's Press, 1989. **L**

Sentimental, melodramatic, interconnected, and at times erotic, stories about a group of women who frequent a lesbian bar.

Awards: Lambda Literary Award, 1989

Subjects: Anthologies • Bars • Dating • Friendship • Love • Lust

Read-Alikes: *Boys in the Brownstone,* by Kevin Scott, is the equivalent read for gay men.

Donoghue, Emma.

The Mammoth Book of Lesbian Short Stories. New York: Carroll & Graf, 1999. **L**

Thirty tumultuous and tempting stories span different phases of womanhood and passages of time.

Subjects: Anthologies • Dating • Friendship • Love • Lust • Sex

Read-Alikes: For more lesbian love stories, readers should check out Irene Zahava's *Love Shook My Heart.*

Ebershoff, David.

🎗 *Rose City: Stories.* New York: Penguin, 2002. **G**

Pasadena, California, a/k/a Rose City, is the locale for seven stories about gay men who, for various reasons, lead unfulfilling lives.

Awards: Ferro-Grumley Award, 2002

Subjects: Anthologies • California

Holleran, Andrew.

In September the Light Changes. New York: Hyperion Press, 1999. **G**

Sixteen stories gallop over two tumultuous decades, from the torrid sexual freedom of the 1970s through the chilly bleakness of the AIDS-shrouded 1980s–1990s. The stark writing style conveys a sense of nostalgic detachment akin to memories.

Subjects: Aging • Anthologies • Love • Lust

Jones, John Sam.

Welsh Boys Too. Cardiff, Wales: Parthian Books, 2000. **G**

> The diverse country of Wales is the setting for eight stories about the lives of gay men. The stories cover family relationships, revenge, homophobia, and grief, each with a distinctly Welsh feel.
>
> **Subjects:** Anthologies • Wales
>
> **Read-Alikes:** *Fishboys of Vernazza* is Jones's follow-up volume. Welsh history buffs may enjoy Doris Grumbach's *Ladies,* a fictionalized version of the Ladies of Llangollen.

Kenan, Randall.

🎗 *Let the Dead Bury Their Dead and Other Stories.* San Diego: Harcourt Brace Jovanovich, 1992. **G**

> Twelve short stories about a town fraught with secrets, where the living speak to the dead, animals speak to farmers, and fiction masquerades as scholarly nonfiction.
>
> **Awards:** Lambda Literary Award, 1992; Ferro-Grumley Award, 1993
>
> **Subjects:** African Americans • Anthologies • North Carolina

Leavitt, David.

Family Dancing. New York: Knopf, 1984. **G B**

> Leavitt turns the spotlight on families in all their splendor and horror. Here is a compilation of short stories in which husbands leave wives and children are affected by parental discord. Some sad moments tempered by sensitive writing.
>
> **Subjects:** Anthologies • Families
>
> **Read-Alikes:** Ivan E. Coyote's short stories in *Close to Spider Man* are about young lesbians and their families.

The Marble Quilt. Boston: Houghton Mifflin, 2001. **G**

> Nine stories of broken lives. In the title story, Vincent talks to the Italian police about his dead lover; in "The Black Box," Bob's lover has died in a plane crash; and a young man is obsessed with contracting AIDS in "The Infection Scene."
>
> **Subjects:** Anthologies • Death and dying • Families
>
> **Read-Alikes:** *Interesting Monsters,* by Aldo Alverez, presents sixteen short stories revolving around a couple.

A Place I've Never Been. New York: Viking, 1990. **G L B**

> Short stories dominated by relationship conflicts form the crux of this collection. Find a lesbian attending the marriage of an ex-lover, a straight couple having an affair, and a married man attracted to a gay man. Something for everyone.
>
> **Subjects:** Anthologies • Grief • Love
>
> **Read-Alikes:** *Ordinary Genius,* by Thomas Fox Averill, features stunning stories about twins, neighbors, parent–child relationships, and musicians.

Mordden, Ethan.

Buddies Cycle.

Mordden mines tales from his life and those of friends to construct snapshot-like stories about a group of friends—Dennis, Little Kiwi, Carlos, and Bud—exploring gay city life. The laugh-out-loud stories are mostly about looking for love and developing a circle of friends who become an adopted family. Easy reading level appropriate for older young adults or adults with literacy limitations.

Subjects: Anthologies • Dating • Friendship • Humor • Love • Lust • New York City

Read-Alikes: Alison Bechdel's *Dykes to Watch Out For* and Eric Orner's *Mostly Unfabulous Social Life of Ethan Green* follow a cadre of characters in comic strip form.

I've a Feeling We're Not in Kansas Anymore. New York: St. Martin's Griffin, 1996 (1985).

> Bud narrates the interconnected stories about his best friend and upstairs neighbor Dennis, the latter's lover, Virgil a/k/a Little Kiwi, and their hunky, party-hearty friend Carlo.

Buddies. New York: St. Martin's Press, 1986.

> New York City friends Dennis, Little Kiwi, Carlos, and Bud are still looking for love, but are also debating sex, psychology, and politics.

Everybody Loves You. New York: Saint Martin's Griffin, 1988.

> Intended to be the final volume of the series, its tone is a bit serious but funny nevertheless. Little Kiwi displays deeper emotional maturity, seeking to separate himself from the career-befuddled Dennis, Carlo becomes less self-centered, and the friends take in a newcomer, Cosgrove.

Some Men Are Lookers. New York: St. Martin's Press, 1997.

> Kiwi insists on being called Virgil as he launches a cabaret act with Cosgrove. Carlo introduces the duo to a club owner who books their act, thus leading Virgil into an affair with the club's owner. Dennis is devastated and leaves Virgil for a new lover, and Bud convinces Cosgrove a trip to Italy will heal the hurt.

How's Your Romance? New York: St. Martin's Press, 2005.

> The gang is all here. They have seen it and done it all; survived the disco, drug-laden 1970s and miraculously escaped the AIDS epidemic of the 1980s, and now they stand poised on the brink of a new millennium. As each character ages, reconciliations and romances move in unexpected directions, colliding with a younger set of characters.

Raphael, Lev.

Dancing on Tisha B'av. New York: St. Martin's Press, 1990. **G**

Jewish holidays collide with Gay Pride Parades in these nineteen short stories about being Jewish and homosexual.

Awards: Lambda Literary Award, 1990

Subjects: Anthologies • Jews

Read-Alikes: Gay and straight, Jew and Gentile, mix it up in Aaron Hamburger's *View from Stalin's Head.*

Robson, Ruthann.

🌿 *Eye of a Hurricane.* Ithaca, NY: Firebrand Books, 1989. **L**

These thirteen short stories cover a broad range of topics, from feminism to parenting.

Awards: Ferro-Grumley Award, 1990

Subjects: Anthologies • Death and dying • Feminism • Parenting

Read-Alikes: For more short stories, readers may want to try the *Penguin Book of Lesbian Short Stories,* edited by Margaret Reynolds.

Surkis, Alice, and Monica Nolan, eds.

The Big Book of Lesbian Horse Stories. New York: Kensington, 2002. **L**

Eight campy stories packaged like a dime store novel and set against the backdrop of various twentieth-century historical events, such as the Great Depression and the Stonewall Riots. Love for horses and Sapphic desire combine.

Subjects: Anthologies • Love • Lust • Pets

Wilson, Barbara.

Salt Water and Other Stories. Los Angeles: Alyson Books, 1999. **L**

The many forms of love—passionate, violent, unrequited, temporary, long distance, intercultural—are the central theme in these nine stories. Reimagined fairy tales are employed as a literary device to create a sense of fun and the unattainable.

Subjects: Anthologies • Fairy tales • Love

Short Story Anthologies (Multiple Authors)

Bouldrey, Brian, ed.

Best American Gay Fiction. Boston: Little, Brown, 1997. **G**

Looking for something new to read? Here are twenty-one stories by overlooked writers such as Kolin M. Ohi, Tom House, Kevin Killian, Andrew Sean Greer, Jim Provenzano, Adam Klein, and Peter Weltner. Includes book excerpts, bits of biography, and short stories.

Subjects: Anthologies • Dating • Friendship • Love • Lust • Sex

Carbado, Devon, Dwight McBride, and Don Weise, eds.

🏆 *Black Like Us: A Century of Lesbian, Gay, and Bisexual African American Fiction.* San Francisco: Cleis, 2002. **G** **L** **B**

Divided into three sections, each beginning with a critical essay, the works of thirty-six authors are presented, with biographical data. Valuable for reviving interest in lesser-known authors such as Owen Dodson.

Awards: Lambda Literary Award, 2002; Independent Publisher Book Award, 2003

Subjects: African Americans • Anthologies

Read-Alikes: Shawn S. Ruff's *Go the Way Your Blood Beats* contains thirty-two excerpts by African American GLBT authors.

Drake, Robert, and Terry Wolverton, eds.

Circa 2000: Lesbian Fiction at the Turn of the Millennium. Los Angeles: Alyson Books, 2000. **L**

GLBT's heavy hitters are here, including Dorothy Allison, Emma Donoghue, Achy Obejas, Gerry Gomez Pearlberg, and Sarah Schulman, but there are also some fun, fresh voices from Larissa Lai, Beth Brant, and Rebecca Brown.

Subjects: Anthologies • Dating • Friendship • Love • Relationships • Sex

Hemphill, Essex, ed.

🏆 *Brother to Brother: New Writings by Black Gay Men.* Boston: Alyson Publications, 1991. **G**

A groundbreaking work consisting of short stories and poetry reflecting the pain of racism, the joy of love, and the sorrows of loss. Includes works by Larry Duplechan and John Keene.

Awards: Lambda Literary Award, 1991

Subjects: African Americans • Anthologies

Read-Alikes: *Freedom in This Village,* by E. Lynn Harris, anthologizes forty-seven works by African Americans.

Holoch, Naomi, Joan Nestle, and Nancy Holden, eds.

🏆 *The Vintage Book of International Lesbian Fiction.* London: Vintage, 1999. **L**

Marguerite Yourcenar, Anchee Min, Alifa Rifaat, Jeanne d'Arc Jutras, Yasmin Tambiah, Ngahuia Te Awekotuku, and Dionne Brand are virtually unknown to many American readers, but the thirty-five selections located herein represent a potpourri of cross-cultural lesbian experiences.

Awards: Lambda Literary Award, 1999

Subjects: Anthologies • Dating • Friendship • Love • Lust

Read-Alikes: *Desire High Heels Red Wine,* by Timothy Archer, is a Canadian anthology.

Karlsberg, Michele, and Karen X Tulchinsky, eds.

To Be Continued. Ithaca, NY: Firebrand Books, 1998. **L**

> Eleven suspenseful stories intentionally designed to continue in a future volume are sufficiently self-contained to prove satisfying. Spanning time and culture are vampires, princesses, witches, and weddings from authors such as Carla Trujillo, Lucy Jane Bledsoe, Jewell Gomez, Jess Wells, and Judith Katz, and Cecilia Tan.
>
> **Subjects:** Anthologies • Dating • Friendship • Love • Lust • Sex
>
> **Read-Alikes:** To find out how the stories end, readers should see *To Be Continued: Take Two,* also edited by Karlsberg and Tulchinsky.

Leyland, Winston, ed.

🎗 *Now the Volcano: An Anthology of Latin American Gay Literature.* San Francisco: Gay Sunshine Press, 1979. **G**

> Poems, short stories, and novel excerpts from Brazil, Colombia, and Mexico are featured in this groundbreaking work. Authors such as Luis Cernuda and Adolfo Caminha are introduced with a biographical essay, and poetry is presented in the original language and English translation.
>
> **Awards:** Stonewall Book Award, 1980
>
> **Subjects:** Anthologies • Hispanics
>
> **Read-Alikes:** For a contemporary American collection, readers should try Manuel Munoz's *Zigzagger.*

Manrique, Jaime, and Jesse Dorris, eds.

Besame Mucho: An Anthology of Gay Latino Fiction. New York: Painted Leaf Press, 1999. **G** **T**

> Adan Griego, Erasmo Guerra, Larry La Fountain-Stokes, Jaime Cortez, Alex R. Silva, and Emanuel Xavier are a few of the undiscovered Latino writers found in this collection of seventeen stories.
>
> **Subjects:** Anthologies • Hispanics
>
> **Read-Alikes:** For more writings by gay Latinos, readers should try *Virgins, Guerrillas and Locas,* edited by Jaime Cortez.

Morrow, Bruce, and Charles H. Rowell, eds.

Shade: An Anthology of Fiction by Gay Men of African Descent. New York: Avon, 1996. **G**

> Issues of sex and race are explored in twenty-three short stories by Melvin Dixon, James Earl Hardy, A. Cinque Hicks, John Keene Jr., Jaime Manrique, Bil Wright, and Samuel R. Delany.
>
> **Subjects:** African Americans • Anthologies • Friendship • Love • Lust • Race relations • Sex

Quinn, Jay.

Rebel Yell Series. G

Fictional literature on gay Southern life is sorely lacking, and <u>Rebel</u> contributes a collection of short stories, many of which seem like memoirs. The stories range from iced tea sweetness to bourbon- and humidity-drenched erotica.

Subjects: Anthologies • Southern States

Read-Alikes: Roy Wood's 1985 publication *Restless Rednecks* is perhaps the earliest collection of gay Southern stories, although most are personal recollections.

Rebel Yell. New York: Southern Tier Editions/Harrington Park, 2001.

Editor Quinn brings together fourteen stories emphasizing home and family. Featured are Robin Lippincott, Jameson Currier, Walter Holland, John Trumbo, Andrew Beierle, George Singer, and Jeff Mann.

Rebel Yell 2. New York: Southern Tier Editions/Harrington Park, 2002.

Twenty-two stories continue to build on the Southern, gay male theme. Lippincott, Currier, and Mann are back, along with Picano and lesser-known writers.

Schimel, Lawrence, ed.

Kosher Meat. Sante Fe, NM: Sherman Asher, 2000. G

A variety of voices employ different literary styles, exploring what is to be Jewish and gay.

Subjects: Anthologies • Jews

Read-Alikes: In Evelyn Torton Beck's *Nice Jewish Girls*, lesbians explore their Jewish identity.

Trujillo, Carla, ed.

🌹 *Chicana Lesbians: The Girls Our Mothers Warned Us About.* Berkeley, CA: Third Woman Press, 1991. L

An anthology of stories and poetry about the Hispanic lesbian experience, including multiple pieces from the editor, Gloria Anzaldúa, Ana Castillo, Cherríe Moraga, Terri de la Peña, Emma Pérez, and Karen T. Delgadillo.

Awards: Lambda Literary Award, 1992

Subjects: Anthologies • Hispanics • Race relations • Sex

White, Edmund, and Donald Weise, eds.

🌹 *Fresh Men: New Voices in Gay Fiction.* New York: Carroll & Graff, 2004. G

This collection of twenty stories from up-and-coming young authors features a variety of styles and a diversity of characters exploring love, lust, betrayal, isolation, and illness.

Awards: Lambda Literary Award, 2004

Subjects: Anthologies • Dating • Friendship • Love • Lust • Sex

Read-Alikes: Readers should see the stories in *Contra/Dictions,* edited by Brett Josef Grubisic, and also try the sequel, *Fresh Men 2.*

Woelz, Karl, ed.

M2M. San Francisco: AttaGirl Press, 2003. **G**

An anthology of nineteen pieces, ranging from truly poetic to ordinary, features authors Andrew Holleran, Edmund White, Felice Picano, Paul Lisicky, Mitch Cullin, Tom House, and Robin Lippincott.

Subjects: Anthologies • Dating • Love • Lust • Sex

Read-Alikes: For a mix of gay and lesbian short stories, readers should try *Pills, Thrills, Chills and Heartbreak,* by Michelle Tea and Clint Catalyst.

Chapter 6

Coming Out

Definition

The phrase "coming out," originally used to describe the formal debut of young women into fashionable society, refers in this context to the admission to one's self and others of a same-sex orientation.

Description and Characteristics

Works of literature classed as "coming out" stories are easily identified, because one of the plot lines will be the growth of awareness in the narrator of attraction to his or her own gender, or the description of the process in one or more characters by the author from a perspective other than that of the first person. There will usually be an account of the first experience of some form of same-gender erotic activity, and reflection on how the persons involved felt at the time and coped with the consequences.

History and Development

A primary difficulty with examining the history of this type of writing is that "coming out" in the gay sense is a product of the gay liberation movement rhetoric of the early 1970s, although it has since been generalized to cover admissions of specific identities of many sorts outside the GLBT communities. Within GLBT literature, Radclyffe Hall's *The Well of Loneliness* is seen by many as having initiated the genre, and during the homophile era of the 1950s, much of the short fiction published in the pioneering lesbian journal *The Ladder* contained elements of self-revelation. Following the beginning of the gay liberation movement at the Stonewall Riots in New York City in 1969, the act of coming out was seen to be both a personal liberation and a political tactic to challenge stereotypes of homosexuals. Much of the early monographic writing in this area was nonfiction, examples being Arthur Bell's account of the New York Gay Activist Alliance, *Dancing the Gay Lib Blues: A Year in the Homosexual Liberation Movement* (1971) and Arnie Kantrowitz's *Under the Rainbow: Growing Up Gay* (1977). Collections of personal accounts began to appear in the late 1970s, beginning with the landmark collection *Word Is Out: Stories of Some of Our Lives* (1978), and have continued to be popular since that time. It is against this background that fiction dealing with the coming out process and its events should be considered.

Issues for the Readers' Advisor

The question of how to handle the provision of coming out literature to the public is one of the more problematic ones for a readers' advisor, due to the range of possible motivations behind the inquiries. Patrons may be inquiring about such titles for themselves and not wish to reveal that fact, or may be seeking such books to assist either themselves or a friend or family member who is dealing with the unexpected emotional upset triggered by an act of disclosure. An effective way of judging the situation is to ask the patron if he or she has read such materials before or is familiar with what the phrase "coming out" means. A positive response may indicate that the reader will be less threatened by a work of fiction than might otherwise be the case. It is also possible that the patron is asking for more specific information that might not be contained in a work of fiction, but rather in a more general book on gay rights.

Patrons and librarians should be aware that the concept of coming out is represented by the heading "coming out (sexual orientation)" in the Library of Congress classification system. A simple search under "coming out" in the subject index of most library catalogs will place the user in proximity to the desired term, resulting in little difficulty locating additional reading materials.

Chapter Organization

The titles in this chapter can be considered general fiction books that neatly fit the theme of "coming out." They are divided into sections for novels, short story collections by a single author, and short story anthologies by multiple authors, and then arranged alphabetically by author name. Also, the entries in this chapter serve as read-alikes for one another, as they all deal with the same theme. Readers who enjoy the books listed here may find other enjoyable reads in chapter 9, "Romance," and chapter 5, "General Fiction." For true stories about coming out, refer to chapter 16, "Life Stories," and for dramatic representations, see chapter 15.

Sources

McNaron, Toni A. H. " Coming Out Stories." In *Gay and Lesbian Literary Heritage,* edited by Claude J. Summers, 173–75. New York, Henry Holt, 1995

Plummer, Kenneth. "The Modernisation of Gay and Lesbian Stories." In *Telling Sexual Stories,* 81-96. New York: Routledge, 1995.

Novels

Alther, Lisa.

🎗 *Other Women.* New York: Knopf, 1996 (1984). **L**

Caroline Kelly is an other-oriented woman whose work and life seem to have come to a halt. Her work as a nurse no longer gives her satisfaction, and her partner wants to end their relationship without moving out. To cope with her depressions, she seeks out feisty psychologist Hannah Burke, and the two women surprise each other by mutual exploration of personal darknesses. Very readable and quick paced.

Awards: Publishing Triangle's 100 Best Lesbian and Gay Novels, Reader's Choice

Subjects: Couples • Healthcare workers • Mental health • Parenting • Vermont

Read-Alikes: Readers who enjoyed this title may want to seek out *Kinflicks* and *Original Sins*, Alther's first two novels.

Alumit, Noel.

🎗 *Letters to Montgomery Clift: A Novel.* Los Angeles: Alyson Books, 2003 (2002). **G**

Bong Bong, a Filipino teen, is sent to the United States to escape persecution. Longing for the arrival of his mom, he finds comfort in old Montgomery Clift movies. Idolization becomes a cultlike obsessiveness, and a secret pushes Bong over the edge. Alumit masterfully weaves Filipino culture, refugee issues, and personal struggle into an engaging story.

Awards: Stonewall Book Award, 2003; *ForeWord Magazine*'s Book of the Year Award, 2002

Subjects: Families • Filipinos • Immigrants • Missing persons

Read-Alikes: Shay Youngblood's debut novel *Soul Kiss* is about a young woman abandoned by her mother and forced to live with her spinster aunts.

Benduhn, Tea.

Gravel Queen. New York: Simon & Schuster, 2003. **G** **L** **Teen**

For three young friends, the summer between junior high and high school becomes one of discovery. Fred has known he was gay for years, but when Neila moves into town, his friend Aurin finds herself attracted to her and must face the perplexing questions of what being gay or lesbian means, and how one finds out who one is.

Subjects: Friendship • North Carolina • Students, high school

Read-Alikes: In *November Ever After*, by Laura Torres, Amy reexamines her close friendship with Sara when Sara falls in love with another classmate, Anita.

Boock, Paula.

Dare, Truth or Promise. Boston: Houghton Mifflin, 1999 (1997). **L** **Teen**

Louie and Willa meet at the local fast-food joint and are instantly attracted to one another. For Louie this is a new experience, and her friends, family, and church all have different ideas about what she should do and how she should feel. Meanwhile, Willa's baggage from a previous relationship makes trusting Louie difficult.

Subjects: Dating • Love • New Zealand • Students, high school

Read-Alikes: *Rosemary and Juliet*, by Judy MacClean, has two apparently star-crossed high schoolers—one an out lesbian, the other the minister's daughter—falling in love.

Bram, Christopher.

Almost History. New York: Donald I. Fine, 1992. **G**

Jim Goodall is a member of the Foreign Service whose main posting has been to the countries of Southeast Asia; but he feels himself to be, as he puts it, "a houseguest of history." This novel follows Jim's career from the 1950s witch-hunts in the State Department to the overthrow of the Marcos regime, along with his gradual coming to terms with his identity as a gay man. An unusual blending of the idea of coming out with other questions of identity and how it is defined.

Subjects: Families • Filipinos • Homophobia • Politics

Read-Alikes: Angus Wilson's *As If By Magic* is another book that looks at the developing world through the eyes of a closeted gay man.

Brantenberg, Gerd. Translated by Margaret Hayford O'Leary.

🏆 *The Four Winds*. Seattle: Women in Translation, 1996. **L**

Meet Inger, a Norwegian student, as she graduates from high school, fervently hoping the catastrophe inside her—attraction to women—will disappear. However, nothing—not working as a nanny, sleeping with men, or university—removes her desires. Richly drawn secondary characters enhance the story, which thaws as slowly as a fjord.

Awards: Publishing Triangle's 100 Best Lesbian and Gay Novels, Reader's Choice

Subjects: Families • Norway • Students, college

Brett, Catherine.

S.P. Likes A.D. Toronto: Women's Press, 1989. **L** **Teen**

Stephanie Powell is drawn to high school classmate Ann Delaney but is not sure how to sort out her feelings. Through an art project, she meets an older lesbian couple and begins to unravel the knot in her heart.

Subjects: Couples • Friendship • Students, high school

Brown, Todd.

Entries from a Hot Pink Notebook. New York: Washington Square, 1995. **G** **Teen**

Ben Smith is thirteen years old, starting high school, and the youngest child in a badly dysfunctional family. In his freshman year he starts a relationship with a classmate, only to be forcibly outed when another student takes a picture of them kissing.

Subjects: Families • Homophobia • Maine • Students, high school • Substance abuse

Read-Alikes: In Eric Goodman's *Child of My Right Hand*, Simon is harassed by his high school classmates after coming out, although his family stands behind him.

Cart, Michael.

My Father's Scar. New York: St. Martin's Press, 1998 (1996). **G** **Teen**

> In a series of episodes, Andy Logan tells the story of his life and his growth from high school, where a friend came out as gay and was savagely beaten, to college, where he sheds the weight of his past.
>
> **Subjects:** Families • Homophobia • Relationships, parent–child • Religion • Running • Students • Substance abuse
>
> **Read-Alikes:** *Stuck Rubber Baby*, by Howard Cruse, is a graphic novel whose narrator's emergence from the closet is catalyzed by the lynching of a former lover.

Chambers, Aiden.

Dance on My Grave. London: Red Fox , 1995 (1982). **G**

> An unlikely love affair begins when Hal is rescued from an overturned sailboat, leading him eventually to fulfill a vow to his deceased lover that lands him in the newspapers and in court. British slang and cultural references may make this a challenging read for American readers.
>
> **Subjects:** England • Literature • Masculinity • Motorcycles
>
> **Read-Alikes:** In *A Separate Peace*, by John Knowles, Gene shows a near-obsessive affection for Phineas.

Chbosky, Stephen.

The Perks of Being a Wallflower. New York: Simon & Schuster, 1999. **G** **Teen**

> Told in the form of a series of letters, this is the story of a high school freshman whose best friend commits suicide. As his story unfolds, he gradually moves from being an outsider living through others, to claiming his own feelings, including how he feels about sex with men. Very detailed and worth the effort.
>
> **Subjects:** Death and dying • Families • Homophobia • Pennsylvania • Sexual abuse • Students, high school • Violence

Donovan, Stacey.

Dive. Lincoln, NE: IUniverse, 2001 (1994). **L** **Teen**

> Virginia feels overwhelmed. When her dog is injured, her mother refuses to pay for veterinary care, obliging Virginia to work for the veterinarian to pay off the bill. When her father is diagnosed with a terminal illness, she turns to a new friend for support, a bond that develops into love.
>
> **Subjects:** Death and dying • Families • Substance abuse

Downing, Michael.

Breakfast with Scot. Washington, DC: Counterpoint, 1999. **G**

> Eleven-year-old Scot, complete with makeup kit and costume trunk, is sent to live with Uncle Ed and his partner. Suddenly everyone's life is turned upside down, as Ed attempts to parent the already sensitive Scot. A charming story.

Subjects: Adoption • Families • Parenting

Read-Alikes: In *Unexpected Child*, by Patricia Grossman, Meg Krantz is forced into motherhood when she becomes the guardian of a young girl whose father has succumbed to AIDS. David Gerrold fictionalized his story of adopting a young boy in *The Martian Child*.

Esposito, Michelene.

Night Diving. Duluth, MN: Spinsters Ink, 2002. **L**

Thirty-year-old Rose Salino is not having a good year. On the same day, she is forced to deal with the end of her relationship and the loss of her professional job as a chef, and on top of that, her grandmother dies. This chain of events brings Rose back to her childhood home for her grandmother's funeral, where she meets again her first love. Rose begins to dive into her own night to make some choices about her future. This is a book about shocks and the power of the growth that can come from coping with them. Rose can serve as an example in discouraging times.

Subjects: Friendship • Relationships • Sexual abuse

Read-Alikes: In Erin Dutton's *Sequestered Hearts*, an artist abruptly withdraws to her childhood home but finds love with the journalist who follows her to get the story.

Feinberg, Leslie.

Stone Butch Blues. Los Angeles: Alyson Books, 2003 (1993). **L T**

Jess Goldberg is born into the blue-collar world of upstate New York in the 1950s, only to find as she grows up that her masculine ways make people wonder what gender she is. Finding the lesbian bars of the pre-Stonewall era, with their butch-femme social structure, allows her to begin to fit in as a "stone butch," but as police harassment builds, she decides to take hormone shots and have cosmetic surgery to pass as a man in the worlds of work and love. The first serious novel to frankly explore the issues faced by gender identity, this is an underground classic that has gained a wide audience.

Awards: Lambda Literary Award, 1993; Stonewall Book Award, 1994; Publishing Triangle's 100 Best Lesbian and Gay Novels, Reader's Choice

Subjects: Cross-dressing • Gender identity• Homophobia • New York State • Sex change • Stereotypes

Read-Alikes: An insightful, nonfiction look at transitioning from female to male is Max Wolf Valerio's *The Testosterone Files*.

Ferris, Jean.

Eight Seconds. San Diego: Harcourt, 2002 (2000). **G Teen**

According to John and his friends, the rodeo is a place where real men prove their masculinity; bull riding is not for sissies. John must rethink the definition of masculinity, sexuality, and friendship when his friendship with Kit, a gay cowboy, becomes the target of rumors.

Subjects: Friendship • Homophobia • Rodeo

Read-Alikes: In *Just a Boy*, by Rob Clinger, Jove, a closeted high school wrestler, reacts badly when his next door neighbor (and secret crush) is outed.

Frame, Ronald.

The Lantern Bearers. Washington, DC: Counterpoint, 2001 (1999). **G**

Neil Pritchard is dying, but he must finish his book about Scottish composer Euan Bone. While writing, Neil reflects on his boyhood encounters with Bone during summer vacation on the coast of Scotland. Fourteen-year-old Neil works with Bone on a musical compilation, and in the process falls in love. The collaboration ends abruptly. Crushed, the boy lies about his relationship with the composer, and tragedy follows.

Subjects: Music • Scotland

Read-Alikes: The musical director in Alexander Chee's first novel, *Edinburgh*, molests Korean American choirboy Fee.

Futcher, Jane.

Crush. Los Angeles: Alyson Books, 1995 (1981). **L**

It is senior year at a private and very upscale boarding school for girls in the 1960s, and Jinx, who has always been on the sideline, deeply involved with her art, suddenly finds herself being sought as a friend by one of the most popular girls. Jinx realizes she is attracted to the girl and pursues it into a very unequal relationship that tests her courage.

Subjects: Art and artists • Friendship • Relationships • Students, high school

Garden, Nancy.

🏆 *Annie on My Mind.* New York: Farrar, Straus & Giroux, 2007 (1982). **L** **Teen**

Annie and Liza meet accidentally, become friends, and slowly realize their feelings for each other. Their relationship remains a secret until they are caught and forced to denounce their love. A sweet love story.

Awards: Publishing Triangle's 100 Best Lesbian and Gay Novels, Reader's Choice

Subjects: Dating • Homophobia • Love • Students, high school

🏆 *Good Moon Rising.* Lincoln, NE: IUniverse, 2005 (1996). **L** **Teen**

Jan and Kerry meet as cast members in the school play and fall in love. Their developing relationship becomes an excuse for homophobia that threatens to ruin the play. Can the play and the relationship succeed?

Awards: Lambda Literary Award, 1996

Subjects: Dating • Homophobia • Love • Students, high school • Theater

Read-Alikes: *Talk*, by Kathe Koja, uses the backdrop of a high school play in trouble for the story of a young man's coming out story.

The Year They Burned the Books. New York: Farrar, Straus & Giroux, 1999. **L** **Teen**

Censorship and homophobia converge when Jamie's editorial in the student newspaper causes quite a stir and initiates a series of events, including book burning, textbook removal, and harassment. Complicating matters are Jamie's friendship with the openly gay Terry and a sudden attraction to Tessa.

Subjects: Censorship • Hate crimes • Homophobia • Students, high school

Read-Alikes: In Alex Sanchez's *So Hard to Say*, Xio develops a powerful crush on new student Frederick—who keeps avoiding her advances as he pines for soccer teammate Victor.

Gilgun, John.

Music I Never Dreamed Of. New York: Amethyst Press, 1989. **G**

It's the 1950s, and the newspapers are full of gloomy news about the McCarthy hearings and the threat of communism. In Boston, nineteen-year-old Steve Riley becomes aware of his gay identity in a blue-collar world of expectations that do not fit him, and never will. This novel was written thirty years before it was published.

Subjects: 1950s • Class conflict • Families • Homophobia • Massachusetts • Religion • Stereotypes

Read-Alikes: *Quatrefoil*, by James Barr, is also set in the same time period.

Grumbach, Doris.

🏵 *Chamber Music.* New York: W. W. Norton, 1993 (1979). **G** **L**

Told as a memoir by a ninety-year-old widow and founder of an artist's colony, the tale of the lives and loves of Robert and Caroline Maclaren takes the reader deftly into the world of late Victorian America. The quiet awareness of same-sex love affairs is an interesting study in manners. Grumbach based the story on the lives of the American composer Edward MacDowell and his wife.

Awards: Publishing Triangle's 100 Best Lesbian and Gay Novels, Reader's Choice

Subjects: Art and artists • Families • Music • New York State

Read-Alikes: Readers who enjoyed this should try Grumbach's other works for a taste of the range of her abilities. For a novel set in the same period, readers should check out *The House on Brooke Street*, by Neil Bartlett.

Guerra, Erasmo.

🏵 *Between Dances.* New York: Painted Leaf Press, 2000. **G**

A trip into the gritty night world of New York City as seen through the eyes of a bar dancer, who falls in love and struggles to keep his dreams alive.

Awards: Lambda Literary Award, 2001

Subjects: Bars • Dancing • Hispanics • New York City • Sex workers·

Read-Alikes: John Rechy's *City of Night* and *Sexual Outlaws* have the same flavor of shadows and smoke.

Guy, Rosa.

Ruby. East Orange, NJ: Just Us Books, 2005 (1976). **L**

It is the 1970s, and Ruby Cathy is an immigrant from the West Indies living in Harlem. Her mother is dead, and her father is obsessed with running his business and protecting his family. Ruby wants to connect to the new world around her but has limited success, until she becomes involved with Daphne, who blends love with the energy of revolution. Ruby's world is then transformed. Powerful and lyrical.

Readers will find that the patois of the islands gives the text an interesting flavor.

Subjects: Caribbean • New York City • Politics • Relationships, parent–child • Students

Hall, Lynn.

Sticks and Stones. New York: Dell, 1977 (1972). **G**

Musically talented Tom Naylor finds himself in a small town on the Mississippi as a consequence of his parents' divorce. He finds a kindred spirit in an older boy just returned from the Air Force, only to become the subject of rumors that eventually force him to confront his own sexuality and identity.

Subjects: Families • Music • Stereotypes

Hartinger, Brent.

Geography Club Series. **G L B Teen**

Meet Russel and his best friend Min as they begin high school and journey to self-discoveries that will test them as individuals and as friends.

Subjects: Asians • Friendship • Race relations • Students, high school

Read-Alikes: In Alex Sanchez's *Getting It*, help in forming a gay–straight alliance in their high school is the reward Carlos offers to openly gay Sal, if Sal will help Carlos hook up with the girl of his dreams.

The Geography Club. New York: HarperCollins, 2004 (2003).

In a chat room, Russel Middlebrook discovers that there are a number of other gay and lesbian students at his high school. The group decides to hide in plain sight and form an after-school organization, for which they create a nerdy image by naming it the "Geography Club" to keep its true purpose secret. Nevertheless, as they learn, life has a way of exposing secrets.

The Order of the Poison Oak. New York: HarperCollins, 2006 (2005).

Russel, Min, and Gunnar are back, as counselors at a camp for burn victims. Because of his homosexuality, Russel easily identifies with his young charges' feelings of rejection and creates the Order of the Poison Oak as a vehicle for helping the children to cope with life's challenges.

Split Screen. New York: HarperTeen, 2007.

Russel struggles with his parents' reaction to his homosexuality, his attraction to multiple persons, and a job on a horror film set. Meanwhile, Min must decide how important it is to have an "out" girlfriend. The two stories converge in surprising ways in this flip-book.

Hautzig, Deborah.

Hey, Dollface. New York: Knopf, 1989 (1978). **L** **Teen**

Valerie Hoffman begins a new school year at an exclusive high school for girls in New York City and meets fellow rebel Chloe Fox. Together, they cope with deaths in their families, their growing friendship, and an obsession with *Vogue,* as they explore the city and their own hearts.

Subjects: Death and dying • New York City • Students, high school

Hines, Sue.

Out of the Shadows. London: Livewire, 2001 (1999). **G** **L** **Teen**

In a contemporary Australian high school, life becomes complicated for Rowanna, who's already spent years coping with the loss of her mother and living with her mother's partner. Her relationship with Mark, the school athlete, alters when he becomes interested in a new girl, Jodie. Meanwhile, Jodie has found a new love, but not who Mark expects.

Subjects: Australia • Love • Parenting • Relationships, parent–child • Students, high school

Read-Alikes: *Sevens: Exposed*, by Scott Wallens, tells how high school football star Jeremy stopped dating Tara when he met Josh.

Holleran, Andrew.

🌸 *Dancer from the Dance.* New York: HarperTrade, 2001 (1978). **G**

Two men with opposite personalities fall into and out of love, in this surreal and poignant depiction of the gay subculture of the Fire Island summer community and the dance bars of Manhattan as they were in the years just prior to the appearance of AIDS. The whole is presented as a novel sent from one friend to another. *Dancer* has come to be seen as a classic read in the genre of gay male fiction. The title is based on a poem by William Butler Yeats.

Awards: Publishing Triangle's 100 Best Lesbian and Gay Novels

Subjects: Bars • Dancing • New York City • Stereotypes • Substance abuse

Read-Alikes: Other works using letters to tell a story include Edmund White's *Nocturnes for the King of Naples* and Richard Zimler's *Unholy Ghosts.*

Kenan, Randall.

🌸 *A Visitation of Spirits.* New York: Vintage, 2000 (1989). **G**

This is a beautifully drawn tale of a young gay man growing up in a church-oriented family in North Carolina's tobacco country. The sections of the book that recount his efforts at sorcery make for eerie reading.

Awards: Publishing Triangle's 100 Best Lesbian and Gay Novels

Subjects: African Americans • North Carolina • Race relations • Religion • Spirituality

Read-Alikes: In *The God Box,* by Alex Sanchez, Paul isn't sure what to make of new student Manuel, like Paul a professed Christian but gay.

Kerr, M. E.

"Hello," I Lied. New York: HarperCollins, 1997. **G** **B** **Teen**

Trapped in the home of a retired rock star because of his mom's housekeeping job, straight-acting Lang contemplates coming out, a decision complicated by his recent attraction to a girl. Would it be a lie not to mention that he thinks he is gay?

Subjects: Music • Students, high school

Read-Alikes: Youth questioning their sexual orientation is the topic of Alex Sanchez's *So Hard to Say.*

Ketchum, Liza.

Blue Coyote. Lincoln, NE: IUniverse, 2004 (1997). **G** **Teen**

In this companion volume to *Twelve Days in August*, Alex Beekman is the child of a constantly moving family. When his writer father transplants the family to Vermont and later returns to Los Angeles, Alex takes this chance to try to track down his best friend, who has disappeared after coming out to his family. The search forces Alex to consider his own sexual identity as well.

Subjects: Body modification • California • Families • Surfing

Read-Alikes: In Jay Quinn's *Metes and Bounds,* Matt is another gay surfer who comes of age with the help of a friend and away from his family.

Twelve Days in August. Lincoln, NE: IUniverse, 2004 (1995). **G** **Teen**

Into the close-knit world of small-town Vermont come Rita and Alex Beekman, who quickly upset Todd O'Connor's sense of reality. When Alex turns out to be a talented soccer player, another member of the team starts a whispering campaign that he is gay, and Todd learns some harsh lessons about family, friendship, and loyalty. Fast-paced with good characterization. The original publication credited Liza Ketchum Murrow as the author.

Subjects: Families • Friendship • Homophobia • Soccer • Vermont

Read-Alikes: Jim Provenzano's *Pins* is a powerful novel of homophobia in sports, based on real-life incidents in New York in 1992.

Kringle, Karen.

Vital Ties. San Francisco: Spinsters Book Co., 1992. **G** **L**

Written by a working dairy farmer in western Wisconsin, this novel follows the lives and fortunes of two highly independent rural farmwomen and their families over several decades, as they move into and out of marriages; face death, AIDS, and the legacies of Vietnam; and ultimately recognize what they mean to each other. The details of the major issues facing U.S. farmers from the 1960s through the 1980s give this novel added power.

Subjects: AIDS • Couples • Families • Farmers • Wisconsin

Read-Alikes: Readers who want a similar tale should look at the classic *Patience and Sarah,* by Isabel Miller, about two women in the nineteenth century who forge a life for themselves.

Leavitt, David.

🏵 *The Lost Language of Cranes.* London: Penguin, 1988 (1986). **G**

In this novel about choices and coming to terms with one's self, Philip, seriously in love for the first time, comes out to his parents and unwittingly opens the door on his father's secret.

Awards: Publishing Triangle's 100 Best Lesbian and Gay Novels, Reader's Choice

Subjects: Books to film • Families • New York City • Secrets

Read-Alikes: *The Beauty of Men,* by Andrew Holleran, features a middle-aged man who has failed to come out.

Levin, Jenifer.

🏵 *The Sea of Light.* New York: Plume, 1994 (1993). **L**

Set in the world of competitive collegiate swimming, this is the tale of three women whose lives are intertwined: a coach who has lost her lover, a rising star athlete who dreads telling her parents she is a lesbian, and a once-hopeful survivor of a team plane crash, who wants and fears to learn to live again. The well-drawn characters engage the reader's emotions quickly.

Awards: Publishing Triangle's 100 Best Lesbian and Gay Novels, Reader's Choice

Subjects: Couples • Friendship • Students, college • Swimming

Read-Alikes: *A Secret Edge*, by Robin Reardon, tells the intertwined story of two high school track stars who fall in love despite their differences.

Lisicky, Paul.

Lawnboy. Saint Paul, MN: Graywolf, 2004 (1999). **G** **Teen**

After a fling with a much older neighbor, seventeen-year-old Evan lives and works with his older brother in a rundown central Florida hotel, where he forms a profoundly affective relationship with his brother's sometime lover, Hector. A long, humid coming-of-age story.

Subjects: AIDS • Coming-of-age • Florida • Siblings

Read-Alikes: In Jim Grimsley's *Boulevard,* Newell is an aimlessly wandering Southern young man searching for his identity.

Malloy, Brian.

The Year of Ice. New York: St. Martin's Press, 2003 (2002). **G** **Teen**

Secrets are part of Kevin's life. While keeping his affection for a classmate a secret, Kevin slowly uncovers a jumble of family secrets, including his father's complicity in the death of his mother.

Subjects: Minnesota • Relationships, parent–child • Secrets • Students, high school

Read-Alikes: In Greg Lilly's *Fingering the Family Jewels,* Derek learns some dark family secrets as he investigates his father's role in a lynching.

McGehee, Peter.

Beyond Happiness: The Intimate Memoirs of Billie Lee Belle. Regina, SK: Coteau Books, 1993 (1985). **G**

> In less than a hundred pages, the reader is introduced to the life and adventures of Billie Lee Belle, a spunky and determined Arkansas queen who is the despair of his very traditional family. Based on the author's life.
>
> **Subjects:** Arkansas • Autobiographical fiction • Families • Stereotypes

Mosca, Frank.

All-American Boys. Boston: Alyson Publications, 1983. **G** **Teen**

> Neil Melisch finds his first gay love and gets an education in courage and trust, against the backdrop of small-town California.
>
> **Subjects:** California • Families • Homophobia • Love • Martial arts • Violence
>
> **Read-Alikes:** In *Clay's Way*, by Blair Mastbaum, fifteen-year-old Sam finds first love with the slightly older, equally adrift Clay, as they fight together against the conformity of middle-class suburbia.

Mullins, Hilary.

🎗 *The Cat Came Back.* Tallahassee, FL: Naiad Press, 1993. **L** **Teen**

> Tomboy Stevie Roughgarden is isolated at her exclusive private school, both by the processes of being a teenager and her total involvement with the girl's hockey team, which she captains. When her friendship with a new classmate, Andrea Snyder, deepens, she begins a new process of self-discovery and liberation. A very well told story of the perils and courage of coming out and the power of dreams.
>
> **Awards:** Lambda Literary Award, 1993
>
> **Subjects:** Couples • Feminism • Hockey • Sexual abuse • Students, high school • Teachers
>
> **Read-Alikes:** Stevie learns to accept herself through reading Rita Mae Brown's *Rubyfruit Jungle*.

Murphy, Timothy.

Getting Off Clean. New York: St. Martin's Press, 1998 (1997). **G** **Teen**

> High school senior Eric Fitzpatrick has it all: good grades, the determination to make it to college, and the ambition to fit in. The only problem he has is that he's gay, just coming out, and in love with a student at the exclusive prep school outside town, who happens to be black. When the community becomes racially polarized, the two must make some difficult choices.
>
> **Subjects:** Families • Hispanics • Massachusetts • Murder • Race relations • Students, high school

Myracle, Lauren.

Kissing Kate. New York: Speak, 2007 (2003). **L** **Teen**

Kate has been Lissa's best friend since seventh grade, but one night at a party, she initiates a kiss that leaves Lissa responding strongly—and wondering how to sort out her own identity. Through her delivery work, she gets to know a New Age classmate, Ariel, who offers her alternative ways of thinking about who she is and who she may be. Good use of New Age cultural themes

Subjects: Friendship • Love • Students, high school

Read-Alikes: In *November Ever After*, by Laura Torres, Amy wonders if she wants to stay friends with Sara, when Sara falls in love with their classmate, Anita.

Park, Jacquelyn Holt.

A Stone Gone Mad. Los Angeles: Alyson Books, 1996 (1991). **L**

Emily Stolle is a high school student in 1948, when she is caught with another girl and sent away to a series of private schools and women's colleges by her family, who impose strict limits on the way they will view her. Her road leads from the fields of Virginia, through the streets of Washington and New York, to a house in Provincetown. Along the way she learns to accept who she is and how she loves.

Subjects: Couples • Families • Friendship • Homophobia • Stereotypes

Peters, Julie Ann.

Keeping You a Secret. New York: Little, Brown, 2005 (2003). **L** **Teen**

Holland is a popular student with good grades, a great boyfriend, and good relationships with her family, yet CeCe, who wears T-shirts with sayings like "IM1RU," intrigues her. When Holland befriends CeCe, she finds her future deviating from her plan.

Subjects: Dating • Homophobia • Love • Secrets • Students, high school

Read-Alikes: Readers should try Maureen Johnson's *Bermudez Triangle* for the story of three girls whose friendships are tested when two of the friends fall in love.

Piercy, Marge.

🌻 *The High Cost of Living.* New York: FawcettCrest, 1985 (1978). **G** **L**

The action in this novel of urban academic life centers around three main characters: Leslie, an ardent lesbian feminist whose lover has left her; Bernie, a former hustler trying to reform; and Honor, a beautiful teenager desired by them both, who is in love with her own dreams. Piercy's novel contains a mixture of feminism and reality.

Awards: Publishing Triangle's 100 Best Lesbian and Gay Novels, Reader's Choice

Subjects: Families • Michigan • Students, college • Theater

Reed, Gary.

🌻 *Pryor Rendering.* New York: Plume, 1997 (1996). **G**

Charlie Hope's world has always been the small town of Pryor, Oklahoma, dominated by the meat processing plant where his grandfather and many men of the town work. He grows up in the shadows of the past, until he meets Dewar, a boy from the local orphanage, and begins to see beyond the boundaries of his life. Lyrical and gritty.

Awards: Publishing Triangle's 100 Best Lesbian and Gay Novels, Reader's Choice

Subjects: Families • Friendship • Oklahoma • Religion

Read-Alikes: For a similar small-town atmosphere, readers may want to try *Bastard Out of Carolina,* by Dorothy Allison.

Rees, David.

In the Tent. Boston: Alyson Publications, 1985 (1979). **G** **Teen**

At seventeen, Tim is increasingly aware of his attraction to other boys, but he agrees to go hiking with three classmates for a holiday. Bad weather forces them to hole up in a tent, where Tim resolves his conflicts with the help of a historical fantasy. The British terminology may be unfamiliar to American readers.

Subjects: England • Friendship • Students, high school

Read-Alikes: In John Fox's *The Boys on the Rock,* sixteen-year-old Billy finds his first love and the courage to come out to his classmates.

Revoyr, Nina.

The Necessary Hunger. New York: St. Martin's Press, 1998 (1997). **L** **Teen**

Two high school women's basketball players, rivals on the court and lovers off it, find themselves in a strange situation when their parents move in together and they must live under one roof while keeping their secret, if they can.

Subjects: African Americans • Asians • Basketball • California • Families • Friendship

Read-Alikes: Rita Rashad's *Love at Half-Court* is the coming out story of African American high school basketball star Kendra.

Reynolds, Marilyn.

Love Rules. Buena Park, CA: Morning Glory Press, 2003. **G** **L** **Teen**

When her best friend Kit comes back to high school from a summer spent in San Francisco and subsequently comes out as a very open lesbian, Lynn tries to be supportive, only to see antigay harassment escalate as her own interracial romance with a football star draws fire.

Subjects: African Americans • Friendship • Homophobia • Race relations • Stereotypes • Students, high school • Violence

Read-Alikes: In *Tips on Having a Gay (ex-) Boyfriend,* by Carrie Jones, Belle stands behind her ex-boyfriend Dylan after his private coming out to her and a few close friends is leaked.

Russell, Paul.

🎗 *The Coming Storm.* New York: St. Martin's Press, 2000 (1999). **G** **Teen**

A private school in upstate New York is the setting for this exploration of a student coping with his own sexual identity and the impact his search has on the formally structured world around him and on several of the faculty and staff.

Awards: Ferro-Grumley Award, 2000

Subjects: New York State • Students, high school • Teachers

Read-Alikes: In Christopher Rice's *The Snow Garden,* a private college campus is roiled as a result of a series of affairs between a closeted professor and his favored students.

Ryan, Sara.

Battle Hall Davies Series. **L B** **Teen**

The unusually named protagonist comes of age and discovers her sexuality.

Subjects: Coming-of-age • Love • Relationships • Students

Read-Alikes: In E. Lockhart's *Dramarama,* gifted students go to a theater camp for a summer of growing up and coming out.

Empress of the World. New York: Speak, 2003 (2001).

Nic's summer camp experience yields love—with a girl, Battle. The unexpected feelings are confusing; is Nic bisexual? Lesbian? Ultimately, the girls must learn to accept their feelings and disregard society's labels. Written from Nic's perspective, in journal format.

Rules for Hearts. New York: Viking, 2007.

Battle is back again, this time as an eighteen-year-old preparing for college and caught up in a family drama involving her estranged brother, Nick. While she visits Nick at his co-op, Battle discovers the intensity created by living with a group, as well as the pain of ambiguous love.

Saba, Umberto.

Ernesto. London: Paladin, 1989 (1975). **G B**

Set in the author's home city of Trieste, Italy, this novel takes place in 1898, beginning when sixteen-year-old Ernesto has an affair with an older man in his twenties. Eventually he falls in love with another teenager, but is attracted to his sister at the same time. *Ernesto* was kept a secret by the author, the novelist Umberto Poli, and was published twenty-two years after being written and eighteen years after the author's death. It was made into a film in 1979.

Awards: Publishing Triangle's 100 Best Lesbian and Gay Novels, Reader's Choice

Subjects: Italy • Books to film • Love triangles

Read-Alikes: Readers may enjoy the darkly humorous world of Naples in Joseph Caldwell's *Uncle from Rome,* another work set in Italy.

Sanchez, Alex.

Rainbow Boys Series. **G** **Teen**

Follow a trio of young friends through their high school years as they cope with coming out, first loves, and homophobia.

Subjects: Friendship • Students, high school • Virginia

Read-Alikes: A younger set fights for their rights in James Howe's *Misfits* and its companion, *Totally Joe.*

Rainbow Boys. New York: Simon Pulse, 2003 (2001).

> The "boys" of the title are in fact three gay high school seniors whose lives are lived in three different social spaces, spanning the range of possible situations from having a girlfriend to being out and "in your face" about their sexual identities. As the year goes on, each comes out in his own way and to his own degree. They then must deal with their feelings about each other as well, and face problems ranging from sexual predators to prejudice.

Rainbow High. New York: Simon Pulse, 2005 (2003).

> Jason, Kyle, and Nelson face complicated futures, involving everything from the impact of college on relationships to learning their HIV status and learning to live an out life.

Schwab, Rochelle H.

A Departure from the Script. Alexandria, VA: Orlando Place Press, 2002. **L**

> Jenny is a nice Jewish girl who announces that she is in love and wants to have a traditional Jewish wedding—with a woman. Jenny's parents have mixed reactions to the news. Mom does her best to cope with the situation, but dad thinks Jenny just needs to meet the right man. A humorous look at a family's reaction to the coming out process.

> **Subjects:** Humor • Jews • Relationships, parent–child

> **Read-Alikes:** Another humorous take on coming out is *Absolutely, Positively Not,* by David LaRochelle.

Scoppettone, Sandra.

Happy Endings Are All Alike. Los Angeles: Alyson Books, 2000 (1978). **L**
Teen

> Two young women fall in love in high school, but their relationship generates confusion and finally violence based on prejudice. A classic young adult book about lesbian love.

> **Subjects:** Families • Homophobia • Sexual abuse • Students, high school • Violence

Selvadurai, Shyam.

🎗 *Funny Boy.* Toronto: Emblem Editions, 2004 (1994). **G**

> Arjun, the child of a wealthy Tamil family in Colombo, refuses to act in gender-appropriate ways: he wears saris and plays with dolls. In an effort to reform him, his father sends him to a private school, where he proceeds to break yet another cultural taboo by entering into a relationship with a Sinhalese. His evolution from child to adult is set within the seven years that culminated in the anti-Tamil riots of 1983, which drive his family into exile. An interesting look at coming out in a non-Western culture.

> **Awards:** Lambda Literary Award, 1996; Publishing Triangle's 100 Best Lesbian and Gay Novels

> **Subjects:** Humor • Cross-dressing • Refugees • Sri Lanka • Stereotypes

Read-Alikes: Another look at non-Western gay life can be found in Lawrence Chua's *Gold by the Inch*.

Shyer, Marlene Fanta.

Rainbow Kite. Tarrytown, NY: Marshall Cavendish, 2002. **G** **Teen**

Bennett is fifteen and becoming socially isolated at school, dropping out of activities, disappointing his father, and losing friends, until he makes a new one in Jeremy, a new neighbor hooked on kite building. The boys plan a large rainbow kite to be flown at their eighth-grade graduation, but a hate crime separates them and leads Bennett to try to kill himself. This act sparks the beginnings of resolution and balance for Bennett and his family, with the help of two lesbians from down the block. Smoothly written, although somewhat clichéd.

Subjects: Death and dying • Families • Homophobia • Relationships, parent–child • Students • Swimming

Soehnlein, K. M.

🎗 *The World of Normal Boys.* New York: Kensington, 2001 (2000). **G** **Teen**

Robin's family is a bit dysfunctional. His brother is seriously injured, his dad is abusive, and his mom drinks too much. In the midst of this family chaos, Robin attempts to fit in at school and to be normal, but an attraction to boys challenges his understanding of what "normal" is.

Awards: Lambda Literary Award, 2000

Subjects: Families • New Jersey • Students, high school

Read-Alikes: In Jim Grimsley's *Dream Boy*, Nathan finds solace for his violent home life at school and in love.

Stark, Elizabeth.

Shy Girl. Seattle: Seal Press, 2000 (1999). **L**

A phone call from her mother pulls butch lesbian body modification artist Alta Corral back into a past she would rather ignore. When her estranged lover's mother has a stroke, the two women must face who they have become in five years apart—and who they can be again—as they care for her.

Subjects: California • Death and dying • Motorcycles • Pregnancy • Relationships, parent–child

Steinhofel, Andreas, and Alisa Jaffa.

The Center of the World. New York: Delacorte Press, 2005. **G**

In an old mansion on the edge of a small German town, Phil and his sister Dianne grow up in a blend of fairy tale isolation and reality. Phil knows he is attracted to athletic Nicholas, and enjoys his friend Katja. After he and Nicholas begin a relationship, tensions build within the family, and old secrets begin to awaken.

Subjects: Families • Germany • Relationships, parent–child

Stoehr, Shelly.

Tomorrow Wendy: A Love Story. Lincoln, NE: IUniverse, 2003 (1998). **L**
Teen

> At seventeen, Cary seems to have an ideal life: good looks, a boyfriend, and no financial worries. The only problem is her attraction to green-haired Wendy, whom she thinks could love her as her boyfriend does, but who happens to be his sister. Deft use of humor.
>
> **Subjects:** Love triangles • Relationships • Students, high school
>
> **Read-Alikes:** In *Execution Texas: 1987*, by D. Travers Scott, Seeger King enjoys the affections of both Kent and Cordelia.

Stollman, Aryeh Lev.

🎗 *The Far Euphrates.* New York: Riverhead Books, 1998 (1997). **T**

> Alexander grows up in Windsor, Ontario, in a Jewish community filled with beauty as well as shadows of the Holocaust, and he is marked by both. In seeking his own identity, he collides with his father's dreams of scholarship, mental illness, and the limits of hope, eventually achieving a balance with his faith.
>
> **Awards:** Lambda Literary Award, 1997
>
> **Subjects:** Canada and Canadians • Coming-of-age • Holocaust • Jews

Sullivan, Mary W.

What's This About Pete? Nashville: T. Nelson, 1976. **G**

> Peter Hanson is small in stature, dreams of riding his mechanic dad's Harley, and on occasion helps his seamstress mother when orders pile up. His mix of abilities and interests only serves to complicate his search for an identity, and when one of his macho biking buddies catches him sewing, matters come to a head, especially with his girlfriend. A prime example of the type of novel that treats the coming out process as something that happens to both gay and heterosexual adolescents.
>
> **Subjects:** Motorcycles • Stereotypes • Students
>
> **Read-Alikes:** A good-humored look at coming out is David LaRochelle's *Absolutely, Positively Not.*

Taylor, William.

The Blue Lawn. Auckland, New Zealand: HarperCollins, 2004 (1994). **G**
Teen

> Opposites attract when clean-cut rugby star David is attracted to the rebellious outsider Theo. They spend a summer landscaping grandmother's lawn, until she suspects their friendship is too familiar and sends the boys home.
>
> **Subjects:** Landscaping • New Zealand • Rugby • Students, high school
>
> **Read-Alikes:** Kirk Read's autobiographical and amusing *How I Learned to Snap* has the same sense of adolescence on the brink.

Jerome. Los Angeles: Alyson Books, 1999 **G** **L**

Written as a series of e-mail messages, faxes, and letters between two students in the United States and New Zealand, which begin as an attempt to share and cope with the suicide of a friend, this novel follows their mutual growth into acceptance of their sexual identities. An unusual approach that works very well.

Subjects: Computers • Death and dying • Friendship • New Zealand • Students, high school

Read-Alikes: In *Just a Boy*, by Rob Clinger, Jove, a closeted high school wrestler, reacts badly when his next door neighbor (and secret crush) is outed.

Pebble in a Pool. Los Angeles: Alyson Books, 2003. **G**

In this concise but powerful story from New Zealand, Paul Carter is expelled from his home by his preacher father for speaking out on behalf of a murdered gay classmate, and moves in with an older friend. His evolving awareness of his gay identity and the many ways of being a man contrast with his friendship with the class star athlete, who is confined to a wheelchair after an automobile accident.

Subjects: Disability • Families • New Zealand • Relationships, parent–child • Religion • Students, high school

Read-Alikes: In Alex Sanchez's *The God Box*, Paul learns to reconcile his Christian beliefs and his friendship with a gay student.

Tea, Michelle.

Valencia. Emeryville, CA: Avalon, 2000. **L**

In her second novel, Tea takes the reader inside the mind and heart of a young and very out lesbian in the complex world of San Francisco's dyke culture, following her loves, frustrations, sorrow, and victories over the course of a year.

Subjects: California • Feminism

Read-Alikes: Myriam Gurba's *Dahlia Season* is a collection of short stories and a novella about a young Chicana dyke into the goth scene.

Tóibín, Colm.

❀ *The Story of the Night.* New York: Simon & Schuster, 2005 (1996). **G**

Richard Garay grows up in two kinds of isolation: from his own relatives and from the country he lives in, Argentina under the regime of the generals. As he matures and moves abroad, it is his dual heritage that leads him out into a world where nothing has the possibility of enduring, except love. Well-written and surreal.

Awards: Publishing Triangle's 100 Best Lesbian and Gay Novels; Ferro-Grumley Award, 1998

Subjects: AIDS • Argentina • Politics • Stereotypes

Read-Alikes: Another surreal look at Argentina during the 1970s is Manuel Puig's *The Kiss of the Spiderwoman.*

Walker, Kate.

Peter. Boston: Houghton Mifflin, 2001 (1991). **G**

The title character, interested in riding his motorbike and hoping to become a professional photographer, is drawn to a friend of his older brother, complicating an already confused emotional situation.

Subjects: Australia • Families • Motorcycles • Photography • Stereotypes

Read-Alikes: Eddie de Oliveira's *Lucky* tells how British teen Sam comes to accept his attraction to both men and women—and to recognize his good fortune in this.

Watts, Julia.

🔥 *Finding H.F.* Los Angeles: Alyson Books, 2001. **G** **L** **Teen**

Sixteen-year-old Heavenly Faith Simms (the H. F. of the title) has been raised by her grandmother after her birth mother abandoned her. The discovery of her mother's address in Florida makes her decide to track her down, and she leaves her home in Kentucky in the company of her friend Bo, a gay boy with an extremely ratty car, only to find new meanings for family along the way. Humorous.

Awards: Lambda Literary Award, 2002

Subjects: Florida • Relationships, parent–child • Religion • Humor

Read-Alikes: *How I Learned to Snap*, by Kirk Read, has the same madcap air, as three friends discover themselves in the clubs and suburbs of Dallas.

Wersba, Barbara.

Whistle Me Home. New York: Henry Holt, 1997. **G** **Teen**

Told from the viewpoint of Noli Brown, an East Hampton junior, this is the story of TJ Brown, the new boy in school who seems to excel at everything, except falling in love with her. The title refers to an incident on Noli and TJ's first date.

Subjects: Friendship • New York State • Students, high school • Substance abuse

Read-Alikes: In *Tips on Having a Gay (ex-) Boyfriend*, by Carrie Jones, Dylan is abandoned by many of his friends when he comes out, but his ex-girlfriend Belle supports him.

White, Edmund.

Edmund White Series. **G**

White employs a nameless narrator in these two works, designed to be fictional accounts of his personal struggles with his sexuality, family, and society's norms.

Subjects: Autobiographical fiction • Coming-of-age • Students

Read-Alikes: Martin Schecter's *Two Halves of New Haven* and Robert Rodi's *Closet Case* also deal with resolving family relationships and individual identity.

🔥 *A Boy's Own Story.* New York : Modern Library, 2002 (1982).

In the 1950s, a young man grapples with his feelings of isolation and same-sex attraction. Unsuccessful attempts to affect masculinity are compounded by crushes on teachers and fellow students, sibling taunting, and family dysfunctions. A familiar plot, poetically rendered.

Awards: Publishing Triangle's 100 Best Lesbian and Gay Novels

🎗 *The Beautiful Room Is Empty.* New York: Vintage, 1994 (1988).

In this sequel, the narrator enjoys the freedoms of college but continues to be conflicted over his sexuality. In New York City on the eve of the Stonewall Riots, the man experiences a turning point, arriving at self-acceptance and simultaneously coming out.

Awards: Lambda Literary Award, 1988

White, Patrick.

🎗 *The Twyborn Affair.* London: Vintage, 2000 (1979).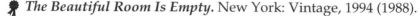

The tale of Australian Eddie Twyborn, who moves from a male to a female identity and back again across the years, beginning just before World War I and ending during the London blitz. Along the way, he becomes the "wife" of a Greek, works on a sheep ranch in the Outback, and takes on the persona of a madam in an exclusive brothel.

Awards: Publishing Triangle's 100 Best Lesbian and Gay Novels, Reader's Choice

Subjects: Australia • Cross-dressing • England • Humor • Stereotypes

Read-Alikes: This comedy of manners is reminiscent of Oscar Wilde's *The Importance of Being Earnest*, particularly as drawn in the graphic novel by Tom Bouden.

Wieler, Diana.

Bad Boy. New York: Delacorte Press, 1992 (1989). **G** **Teen**

A. J., who has finally made it into playing semiprofessional hockey, is faced with his best friend's admission of gay identity and the homophobia of the sports world. He explores his own identity and comes to some unexpected conclusions.

Subjects: Canada and Canadians • Families • Friendship • Hockey • Stereotypes • Violence

Read-Alikes: Robin Reardon's *A Secret Edge* tells how members of a high school track team support each other as they discover their sexual preferences.

Winterson, Jeanette.

🎗 *Oranges Are Not the Only Fruit.* New York: Grove Press, 1997 (1985). **L**

Adopted into a religious household, Jeanette's life revolves around the church, until her unconventional sexuality challenges faith and family. Forced from her home and lover, she eventually obtains personal peace, yet family and church remain unforgiving. A semiautobiographical novel.

Awards: Publishing Triangle's 100 Best Lesbian and Gay Novels

Subjects: Books to film • Fairy tales • Religion

Wittlinger, Ellen.

🎗 *Hard Love.* London: Simon & Schuster, 2004 (1999). **L** **Teen**

John Galardi has retreated from the world emotionally to cope with the consequences of his parents' divorce and has created his own 'zine to express himself.

Then he meets Marisol, an openly lesbian 'zine writer, and his world begins to expand. The mixture of magazine typefaces with regular print makes the book visually active.

Awards: Lambda Literary Award, 2000

Subjects: Authors • Divorce • Families • Massachusetts

Read-Alikes: Francesca Lia Block's *Weetzie Bat* also looks at the issue of gay–straight friendship from the straight-but-not-narrow perspective.

Yamanaka, Lois-Ann.

Name Me Nobody. New York: Hyperion, 2000 (1999). **L** **Teen**

The island world of Hawaii is the setting for this unusual novel that follows two unlikely friends as they move in and out of love with each other. The story is particularly good at depicting and relating the complex web of racial attitudes and histories woven across Hawaii for its Japanese immigrants.

Subjects: Asians • Coming-of-age • Friendship • Hawaii • Race relations • Softball

Yates, Bart.

Leave Myself Behind. New York: Kensington Publishing, 2004 (2003). **G**

When Noah York and his poet mother move to the small college town of Oakland, New Hampshire, after his father's death, they find their house was formerly the residence of a peculiar local faculty member. In the process of rehabbing the house, they discover a series of artifacts and poems hidden in mason jars inside the walls, which sets them on the trail of a decades-old mystery about another woman poet. Noah's own discovery of a powerful relationship with a classmate and the price he pays mark the beginning of a time of painful changes.

Subjects: Authors • Families • Homophobia • Literature • Mental health • Sexual abuse • Violence

Read-Alikes: In *Girl Walking Backwards*, by Bett Williams, Skye learns some important life lessons from her tumultuous affair with a moody goth girl.

Short Story Collections (Single Author)

Woolley, Tom.

🎗 *Toilet.* San Francisco: Suspect Thoughts Press, 2005. **G**

An anthology of ten stories connected by the life experience of the narrator, as he seeks love and connection in the wilds of Manhattan.

Awards: Publishing Triangle's 100 Best Lesbian and Gay Novels, Reader's Choice

Subjects: Anthologies • Humor • New York City • Sex workers

Read-Alikes: Mack Friedman's *Setting the Lawn on Fire* follows narrator Ivan through his travels on a journey of sexual and aesthetic exploration that ends with him as a hustler. *The Wild Creatures*, by Sam D'Allesandro, collects poems and stories with the same dark eroticism.

Short Story Anthologies (Multiple Authors)

Bauer, Marion Dane, ed.

🏵 *Am I Blue?: Coming Out of the Silence.* New York: HarperCollins, 1995 (1994). **G** **L** **Teen**

A unique collection of sixteen stories written by leading authors in the young adult field, which takes as its theme the life experiences gay and lesbian young adults encounter and the ways they react and cope. This was the first anthology of short stories specifically created to tell the story of lesbian and gay young adults. Part of the sales from the book went to support the organization Parents, Families and Friends of Lesbians and Gays (PFLAG). An easy and engrossing read.

Awards: Stonewall Book Award, 1995

Subjects: Anthologies • Homophobia • Stereotypes • Students

Grima, Tony, ed.

Not the Only One: Lesbian and Gay Fiction for Teens. Boston: Alyson Publications, 1995. **G** **L** **Teen**

A multi-ethnic short story collection featuring teens at various stages of accepting their homosexuality. If readers are looking for something new, these overlooked stories by undiscovered authors will do the trick.

Subjects: Anthologies

Read-Alikes: *Growing Up Gay*, by Bennett L. Singer, contains fiction and autobiographical essays.

Moore, Lisa C., ed.

🏵 *Does Your Mama Know?* Decatur, GA: RedBone, 1997. **L**

A collection of coming out poems and stories with a uniquely African American lesbian voice.

Awards: Lambda Literary Award, 1997

Subjects: African Americans • Anthologies

Read-Alikes: There is no parallel collection of coming out stories for African American gay men. Readers are advised to consult *Black Like Us* and *Go the Way Your Blood Beats*.

Singer, Bennett L, ed.

Growing Up Gay. New York: New Press, 1994. **G** **L**

In this unique collection of more than fifty stories, essays, and poems, a range of established gay and lesbian writers recount their own combined coming out and growing up experiences. Writers represented include Essex Hemphill, Rita Mae Brown, David Leavitt, Aaron Fricke, Radclyffe Hall, and Quentin Crisp. Useful as an introduction to the works of the contributors, as some entries are excerpts from longer stories and novels.

Subjects: Anthologies • Authors • Coming-of-age

Read-Alikes: *Two Teenagers in Twenty*, edited by Ann Heron, is a compilation of autobiographical essays by GLBT teens.

1

2

3

4

5

6

7

8

Chapter 7

HIV/AIDS and Other Health Issues

Definition

Included here are literary works in which a disease or infection of some type is a dominant theme or plot element, often featuring prominently in the personal history of one or more characters. Most of the titles in this chapter focus on the theme of HIV/AIDS, although a few titles deal with other health conditions.

Description and Characteristics

Health literature is usually marked by the presence of one or more specific conditions, which are not always explicitly stated or are treated in a low-key fashion, as in the boy narrator's account of *Losing Uncle Tim*. This can be done through the use of individual symptoms described without a medical context, or references to people or events associated with the condition can also be made to introduce the subject as a plot element to give more depth to the story.

History and Development

The titles in this chapter are grouped around a theme. That theme is so powerful and prevalent in GLBT literature that it deserves separate recognition. Most gay and lesbian fiction in print that deals with health issues dates from the 1980s, with gay male literature centered on the AIDS pandemic and lesbian literature focusing on breast cancer. Prior to that time, health concerns were primarily present in fiction as incidental background color, often as common venereal diseases such as syphilis or gonorrhea, or, less commonly, the belief that being homosexual automatically classified one as mentally ill, a position not reversed by the American Psychological Association until 1972.

The full range of emotions generated by the emergence of AIDS made its expression in literature inevitable and inescapable, with the appearance of two plays, Larry Kramer's *The Normal Heart* and *As Is* by William Hoffman, in 1985 marking the formal beginning of this category of literature. Although much of the writing on AIDS in the

1980s was political or factual in nature, fiction authors also took up the challenge of translating experience into prose. One of the earliest examples is the well-illustrated children's book *Losing Uncle Tim*, issued in 1987, followed quickly in 1989 by the dark comedy *Eighty-Sixed* by David Feinberg and John Weir's *The Irreversible Decline of Eddie Socket*. The 1990s witnessed the production of the bulk of AIDS fiction written to date, works that reflected the gradual shift in the social perception of the disease from unknown threat to a partially manageable condition not instantly fatal. The degree of politicization of the disease also varies, with the more extreme expressions shown in the earlier works moderating into quieter if no less intense expression in more recent publications.

Issues for the Readers' Advisor

The main problem facing librarians when choosing fiction related to any disease is the degree of detail provided, which can range from clinical descriptions to very general terms, and ascertaining how much detail the reader wishes to find. Many of the works classed as health-related assume a degree of awareness of individual diseases that the patron may or may not possess. If the reader does not have enough background, he or she may be unable to pick up on the more subtle shadings of character and plot or, in some cases, the environment in which the story takes place. The widespread nature of misinformation about a particular condition (lamentably abetted by the Internet) may also be a factor, as the librarian may face a patron convinced that a myth is in fact true, and have to contend with selecting a work may both entertain and challenge deep-seated attitudes. An effective means of dealing with this class of literature would be for the readers' advisor to direct the patron to general background information on the disease or conditions featured in the specific book as a standard part of the reference interview, which leaves the user free to pursue the data without having to ask for it.

Chapter Organization

The entries in this chapter are divided into four sections. First are books about HIV/AIDS, followed by those dealing with other illnesses. The last two sections are short story collections by a single author and short story anthologies by multiple authors. The HIV/AIDS entries serve as read-alikes for each other or utilize the terms "AIDS (disease)" combined with "biography" or "autobiography" in the Library of Congress Subject Headings. Readers desiring to learn more about the health struggles of specific GLBT individuals should consult chapter 16, "Life Stories."

Sources

Cady, Joseph. "AIDS Literature." In *Gay and Lesbian Literary Heritage,* edited by Claude J. Summers, 16–20. New York: Holt, 1995.

Kruger, Steven F. *AIDS Narratives: Gender and Sexuality, Fiction and Science*. New York: Garland Publishing, 1996.

Literature, Arts & Medicine Database: http://litmed.med.nyu.edu/ (accessed October 15, 2007). An annotated, searchable database exploring the links between medicine, disease, and the arts.

Nelson, Emmanuel S. *AIDS—The Literary Response*. New York: Twayne Publishers, 1992.

Pastore, Judith. *Confronting AIDS through Literature: The Responsibilities of Representation*. Urbana: University of Illinois Press, 1993.

Sánchez, Alberto Sandoval. "Breaking the Silence, Dismantling Taboos: Latino Novels on AIDS." *Journal of Homosexuality* 34, nos. 3–4 (1998): 155–75.

Teasley, Alan B. "YA Literature about AIDS: Encountering the Unimaginable." *ALAN Review* 20, no. 3 (Spring 1993): 18–23.

Wright, Les K., with Deborah Landau. "Literature." In *Encyclopedia of AIDS*, 328–32. Chicago: Fitzroy Dearborn, 1998.

HIV/AIDS

Alameddine, Rabih.

Koolaids: The Art of War. New York: Picador, 1998. **G**

This challenging first novel by a Lebanese expatriate artist skillfully combines the horrors of the ongoing conflict in his homeland (and Beirut, in particular) with the experiences of a young gay Arab. Samir faces the equally terrifying scenes of the AIDS pandemic, the memories of watching both family and country fight to survive, and a painter whose abstract works are seen as expressions of the war. The collage-like structure makes it difficult to tell whose voice is speaking.

Subjects: AIDS • Arabs • Art and Artists • Families

Read-Alikes: *Funny Boy*, by Shyam Selvadurai, and *Teranesia*, by Greg Egan, both have main characters deeply affected by the civil wars they escaped as youths.

Baker, James Robert.

🎖 *Tim and Pete.* Los Angeles: Alyson Books, 2001 (1993). **G**

Two separated lovers are reunited in a subversive odyssey across nighttime Los Angeles, where they encounter a quartet of HIV-positive men bent on committing crimes of revenge. The lovers' journey takes them into their past and toward a different future. A vivid depiction of the urban music cultures of the city.

Awards: Publishing Triangle's 100 Best Lesbian and Gay Novels, Reader's Choice

Subjects: AIDS • California • Couples • Homophobia • Music

Read-Alikes: Mark Zimmerman's *Hostage* has an HIV-positive man out to settle a score with a politician who blocked AIDS funding. Bret Easton Ellis's *Glamorama* features a pansexual gang of decadent models turned terrorists.

Bram, Christopher.

In Memory of Angel Clare. London: GMP, 1991 (1989). **G**

Haunted by the AIDS-related death of his lover Clarence, Michael hopes that a European escape will help him with his grief. Upon returning to America, he enters into the process of growing beyond his grief and beginning a new relationship. The character portrayals echo the novels of manners of Henry James.

Subjects: Couples • Grief • Love

Read-Alikes: Terrence McNally's play *Love! Valour! Compassion!* also shows a circle of friends working to console those in their number affected by HIV.

Brown, Rebecca.

🎗 *Gifts of the Body.* New York: HarperPerennial, 1995 (1994). **G L**

Written by a caregiver with direct experience of the myriad changes AIDS can make in both body and mind, this series of interwoven stories offers a new appreciation of human courage and vulnerability.

Awards: Lambda Literary Award, 1995

Subjects: AIDS • Death and dying • Healthcare workers • Relationships

Read-Alikes: Katrina Kittle's *Traveling Light* tells the story of a young woman caring for her brother, who is dying of AIDS in their Ohio hometown.

Caldwell, Joseph.

The Uncle from Rome. New York: Penguin, 1993 (1992). **G**

Michael Ruane, in Naples to sing a supporting role in *Tosca* after the death of his lover from AIDS, is asked by the diva of the company to pose as "the uncle from Rome" at a friend's wedding. The role becomes a real one for Michael as he seeks to deal with not only his temporarily adopted family and his past grief but also the colorful, infuriating, and often contradictory city and a new love affair.

Subjects: AIDS • Grief • Italy • Music • Relationships

Read-Alikes: In Paul Monette's *Afterlife*, men who have lost their partners to AIDS learn to embrace life again.

Currier, Jameson.

Where the Rainbow Ends. Woodstock, NY: Overlook Press, 2001 (1998). **G L**

This elegantly written novel tracks a group of friends in New York City from the late 1970s to the 1990s, telling their histories as seen by one of them, Robbie Taylor. The damage wrought by the coming of AIDS is countered by the support of this chosen family. Robbie later leaves New York for California and finds a new lover and a role as parent to a lesbian friend's child, which he helped create.

Subjects: AIDS • Artificial insemination • California • New York City • Parenting

Read-Alikes: *Like People in History*, by Felipe Picano, also takes the long view, tracing the connected lives of two gay cousins from the 1950s to the early 1990s.

Feinberg, David B.

B. J. Rosenthal Books. **G**

B. J. Rosenthal narrates his search for love and stability in a city changed forever by the advent of AIDS.

Subjects: AIDS • Homophobia • Humor • Mental health • New York City

Read-Alikes: Paul Rudnick's *Jeffrey* is another amusing look at love in the time of AIDS.

🎗 *Eighty-Sixed.* New York: Grove Press, 2002 (1989).

B. J. Rosenthal takes the reader on a detailed journey through his personal life in the New York gay culture, depicting the world before and after AIDS, as he looks for love.

Awards: Lambda Literary Award, 1989; Stonewall Book Award, 1990

Spontaneous Combustion. New York: Viking, 1991.

B. J. continues to search for love, even as he deals with seroconverting and joins ACT UP.

Fox, Paula.

The Eagle Kite. New York: Orchard Books, 1995. **G** **Teen**

At the beginning of Liam's freshman year, his father is diagnosed with AIDS and leaves their apartment to live in a rural area. As he deals with his father's approaching death, Liam is forced into a new awareness of his own awakening sexuality, his father's past, and the complex web of emotions that binds his family together and keeps them apart.

Subjects: AIDS • Families • New York City • Relationships, parent–child

Read-Alikes: In A. M. Homes's *Jack*, the sixteen-year-old title character has to deal with the sudden revelation that his father is gay.

Gurganus, Allan.

Plays Well with Others. New York: Vintage, 1999 (1997). **G**

Narrator Hartley Mims and his friends and lovers dream of artistic success, only to find their efforts sabotaged by the arrival of AIDS. Hartley finds literary success in retelling their heroic struggles. Autobiographical shadings color this comic, episodic novel about immense tragedy.

Subjects: AIDS • Art and artists • New York City

Read-Alikes: *What We Have Lost*, edited by Edmund White, is a moving nonfiction collection of elegies for artists who succumbed to AIDS.

Hoffman, Amy.

Hospital Time. Durham, NC: Duke University, 1997. **G** **L**

Hoffman cared for her friend Mike Riegle during his struggle with AIDS. The emotionally elusive and doggedly self-determined patient rebuffed all help but Hoffman's, forcing her to examine herself and the nature of friendship in this shared story of patient–caregiver suffering.

Subjects: AIDS • Autobiography • Death and dying • Hoffman, Amy • Riegle, Mike

Read-Alikes: *Traveling Light,* by Katrina Kittle, is a sentimental, fictionalized examination of how a biological sister cares for and copes with the slow death of her brother from AIDS.

Johnson, Fenton.

🎬 *Geography of the Heart.* New York: Pocket Books, 1997 (1996). **G**

Johnson's account of life with long-term partner Larry and the painful reality of Larry's AIDS-related death is so beautifully rendered it will bring tears to your eyes. A moving memoir of love.

Awards: Lambda Literary Award, 1996; Stonewall Book Award, 1997

Subjects: AIDS • Autobiography • Couples • Death and dying • Johnson, Fenton • Rose, Larry

Read-Alikes: *As Is,* by William Hoffman, is another moving tale of love and sacrifice in the age of AIDS.

🎬 *Scissors, Paper, Rock.* New York: Washington Square Press, 1994 (1993). **G**

This is not a novel so much as a matrix of interwoven, captivating stories, told across the years by the members of the Hardin clan of Kentucky and their school-teacher neighbor, Miss Camilla Perkins. Among the stories told about the seven children is that of Rafe, the youngest, who leaves a good library job in San Francisco to come home, and dies of AIDS. Readers will find themselves caught up in the telling.

Awards: Publishing Triangle's 100 Best Lesbian and Gay Novels, Reader's Choice

Subjects: AIDS • California • Families • Kentucky • Librarians

Read-Alikes: Peter McGehee's *Boys Like Us* and *Sweetheart* star a young man from the South, now living in Toronto, who finds his Arkansas roots a surprising source of strength. McGehee's lover, Doug Wilson, completed the trilogy with *Labour of Love* after McGehee died of complications from AIDS.

Jordan, MaryKate. Illustrated by Judith Friedman.

🎬 *Losing Uncle Tim.* Niles, IL: A. Whitman, 1989. **G** **Teen**

In this picture book, attractive watercolor illustrations in muted tones accompany a text appropriate for nearly any age group. Daniel is upset to learn that his beloved Uncle Tim has AIDS. Daniel's feelings, questions, and fears are addressed by his parents and Uncle Tim. A useful story for explaining any terminal illness to a child.

Awards: Lambda Literary Award, 1989

Subjects: AIDS • Death and dying • Families

Read-Alikes: A young girl's uncle has AIDS in Lesléa Newman's *Too Far Away to Touch.*

Kerr, M. E.

Night Kites. New York: HarperCollins, 1987 (1986). **G** **Teen**

A deftly woven story of a young man's coming-of-age in the late 1980s and the emotional challenges he faces, one of which is coping with the revelation that his idolized older brother is gay and has contracted AIDS. Eric's tale of how his family reacts to this news offers a window into how society in general perceived the disease at that time and common misconceptions about it.

Subjects: AIDS • Coming-of-age • Coming out • Families • Homophobia • Stereotypes

Read-Alikes: *Earthshine,* by Theresa Nelson, features a twelve-year-old girl hoping for a miracle cure for her father's AIDS.

Monette, Paul.

🏆 *Halfway Home.* New York: Kensington, 2003 (1991). **G**

Performance artist Tom Shaheen is staying in one of the few remaining coastal California mansions while coping with AIDS. When his estranged brother and family find it necessary to reenter his life, they collide both with the realities of the disease and with Tom's gay identity.

Awards: Stonewall Book Award, 1992

Subjects: AIDS • California • Families • Friendship • Love • Performance art • Relationships, parent–child

Read-Alikes: In *Comfort and Joy*, by Jim Grimsley, HIV positive hemophiliac Danny takes his lover home with him for the holidays, forcing his family to recognize his homosexuality.

Peck, Dale.

🏆 *Martin and John.* New York: Farrar, Straus & Giroux, 2006 (1993). **G**

This novel within a novel presents the story of the evolution of the title characters and their families from frequently shifting perspectives. John, the surviving partner of AIDS victim Martin, recounts his and Martin's pasts and creates fictionalized versions of their lives as a way to work through his life and grief. The shifting between the reality and fiction of their relationship forces the reader to build a coherent tale out of the pieces of a life and a love.

Awards: Publishing Triangle's 100 Best Lesbian and Gay Novels, Reader's Choice

Subjects: AIDS • Families • Grief • Love

Picano, Felice.

🏆 *Like People in History.* New York: Penguin, 1996 (1995). **G**

The intertwined life stories of two gay cousins from childhood to maturity, their loves, and the losses brought to them by AIDS. A detailed evocation of the urban gay cultures of San Francisco and New York as they changed over the years of AIDS.

Awards: Ferro-Grumley Award, 1996; Publishing Triangle's 100 Best Lesbian and Gay Novels, Reader's Choice

Subjects: AIDS • California • Coming-of-age • Families • New York City

Read-Alikes: Ethan Mordden's *How Long Has This Been Going On* captures the same sense of urbanity over a forty-year period, which culminates at the height of the AIDS crisis.

Price, Reynolds.

The Promise of Rest. New York: Scribner, 1997 (1995). **G**

The Mayfield family must admit and explore a range of unpleasant truths, both present and past, when their son and family heir comes home to North Carolina to die. Questions of racism, unrequited love, and the need for fulfillment of family and personal obligations arise in polished prose with a definite Southern flavor.

Subjects: AIDS • Families • North Carolina • Race relations

Read-Alikes: Family secrets and issues emerge in William Mann's *All-American Boy*, as Wally returns to his bucolic home to care for his mother.

Russell, Paul.

🏵 *Sea of Tranquility.* New York: St. Martin's Press, 2003 (1994). **G**

Allen Cloud is an astronaut in 1970, training for a lunar mission, when he learns in one day that his son Jonathan is gay and that his wife has decided to leave him. This novel follows the journeys of father and son as they travel across space and explore the distances within themselves, as Jonathan faces his death from AIDS and his father faces the responsibilities and glories of life.

Awards: Publishing Triangle's 100 Best Lesbian and Gay Novels

Subjects: AIDS • Astronauts • Families • Relationships, parent–child

Ryman, Geoff.

🏵 *Was.* London: Gollancz, 2007 (1992). **G**

A darkly fascinating tale of interwoven themes from the *Wizard of Oz* portrays the real Dorothy, her austere aunt and abusive uncle, and pioneer life in Manhattan, Kansas. Dorothy's eventual descent into mental illness brings her into contact with Bill Davison, who becomes a psychiatrist and later treats a man who was to have played the Scarecrow, but is now dying of AIDS. His obsession with the world that was leads him to seek the truth about Oz and Dorothy.

Awards: Publishing Triangle's 100 Best Lesbian and Gay Novels; Gaylactic Spectrum Award: Hall of Fame Inductee, 2002

Subjects: Actors and actresses • AIDS • Healthcare workers • Kansas • Literature • Mental health

Read-Alikes: Armistead Maupin's *Maybe the Moon* tells the story of a little person who had played the part of an alien in a breakthrough movie—and the truths she discovers when reunited with her gay costar.

Weir, John.

🏵 *The Irreversible Decline of Eddie Socket.* New York: InsightOut Books, 2001 (1989). **G**

Hailed upon its publication in 1989 as a promising first novel, this book, in some ways a dark comedy rooted in the gay world's love of superficiality and glamour, tells the story of the gradual fading and death of Eddie Socket from AIDS. Eddie's life seems to be a series of episodes of the movies he is so fond of, and his inner life is disconnected from the reality around him, until his illness forces him to reevaluate his life. Much of the narration is done from the viewpoint of Saul, who relates Eddie's progress to his lover.

Awards: Lambda Literary Award, 1990

Subjects: AIDS • Families • Friendship

White, Edmund.

🎗 *The Married Man.* London: Vintage, 2001 (2000). **G**

The romantic world of expatriate Paris is the setting for this well-crafted love story. Austin, an American from a good Southern family and an expert on furniture, meets two-decade younger Julien, the "married man" of the title, who is in the process of getting a divorce. The novel follows their relationship, from the disclosure by Austin that he is HIV positive through travels in exotic settings as varied as Venice, Morocco, and the Yucatan; and eventually back to the United States, where Austin accepts a teaching position. The gradual shrinking of their world from glittering Paris to the limited space marked out by Austin's care for the dying Julien (who has contracted AIDS) gives this story depth and presence. White's social commentary on the gay subculture is deft and biting.

Awards: Ferro-Grumley Award, 2001

Subjects: AIDS • Families • France • Italy • Mexico • Morocco • Teachers

Read-Alikes: The experiences of Edmund White in Paris are detailed in his nonfiction *Le Flaneur*. Evelyn Waugh's *Brideshead Revisited* has much the same tone.

Other Health Issues

Butler, Sandra, and Barbara Rosenblum.

🎗 *Cancer in Two Voices.* San Francisco: Spinsters, 1996 (1991). **L**

Cancer-stricken Barbara and her partner, Sandra, alternate narration on the physical and emotional pain associated with terminal illness. The mutual suffering and grief of patient and caregiver contrasts with their separate experiences as Jews, and ultimately celebrates living joyfully in the face of mortality.

Awards: Lambda Literary Award, 1991

Subjects: Autobiography • Books to film • Butler, Sandra • Couples • Death and dying • Illness • Jews • Love • Rosenblum, Barbara

Read-Alikes: Audre Lorde's *Cancer Journals* is one of the earliest lesbian cancer memoirs.

DuPrau, Jeanne.

The Earth House. New York: Ballantine, 1993 (1992). **L**

The author and her partner build their dream home in proximity to a Zen Buddhist retreat center. Their plans, disrupted by a cancer diagnosis, shift to introspective matters of mortality and grieving.

Subjects: Autobiography • Couples • Death and dying • DuPrau, Jeanne • Illness • Love • Religion

Read-Alikes: Deb Margolin's *Three Seconds in the Key* is a play depicting her struggle to live with Hodgkins disease.

Searle, Elizabeth.

The Four-Sided Bed. Saint Paul, MN: Graywolf Press, 1998. **G** **L** **B**

After several years of marriage to JJ, Allie begins to discover more of his past as a mental patient. Then Bird and Kin, two of JJ's old friends (and possibly lovers), re-appear in his life with the news that they are getting married. Their reunion forces both JJ and Allie to reexamine the meaning of their relationship and the potential threat of AIDS. Meanwhile, Bird and Kin continue their travels, sending unsettling letters. Shifts of perspective are frequent but deftly handled.

Subjects: AIDS • Families • Mental health

Read-Alikes: In Larry Duplechan's *Tangled Up in Blue,* three close friends work through a love triangle and the specter of AIDS.

Short Story Collections (Single Author)

Barnett, Allen.

The Body and Its Dangers and Other Stories. New York: St. Martin's Press, 1990. **G** **L**

This collection of six stories was Barnett's writing debut, and was well received critically. The central characters of three of the stories are gay men with AIDS, while a fourth story centers attention on a lesbian who has cancer. Powerfully and engagingly written.

Subjects: AIDS • Anthologies • Families • Relationships, parent–child

Read-Alikes: Jameson Currier's *Dancing on the Moon* is a collection of twelve stories about the impact of AIDS on the gay male community.

Short Story Anthologies (Multiple Authors)

Hunter, B. Michael, ed.

🎗 *Sojourner: Black Gay Voices in the Age of AIDS.* New York: Other Countries Press, 1993. **G**

Issued as the second volume of the New York–based journal *Other Countries: Black Gay Voices*, this collection of writings by and about black gay men stands as a testimony to their often-invisible community. Types of material included range from essays and interviews to short stories and poetry.

Awards: Lambda Literary Award, 1993

Subjects: African Americans • AIDS • Anthologies • New York City

Read-Alikes: Readers may also wish to examine the books of poetry by Essex Hemphill and Assoto Saint, as well as Joseph Beam's groundbreaking anthology *In the Life*.

Chapter 8

Historical Fiction

Definition

Works of literature that make significant use of facts, individuals, and settings from local, regional, or world history in their story lines are deemed historical fiction. For the purposes of this volume, the term *historical* applies to both the approach to the story and the era(s) in which it takes place, which may include contemporary society.

Description and Characteristics

Historical fiction either retells the lives of major figures from the point of view of a character who acts as observer and narrator, but who did not actually exist, or places its principal characters in an era whose clothing, politics, food, and customs are used to frame the story. These can range from modern society a few decades ago to cultures known only from manuscripts and ruins, giving the authors of these works considerable flexibility with theme and plotlines. The historical time and place; significant events; and, in the case of GLBT works, moral standards relating to sexuality in general and same-gender relationships in particular, offer readers a place in which contemporary issues may be safely explored.

History and Development

The growth and development of GLBT historical fiction must be understood in the context of the attitudes of the writing community toward homosexuality during the nineteenth and twentieth centuries. In the nineteenth century same-gender bonds were depicted in the disguise of socially accepted forms, such as the love and devotion between sisters. During most of the first half of the twentieth century, historical portrayals of gay men and lesbians in fiction were few and far between, although literary works featuring such characters, not specifically set in another time, continued to appear. The historical element was most frequently co-opted in the pre-Stonewall era through the compiling of lists of famous people who were—or were presumed to have been, often on incomplete evidence—lesbian or gay. Such works were attempting to counter the heavily negative cultural attitudes toward homosexuality, which denied gays and lesbians the capacity to make positive contributions to society. This mindset is discussed in *Homosexuals in History: A Study of Ambivalence in Society, Literature, and the Arts,* by A. L. Rowse (1977).

The explosion of gay and lesbian writing and publication that followed the Stonewall Riots of 1969 also saw a more open use of historical settings, beginning with the groundbreaking work by Isabel Miller, *Patience and Sarah,* in 1972, the same year that Mary Renault's *The Persian Boy* appeared. The decades since have witnessed a selective use of historical settings in gay and lesbian writing by authors both within and outside the GLBT community, with the familiar civilizations of Western Europe and the history of the United States most frequently used. Settings are as varied as the drawing room, the college campus, the pinewoods of the Carolinas, and the circus, and this diversity illustrates both the health of this genre and the possibilities of future evolution.

Issues for the Readers' Advisor

This type of GLBT literature is a mixture of real historical characters known to have had same-gender relationships, an example being Alexander the Great, and settings other than contemporary society in which individuals work out the dynamics of same-sex relationships under different social standards and limits. Advising the reader in this category involves learning whether the patron is familiar with this aspect of the documented past. If not, recommending a novel with a historical setting may serve as a useful bridge to readers accustomed to more mainstream historical fiction and romances that feature heterosexual relationships. The dominance of this type of writing by works set in either Europe or America in the last two centuries also offers access to readers interested in works set in specific eras such as the Victorian.

Patrons should also be advised to explore other sections of this guide for individual works set in a specific historical era, in particular the romance (chapter 9) and fantasy chapters (chapter 10).

Librarians advising readers unfamiliar with this genre can and should emphasize that these books can introduce aspects of the GLBT experience that may be new to the patron and stimulate investigation into the background and accuracy of the times depicted and the data used. Historically motivated readers may also want to consult chapter 4 for additional reading suggestions.

Chapter Organization

The chapter is organized chronologically by era in which the works are set, beginning with the classical civilization of the time of Alexander the Great and then proceeding through the nineteenth and twentieth centuries. The majority of entries are set in either America or Europe, possibly a consequence of the familiarity of these cultural areas to the authors.

Antiquity

Given the influence the classical civilization of Greece and Rome exerted on the historical consideration and cultural definitions of homosexuality, it is surprising to find little fiction dealing with this era. Readers interested in further exploration may wish to consult chapter 4 and 5 for other titles relevant to this period.

Renault, Mary.

🎗 *The Persian Boy.* London: Arrow, 2003 (1972). **G**

Bagoas's family, on the wrong side of a political dispute, is murdered, and the boy is sold into slavery. Castrated and prostituted, Bagoas lands in the camp of Alexander the Great, where loyalty and love mingle, in this vividly detailed mix of fact and fiction.

Awards: Publishing Triangle's 100 Best Lesbian and Gay Novels

Subjects: Alexander the Great • Antiquity • Greece • Love • War

Read-Alikes: Renault's *Fire from Heaven* is a fictionalized account of Alexander's childhood. Readers may also want to try *Memoirs of Hadrian,* by Marguerite Yourcenar, for a love story between Roman Emperor Hadrian and the young Greek Antinous.

Nineteenth-Century United States

The variety of ways in which same-gender relationships occurred in nineteenth century America, coupled with a different perspective on close and loving (although not erotic) friendships between men and women, offer the writer a diverse universe for setting stories. Some of this genre can also be used to introduce social issues and attitudes of the times, such as slavery and prostitution.

Argiri, Laura.

🎗 *God in Flight.* New York: Penguin, 1996. **G**

Elegant writing compensates for scant historical perspective in this nineteenth-century romance novel of idealized Greek love. Professor Doriskos's overwrought relationship with Simon is fraught with illness and fear, driving the professor to create a sculpture that nearly ruins their lives.

Awards: Publishing Triangle's 100 Best Lesbian and Gay Novels, Reader's Choice

Subjects: Connecticut • Students, college • Teachers

Bram, Christopher.

The Notorious Dr. August. New York: William Morrow, 2000. **G B**

Dr. August, aka "Fritz," believes his piano playing is occasionally inspired by unseen forces. Fritz travels the world of the late nineteenth and early twentieth centuries with his bisexual lover, Isaac, a former slave, and together they dupe clients with psychic predictions. Isaac, torn between affection for Fritz and love of a woman, creates a traveling love triangle, with surprising results.

Subjects: African Americans • Interracial relationships • Love triangles • Music • Race relations • Supernatural

Read-Alikes: For more stories imbued with homoerotic interracial relationships, readers should try Anne Rice's *Cry to Heaven* and *Feast of All Saints.*

Spanbauer, Tom.

The Man Who Fell in Love with the Moon. New York: Grove Press, 2000. **G** **B**
Shed epitomizes the saying "bad things happen to good people." A rape leads to murder and prostitution, a search for self leads to Native American roots but almost costs him his life, and love is tainted by the possibility of incest. Taboo topics mix with mythology to produce a sweeping story of underlying despair.

Awards: Publishing Triangle's 100 Best Lesbian and Gay Novels

Subjects: Idaho • Native Americans • Sex workers • Sexual abuse

Read-Alikes: Tom Robbins's *Even Cowgirls Get the Blues* and Chuck Palahnuik's *Invisible Monsters* both involve over-the-top characters breaking taboos in tragic-comedic stories.

Nineteenth-Century Europe

Discussions of controversial subjects have long been safely addressed in literature through the device of being set in a culture other than the audience's. The books listed here place same-gender relationships in a variety of settings in both England and France, ranging from the proper world of Victorian London, to the Napoleonic Wars, to the dubious worlds of the asylum and the theater.

Donoghue, Emma.

Slammerkin. New York: Harcourt, 2001. **L** **B**
Mary Saunders is a fashion-obsessed girl who falls into prostitution and forms a close relationship with her coworker and mentor, Doll. After a misunderstanding, Mary flees to the countryside, leading a double life as servant and prostitute, until her clothing obsession gets the best of her. Based on a true story with implied GLBT content.

Awards: Ferro-Grumley Award, 2002

Subjects: England • Murder • Sex workers

Read-Alikes: *Dress Lodger,* by Sheri Holman, also features a fashion-obsessed prostitute.

Waters, Sarah.

Affinity. New York: Riverhead Books, 2000. **L**
Margaret Prior is a depressed spinster with an unrequited love for her sister-in-law. As therapy, Margaret decides to help the less fortunate at a women's prison, where she falls under the spell of the inmate-spiritual medium Salina. Salina convinces Margaret of her innocence and love, and the two undertake a dan-

gerous scheme. A psychological thriller featuring a love triangle in which not all the participants are aware of each other.

Awards: Ferro-Grumley Award, 2001; Stonewall Book Award, 2001

Subjects: England • Intrigue • Love triangles • Supernatural

🌱 *Fingersmith.* New York: Riverhead, 2002. 🄻
Sue Trinder, raised by a "baby farmer" and a clan of thieves in Victorian London, impersonates a maid in order to steal an inheritance. Love confronts dishonesty as Sue falls for Maud, the intended victim, and the plot twists at breakneck speed, in this immaculately researched gothic novel.

Awards: Lambda Literary Award, 2002

Subjects: Books to film • Crime • England • Intrigue

Read-Alikes: For superbly fashioned plot twists and homoerotic male undercurrent, readers should try Patricia Highsmith's *The Talented Mr. Ripley*.

🌱 *Tipping the Velvet.* New York: Riverhead Books, 1999. 🄻
Nan Astley, a shy oyster shucker, attends the theater, where her enchantment with a male impersonator leads to a career change and love. Ultimately betrayed, Nan is forced into a life of crime and exploitation by wealthy lovers. Superbly drawn setting and characters signaled Sarah Waters's first smash hit. When the made-for-television BBC production aired in the United States, it was significantly edited. Readers should see the Acorn Media release for the complete film.

Awards: Lambda Literary Award, 1999

Subjects: Books to film • Cross-dressing • England • Theater

Read-Alikes: Kathryn Shevelow's biography *Charlotte* is the true story of an eighteenth-century cross-dressing stage actress. In *Mistress Moderately Fair*, by Katherine Sturtevant, Margaret, a playwright, and Amy, an actress, are lovers.

Winterson, Jeanette.

🌱 *Passion.* New York: Atlantic Monthly, 1988. 🄻 🄱
In this fantastical novel, Henri deserts Napoleon's army in the company of Villanelle, who has literally lost her heart to a female lover. Together the pair learn that love is like gambling; win or lose, you continue to play.

Awards: Publishing Triangle's 100 Best Lesbian and Gay Novels

Subjects: Fantasy • Gambling • Soldiers and sailors • War

Nineteenth Century, Other Locations

Although a great deal of research exists on the role and place of gay and lesbian life in cultures outside Western Europe, much of this has been historical in nature. Readers interested in a fictional perspective on these themes should checking headings such as "Homosexuality, Male" and " Lesbianism" by country in the Library of Congress catalog (http://www.loc.gov/), a quick way of obtaining background information.

Powell, Patricia.

The Pagoda. San Diego: Harcourt Brace, 1999. **L B T**

Asian immigrant Lowe's workaholic life is an escape from a secret-steeped reality centered on his Caucasian benefactor, Cecil. The destruction of his business and Cecil's death prompt self-reflection, truthfulness, new dreams, and loves in this melancholy, sometimes repetitive tale set in nineteenth-century Jamaica.

Awards: Ferro-Grumley Award, 1999

Subjects: Asians • Caribbean • Immigrants • Race relations • Secrets

Twentieth-Century United States

This is the largest group of historical GLBT fiction yet produced and reflects the concerns and issues of a wide variety of regional writers and mainstream authors who chose to feature gay and lesbian characters.

Arnold, Madelyn.

Bird-Eyes. New York: St. Martin's Press, 2000. **G L**

Institutionalized for being "incorrigible"—read lesbian—Latisha relates her experiences in this character-driven story. Bits and pieces are revealed in a disjointed, stream-of-consciousness style eerily evocative of mental health dysfunction. The pre-Stonewall (1963) attitude that equated homosexuality with mental illness is clearly evident.

Awards: Lambda Literary Award, 1988

Subjects: 1960s • Mental health • Students, high school

Read-Alikes: *Bird-Eyes* is reminiscent of *Girl Interrupted*, by Susanna Kaysen. Readers may also want to try *Entwined*, by Beatrice Stone, which focuses on the relationship between an elderly woman and a young lesbian in a mental hospital.

Boyd, Blanche McCrary.

Ellen Larrain Series. **L B**

Tomboy-heroine Ellen Larrain comes of age during the social upheavals of the 1960s and 1970s and partakes heavily in the various social-political movements of the period.

Subjects: 1960s • 1970s • Coming-of-age • Coming out • South Carolina • Substance abuse

Read-Alikes: Francine Prose's *Hunters and Gatherers* takes a similarly wry look at feminism.

The Revolution of Little Girls. New York: Vintage Books, 1992.

In this disjointed prequel to *Terminal Velocity*, Ellen describes her train-wrecked life loving Nicky, alcohol, and other women.

Awards: Lambda Literary Award, 1992; Ferro-Grumley Award, 1992

Terminal Velocity. New York: Random House, 1999.

It is the 1970s, and Ellen has left her husband to join a feminist/lesbian commune, where she falls in love with Jordan, a fugitive. Running from the law, drugs, and alcohol abuse take a toll on the relationship and the psyches of both women, with tragic results. A potpourri of disjointed plots.

Awards: Lambda Literary Award, 1998

Bradley, Marion Zimmer.

The Catch Trap. New York: Ballantine, 1979. **G**

In the relatively quiet, post–World War II era, the excitement of the circus comes vividly to life in this story featuring Tommy, who dreams of becoming a trapeze artist, and Mario Santelli of the famous Flying Santellis. Mario takes Tommy under his wing, and the two have an illicit, sometimes violent, love affair, in this mid-twentieth-century novel.

Subjects: 1940s • 1950s • Circus • Families • Homophobia, self-directed • Love • Secrets

Bram, Christopher.

🏵 *The Father of Frankenstein.* New York: Dutton, 1995. **G**

Weakened by a stroke, movie director James Whale asks Clayton Boone, a surly, straight World War II veteran and gardener, to sit for some sketches. As he draws, Whale shares with Boone stories of his life and Hollywood career, which spans the early twentieth century. Finally, Whale takes advantage of their growing bond to ask a final, shocking favor of Boone. The 1998 film *Gods and Monsters* was based on this book and won one of the three Academy Awards for which it was nominated.

Awards: Publishing Triangle's 100 Best Lesbian and Gay Novels

Subjects: 1950s • Books to film • California • Death and dying • Homophobia • Whale, James

Read-Alikes: Katherine Forrest's police procedural, *Beverly Malibu,* explores 1950s Hollywood. Additional information on James Whale can be found in the biography by James Curtis, *James Whale: A New World of Gods and Monsters.*

Chabon, Michael.

The Amazing Adventures of Kavalier and Clay. New York: Random House, 2000. **G** **B**

At the dawn of World War II, cousins Sam and Joe create The Escapist superhero as an outlet for personal demons. The Escapist battles Hitler on Joe's behalf and forces Sam out of the closet. Escapism and the search for happiness are primary themes in this fictional novel masquerading as history, complete with fabricated footnotes.

Subjects: 1940s • Comic strips • Jews • Love triangles • Magic

DeLynn, Jane.

🏵 *In Thrall.* Madison: University of Wisconsin Press, 2004. **L**

It is the 1960s, and Lynn thinks she is the only homosexual in school, a fear she confides to an English teacher. The shared secret develops into a crush and a subsequent relationship. The teacher hopes Lynn is just going through a phase, as do Lynn's parents when they find out about the situation. A classic motif presented in simplistic style.

Awards: Publishing Triangle's 100 Best Lesbian and Gay Novels

Subjects: 1960s • Students, high school • Teachers

Read-Alikes: In *Pages for You,* by Sylvia Brownrigg, Flannery Jansen's attraction to her college professor has a sophisticated, almost ethereal feeling.

Drury, Joan M.

Those Jordan Girls. Duluth, MN: Spinsters Ink, 2000. **L**

The unconventional women of the Jordan clan relate their individual yet inter-linked personal histories through ten-year-old narrator Maddie. Part social history of the twentieth century up through the 1950s and part fictionalized family history. The reader will experience history with a warm, fuzzy, family feeling.

Subjects: 1900–1950s • Families • Feminism

Read-Alikes: In *Altar Music,* by Christin Lore Weber, the Pearson women are Minnesota neighbors to the Jordan girls.

Dykewomon, Elena (pseud. of Elana Nachman).

🎗 *Beyond the Pale.* Vancouver, BC: Press Gang, 1997. **L**

Follow Jewish immigrants Chava, Rose, Gutke, and Dovida from the Russian po-groms to New York City at the beginning of the twentieth century. Reality confronts the women as each struggles to adapt, find hope, and love in a gritty city teeming with socialism, labor unions, and poor working conditions.

Awards: Lambda Literary Award, 1997; Ferro-Grumley Award, 1998

Subjects: 1900–1920s • Cross-dressing • Immigrants • Jews • New York City

🎗 *Riverfinger Women.* Tallahassee, FL: Naiad Press, 1974. **L**

An all-girl boarding school during the turbulent 1960s is the setting for the struggles of Inez, Peggy, and Abby. Feminism, antiwar sentiments, and basic adolescent urges are "documented" with fictitious historical fragments such as flyers and newspaper articles.

Awards: Publishing Triangle's 100 Best Lesbian and Gay Novels

Subjects: 1960s • Jews • Love triangles • Sexual abuse • Students, high school

Eugenides, Jeffery.

Middlesex. New York: Farrar, Straus & Giroux, 2002. **T**

Cal (Calliope), a second-generation Greek American, spends his first fourteen years as a girl, only to discover he is a hermaphrodite. Cal's gender identity twists and turns during eighty years of family history, beginning in the 1920s and continuing through the dawn of the twenty-first century. Sweeping details and characterizations draw in the reader.

Subjects: 1920–2000 • Families • Greece • Hermaphrodites • Michigan • Secrets

Grimsley, Jim.

Boulevard. Chapel Hill, NC: Algonquin Books, 2002. **G**

Newell, an unbelievably naïve young man from the rural South, confronts the challenges of big city life in 1970s New Orleans.

Subjects: 1970s • Louisiana

Read-Alikes: *Hey, Joe,* by Ben Neihart, follows the New Orleans wanderings of teen Joe Keith. Jane Hamilton's *Short History of a Prince* and Shyam Selvadurai's *Funny Boy* also feature young men coming to terms with homosexuality.

Hansen, Joseph.

Nathan Reed Series. **G**

Nathan Reed comes of age and comes out in 1940s-era Los Angeles, finding friendship, love, and mystery.

Subjects: 1940s • California • Friendship • Love • Intrigue • Murder • Politics

Jack of Hearts. New York: Dutton, 1995.

Meet Nathan, a recent high school graduate, as he tries junior college and discovers his sexuality in pre–World War II California.

🎗 *Living Upstairs.* New York: Dutton, 1993.

A large cast of characters populates this love story centered on Nathan, now a struggling artist, and his roommate Hoyt. Hoyt's frequent and unexplained disappearances worry Nathan, especially when the FBI snoops around and a friend ends up dead. Subtle eroticism coupled with a cliffhanger ending.

Awards: Lambda Literary Award, 1993

Hinton, Gregory.

The Way Things Ought to Be. New York: Kensington, 2003. **G** **B**

Things in King's life are not as they should be, in this character-driven story set in 1970s-era Colorado. A serious young writing student, he faces typical college-related challenges, including failed love affairs, roommate difficulties, and family problems. Ultimately, King creates a circle of friends and finds a sense of community.

Subjects: 1970s • Colorado • Friendship • Students, college

Read-Alikes: In Tom Spanbauer's *In the City of Shy Hunters,* Will creates a family from friends and searches for love just as the AIDS crisis is developing.

Hucklenbroich, Frankie.

Crystal Diary. Ithaca, NY: Firebrand Books, 1997. **L**

Follow streetwise Nicky for thirty years as she progresses from baby butch to stone cold butch, substance abuser, thief, and pimp and eventually to an understanding of love and a form of personal redemption. A rapid-fire, speed-induced, stream-of-consciousness style, autobiographical novel set between the 1950s and 1970s.

1

2

3

4

5

6

7

8

Subjects: 1950–1970s • Autobiographical fiction • Butches • Femmes • Substance abuse

Read-Alikes: Lillian Faderman's autobiography, *Naked in the Promised Land*, reads like Hucklenbroich's story from the viewpoint of Nicky's lover Jill. For more butch/femme stories, both fictional and true, Joan Nestle's *Persistent Desire* should not be missed.

Katz, Judith.

The Escape Artist. Ithaca, NY: Firebrand Books, 1997. **L T**

Sofia, a shy Polish-Jewish girl, lusts for her girlfriend, but finds herself on the way to pre–World War I America engaged to a businessman with less than honorable intentions. A cross-dressing magician befriends Sofia, and that's when the adventure—and love—begin.

Subjects: 1900s • Cross-dressing • Jews • South America

Read-Alikes: Dinitia Smith's *Illusionist* is a cross-dressing magician, wooing women and angering townspeople.

Larson, Rodger.

What I Know Now. New York: Henry Holt, 1997. **G Teen**

A gardening project introduces teenage Dave to Gene, a slightly older man who becomes a combination father figure and mentor. Struggling with his parents' separation, which in the 1950s was uncommon, Gene represents hope, tenderness, and another form of masculinity, in this languid summer reverie. Appropriate for reluctant adult readers.

Subjects: 1950s • California • Families • Landscaping

Read-Alikes: Pacing and slow revelations also characterize Paul Lisicky's *Lawnboy*.

Merlis, Mark.

🌣 *American Studies.* Boston: Houghton Mifflin, 1994. **G**

The hospitalized Reeve contrasts his situation with the politically motivated attack on his mentor, Tom. The complex story evolves over a three-day period during the 1950s, effortlessly moving between past and present, spanning fifty years of gay history with a subtlety rarely seen in a debut novel. The life of Harvard literature professor F. O. Matthiessen served as the basis for this story.

Awards: Ferro-Grumley Award, 1995

Subjects: 1950s • McCarthyism • Students • Teachers

Muhanji, Cherry.

🌣 *Her.* San Francisco: Aunt Lute Foundation, 1990. **G L B T**

A constellation of characters revolves around Kali and her mother-in-law Charlotte in this novel set in the mid-twentieth-century. The story, driven by the women's multilayered personalities, demonstrates the interrelations, dependencies, and betrayals among a neighborhood of African American women.

Awards: Lambda Literary Award, 1991; Ferro-Grumley Award, 1991

Subjects: 1960s • African Americans • Michigan • Sex workers

Revoyr, Nina.

🏵 *Southland.* New York: Akashic Books, 2003. **L**

Jackie, a Japanese American law student, seeks information about an unknown heir mentioned in her grandfather's will and uncovers a murder mystery in the process. Alternating chapters move effortlessly between the 1960s and 1990s in this ambitiously plotted novel with scant GLBT content.

Awards: Lambda Literary Award, 2003; Ferro-Grumley Award, 2004

Subjects: 1960s • 1990s • Asians • California • Intrigue • Race relations

Schulman, Sarah.

Shimmer. New York: Avon, 1998 **L**

Mid-twentieth-century perspectives on racism, homophobia, and communism are revealed in the lives of a Jewish lesbian, an upper-class white gossip columnist, and an aspiring black playwright. Their overlapping stories ultimately merge to form a cohesive tale.

Subjects: 1950s • Class conflict • McCarthyism • New York City • Politics • Race relations

Sinclair, April.

Stevie Stevenson Series. **G** **L** **B** **Teen**

Jean "Stevie" Stevenson is a young Chicago woman coming of age and coming out in the face of racism and cultural misunderstandings.

Subjects: 1960s • 1970s • African Americans • Race relations • Students, high school

Read-Alikes: *Sunday, You Learn to Box,* by Bil Wright, features an African American boy growing up in the projects.

Coffee Will Make You Black. New York: Hyperion Press, 1994.

It's the mid-1960s, and twelve-year old Jean Stevenson is beginning to suffer puberty's conflicting emotions and face the typical teenager's questions about herself and her body. Her transition to a young woman is presented in a chatty style, in this well-received debut novel.

Ain't Gonna Be the Same Fool Twice. New York: Hyperion Press, 1996.

Follow Stevie as she discovers her attraction to women and moves through relationships and friendships with a sassy attitude and strong sense of herself. A lighthearted story appropriate for adult literacy situations.

Stadler, Matthew.

Landscape: Memory. New York: Scribner, 1990. **G**

In this richly layered novel, teenage Maxwell attempts to preserve moments through entries in his memory book, especially moments spent with Duncan. A love story set primarily in 1914–1916 and told in di-

8

ary-like entries interspersed with pictures, this tale is supported by strong secondary characters and plots.

Subjects: 1910s • Art and artists • California • Love

Read-Alikes: Stadler's disconcerting endings are similar to the works of James Purdy. Shay Youngblood's *Black Girl in Paris* uses a travel diary as a literary device.

Truong, Monique.

🏶 *The Book of Salt.* Boston: Houghton Mifflin, 2003. **G** **L**

Rejected by a domineering father and expelled from his job because of a homosexual affair, Bính travels to Paris during the 1930s, eventually landing a job as cook to Alice B. Toklas and Gertrude Stein. Fictionalized glimpses into women's lives are interwoven with frequent tantalizing references to food and his sad reminiscences of life in Vietnam, to create the backdrop for Bính's attempts to find love.

Awards: Stonewall Book Award, 2004

Subjects: 1930s • Asians • Authors • Couples • France • Immigrants • Stein, Gertrude • Toklas, Alice B • Vietnam

Walker, Alice.

🏶 *The Color Purple.* New York: Harcourt, 1992. **L** **B**

The color purple, often associated with transformation and self-knowledge, is an apt title for this empathetic portrayal of female affections. Celie, an abused homemaker, finds strength and love with a blues singer in the 1920s and 1930s. Told in letters to her sister and God, this is a must read, a modern classic. The movie by the same title was nominated for eleven Academy Awards, five Golden Globes, and numerous other awards.

Awards: Publishing Triangle's 100 Best Lesbian and Gay Novels; Publishing Triangle's 100 Best Lesbian and Gay Novels, Reader's Choice

Subjects: 1920s • 1930s • African Americans • Books to film • Relationships • Sexual abuse

Read-Alikes: For more novels explicitly portraying love between women of color, readers may want to try Rosa Guy's *Ruby* and Gloria Naylor's *Women of Brewster Place*.

Twentieth-Century Europe

Prior to World War II, Europe hosted a burgeoning homosexual rights movement, which in turn contributed to a greater openness regarding homosexuality in literature. The books in this section draw on various events, especially the violent conflicts of the period.

Cunningham, Michael.

🏶 *The Hours.* New York: Farrar, Straus & Giroux, 1998. **L**

Three woman-centered women leading parallel lives fight conformity, destiny, and despair, but in different eras and countries. In 1920s London, Virginia Woolf rises one morning from the dream that inspires *Mrs. Dalloway* to prepare for a party she will not enjoy. In 1949, a Los Angeles housewife uses *Mrs. Dalloway* to escape planning her husband's birthday celebration. Fifty years later in New

York, a woman plans the perfect party for her closest friend, a male poet dying from AIDS. Finely drawn characters and exquisite writing mark this homage to literary hero Virginia Woolf. The 2002 film based on the book was nominated for nine Oscars and received one.

Awards: Ferro-Grumley Award, 1999; Stonewall Book Award, 1999; Publishing Triangle's 100 Best Lesbian and Gay Novels, Reader's Choice

Subjects: 1920s • 1940s • 1990s • AIDS • Books to film • Relationships • Woolf, Virginia

Read-Alikes: *Three Junes,* by Julia Glass, is a three-part, time and continent sweeping story of one family and the role fate plays in shaping their bonds.

Dijk, Lutz van. Translated by Elizabeth D. Crawford.

Damned Strong Love: The True Story of Willi G. and Stefan K.: A Novel. New York: Henry Holt, 1995. **G** **Teen**

A powerful novel based on the true story of Stefan K., who as a teen in Nazi-occupied Poland fell in love with Willi G., a German soldier. When the authorities discovered their affair, Stefan was sent to a labor camp, where he remained until the war's end. To this day, Stefan has been unable to learn Willi's fate.

Subjects: 1940s • Germany • Nazis • World War II

Read-Alikes: Erica Fischer's *Aimee & Jaguar* is the true story of the love affair between a Jewish woman and a German officer's wife during the Nazi era.

Ebershoff, David.

🏵 *The Danish Girl.* New York: Viking, 2000. **T**

Greta's portrait model canceled on her, so she asks her husband Einar to pose in women's clothes. He discovers he feels right as a woman—Lili—and cross-dresses more and more. With Greta's loving assistance, in 1931 Dresden he becomes the first man to undergo a sex-change operation. Based on a true story.

Awards: Lambda Literary Award, 2000

Subjects: 1930s • Art and artists • Cross-dressing • Denmark • Elbe, Lili • Germany • Sex change

Lippincott, Robin.

Mr. Dalloway. Louisville, KY: Sarabande, 1999. **G** **B**

Richard Dalloway, pining for his lover Robbie, must plan a party to celebrate his wedding anniversary with Clarissa. Robbie, desperately in love with Richard, schemes his way into the celebration. In the final scene of this novel set in the 1920s, Richard holds Clarissa and Robbie as he realizes his future can include them both.

Subjects: 1920s • England • Infidelity • Love triangles • Parties

Read-Alikes: *The House on Brooke Street,* by Neil Bartlett, is also set in the 1920s (in London) and involves a secret love between two men of different classes.

O'Neill, Jamie.

🎗 *At Swim, Two Boys.* London: Scribner, 2001. **G**

Jim and Doyle are adolescent Irish boys who meet and fall in love. Through swimming, the boys grow closer. The Easter Day Uprising of 1916 interrupts the boys' lives and relationship. Abounding with historical detail and elements of class, political, and religious conflict.

Awards: Lambda Literary Award, 2002; Ferro-Grumley Award, 2003

Subjects: 1910s • Ireland • Politics • Swimming

Read-Alikes: Gabriella West's *Time of Grace* uses the Easter Day uprising as a backdrop for a love story between women. England's Civil War is the setting for Maria McCann's *As Meat Loves Salt*.

Chapter 9

Romance

Definition

Romance fiction is marked by a plot structure containing one or more love stories; the histories of their successes, adventures, and failures; and the emotional challenges faced by the individuals involved.

Description and Characteristics

Although many forms of literature deal with the joys and sorrows of love, romance writing is easily recognized by one major element: the belief in the power of true love to overcome all obstacles blocking the achievement of a full and lasting relationship. Exotic settings, whether a different culture or a different time, are frequently used in this genre. Levels of erotic detail vary from innocent to outright erotica.

History and Development

The question of the validity, viability, and lasting quality of same-sex love and relationships has long been a topic of GLBT literature in all forms, beginning in classical times with the love poems of Sappho of Lesbos and the tales of Petronius's *The Satyricon*, and continuing with the lengthy poems of chivalry created during the Middle Ages and into present times.

GLBT romance writing as we know it has its beginnings in the lesbian pulp fiction written in the 1950s, in which reasonably realistic heroines attempted to build lasting happiness as a couple. Although the major writers of this period, Ann Bannon and Valerie Taylor, are sometimes criticized for reflecting the attitude of the day, that homosexuals of either gender could not establish solid and lasting bonds, their works are important as a basis upon which later authors could build. One 1950s author who did give her characters a winning hand in the game of love was Patricia Highsmith, who penned a lesbian version of "happily ever after" in the 1952 novel *The Price of Salt*.

The gay rights movement removed the idea of inevitable doom from homosexual romances, resulting in an explosion of creativity and the reuse of traditional forms of the romance from a lesbian or gay slant. The first major work of this type was Isabel

Miller's *A Place for Us* (later renamed *Patience and Sarah*), a classic historical romance based on the lives of two women in upstate New York. Liberation also brought about the foundation of what would become the major publisher of lesbian romances for the next several decades, Naiad Press. Through Naiad, a host of writers found a venue for the creation and elaboration of the lesbian romance as a distinct genre, and the introduction of lesbian characters into other forms of literature such as detective stories and science fiction, a process that continues in the twenty-first century. The 1980s were a particularly rich time for this new type of romance, marked by landmark works such as Katherine Forrest's *Curious Wine* (considered by many the model story of girl meeting girl) in 1983 and more complex works such as Kathleen Fleming's *Lovers in the Afternoon* (1984).

Gay men can claim a place in the world of romance as well, although the number of romance titles written specifically for them is significantly smaller than the body of women's romance. While such lesbian classics as *Beebo Brinker* were being written in the 1950s, Jay Little was producing similar works for a male audience, exploring and challenging the perhaps most extreme prohibition of the day, that two men could find happiness together, although it must be noted that his novels often lacked the traditional happy ending. The years immediately before the Stonewall Riots of 1969 saw the publication of Richard Amory's Loon Trilogy, another historical romance set in frontier times. The first book in the series, *Song of the Loon* (1966), would later be made into a film. In 1970, Gordon Merrick's *The Lord Won't Mind* brought the full range of standard romance plot and theme alive in a gay male context and became the first frankly gay novel to make the best-seller list of the *New York Times*. Merrick went on to develop his initial characters in the sequels *Forth into Light* and *One for the Gods*.

Even the stereotyped gothic romance was experimented with, as in Vincent Virga's successful 1980 novel *Gaywyck*, which he followed in 2001 with another Victorian-era story, *Vadriel Vail*. This surge of interest in romances among gay men led to the founding of a male equivalent to Naiad, Romentics, in 2003.

Issues for the Readers' Advisor

Romance has always been a popular genre, with a large mass-market audience for both print and electronic formats. Librarians should expect a consistent demand for this type of GLBT material from their clientele. Given the variety of authors and plotlines available, patrons may well have seen notices for or heard about works that have not yet been covered in the professional review media, providing an opportunity for both effective public relations and becoming informed about emerging writers. The extant literature is more heavily oriented toward women than men, although this is beginning to change as new publishing houses appear, and many authors' works cross gender lines. This is a point that patrons should be made aware of, as they may be puzzled about why more material isn't available, not realizing that many works not usually classed as romances have subtle shadings of this genre.

When interviewing a patron who has asked for GLBT romance, it is important to find out exactly what type of romance is being requested. Some direct questions about what romance titles the patron has enjoyed in the past will help you more clearly define what is needed. It may be useful to note that GLBT romances do not always end in a "happily ever after" fashion; some are bittersweet and some are a blend of both.

The diversity in the genre is vast—from highly charged erotica to innocent prairie romances, from historical to contemporary, and covering all types of gender identities. This dichotomy is reflected in this chapter's two subject categories: sweet and spicy. Readers seeking additional love stores are advised to consult chapter 6, as the coming out process is often prompted by a romantic attraction, as well as chapter 8 (on historical fiction) and chapter 5 (on general fiction), for further recommendations.

Chapter Organization

The entries in this chapter are divided into two subject sections, sweet romances and spicy romances, followed by works in a series, short story collections by one author, and short story anthologies by multiple authors. Stories emphasizing love over sex are included with the sweet romances. By contrast, spicy romances blend romance and erotic content and may contain sexual content offensive to some readers.

Sources

Gianoulis, Tina. "Romance Novels." In *glbtq: An Encyclopedia of Gay, Lesbian, Bisexual, Transgender and Queer Culture.* Available at: http://www.glbtq.com/literature/romance_novels,2.html (accessed June 13, 2006).

Wadsworth, Ann. "American Literature: Lesbian, Post-Stonewall." In *Gay and Lesbian Literary Heritage,* edited by Claude Summers, 47 53. New York, Holt, 1995.

Sweet Romances

Bohjalian, Chris.

Trans-Sister Radio. New York: Harmony, 2000. **T**
One family revolves around Dana as he transitions from male to female; they use a radio series to discuss their feelings about and reactions to Dana. Told in a series of transcripts and narratives, Dana's transition becomes the crucible for an exploration of love and sexuality.
Subjects: Cross-dressing • Radio • Sex change

Brownrigg, Sylvia.

🌱 *Pages for You.* New York: Picador, 2002. **L**

The joys of first love are beautifully rendered by Flannery Jansen, a student in love with a teaching assistant. Each day, Flannery writes a page for Anne, reflecting on first kisses, meals, fights, and how life could be if they were together.

Awards: Lambda Literary Award, 2002

Subjects: Age differences • Coming-of-age • Students, college • Teachers

Calderon, Sara Levi. Translated by Gina Kaufer.

Two Mujeres. San Francisco: Aunt Lute, 1991. **L** **B**

Genovesa and Valeria's affair is inhibited by cultural considerations, familial obligations, homophobia, and misogyny. Penniless and forsaken by her family, Valeria must find the strength to choose between her old life and Genovesa. Contains symbolism, Spanish, and dream elements.

Subjects: Age differences • Hispanics • Jews • Love

Cooney, Ellen.

The White Palazzo. Minneapolis, MN: Coffee House Press, 2002. **L**

The *Thelma and Louise* type plot involves two women, a runaway bride, Tara, and the psychic hired to find her, Guida. Despite their differences, the two are unexpectedly attracted to each other.

Subjects: Age differences • Missing persons • Psychics • Supernatural

Read-Alikes: For a fun road trip via motorcycle, drive into Erika Lopez's *Flaming Iguanas* and follow Tomato Rodriguez's quest for love.

Cox, C. Jay

Latter Days. Los Angeles: Alyson Books, 2004. **G**

Opposites attract in this story of a party boy, Christian, who bets friends he can seduce the Mormon missionary neighbor, Aaron. Through his scheming, Christian discovers real feelings for Aaron, while Aaron must choose between faith and family or self-acceptance and love.

Subjects: Books to film • Homophobia • Love • Religion

Donoghue, Emma.

🌱 *Hood.* New York: HarperCollins, 1995. **L**

Pen reflects on her fourteen-year relationship with Cara and its sudden conclusion when Cara died prematurely. Her relationship unrecognized by friends, family, church, and country, Pen must mourn alone or risk disclosing her grief. A tender tearjerker.

Awards: Stonewall Book Award, 1997; Publishing Triangle's 100 Best Lesbian and Gay Novels, Reader's Choice

Subjects: Grief • Ireland

Dorcey, Mary.

🎗 *Biography of Desire.* Dublin, Ireland: Poolbeg Press, 1997. **L** **B**
Katherine and Nina's adulterous affair forces them to choose between their current partners or a life together. Katherine, awaiting Nina in a seaside cottage, endlessly writes a journal reflecting on her entire life and how loving Nina changes everything. Romantic, but lengthy.

Awards: Publishing Triangle's 100 Best Lesbian and Gay Novels, Reader's Choice

Subjects: Gender identity • Infidelity • Ireland

Douglas, Marion.

🎗 *Bending at the Bow.* Vancouver, BC: Press Gang, 1995. **L**
Douglas, a psychologist, weaves a subdued story of grief splashed with symbolism. Surrounded by caring neighbors and childhood memories, Annie mourns her childhood friend and lover, Sylvie. Each neighbor or memory connects to Sylvie and represents a stage in Annie's grieving process

Awards: Publishing Triangle's 100 Best Lesbian and Gay Novels, Reader's Choice

Subjects: Canada and Canadians • Grief

Forrest, Katherine.

🎗 *Curious Wine.* Los Angeles: Alyson Books, 2002. **L** **B**
Lane and Diana meet through mutual friends during a ski weekend in Lake Tahoe. They strike up a quick friendship that evolves into romance. Set in the 1970s, portions of the story are a bit dated, but the romance transcends time. A modern classic.

Awards: Publishing Triangle's 100 Best Lesbian and Gay Novels, Reader's Choice

Subjects: Love • Nevada

Read-Alikes: *Heart on Fire,* by Diana Simmonds, is an Australian-based, love story equivalent.

Garden, Nancy.

Nora and Liz. Tallahassee, FL: Bella Books, 2002. **L** **Teen**
Liz is coming to terms with the end of a long relationship and the death of her parents when she accidentally meets Nora, who is coping with her own aging parents. The two women develop a bond, and their rural town erupts in gossip. The popular juvenile author's first adult novel is simplistic enough for adolescent readers.

Subjects: Love • Families • Relationships, parent-child

Grimsley, Jim.

Comfort and Joy. Chapel Hill, NC: Algonquin Books, 2003. **G**
Proof that opposites attract, Dan is an out HIV positive hemophiliac from a blue-collar family; Ford is a closeted healthy physician from a wealthy family. Relationship doubts and dysfunctions unfold around a family holiday visit, in this discordant romance.

Subjects: Christmas • Couples • Families

Read-Alikes: Dan was featured in Grimsley's stylistically similar *Winter Birds,* also centered about a family holiday.

Hoppenbrouwers, Toke.

🏵 *Autumn Sea.* Portland, ME: Astarte Shell Press, 1996. **L**

Past loves, family relationships, and memories all shape the unnamed narrator, a Dutch woman, and profoundly affect her present relationship with an African American woman. Through travel and flashbacks, the reader watches one relationship progress while reliving the narrator's past.

Awards: Independent Publisher Book Award, 1997

Subjects: Families • Interracial relationships • Travel

Kallmaker, Karin.

🏵 *Maybe Next Time.* Tallahassee, FL: Bella Books, 2003. **L**

Betrayed by love, Sabrina (Bree) throws herself into her career as a professional violinist. Despite fame and fortune, memories interfere with love, until death, an occupational injury, and the appearance of Diana force her to reexamine her life. This multilayered story slips back and forth between past and present.

Awards: Lambda Literary Award, 2003

Subjects: Grief • Hawaii • Infidelity • Music

Read-Alikes: Gerri Hill's *Gulf Breeze* features a career-minded wildlife biologist blindsided by love.

🏵 *Sugar.* Tallahassee, FL: Bella Books, 2004. **L**

While she is bemoaning the difficulty of dating while balancing a career, a fire at Sugar Sorenson's home is the last straw. Just as scorched earth renews nature, the fire reignites Sugar's romantic life. Food motifs abound in this tasty romance.

Awards: Goldie Award, 2005

Subjects: Dating • Food • Love • Lust

Kluger, Steven.

🏵 *Almost Like Being in Love.* New York: HarperCollins, 2004. **G**

High school sweethearts Craig and Travis lose touch for twenty years. Travis, still single, laments the dearth of available men while Craig prepares to marry. Travis embarks on a search to find Craig. Witty.

Awards: Lambda Literary Award, 2004

Subjects: Dating • Politics • Students, high school

Read-Alikes: In James Earl Hardy's *If Only for One Nite,* a class reunion reignites an affair.

Lefcourt, Peter.

The Dreyfus Affair: A Love Story. New York: HarperPerennial, 1993. **G B**

Dreyfus has the American dream: a beautiful wife, money, and fame as a professional baseball player. His sudden, inexplicable love for a teammate jeopardizes everything, from his marriage to the World Series. A quirky, humorous parallel to history's Dreyfus affair.

Subjects: Baseball • Interracial relationships

Read-Alikes: Sports enthusiasts may enjoy E. Lynn Harris's *And This Too Shall Pass*, featuring a gay, African American quarterback.

Levithan, David.

🏵 *Boy Meets Boy.* New York: Knopf, 2003. **G** **B** **T** **Teen**

Paul attends a progressive school where the star football player is a drag queen, and school dances present no problem for the nonheterosexual crowd. A mix-up involving an ex-boyfriend threatens Paul's latest crush, while his lifelong friendship with Joni falls apart. Every gay teen dreams of this high school love story.

Awards: Lambda Literary Award, 2003

Subjects: Dating • Friendship • Love • Students, high school

MacLean, Judy.

🏵 *Rosemary and Juliet.* New York: Alice Street Editions, 2003. **L**

Shakespeare's *Romeo and Juliet* inspired this contemporary love story in which opposites attract. Romey, an out lesbian, and Julie, the preacher's daughter, face parental obstacles to their affair. A cacophony of contemporary societal conflicts contributes to the plot.

Awards: Goldie Award, 2005

Subjects: Religion • Students, high school

Maso, Carole.

🏵 *The American Woman in the Chinese Hat.* Normal, IL: Dalkey Archive Press, 1994. **L** **B**

A hat, a fountain, a swimming pool, and other objects are recurring motifs as Catherine tries to write a novel and recover from a breakup. Shifting narrative, time, and language combine with repetitiveness to create a sense of desperation, which leads to a shocking conclusion.

Awards: Publishing Triangle's 100 Best Lesbian and Gay Novels, Reader's Choice

Subjects: Authors • France • Mental health

Read-Alikes: Jeanette Winterson's *Art and Lies* is equally experimental in terms of style and narration.

McCauley, Stephen.

The Easy Way Out. New York: Simon & Schuster, 1993. **G**

When it comes to relationships, Peter's family takes the path of least resistance, staying in unproductive relationships and marrying friends rather than lovers. Peter's current relationship has devolved into friendship, and he must decide between the comfortable and the unknown. A bittersweet, character-driven, satirical tale.

Subjects: Couples • Families • Friendship • Infidelity • Travel

Read-Alikes: Mark O'Donnell's *Getting Over Homer* is a similarly funny tale of love's uncertainty.

Merrick, Gordon.

🎗 *The Lord Won't Mind.* Los Angeles: Alyson , 1995 (1970). **G** **B**

In the mid-twentieth century, cousins Charlie and Peter, complete opposites in most ways, act on their mutual attraction. Their emotionally charged relationship faces numerous obstacles, including Charlie's marriage, ultimately demonstrating that gay love affairs are not unlike heterosexual affairs. An early, gay Harlequin-style romance.

Awards: Publishing Triangle's 100 Best Lesbian and Gay Novels, Reader's Choice

Subjects: Class conflict • Coming out • Families

Read-Alikes: Charlie and Peter's adventures continue in *One for the Gods* and *Forth into the Light*.

Newbery, Linda.

The Shell House. New York: Dell Laurel-Leaf, 2004. **G** **B**

In 1917 England, Edmund will inherit Graveney Hall only if he produces an heir, which is unlikely because he loves a fellow soldier. Eighty-five years later Greg is attracted to Jordon. Both men struggle with their feelings and religious beliefs, each arriving at a bargain with God. Two stories connected through time.

Subjects: England • Photography • Religion • Soldiers and sailors • War

Read-Alikes: Aidan Chambers uses time to connect the story of two young men in *Postcards from No Man's Land*.

Olshan, Joseph.

🎗 *Nightswimmer.* New York: Berkley Trade, 2000. **G**

Haunted by the uncertainty of Chad's disappearance, Will avoids emotional entanglements until coincidence introduces Sean. Both men must decide to live in the past with their ideal lovers or risk letting go to find new love.

Awards: Publishing Triangle's 100 Best Lesbian and Gay Novels, Reader's Choice

Subjects: Death and dying • Intrigue • Missing persons • Swimming

Read-Alikes: William J. Mann's *Where the Boys Are* features ex-lovers coping with the loss of a friend and searching for a way back to each other.

Outland, Orland.

Different People. New York: Penguin, 2003. **G**

Neighborhood pals Cal and Eric have nothing in common, although Cal has a crush on Eric. As they grow up, multiple variables conspire to keep them apart, but fate has other plans. Convenient plotting covers every conceivable gay topic.

Subjects: AIDS • Substance abuse

Peña, Terri de la.

Faults. Los Angeles: Alyson Books, 1999. **L**
> The "faults" in this story are emotional, physical, and geophysical. Protagonist Tori is guilty of abandoning her lover. Tori's family is guilty of abuse and homophobia. The various plots converge with an earthquake. Some Spanish.
>
> **Subjects:** Earthquakes • Families • Hispanics

Sawyer, Michelle.

They Say She Tastes Like Honey. Los Angeles: Alyson Books, 2003. **L**
> A lighthearted story about sophisticated lipstick lesbian Macy and the travails of daily life. A dying friend sends Macy into a period of self-neglect, until Faith appears. The combination of illness and love creates Macy's cosmic conversion.
>
> **Subjects:** Dating • Illness
>
> **Read-Alikes:** In *Chicken,* by Paula Martinac, a chance meeting with a younger woman also leads to romance.

Schutzer, Amy.

Undertow. Corvallis, OR: Calyx Books, 2000. **L**
> In alternating chapters, Macy and Dotty recount their chance meeting, but must cope with past ghosts before moving forward in their relationship.
>
> **Subjects:** Families • Healthcare workers • Medicine

Wadsworth, Ann.

🏵 *Light, Coming Back.* Los Angeles: Alyson Books, 2001. **L** **B**
> Mercedes Medina has spent most of her adult life in the shadow of her much older husband, a world famous cellist. As she cares for her dying spouse, Mercedes finds herself attracted to a much younger woman. The joy of finding love is contrasted with the pain of losing a loved one.
>
> **Awards:** *ForeWord Magazine*'s Book of the Year Award, 2001
>
> **Subjects:** Age differences • Death and dying • Music
>
> **Read-Alikes:** In Bart Schneider's *Beautiful Inez,* Sylvia Bran is smitten with a married violinist.

Warren, Patricia Nell.

The Wild Man. Beverly Hills, CA: Wildcat Press, 2001. **G**
> Antonio is an aristocratic hero in the brutal, closeted world of Spanish bullfighting when a chance encounter with a peasant, Juan, leads to love. Class differences, oppression from the ultraconservative Franco government, and machismo tear at the relationship.
>
> **Subjects:** Bullfighting • Class conflict • Psychics • Spain • Supernatural

9

10

11

12

13

14

15

16

Read-Alikes: The Spanish Civil War is the backdrop for love between two Englishmen in David Leavitt's *While England Sleeps*.

Front Runner Series. G L Teen

Homosexuality in the world of male athletics presents a unique test to modern American masculinity. These stories challenge assumptions about masculinity by depicting love and loss amid the world of college sports. Although these stories are interrelated, each stands alone.

Subjects: Coming out • Grief • Love • Running • Students, college • Teachers

The Front Runner. Beverly Hills, CA: Wildcat Press, 1995 (1974).

Track coach Harlan Brown leads a quiet, closeted life until three gay runners join the team. Forced from the closet because of an attraction to one of the runners, he walks a thin line between coach and lover.

Awards: Publishing Triangle's 100 Best Lesbian and Gay Novels, Reader's Choice

Harlan's Race. Beverly Hills, CA: Wildcat Press, 1994.

Part mystery, part romance. Warren weaves Harlan's story of grief after the murder of his Olympic-bound lover, Billy. As Harlan slowly heals, he faces new threats from an unnamed disease, those who murdered Billy, and the possibility of getting hurt by loving again.

Billy's Boy. Beverly Hills, CA: Wildcat Press, 1997.

Harlan and Billy's son, John William, is the narrator of this sequel. Young William is seeking answers to his family's history while he simultaneously deals with his emerging sexuality and the disappearance of his best friend. The destructive forces of homophobia and the positive power of family are explored and contrasted.

Watts, Julia.

Phases of the Moon. Tallahassee, FL: Bella Books, 2003. L

This post–World War II novel set in Kentucky features the naïve, backwoods narration of Glenda Mooney, aspiring singing star. Success for Glenda is surprisingly delayed, but music sustains her through difficult times. The *Coal Miner's Daughter* meets *Hee Haw* and Elvis.

Subjects: Age differences • Coming out • Kentucky • Music

Winterson, Jeanette.

Gut Symmetries. New York: Knopf, 1997. L B

Jove and Alice's mutual interest in physics leads to a love affair. When Stella, Jove's wife, discovers the affair, the ensuing confrontation with Alice leads to an affair between the two women. Each character tells his or her story in alternating chapters, threaded together by science as a metaphor for love.

Subjects: Infidelity • Love triangles • Physics • Tarot

Read-Alikes: *Quicksand*, by Jun'ichiro Tanizaki, features a love triangle between two Japanese women and one of their husbands.

🏵 *Written on the Body.* New York: Knopf, 1994. **G L B T**

Winterson brings her plush writing style to this story about an unnamed, gender-neutral, philandering narrator, who has finally found true love with the secret-keeping Louise. When Louise's secret is revealed, the narrator must decide if loving means letting go.

Awards: Lambda Literary Award, 1993; Ferro-Grumley Award, 1994

Subjects: Infidelity • Love triangles • Secrets

Read-Alikes: Winterson uses the gender-neutral narrator technique in *Powerbook*.

Spicy Romances

Andrews, Terry.

🏵 *The Story of Harold.* New York: Holt, Rinehart & Winston, 1974. **G B**

A children's book author is narrator/author of this snide, stylistically formal novel. Terry enjoys kinky escapades, particularly with Jim, who enjoys the sex but does not share Terry's affection. The reader is never quite sure if the tale is memoir or fiction. Terry Andrews was a pseudonym for George Selden Thompson, also known as George Selden.

Awards: Publishing Triangle's 100 Best Lesbian and Gay Novels

Subjects: Authors • Infidelity • Sadomasochism

Bartlett, Neil.

🏵 *Ready to Catch Him Should He Fall.* New York: Dutton, 1990. **G T**

The main story revolves around a tavern and its colorful cast of characters, especially the courtship between an older man known only as "O" and a younger lover, "Boy." Readers will find a densely descriptive and meandering narrative with numerous subplots, including hate crimes and AIDS.

Awards: Publishing Triangle's 100 Best Lesbian and Gay Novels

Subjects: Age differences • AIDS • Bars • Hate crimes

Beierle, Andrew W. M.

🏵 *The Winter of Our Discotheque.* New York: Kensington, 2003. **G**

A fluffy fantasy featuring hunky Tony, an aspiring starlet, and the older has-been, Dallas, set in the age of disco, drugs, and indiscriminate sex. Dallas molds Tony into a star, only to be rejected. A soap opera drama with a carnival-like cast.

Awards: Lambda Literary Award, 2002

Subjects: Actors and actresses • Florida • New York City

Read-Alikes: In Ben Tyler's *Tricks of the Trade,* in Hollywood, it isn't whom you know, it's whom you sleep with.

Benbow, Dave.

Daytime Drama. New York: Kensington, 2003. **G**

A love story/murder mystery set in Los Angeles, featuring Travis and Clay, B-list actors on a soap opera seeking fame and fortune. The romance is intense, almost erotic, but the obvious plotting makes for a blithe beach read.

Subjects: Actors and actresses • California • Intrigue

Read-Alikes: Jon P. Bloch's *Best Murder of the Year* is another Hollywood murder mystery, involving a gossip columnist and the Academy Awards.

Burnett, Allison.

Christopher. New York: Broadway, 2003. **G**

B. K. Troop, a middle-aged fag, relates his obsession with younger neighbor Christopher. Reeling from divorce, Christopher tries to escape his pain through new age healing, sex, and writing, while B. K. sets about a slow seduction. Snide narration tinged with formality.

Subjects: Authors • Friendship • Lust

Esser, Kevin.

🎗 *Dance of the Warriors.* Amsterdam: Acolyte Press, 1988. **G**

Militant religious conservatives control America, enforcing church attendance, criminalizing homosexuality, and euthanizing all dissidents. Amid the turmoil, Ted discovers his illicit sexuality, suffers at the church's hands, and forges a life on society's fringes.

Awards: Publishing Triangle's 100 Best Lesbian and Gay Novels, Reader's Choice

Subjects: Age differences • Religion • Sexual abuse

Read-Alikes: *Wild Boys,* by William S. Burroughs, also deals with religious extremists and gangs of violent teens.

🎗 *Streetboy Dreams.* New York: Sea Horse Press/Calamus Books, 1983. **G**

Peter knows he is gay, but has never had a relationship. Entranced with Gito, Peter wishes to rescue the young man from life on the streets, so he takes him home. Slowly, Peter realizes his desires amount to more than altruism.

Awards: Publishing Triangle's 100 Best Lesbian and Gay Novels, Reader's Choice

Subjects: Age differences • Substance abuse • Teachers

Ford, Michael Thomas.

🎗 *Last Summer.* New York: Kensington, 2004. **G** **L** **T**

Ford switches from humor to fiction in his first novel. Stung by infidelity, a young man escapes to the beach, where a host of characters fall in and out of summer loves with soap opera swiftness.

Awards: Lambda Literary Award, 2003

Subjects: Dating • Friendship • Infidelity • Massachusetts

Read-Alikes: Armistead Maupin's *Tales of the City* appears to have been Ford's model.

Greco, Stephen.

Sperm Engine. San Francisco: Green Candy, 2003. **G**

The author uses short stories, journal entries, memoir, and the occasional, interconnected plot to "propose Eros as a measure of truth."

Subjects: Lust • Sex

Guinan, Doug.

California Screaming. New York: Simon & Schuster, 1998. **G**

Hunky New Yorker Kevin Mahony, on the run from his lover's mafia connections, ends up in Los Angeles, where sex, drugs, glamour, and glitz reign supreme. Kevin fits right in, sleeping his way to fame. Pop culture skewering characterizes this fluffy read.

Subjects: Actors and actresses • California • Photography

Read-Alikes: For another hollow Hollywood adventure, readers may want to try Dennis Hensley's *Misadventures in the (213)*.

Hollinghurst, Alan.

The Folding Star. London: Vintage, 1994. **G**

Obsessed with a young student, Edward resorts to stalking and pursuing unsatisfying affairs. Moving between past and present, the interconnectedness of various lives and memories unravels in a slow, stream-of-consciousness merging of language and lust.

Awards: Lambda Literary Award, 1995

Subjects: Age differences • Belgium • Students, high school • Teachers

Read-Alikes: Colm Tóibín's *The Master* is a stylistically similar, fictionalized account of the life of Henry James.

Indiana, Gary.

Horse Crazy. New York: Grove Press, 1989. **G B**

Indiana's spurning of dialogue conventions allows readers inside the thoughts of the unnamed narrator and creates a feeling of eavesdropping on conversations. A fast-talking former substance abuser, Gregory manipulates the obsessively infatuated narrator into a destructive entanglement. Semiautobiographical.

Subjects: AIDS • Authors • Autobiographical fiction • Love • Substance abuse

Jeffrey, Jon.

Boyfriend Material. New York: Kensington, 2002. **G**

A quartet of stylish, shallow friends navigates New York City, bemoaning the lack of good men. Each gentleman finds love but is never quite happy with the results. Despite the muscled men on the cover, the story is lightweight. A gay man's *Sex and the City*.

Subjects: Dating • Friendship • New York City

Read-Alikes: Readers may want to try Scott Pomfret's *Hot Sauce* for a spicy, rocky relationship tale.

Queen, Carol.

🏵 *Leather Daddy and the Femme: An Erotic Novel.* San Francisco: Down There Press, 2003. **G** **L** **B** **T**

There is a little bit of something for everyone is this story about a straight girl with a broad range of sexual interests. Miranda likes to dress up as a man, Randy, to attract hardcore gay leather daddies. Lusty and literate.

Awards: Firecracker Alternative Book Award, 1999

Subjects: California • Gender roles • Leather • Sadomasochism

Read-Alikes: *Best Bisexual Erotica* has something for everyone. Readers with thick skins may enjoy Pat Califia's *Macho Sluts*.

Russell, Paul.

War Against the Animals. New York: St. Martin's Griffin, 2004. **G**

Retreating to rural life after a long struggle with AIDS, Cameron Barnes hires two gardeners who are brothers, Jesse and Kyle. Cameron and Jesse form an attachment, but Kyle has other, more destructive ideas.

Subjects: Age differences • Landscaping • Siblings

Read-Alikes: *It Had to Be You,* by Timothy James Beck, features a transplanted New York drag queen with a green thumb longing for a neighbor.

Sanders, Lauren.

🏵 *Kamikaze Lust.* New York: Akashic Books, 2000. **L** **B**

Rachael finds sexual liberation while moonlighting as the ghostwriter for a porn star. She gets in touch with her inner porn star, falls for her best friend, and copes with the death of a family member. An existential conflict between life and death, flawed by length.

Awards: Lambda Literary Award, 2001

Subjects: Authors • Death and dying • Friendship • Sex Workers

Read-Alikes: Much shorter is Melissa P.'s *100 Strokes of the Brush Before Bed,* in which the author searches for self-identity through sexual encounters.

Stadler, Matthew.

🏵 *Allan Stein.* New York: Grove Press, 1999. **G**

Dismissed for sexual misconduct, a teacher travels to Paris under the pretense of researching Gertrude Stein's nephew, Allan. The lyrical prose moves between past and present to tell the story of a teacher's forbidden love for a young man.

Awards: Lambda Literary Award, 2000

Subjects: Age differences • France • Teachers

Read-Alikes: In Patrick Gale's *Rough Music,* a young man's reflection on childhood contains shades of abuse.

Works in a Series

Best Gay Erotica. Pittsburgh: Cleis Press, 1996– . **G**
> Issued annually since 1996, this collection features a broad range of stories for all interests and reading levels. Look for works by Felice Picano, Scott O'Hara, and Justin Chin.
>
> **Subjects:** Anthologies • Dating • Erotica • Love • Lust • Sex
>
> **Read-Alikes:** Readers should try *Best Black Gay Erotica* for more stories.

🏆 Best Lesbian Erotica. Pittsburgh: Cleis Press, 1996– . **L**
> This long-running, annual series features stories from established and novice authors. Pat Califia, Joan Nestle, and Kate Bornstein are a few of the more recognizable names.
>
> **Awards:** Lambda Literary Award, 2002 and 2003
>
> **Subjects:** Anthologies • Dating • Erotica • Love • Lust • Sex
>
> **Read-Alikes:** For something more romantic, readers should try *Early Embraces,* by Lindsey Elder.

Best Lesbian Love Stories. Edited by Angela Brown. Los Angeles: Alyson Books, 2003– . **G L B T**
> Star Trek conventions, pride parades, ferry rides, and weddings are just a few of the venues for stories by headliners such as Lucy Jane Bledsoe, Katherine V. Forrest, Carol Guess, Karin Kallmaker, and Ann Wadsworth.
>
> **Subjects:** Anthologies • Dating • Love • Lust • Sex
>
> **Read-Alikes:** *Pillow Talk: Lesbian Stories Between the Covers,* edited by Leslea Newman, contains a mixture of sexy and sweet short stories.

🏆 His: Brilliant New Fiction by Gay Writers. Edited by Robert Drake. Boston: Faber & Faber, 1995– . **G**
> Arab immigrants, guilty pornographers with arson tendencies, and angst while awaiting HIV test results are just a few of the themes found in these stories. Look for stories by Bernard Cooper, Alexander Chee, Patrick Gale, Matthew Stadler, Henri Tran, and David Watmough.
>
> **Awards:** Lambda Literary Award, 1998
>
> **Subjects:** Anthologies • Dating • Love • Lust • Sex

Hot and Bothered. Edited by Karen X.Tulchinsky. Vancouver, BC: Arsenal Pulp Press, 1998– . **L**
> Karen X. Tulchinsky began this series in 1998 and has since produced four volumes, featuring a mix of established authors such as Lucy Jane Bledsoe, Elana Dykewomon, Sarah Schulman, Joan Nestle, Cecilia Tan, and Lesléa Newman, as well as newer writers.
>
> **Subjects:** Anthologies • Dating • Love • Lust • Sex
>
> **Read-Alikes:** Tulchinsky coedited *Tangled Sheets: Stories & Poems of Lesbian Lust* with Rosamund Elwin.

🌹 **Men on Men**. New York: Penguin, 1996– . **G**

Beginning in 1996, this series continues to feature some of the biggest names in gay fiction. Look for stories by Michael Lowenthal, Jamie Manrique, David Rakoff, David Ebershoff, James Purdy, Paul Lisicky, and Jim Grimsley.

Awards: Lambda Literary Award, 1999 and 2000

Subjects: Anthologies • Dating • Love • Lust • Sex

Quickies: Short Short Fiction on Gay Male Desire. Edited by James Johnstone. Vancouver, BC: Arsenal Pulp Press, 1998– . **G**

Stories of a thousand words or fewer about male-male desire. Writers include Doug Ferguson, Shaun Levin, Sandip Roy, Andy Quan, and Daniel Curzon.

Subjects: Anthologies • Dating • Love • Lust • Sex

Wired Hard. Edited by Cecila Tan. Cambridge, MA: Circlet Press, 1994– . **G**

Science fiction and horror stories with erotic twists.

Subjects: Anthologies • Horror • Lust • Science fiction • Supernatural

Read-Alikes: *Flying Cups and Saucers,* by Debbie Notkin, collects thirteen winners of the Tiptree Award.

🌹 **Women on Women.** New York: Plume, 1990– . **L**

Butches, femmes, homophobia, lost loves, and family life are a few of the themes in this series. Includes original stories and reprinted passages from authors such as Willa Cather, Sapphire, Bertha Harris, June Arnold, and Jewelle Gomez.

Read-Alikes: For more stories of Sapphic love, readers may want to try *Love Shook My Heart,* edited by Irene Zahava, and *Heatwave,* by Lucy Jane Bledsoe.

Awards: Lambda Literary Award, 1990 and 1996

Subjects: Anthologies • Dating • Love • Lust • Sex

Short Story Collections (Single Author)

Newman, Lesléa.

She Loves Me, She Loves Me Not. Los Angeles: Alyson Books, 2002. **L**

This charming collection of eleven love stories is infused with wit and warmth that will appeal to readers of all ages.

Subjects: Anthologies • Dating • Love • Lust • Sex

Read-Alikes: For more romantic short stories, readers should try Newman's *Girls Will Be Girls* and Elana Dykewomon's *Moon Creek Road.*

Philips, Ian.

🌹 *See Dick Deconstruct: Literotica for the Satirically Bent.* San Francisco: Atta-Girl Press, 2001. **G T**

Satire, intelligentsia, porn, and poetry combine to form fifteen tales for the Mensa-minded reader.

Awards: Lambda Literary Awards, 2002

Subjects: Anthologies • Dating • Erotica • Love • Lust • Sex

Vickery, Bob.

Cocksure. Los Angeles: Alyson Books, 2002. **G**

Thirty-two stories with some reoccurrence of characters and a variety of styles, including science fiction and horror; however, lust is the main theme.

Subjects: Anthologies • Dating • Erotica • Horror • Love • Lust • Sex

Short Story Anthologies (Multiple Authors)

Califia, Pat, ed.

🎗 *Forbidden Passages: Writings Banned in Canada.* Pittsburgh: Cleis Press, 1995. **G L B T**

A collection of writings and art described by Canadian Customs as "sexually degrading [and] obscene." Leading authors such as Pat Califia, Dorothy Allison, Susie Bright, Dennis Cooper, Diane DiMassa, Marguerite Duras, bell hooks, John Preston, Jane Rule, and David Wojnarowicz are included. Published as a fund-raiser to offset the legal costs of suing Canadian Customs for censoring gay and lesbian publications.

Awards: Lambda Literary Award, 1995

Subjects: Anthologies • Canada and Canadians • Censorship • Erotica

Corinne, Tee A., ed.

🎗 *Intricate Passions.* Austin, TX: Banned Books, 1989. **L**

A multicultural, multigenerational erotic reader featuring stories by Paula Gunn Allen, Chrystos, Terri de la Peña, Kitty Tsui, and many others.

Awards: Lambda Literary Award, 1989

Subjects: Anthologies • Dating • Erotica • Love • Lust • Sex

Read-Alikes: *Wet: True Lesbian Sex Stories,* by Nicole Foster, contains more erotic stories.

Jeffrey, Jon, Chris Kenry, William J. Mann, and Ben Tyler.

All I Want for Christmas. New York: Kensington, 2003. **G**

Four novellas of love, lust, and romance centered on the Christmas holiday. Fun fireplace reading.

Subjects: Christmas • Love • Lust • Sex

Read-Alikes: In Mark O'Donnell's novel *Let Nothing You Dismay*, Tad struggles with the holidays.

Summer Share. New York: Kensington, 2002. **G**

The boys-at-the-beach cartoon cover art matches this lighthearted story collection centered on dating, love, and summer frolicking.

Subjects: Dating • Sex

Read-Alikes: *Man of My Dreams,* by Dave Benbow, contains four stories about finding the ideal guy.

Newman, Lesléa, ed.

Bedroom Eyes: Stories of Lesbians in the Boudoir. Los Angeles: Alyson Books, 2002. **L**

Twenty-one short love stories by authors such as Leslea Newman, Jane Futcher, and Ruthann Robson. Students, teachers, police officers, and neighbors are just a few of the characters populating the stories.

Subjects: Anthologies • Dating • Love • Lust • Sex

Read-Alikes: *Good Parts,* by Nicole Foster, is a collection of fifty-nine erotic episodes.

Schimel, Lawrence, ed.

The Mammoth Book of Gay Erotica. New York: Carroll & Graf, 1997. **G**

Thirty-nine widely varied stories from an international cast of writers unapologetically celebrate the varied facets of gay male sex, from intimate relationships to chance encounters fraught with the thrill of anonymity and the fear of AIDS. Includes stories by Christopher Bram, Neil Bartlett, Michael Thomas Ford, Paul Elliott Russell, and Edmund White.

Subjects: Anthologies • Dating • Erotica • Love • Lust • Sex

Read Alikes: Readers should check out the sequel, *The Mammoth Book of New Gay Erotica.*

Tan, Cecilia, ed.

Sextopia. Cambridge, MA: Circlet Press, 2001. **G L B T**

Eleven intergalactic, utopia/dystopia science fiction stories "where erotic needs and society's rules conflict or interact." Sex soldiers, orgasm-enhancing nanogels, and erotically powered rocketships abound.

Subjects: Anthologies • Erotica • Science fiction • Sex • Supernatural

Tan, Joel, ed.

Queer PAPI Porn. Pittsburgh: Cleis, 1998. **G T**

Rent boys, serial killers, body builders, and drag queens populate this ground-breaking, ethnically oriented anthology.

Subjects: Anthologies • Asians • Erotica • Interracial relationships

Read-Alikes: For more ethnically oriented erotica, readers may want to try David Laurents's *Latin Boys.*

Chapter 10

Fantasy

Definition

Fantasy is marked by inventive, extravagant imagination, not limited by or rooted in the physical laws or recorded history of the known universe. This distinguishes it from science fiction, with which it is often linked, in which action and plot rest upon established scientific facts and principles.

Description and Characteristics

Weaving tales about worlds where the powers of magic and sorcery are commonplace is as old as the human species. In such lands of fantasy, creatures exist that cannot be bound by the known laws of the natural environment or whose existence stems from a whole other order of reality, often outside or interwoven with the basic structure of our own. These beings often represent qualities humans possess but are unwilling to acknowledge or may find uncomfortable addressing. Stories about them frequently permit controversial subjects to be addressed, such as lessons on sustaining human society or the universe and how it came into being. A frequent feature of fantasy is a quest for an object, place, or person, usually with the aim of averting the triumph of darkness but often also interwoven with personal growth and development of insight.

History and Development

Contemporary fantasy writing featuring GLBT characters draws upon several threads of tale and plot elements. These range from retellings of classic myths and fairy stories from across the planet, through detailed lands of alternate reality, to magic as a living force and stories set in worlds based on historical eras reaching from ancient Egypt and Sumeria to the Renaissance and the future. Fantasy literature possesses a time-hallowed respectability, rooted partly in traditional folklore and children's collections, such as the works of Hans Christian Andersen and the Brothers Grimm. Its half-familiar nature made the expansion of this genre into adult fiction more acceptable to the reading public and Western culture in general. The iconography of fantasy tales lends them their flexibility with regard to asking questions of gender and sexuality, as gods and beings outside the realm of humanity may possess qualities and pose questions seldom allowed in mainstream writings. Contemporary fantasy began to flower with the appearance of the first issue of *The Magazine of Fantasy and Science Fiction* in 1950, in which many stories later anthologized were first published, and the 1970s era served as the incubation decade for many writers. An excellent example of modern myth-making is Diane Duane's three-book series <u>The Tale of the Five</u>, published between 1979 and 1992, whose heroes are a prince and his male lover, fighting to keep the world in balance and create an extended family of their own. This series presaged the appearance between 1994 and the early twenty-first century of the bulk of GLBT fantasy titles in a variety of subgenres, created by a mixture of established writers such as Mercedes Lackey and emerging writing talents. Anthologies of scattered examples of GLBT fantasy stories appeared in the late 1990s, beginning with *Swords of the Rainbow* in 1996 and including a volume in the <u>Bending the Landscape</u> series.

Issues for the Readers' Advisor

The sheer wealth of options in the fantasy genre (and the difficulty of setting clear limits to its inhabitants, who often appear in other types of literature such as horror and science fiction, in various guises) poses unique problems for patrons who know what they want but are unfamiliar with the full extent of the field. The best approach to take is to define their interest by subgenre or theme, such as magic or alternative worlds, and then introduce them to the major writers whose work has been structured around these concepts.

Chapter Organization

High fantasy—epic adventures of folk on a quest and the world in the balance—is the first and largest section of this chapter. A roughly chronological order follows: the mythic past (action-oriented sword and sorcery stories set in the time of legend), followed by stories based on folk or fairy tales of medieval times, then Renaissance-era tales, fantasies set in contemporary or near-future worlds, time travel/alternative universe stories and finally, a section on short stories. Rounding out the chapter are short story collections and anthologies.

Sources

Garber, Eric, and Lyn Paleo. *Uranian Worlds: A Guide to Alternative Sexuality in Science Fiction, Fantasy and Horror.* 2nd ed. Boston: G.K. Hall, 1990.

GLBT Fantasy Fiction Resources, http://www.glbtfantasy.com/ (accessed February 11, 2008). Fantasy and science fiction books are reviewed and complemented by essays, reading lists, news, and author interviews.

Marchesani, Joseph. "Science Fiction and Fantasy." In *Gay and Lesbian Literary Heritage,* edited by Claude J. Summers, 638–44. New York, Henry Holt, 1995.

Stableford, Brian, and Peter Nichols. "Fantasy." In *Encyclopedia of Science Fiction,* edited by John Clute and Peter Nichols, 407–11. New York: St. Martin's Griffin, 1993.

High Fantasy

This variant of fantasy (sometimes known as "epic fantasy") is rooted in epic poems and sagas, the oldest known genre of literature, which began with the Sumerian *Epic of Gilgamesh* and the title character's quest for the survivor of the Great Flood. Such stories are marked by a dangerous quest pursued by a hero or heroes, whose goals are returning their worlds (and sometimes, the universe itself) to stable order and purpose.

Duane, Diane.

★ The Tale of the Five. G B

Herewiss rallies opposition to the evil forces of Shadow, even as he seeks the knowledge and training to be an effective mage and a strong support to his lover, rightful heir to the throne.

Awards: Gaylactic Spectrum Hall of Fame, 2003

Subjects: Dragons • Intrigue • Magic • Relationships • Sexual abuse

Read-Alikes: In Steven Perry's <u>Matador Series</u>, a small group learns mental disciplines and rallies opposition to the corrupt and evil Galactic Federation.

The Door into Fire. New York: Dell, 1979.

Herewiss employs his skills at sorcery and the friendship of Sunspark, a fire elemental, to rescue his lover, Freelorn. Then he must choose between following Sunspark and learning to control the Power of Flame, or helping Freelorn regain his lost kingdom from the Shadow.

The Door into Shadow. New York: Tom Doherty Associates Book, 1985.

In the second book in the series, the saga continues as Freelorn, Sunspark, and Herewiss are joined by sorceress and dragonspeaker Segnbora and warrior queen Eftgan in the struggle against the forces of Shadow.

The Door into Sunset. New York: TOR, 1993.

Freelorn returns to Arlen in disguise, seeking the secret of the land's oppression, while Herewiss goes to the capital ahead of Eftgan and her army. Segnbora rallies the dragons behind her in the war against the Shadow.

Fletcher, Jane.

Lorimar's Chalice. Austin, TX: Fortitude Press, 2002. L

The rulers of Storensteg, a profoundly heterosexist matriarchy, discover that heir apparent Tevi is a lesbian; and send her out of the kingdom on a hopeless quest to recover a stolen chalice. She is joined on this quest by the wizard Jemeryl; as the women face danger and treachery together, they fall in love.

Subjects: Intrigue • Magic

Read-Alikes: In R. C. Brojim's *Cognate,* known GLBT members of humanity's space exploration forces are put out of the way into second-class units with low priority or impossible missions.

Flewelling, Lynn.

Nightrunners Series. G B

Exiled elf and assassin/spy Seregil takes on the human orphan Alec as his apprentice. Over the years together fighting for their city of Skala, the two develop a deepening love and become partners.

Subjects: Intrigue • Magic

Read-Alikes: In Nicole Griffith's *Slow River,* Lore, left for dead on the streets, is rescued and comes to depend on the criminal Spanner. Robin Hobb's Assassins Trilogy tells the story of FitzChivalry, a royal bastard whose training as an assassin becomes useful in overthrowing a usurper.

Luck in the Shadows. New York: Bantam Books, 1996.

> Spy, master thief, and minor aristocrat Seregil takes young orphan Alec as his apprentice. When their city of Skala is threatened by an evil Necromancer, Seregil's ex-lover Nysander recruits them to the side of the challenged queen.

Stalking Darkness. New York: Bantam Books, 1997.

> Alec, Seregil, and Nysander join forces once again to thwart plans of Skala's enemies to incarnate a dark god.

Traitor's Moon. New York: Bantam Books, 1999.

> Accompanied by their dying queen's daughter, Seregil and Alec seek aid for Skala from the mysterious, elvish people of Aurenun, a land from which Seregil was banished years before.

Grimsley, Jim.

Kirith Kirin. Atlanta, GA: Meisha Merlin, 2000. G

In a land ravaged by the usurping Blue Queen, young Jessex escapes to the forces of the rightful king, Kirith Kirin. As he grows in magical and combat skills, Jessex also comes to love and be loved by Kirith Kirin.

Subjects: Intrigue • Magic • Religion

Read-Alikes: In Chris Anne Wolfe's *Fires of Aggar*, an Amazon and the queen she protect from invaders fall in love.

Huff, Tanya.

Quarters Series. G L B T

Bards work magic by singing requests to elemental spirits. This is a world in which bisexuality is the norm, and the author is able to explore other dimensions of love—romance, lust, platonic—against a Byzantine backdrop of intrigue.

Subjects: Assassins • Magic • Music • Possession • Religion

Read-Alikes: Marion Zimmer Bradley's <u>Darkover</u> series presents a similarly medieval world, but in a psychic, science fiction milieu.

Sing the Four Quarters. New York: DAW Books, 1994.

During a power struggle with her brother, the king, Annice is disinherited. She becomes a bard, able to sing to the spirits of the four elements, and lover of another female bard. When Annice learns that she is pregnant with the child of a falsely condemned traitor, she is forced to reenter the murky world of politics.

Fifth Quarter. New York: DAW Books, 1995.

Gyhard escapes brother and sister assassins Bannon and Vree by stealing Bannon's body. By taking his spirit into her body, Vree saves Bannon and sets off in pursuit. Meanwhile, Gyhard is seeking Prince Otavas, hoping to take his body and throne, but Kars, a necromancer (and singer of the forgotten fifth element) has kidnapped the object of his obsessive love, Prince Otavas.

No Quarter. New York: DAW Books, 1996.

Bannon has regained his body and is in hot pursuit of Vree, who is looking for help for Gyhard, her new love. Karlene joins the three to stop the evil Kars.

The Quartered Sea. New York: DAW Books, 1999.

Benedikt, who can only sing the spirit of water, is shipwrecked in a distant, dangerous country, while his lover, Bannon, plans his rescue.

Lackey, Mercedes.

The Last Herald Mage Trilogy. ▣

This trilogy is part of Lackey's larger <u>Velgarth Series</u>, all of which take place over a 3,000-year span, mostly in and around the country of Valdemar. The main character of this trilogy is a gay man, Vanyel, who struggles with his sexuality, love, and loneliness as he grows into his land's last defense against evil.

Subjects: Death and dying • Intrigue • Magic • Murder • War

Read-Alikes: The <u>Silent Empire</u> series, by Stephen Harper, features another abused young man whose powers prove essential to the defeat of evil.

Magic's Pawn. New York: DAW Books, 1989.

Vanyel's father wanted him to be a man, a fighter, but Vanyel has other ideas. At age sixteen he is sent away to train with his aunt, a powerful magic user who finds Vanyel could become the strongest Herald-Mage ever.

Magic's Promise. New York: DAW Books, 1990.

Twelve years later, the Herald-Mage Vanyel investigates a murder apparently committed by Herald and Prince Tashir. As evidence mounts against Tashir, Vanyel and his magical Companion begin to suspect a conspiracy designed to plunge Valdemar into civil war.

🌲 *Magic's Price.* New York: DAW Books, 1990.

> Valdemar's king is dying, and its enemies are circling. One after another, the Herald-Mages are eliminated, until only Vanyel is left to fight the darkness.
>
> **Awards:** Lambda Literary Award, 1990

Lynn, Elizabeth A.

Dragon Series. G B

Dragonlord Karadur battles his brothers for the power of the Dragon birthright, unintentionally harming his subjects and his loved ones.

Subject: Dragons • Magic • Shapeshifters • Siblings • Violence

Read-Alikes: In Anne Rices's <u>Vampire Chronicles</u>, Louis and Lestat struggle to come to terms with their predatory natures, much as Karadur struggles with his Dragon impulses.

Dragon's Winter. New York: Ace Books, 1998.

> Evil sorcerer Tenjiro envies the power of his brother Karadur, weredragon and king, and lures away Karadur's lover, the musician Azil.

Dragon's Treasure. New York: Ace Books, 2003.

> Marauding outlaws attack a farm under the protection of Dragon-Lord Karadur, who takes a fierce vengeance for the deaths of his people. Maia survives the dragonfire but leaves the bandit life to dispense herbs and healing; a chance meeting between her and Karadur leads to romance but threatens his kingdom and his true love, Azil.

Marks, Laurie J.

Elemental Logic Saga. G L

The land of Shaftal has been invaded by the Sainnites, who subjugate the population and try to wipe out magic. But magic continues to express itself in the Shaftali DNA, and a new but flawed earth witch emerges to restore the balance.

Subjects: Families • Magic • Slavery • Substance abuse • War

Read-Alikes: Liz Williams's *Ghost Sister* has as its main character another who is cut off from the land—and suffers greatly for it.

🌲 *Fire Logic.* New York: Tor, 2002.

> After the death of their earth witch, Harld G'deon, the Shaftal lose ground to the conquering Sainnites. When Zanja, last survivor of a tribe slaughtered by the Sainnites, joins the Paladins, she draws together the crucial folk to resist the invasion: Emil, like Zanja a Paladin and gifted with Fire Logic; Karis, a blonde giant metalsmith skilled in healing and possessed of Earth Logic; and the seer Emric.
>
> **Awards:** Gaylactic Spectrum Award, 2003

🌲 *Earth Logic.* New York: Tor Books, 2004.

> Twenty years after the death of Harlad G'deon, Shaftal remains leaderless, though rumors abound of a new earth witch able to rule in his place. Karis, the lost G'deon, is reluctant to lead, unwilling to make matters worse by intervening. However, with troops claiming to act in the G'deon's name butch-

ering a Sainnite garrison, and a strange sickness descending upon Sainnite and Shaftal alike, Karis must use her powers or lose the land.

Awards: Gaylactic Spectrum Award, 2005

Water Logic. Northampton, MA: Small Beer Press, 2007.

A new government forms in the war-torn land of Shaftal but the elemental forces are still unbalanced, and former foes cannot let go of their hatred. Salvation may come in the powers of a time-tossed fire witch.

Weis, Margaret.

Dragonvarld. G L B

Dragons and men have long stayed apart. A group of discontents, though, lays plans to subjugate humanity under their dragon rule.

Subjects: Dragons • Intrigue • Magic • Religion • Siblings

Read-Alikes: Tracy Hickman has cowritten the several series of the <u>Dragonlance</u> books with Weis. Readers should try the <u>Dragonlance Chronicles</u> or the <u>Dragonlance Legends</u> to start.

Mistress of Dragons. New York: Tor, 2003.

In the Dragonvarld, most dragons hold themselves aloof from human affairs. Nevertheless, when renegade dragons with a taste for human blood seize power over a small kingdom, the Parliament of Dragons sends forth an emissary, Draconas, to bring them to justice, with whatever human help he can muster.

The Dragon's Son. New York: Tor, 2004.

The last high priestess of Seth died giving birth to two children: Marcus, the son of the king of Idlyswylde, and Ven, the son of an evil dragon. Marcus goes on to live at the court of his father, while the embittered woman who had been the lover of the high priestess cares for Ven. Still, the dragon magic that both inherited from their mother could be their doom, as renegade dragons hunt them down.

Master of Dragons. New York: Tor, 2007.

Some dragons continue to conspire to bring about war with humans, but the Dragon Parliament is split. Ven and Marcus try to gather information about the conspiracy, warn humanity, and gather allies for the conflict—but the renegade dragons may already be too strong to stop.

Mythic Past

These are stories based in the distant past, when gods and heroes walked the Earth. Some are rooted in recognizable myths such as those of Greece or Rome (such as Mark Merlis's *Arrow's Flight*) or weave an alternative world into being, as do Delany's <u>Neveryon</u> books.

Constantine, Storm.

Thorn Boy. Eureka, CA: Stark House Press, 2002. **G**

Akaten, the captured lover of his defeated enemy, intrigues King Alofel. Darien, long the king's favorite, schemes to keep his own position secure, but is himself captivated by Akaten's charms.

Subjects: Jealousy • Religion • Slavery

Read-Alikes: In Eleanor Arnason's *Ring of Swords,* love develops between a captured human and an alien soldier.

Delany, Samuel.

Return to Neveryon Series. **G** **L** **B**

The oldest city in the world, Neveryon governs an empire that is slowly declining. The main character in these interwoven stories is Gorgik, who rises to become a top official in the government but never forgets he was once a slave.

Subjects: Feminism • Intrigue • Sadomasochism • Slavery

Read-Alikes: Starhawk's *The Fifth Sacred Thing* also takes us through the start of a new civilization. The Emirate Novels, by Severna Park, provide another strong look at imperialism fueled by slavery.

Tales of Neveryon. Middletown, CT: Wesleyan University Press, 1993 (1979).

Civilization has just begun to impose itself on the world, but already Neveryon is old. Gorgik is released from slavery, but still finds its trappings arousing. Old Venn wistfully watches the matriarchy being supplanted.

Neveryona: or, The Tale of Signs and Cities. Middletown, CT: Wesleyan University Press, 1993 (1983).

Pryn runs away from her mountain village to join Gorgik in his fight against slavery. Later she journeys to the south, learning about the cultures that support the fabled city.

Flight from Neveryon. Middletown, CT: Wesleyan University Press, 1994 (1985).

Gorgik leads a slave revolt and rises to power in the government.

The Bridge of Lost Desire (aka Return to Neveryon). Middletown, CT: Wesleyan University Press, 1994 (1987).

In three interconnected stories, Gorgik relates to a young barbarian his struggle to free the slaves.

Merlis, Mark.

🏹 *An Arrow's Flight.* New York: St. Martin's Press, 1998. **G**

Phyrrus, Achilles's gay son, left home to take up hustling and erotic dancing in the big city. But he is essential to the Greek plan to conquer Troy, so Odysseus sets off to convince him to do his duty. Modern concerns—AIDS, guerrilla warfare, homophobia, male bonding—combine with classical mythology to produce a story halfway between Greek mythology and fantasy.

Awards: Lambda Literary Award, 1998; Publishing Triangle's 100 Best Lesbian and Gay Novels

Subjects: AIDS • Antiquity • Duty • Mythology • Sex workers • War

Read-Alikes: In her <u>Alexander the Great</u> trilogy, Mary Renault shows the passage of history into legend. Readers should also see Eric Shanower's *Age of Bronze* for a gay-friendly recital of the events of the Trojan War,

Folk and Fairy Tales

As the genre of fantasy most familiar to many readers from childhood, the use of fairy tale themes are a natural fit for writers utilizing GLBT themes and characters, as these worlds are by definition beyond the limits of the human realm. Approaches to GLBT fantasy have varied from take-offs of folktales from the corpus of Western European folklore to variations on later stories crafted by known writers such as Hans Christian Andersen and the introduction of sprightly beings from Asia, such as the fox spirits.

Kerr, Peg.

Wild Swans. New York: Aspect/Warner Books, 1999. **G**

Seventeenth-century Eliza, cast out of her father's house, works to save her brothers from a curse that transforms them into swans each dawn, but her efforts convince the townsfolk that she is a witch. Elias, living as a hustler with AIDS in the twentieth century, is saved from the streets by Sean. Both Elias and Eliza labor to understand the scorn of society and the pain they endure for love.

Awards: Gaylactic Spectrum Award, 2000.

Subjects: AIDS • Love • Magic

Read-Alikes: Michael Cunningham's *The Hours* also shows us parallel lives across time, using AIDS as the modern foil to past oppressions.

Lai, Larissa.

When Fox Is a Thousand. Vancouver, BC: Arsenal Pulp Press, 2004 (1995). **L**

In this retelling of Chinese folklore, the spirit of a fox haunts a young woman in Vancouver. This same spirit, centuries before, had troubled a T'ang Dynasty poet accused of killing her maidservant.

Subjects: Coming-of-age • Ghosts • Murder

Read-Alikes: In *The House at Pelham Falls*, by Brenda Weathers, a ghost haunts a modern woman on sabbatical, seeing in her the love she lost in pioneer days.

Sherman, Delia.

Through a Brazen Mirror: The Famous Flower of Servingmen. Cambridge, MA: Circlet Press, 1999. **G L T**

A young man takes a job in the castle kitchen, his hard work and good looks coming to the attention of the amorous king. But this young man is actually a woman, hiding from a sorceress who wants her dead.

Subjects: Coming-of-age • Cross-dressing • Magic • Sexual abuse

Read-Alikes: *Mission Child*, by Maureen McHugh, features a young woman fleeing violence who finds not only a measure of safety but also a deep satisfaction living as a man.

Renaissance

In keeping with writers of more mainstream historical fiction, GLBT fantasy has taken on the colorful, complex world of the Renaissance city-states as a setting for its stories as well. The themes of rebirth or renewal of civilizations and personal honor appear frequently.

Kushner, Ellen, and Delia Sherman.

Riverside World. G L B
In a land without a king, the nobles and the wealthy merchants have taken power—but who among them holds that power is dependent on constant scheming and betrayal, as alliances form and break. However, protocol counts for everything, so the way to eliminate your opponents is to force them into a duel they cannot win.

Subjects: Coming-of-age • Intrigue • Soldiers and sailors

Read-Alikes: Guy Gavriel Kay's *The Lions of Al-Rassan*, set in an alternate Iberian Peninsula, shares both the intrigue and the honor found in Riverside. Sarah Monette's *Melusine* is set in a metropolis with a bit more magic, but that could be the city's downfall, too.

Kushner, Ellen.
🏵 *Swordspoint*. New York: Bantam Books, 2003 (1987).
Master swordsman Richard St. Vier is a duelist for hire, settling affairs of honor for the moneyed classes of his city. Factional infighting and intrigue put Richard's lover, the cynical ex-scholar Alec, in need of rescue.

Awards: Gaylactic Spectrum Award Hall of Fame, 2001.

The Privilege of the Sword. New York: Bantam Books, 2007.
Alec, now Duke of Tremontaine, has his ex-lover, Richard St. Vier, train his niece Kate in swordplay. She returns the favor by lunging into the intrigue of Riverside and forestalling plots against Alec—and coming to the aid of a damsel in distress.

Kushner, Ellen, and Delia Sherman.
The Fall of the Kings. New York: Bantam Books, 2002.
Generations ago, a council of nobles overthrew the decadent kings and their wizard counselors. Now, some twenty years after the events of *Swordspoint*, a historian and his students researching the deposition attract the unwelcome attention of the aristocrats.

Lynn, Elizabeth.

The Chronicles of Tornor. G L T Teen
Tornor Keep protected the northern edge of the kingdom of Tornor. With its fall to invaders, the old traditions are shattered, but the Keep remains a symbol to the people of the South. There are long gaps in time between the books.

Subjects: Duty • Intrigue • Magic • Siblings • War

Read-Alikes: Marion Zimmer Bradley's <u>Darkover</u> series involves a medieval culture in which psionics replaces magic as the special power protecting the land.

The Watchtower. New York: Berkley Publishing, 1979.

> Col Istor storms Tornor Keep, capturing Ryke, commander of the keep's guard, and Prince Errel. To ensure Ryke's aid in holding Tornor Keep, Errel is kept secure and safe—but as Istor's fool. Inwardly raging at this mistreatment of his prince, Ryke plots with two supposedly neutral southerners to escape the frozen north.

The Dancers of Arun. New York: Berkley Publishing, 1979.

> Many years after the events of *The Watchtower*, three-year-old Kerris survives a vicious attack, but suffers the loss of much of his family and his right arm. He recovers at Tornor Keep, suffering occasional fits that turn out to be the first stirrings of his magic powers. Eventually, Kerris reunites with his brother and his band of warriors, learns to control his witchcraft, and comes to terms with the pain of his past.

The Northern Girl. New York: Berkley Publishing, 1980.

> The young bondswoman Sorren has dreams and visions of a long-ago northern fortress, Tornor Keep. A civil war is brewing, and both sides want Sorren for her power to see the past.

Marks, Laurie J.

Dancing Jack. New York: DAW Books, 1993. **L**

> In a devastated kingdom, Ash leaves her farm in search of the remnants of her family. Her last relative, a nephew, has joined a doomed rebellion. As she journeys to rescue him, she is reminded of her own role in her land's ruin.

Subjects: Duty • Families • Illness • War

Read-Alikes: A ruined land is also the backdrop to the <u>Hefn</u> series. In Starhawk's *The Fifth Sacred Thing,* both the invading army and the resistance carry within themselves the seeds of their own destruction.

Pinto, Ricardo.

<u>The Stone Dance of the Chameleon.</u> **G**

> Carnelian is a member of the House of Suth (whose symbol is the chameleon) in a hierarchical, bureaucratic land of fantasy. When the Emperor dies, the secession is challenged, and Carnelian and his lover, the rightful heir, go into hiding to plot their return to power.

Subjects: Class conflict • Intrigue • Religion • Ritual • Slavery

Read-Alikes: The intricate etiquette of the court is echoed in Samuel Delany's *Stars in My Pockets Like Grains of Sand*. Like Osidian, the patriarchal invaders in Starhawk's*The Fifth Sacred Thing* are driven by lust for power and revenge.

The Chosen. New York: Tor, 1999.

> After the death of the Emperor of the Three Lands, young aristocrat Carnelian and his father return from the distant holding of their exile

to the glittering, hierarchical, and intensely ritualistic seat of power of the Chosen in Osrakum. An innocent among the protocol and the struggle for power, Carnelian finds forbidden knowledge and forbidden love.

The Standing Dead. New York: Tor, 2003.

Petty corruption saves Carnelian and his royal lover Osidian from certain death; the free men of the plains save them from slavery. Although Carnelian comes to love these people of the land, Osidian is blind to everything but his plans for vengeance.

Rivers, Diana.

Hadra Series. L

The Hadra are strong women, with psychic powers that allow them to communicate with each other and with their horses. This series tells their history, starting with their emergence among the Zarns and the establishment and evolution of a separate society over several centuries.

Subjects: Feminism • Psychics • War

Read-Alikes: The Holdfast Chronicles, by Suzy McKee Charnas, explores the development of a separate women's society, also dependent on a special relationship with their horses. Starhawk's *The Fifth Sacred Thing* shows a society deeply connected to nature and the land, opposed by a patriarchal, exploitative civilization.

Daughters of the Great Star. Boston: Lace Publications, 1992.

The Zarns begin to fear the psychic powers of the women who will become the Hadra. The women escape to build their own society.

The Hadra. Boston: Lace Publications, 1995.

The Hadra make their way downriver to find a safe location for their city and prepare to defend themselves against the Zarns.

Clouds of War. Ferndale, MI: Bella Books, 2002.

The strong city of Zelindar was built near the sea, but the Zarns threaten to retake the land and subjugate the women.

The Red Line of Yarmald. Ferndale, MI: Bella Books, 2003.

The Hadra, the Koomir, and the Wanderers join together to protect their land.

Journey to Zelindar. Denver: Lace Publications, 1987.

Two centuries after the events in *Red Line,* a refugee is saved by the Hadra and brought to Zelindar.

Scott, Melissa.

Astreiant Series. G

Gay detectives Nicolas Rathe and Phillip Eslingen solve crimes involving magic, in the city of Astreiant.

Subjects: Intrigue • Law enforcement personnel• Magic

Read-Alikes: *Melusine,* by Sarah Monette, is set in a city very like Astreiant, with wide use and acceptance of magic. In a more modern setting, *Unshapely Things,* by Marc Del Franco, has an ex-druid private investigator called in by the police when a serial killer starts going after fairy gigolos.

Point of Hopes. New York: Tor, 1995.

> Pointsman Nicolas Rathe, necromancer Istre b'Estorr and ex-soldier Phillip Eslingen investigate the cases of a large number of missing children, toiling through magical, religious, and political interference to solve the mystery and stave off disaster.

Point of Dreams. New York: Tor, 2001.

> A new play, based on a magical text, is all the rage in Astreiant, when several murders add to the chaos. Nicolas Rathe and Phillip Eslingen, now lovers, look for connections.

Contemporary Magic

With the huge popularity of mass media programs featuring contemporary practitioners of magic that actually works, such as *Charmed* and *Buffy the Vampire Slayer*, it is not surprising that GLBT themes have been woven into this matrix as well. Works of this kind are marked by the juxtaposition of two realities, one in which magic actually works and our own familiar space, where magic is a myth. The collision of these two universes generates the spice and color that mark their pages.

Block, Francesca Lia.

🕯 **Weetzie Bat Series.** G L B T Teen

Weetzie Bat finds a Secret Agent Lover Man and guides her multicultural extended family through a magical world with very modern problems.

Awards: Gaylactic Spectrum Hall of Fame, 2001

Subjects: California • Coming-of-age • Families • Love

Read-Alikes: Jaime Hernandez's *Locas* has the same intense, zany outlook and willing acceptance of the surreal.

Weetzie Bat. New York: Harper & Row, 1989.

> Weetzie Bat grooves, lives, and loves in Shangri-LA, a magic land just a twist away from mundane California. With her Slinkster Dog and best friend Dirk, she goes looking for her Secret Agent Lover Man.

Witch Baby. New York: HarperCollins, 1991.

> The love child of Secret Agent Lover Man and a voodoo queen, Witch Baby is accepted by Weetzie and the gang as their own child. Somehow, Witch Baby does not feel she belongs.

Cherokee Bat and the Goat Guys. New York: HarperCollins, 1992.

> Cherokee Bat, her half-sister Witch Baby, Raphael, and Angel Juan take their band, the Goat Guys, to a new level—but also face the dark side of fame.

Missing Angel Juan. New York: HarperCollins, 1993.

> Angel Juan leaves the Goat Guys for a solo career in New York, leaving behind his heartbroken girlfriend, Witch Baby. She follows him, and with help from family ghosts, angels, and street people, both she and Angel Juan find themselves ready to face the pain of their pasts.

Baby Be-Bop. New York: HarperCollins, 1995.

> This is Dirk's story, from before he met Weetzie Bat. Living with his Grandma Fifi, he struggles with coming out and losing a friend and gets bashed into unconsciousness—but in his coma, ghosts of his family visit him and give him the strength and support he needs.

Necklace of Kisses. New York: HarperCollins, 2005.

> Weetzie is now forty; Secret Agent Lover Man has morphed into Max. The love and enchantment they shared is fraying. Weetzie checks into an LA motel, and with the help of some magic and mundane kisses, she rediscovers herself.

Brownrigg, Elizabeth.

Falling to Earth: A Novel. Ithaca, NY: Firebrand Books, 1998. **L** **T**

> Alice tries to compartmentalize her life, staying in the closet to preserve her career. Nevertheless, her insistence on having her private life separate from her job keeps her from having a private life. Then Phoebe, her guardian angel, asks Alice to write the stories Phoebe tells her—and both learn what it means to be truly human.

Subjects: Angels • Coming out • Doppelgängers • Midlife crisis

Read-Alikes: In Richard Bowes's *Minions of the Moon*, a man struggles with his shadow self as he works through midlife crisis. In *The Vintner's Luck*, by Elizabeth Knox, a special angel afflicts and enchants a farmer's life.

Galford, Ellen.

🏵 *The Dyke and the Dybbuk: A Novel.* Seattle, WA: Seal Press, 1993. **L**

> A centuries-old curse comes down on the head of a Jewish lesbian, but she finds common ground with the demon that possesses her.

Awards: Lambda Literary Award, 1994

Subjects: Humor • Politics • Possession • Religion

Read-Alikes: A similar sense of humor animates *Singling Out the Couples,* by Stella Duffy.

Hartman, Keith.

Gumshoe Series. **G**

> Private investigators Drew Parker and Jen Gray work in a twenty-first century where magic actually works. Their city, Atlanta, is riven into several competing factions along the familiar fault lines of religion and homosexuality.

Subjects: Families • Georgia • Law enforcement personnel • Magic • Murder • Religion • Vampires

Read-Alikes: Rachel Pollack's *Temporary Agency* involves some detective work to keep evil forces at bay. Tanya Huff's <u>Blood Books</u> series, too, has police and private investigators, with help from the undead, solving supernatural crimes.

 The Gumshoe, the Witch, and the Virtual Corpse. Decatur, GA: Meisha Merlin Publishing, 1999.

> Gay P.I. and possible shaman Drew Parker is looking for Jen Gray, his missing business partner. Disinterred, desecrated corpses start appearing in city graveyards; the Christians blame the Wiccans, but Drew has a hunch something else is going on.
>
> **Awards:** Gaylactic Spectrum Award, 2000

Gumshoe Gorilla. Decatur, GA: Meisha Merlin Publishing, 2001.

> Drew Parker and Jen Gray look into a controversy surrounding a set of genetically engineered quintuplet movie stars, while Drew tries to help his friend Daniel figure out his new boyfriend.

Pierce, David M.

Elf Child. Binghamton, NY: Haworth, 2003. **G**

> Eric's mother only wants the best for her son, so when she senses his new beau has a secret, she does some detective work. She's right; Russ is hiding something: He is a changeling, effectively immortal—and his mother doesn't entirely approve of the relationship, either
>
> **Subjects:** California • Coming-of-age • Elves • Violence
>
> **Read-Alikes:** In Ulysses Dietz's *Desmond* and Elizabeth Knox's *The Vintner's Luck*, immortal beings fall in love with humans. Edwin Clark Johnson's *Secret Matter* involves romance with an alien from an alternate Earth.

Pollack, Rachel.

Godmother Night. New York: St. Martin's Press, 1996. **L**

> Three women's lives are woven together and pulled apart by Mother Night—death personified—and her quintet of red-haired motorcyclists. Elements of classic fairy tales, myth, and magical realism all emerge in the story as each woman learns from her bargain with Mother Night.
>
> **Subjects:** Death and dying • Parenting • Religion • Supernatural
>
> **Read-Alikes:** Jeannette Winterson's *The Powerbook* develops interconnected stories of feminist empowerment.

Richardson, Bill.

Waiting for Gertrude. Vancouver: Douglas & McIntyre, 2001. **G L**

> In Paris's Père Lachaise cemetery, several of the famous deceased are being reborn, personalities intact, as cats. Oscar Wilde pines after Jim Morrison, Marcel Proust investigates a series of mysterious thefts, and Alice B. Toklas longs for her beloved Gertrude Stein to assume feline form.
>
> **Subjects:** Humor • Pets • Reincarnation • Stein, Gertrude • Toklas, Alice B.

Read-Alikes: *The Fur Person*, by May Sarton, tells the story of a cat who settles down with May Sarton and her partner in Massachusetts. Another fun look at gay life, from the point of view of pets, is Ralf König's *Roy & Al*.

Ryman, Geoff.

Lust, or No Harm Done. London: Flamingo, 2001. **G** **B**

Michael finds a unique power to go with his midlife crisis: He can call forth a living, intelligent, but temporary, double of anyone for whom he lusts. His work and real relationships don't hold up well under the strain, though he eventually redeems himself by coming to terms with his past.

Subjects: Coming-of-age • Doppelgängers • Families • Midlife crisis • Wishes

Read-Alikes: Paula Martinac's *Out of Time* also shows a person damaging career and friendships by focusing too strongly on the truly unattainable.

Springer, Nancy.

🏵 *Larque on the Wing.* New York: Morrow, 1994. **G** **T**

Larque has always coped with life by spinning off doppelgangers, aspects of her personality made flesh. When she hits forty and a midife crisis, her psychic doubles guide her through her voyage of self-discovery and transformation.

Awards: James Tiptree, Jr. Memorial Award, 1994

Subjects: Art and artists • Doppelgängers • Midlife crisis

Read-Alikes: Elizabeth Knox's *The Vintner's Luck* has supernatural beings helping the main characters navigate midlife.

Time Travel and Alternate Earths

Time travel is perhaps the most fantastic concept ever offered to the reading public, with its potential to alter the most basic fabric of existence and rewrite what has been. The idea of alternate Earths inhabiting dimensions as close to our own as the back of a shadow offers intriguing opportunities for interdimensional love and adventure.

Adams, Laura.

Tunnel of Light Series. **L**

Autumn and Ursula were lovers in a past life, and their reunion is fought by the same dark powers that separated them 1,500 years ago.

Subjects: Reincarnation • Religion • Time travel

Read-Alikes: *The House at Pelham Falls*, by Brenda Weathers, has a darker link to past love.

Sleight of Hand. Ferndale, MI.: Bella Books, 2001.

Bonded during past lives, Autumn and Ursula live today half a world apart. Autumn begins to remember her medieval life with Ursula, but a dark force keeps Ursula from remembering their love.

Seeds of Fire. Ferndale, MI.: Bella Books, 2002.

Autumn has rescued Ursula from the darkness that took her away from her circle of past-life friends. The contemporary incarnations of those friends still struggle against an ancient evil, not knowing Ursula has survived.

9

Anthony, Mark.

The Last Rune Series. G B

Earth and its alternate reality, Eidh, are both threatened by the same sinister powers. A bartender from Earth steps forward to protect both worlds.

Subjects: Illness • Intrigue • Magic • Religion

Read-Alikes: A similar epic scale animates the <u>Matador Series</u>, by Steve Perry.

10

Beyond the Pale. New York: Bantam Books, 1998.

Bartender Travis Wilder and ER doctor Grace Beckett slip across the worldlines into Eldh, an alternate Earth where magic works. They find themselves central to the fight to preserve both worlds from a dangerous evil.

11

The Keep of Fire. New York: Bantam Books, 1999.

The Burning Plague sweeps across Eldh, and Travis returns to his saloon in Colorado hoping to find some sort of cure. However, the sickness follows him back to Earth—and so does the evil he and Grace had fought in Eldh.

12

The Dark Remains. New York: Bantam Books, 2001.

Grace and Travis bring the Eldhish knight Beltan back to Earth to get help pulling him from his coma. The Duratek Company, in league with the sinister forces threatening Earth and Eldh, kidnaps Beltan and prepares to experiment on him. As Grace and Travis work to find and save Beltan on Earth, Eldh descends into chaos.

13

Blood of Mystery. New York: Bantam Books, 2002.

Travis and three friends are dropped into 1880s Colorado and must search for a way back to their own time. Grace remains in contemporary Eldh, seeking the sword that will allow her to defeat the Pale King.

14

The Gates of Winter. New York: Bantam Books, 2003.

In both worlds, heroes and villains alike seek Runemaster Travis. Meanwhile, the dark side has brought forth another runemaster, setting up an ultimate confrontation at the Gate Between Worlds.

15

The First Stone. New York: Bantam Books, 2004.

The Dark God, his Pale King, and his minions at Duratek defeated, the people of Eldh and Earth enjoy several years of peace. But the worlds are coming closer together, and both watch their skies eaten by antimatter. Only Travis can save the worlds, but he is occupied in the search for his kidnapped daughter.

16

Baudino, Gael.

🌱 *Gossamer Axe.* New York: Penguin, 1990. **L**

Chairiste makes magic with her music in sixth-century Ireland, but when she and her lover sneak into the realm of Faerie to take in a concert, only Chariste makes it back out. For centuries she wanders the Earth, unable to find magic of enough power to break her lover free—until she discovers the music of heavy metal.

Awards: Lambda Literary Award, 1990

Subjects: Magic • Music • Religion

Read-Alikes: In Anne Rice's *The Vampire Lestat* and *The Queen of the Damned*, music is used to raise the undead. In *Unshapely Things*, by Marc Del Franco, an inimical faerie court comes back to trouble humanity.

Carey, Jacqueline.

Kushiel's Legacy. **G** **B** **L** **T**

In an alternate Europe with a radically different religion, a courtesan becomes an agent of the crown of the most civilized state, Terre D'Ange.

Subjects: Intrigue • Religion • Sadomasochism • Slavery

Read-Alikes: The epic sweep and eroticism of this trilogy are matched by Storm Constantine's Wraeththu series. Gay Gavriel Kay also created an alternate France, in *A Song for Arbonne*.

Kushiel's Dart. New York: Tor, 2001.

Phedre was born an anguissette, that is, able to find pleasure in pain. Trained as a courtesan, she becomes bondswoman to Anafiel Delaunay, a noble diplomat and spymaster. After Anafiel's assassination, Phedre must face the enemies of her land of Terre d'Ange, with the help of a few close companions.

Kushiel's Chosen. New York: Tor, 2002.

Phedre is now Comtesse de Montreve, a peer of the realm of Terre d'Ange. Her forays to court and journeys abroad cause tension with her lover and apostate monk, Joscelin, but give her the means to thwart another conspiracy against the crown.

Kushiel's Avatar. New York: Tor, 2003.

Phedre's archnemesis, Melisande Shahrizai, asks her for help in freeing Melisande's son. In exchange, Melisande will assist Phedre in locating a magical device that will lift a curse on her childhood friend, Hyacinthe. However, can the cunning, traitorous Melisande be trusted?

Short Stories

Anthologies and collections of GLBT fantasy stories are in less abundant supply than might be supposed, with most writers in this genre crafting tales requiring a broader canvas for their plots and characters than one story can contain. All of the following were published between 1996 and 1998, and their selections reflect an editorial combination of both mainstream GLBT authors, such as Jewelle Gomez, and a new frankness about content, a good example being Lawrence Schimel's *Drag Queen of Elfland*.

Short Story Collections (Single Author)

Donoghue, Emma.

Kissing the Witch. New York: HarperCollins, 1997. **L**

Thirteen fairy tales are connected and retold in a fascinating, feminist, and frequently lesbian retelling of the Brothers Grimm.

Subjects: Anthologies • Feminism • Magic

Read-Alikes: *The Powerbook* has a similar structure, several loosely connected tales combining to create a complete story. *Once Upon a Dyke* is a collection of four fairy tales as reinterpreted by authors Karin Kallmaker, Therese Szymanski, Julia Watts, and Barbara Johnson.

Schimel, Lawrence.

The Drag Queen of Elfland and Other Stories. Cambridge, MA: Circlet Press, 1997. **G L T**

This first collection of Lawrence Schimel's work presents seventeen stories of GLBT dark fantasy, humor, and fairy tales. Schimel does not create separate fantasy realms; instead, he shows the hidden magic of our own world.

Subjects: Anthologies • Erotica • Humor • Magic • Supernatural

Read-Alikes: *Bending the Landscape: Horror*, edited by Nicola Griffith, would be a good match, with its strong leavening of dark fantasy.

Short Story Collections (Multiple Authors)

Garber, Eric, and Jewelle Gomez, eds.

Swords of the Rainbow. Los Angeles: Alyson Books, 1996. **G L B**

Most of these fourteen stories are fantasy, but a few are science fiction; all explore speculative fiction from a gay or lesbian perspective. Among the authors are Tanya Huff, Lawrence Schimel, and Dorothy Allison.

Subjects: Anthologies • Magic • Supernatural

Read-Alikes: *Worlds Apart*, edited by Camilla Decarnin, Eric Garber, and Lyn Paleo, is slightly more weighted to science fiction but includes fantasy authors such as Edgar Pangborn, Elizabeth Lynn, and Marion Zimmer Bradley.

Griffith, Nicola, ed.

🎗 *Bending the Landscape: Fantasy.* Clarkston, GA: White Wolf, 1997. **G L**

Gay, lesbian, and straight writers explore GLBT themes in fantasy in this collection of twenty-two original stories.

Awards: Lambda Literary Award, 1997

Subjects: Anthologies • Magic • Supernatural

Read-Alikes: A companion volume in the <u>Bending the Landscape</u> series, *Bending the Landscape: Horror,* also edited by Nicola Griffith, covers several works of fantasy.

Schimel, Lawrence, ed.

Things Invisible To See: Gay and Lesbian Tales of Magic Realism. Cambridge, MA: Circlet Press, 1998. **G** **L**

A fey sensibility illuminates the mundane with magic in this collection of previously published stories by established GLBT authors. Notably, seven of the eleven authors represented are women.

Subjects: Anthologies • Magic • Supernatural

Read-Alikes: *What Did Miss Darrington See?,* edited by Jessica Amanda Salmonson, has a bit of the magically real in it, particularly in the title story. So, too, does Jeanette Winterson's *The Powerbook.*

Chapter 11

Science Fiction

Definition

The phrase "science fiction" (SF) came into general usage during the 1930s to designate that body of literature in which known and accepted scientific knowledge was mingled with elements of adventure and romance, exploring possible futures through narratives incorporating threads of speculation and projection. Debate over the precise meaning of the phrase continues among fans and the writers who create it.

Description and Characteristics

Ask a reader to describe science fiction, and you will quite probably get a list of authors' names in reply, a situation reflecting the sense that everyone *knows* what SF is, so all that is necessary to answer the question is to offer examples. Beyond the popular images of such creations as the *Star Trek* universe is a genre whose works exhibit shared features of plot and structure. These include the extension of present social and technological trends into future societies, with an array of social systems formed around widely differing philosophies; the collision of various species (some with multiple genders); and the problems of communication, with combinations of physical and emotional realities not possible on Earth. Underlying it all lies the challenge of the unknown.

History and Development

Science fiction's pedigree reaches back to Lucian of Samosata's tale *Icaromenippus*, about a journey to the moon dating to AD 160, but the genre owes much of its present flavor and structure to science adventure tales written in the late nineteenth century. Classic examples familiar to many readers are H. G. Wells's 1898 novel *War of the Worlds,* infamous for its terrifying radio adaptation broadcast by Orson Welles the day before Halloween in 1938 and recast by Hollywood in film form in 1953 and 2005, and the prophetic tales of Jules Verne, such as *20,000 Leagues Under the Sea* and *Off on a Comet*, which depict submarines and interplanetary travel.

The most immediate ancestors of contemporary science fiction were the pulp magazines of the 1930s and 1940s, such as *Amazing Stories*, in which the earliest work by writers who would later become major names in the field was disseminated to a mass audience. It was among this audience that the idea of this type of writing as a separate genre possessing value and vitality quickly took root. The technological explosion prompted by and continuing after World War II further stimulated the growth of the genre. The role of sexuality was consciously downplayed by many writers, the most blatant depictions often being the threatened heroines on the covers of the magazines. Same-gender relationships were confined to the deep friendships of the male characters.

This traditional approach began to erode in the 1950s—with the aging of the original core readership—in such works as Theodore Sturgeon's 1953 story "The World Well Lost," with its pair of gay alien refugees (which the first editor not only rejected, but made an effort to prevent from being published anywhere), and Philip Jose Farmer's 1952 tale "The Lovers," which features a human–alien relationship. The majority of SF authors did not explore the possibilities of this subtext until the late 1960s, when the impact of the civil rights movement, the well-publicized counterculture, and the push for greater social equality (including the birth of the American gay rights movement in 1969) began to appear in a variety of frank and thoughtful works. This decade initiated a period of intense examination of the impact of technologies on previously muted topics such as gender, reproduction, cloning, and changing sex, which marked the SF of the next four decades of the twentieth century with a greater depth and challenge for the reader.

Writers such as Ursula Le Guin, Joanna Russ, Sally Miller Gearhart, and Samuel Delany crafted a wide variety of tales about alternative sexualities spread among the stars and within future societies, ranging from the feminist utopia of *The Wanderground* to the shifting gender of the hero/heroine of *Triton*, and worlds in which the inhabitants can manifest both genders, such as in Le Guin's *The Left Hand of Darkness*. The ultimate impact of technology on sexuality is also explored in this genre, for example through the human/android relationship of the lovers in C. J. Cherryh's three-volume *Cyteen* (1988). The common ground for GLBT literature and the multileveled works of SF fiction lies in their joint claim on and recognition of the need to explore alternative models of gender and sexual form to better comprehend their true natures.

Issues for the Readers' Advisor

Given the broad scope of science fiction and its various subgenres and themes, the librarian should find out what aspects of the field interest the patron most, a matter easily done during the reference interview by asking what the person has already read and enjoyed. Patrons introduced to the subject by television programs such as *Babylon 5, Farscape*, or the offerings of the SCI FI Channel will have a very different set of expectations from those who saw films such as *Alien* and *Dune* or stumbled across the writings of Ray Bradbury or Arthur C. Clarke.

Chapter Organization

Alien worlds, computers and artificial intelligence, genetic modification, and alternate worlds and time travel are the first themes this chapter examines, followed by the softer science of psionic powers. Then science fiction novels are classified by action-oriented space opera, the science fiction/mystery cross of futurecrime, and visions of utopia/dystopia. Short story collections by single authors and short story anthologies by multiple authors round out the chapter.

Sources

Cadora, Karen. "Science Fiction." In *Lesbian Histories and Cultures,* edited by Bonnie Zimmerman, 674–75. New York: Garland, 2000.

Garber, Eric, and Lyn Paleo. *Uranian Worlds: A Guide to Alternative Sexuality in Science Fiction, Fantasy and Horror.* 2nd ed. Boston: G.K. Hall, 1990.

Marchesani, Joseph. "Science Fiction and Fantasy." In *Gay and Lesbian Literary Heritage,* edited by Claude J. Summers, 638–44. New York: Henry Holt, 1995.

Pearson, Wendy. "Science Fiction and Queer Theory." In *Cambridge Companion to Science Fiction,* edited by Edward James and Farah Mendlesohn, 149–60. New York, Cambridge University Press, 2003.

Alien Worlds

Worlds in which traditional boundaries are challenged by different but equally valid realities have been a staple of SF writing from the start. Writers exploring GLBT themes in this area centered their attention on the possible permutations that could be rung upon gender, offering their readers planets whose inhabitants (1) manifest the usual two genders familiar to Earth, but expressed as a matter of conscious choice, as in James Alan Gardner's *Commitment Hour*; (2) possess more than one gender option in the course of their normal life spans; or (3) have formed a society comprising multiple genders working in a dynamic harmony. The explanations for changing gender range from a natural mutation adapting the human species to new conditions, as in the novels about the planet Mictlan by Stephen Leigh, to the pressures of disease, as in Nicola Griffith's *Ammonite.*

The collision between traditionally two-gendered humans and the inhabitants of other cultures also offers a new stage upon which arguments about the function and limits of gender can be presented in a nonthreatening context.

Gardner, James Alan.

Commitment Hour. New York: Avon Eos, 1998. **T**

In Tober Cove, a community of farmers and fishermen, each adolescent annually swaps between male and female, deciding upon entering adulthood which gender suits him or her best. Fullin and Caddie stand on the edge of the Commitment Hour, waiting to make their irrevocable choice, when a visiting anthropologist and one of the rare Tober Covers who chose to be intersexed pay a visit.

Subjects: Gender roles • Hermaphrodites • Religion • Sex change

Read-Alikes: In Octavia Butler's <u>Xenogenesis Series</u>, aliens with three genders land on war-devastated Earth and attempt to merge genetically with humans—saving the race while changing it forever.

Griffith, Nicola.

🦂 *Ammonite.* New York: Ballantine Books, 2002. **L** **T**

A mysterious plague nearly destroys a colony, killing all the men and most of the women. The remaining women, altered by the virus, develop a unique culture, coexisting with the planet and reproducing with each other. Centuries later, when the planet is rediscovered and targeted for exploitation, the plague is still a threat. An experimental vaccine could hold the key to ending the planetary quarantine, but at what cost?

Awards: Lambda Literary Award, 1992; James Tiptree, Jr. Memorial Award, 1993

Subjects: Ecology • Genetic modification • Hermaphrodites • Illness

Read-Alikes: The <u>Hadra Series</u>, by Diana Rivers, describes another all-women society linked by psychic communication.

Le Guin, Ursula K.

🦂 *The Left Hand of Darkness.* New York: Ace, 1987 (1969). **T**

Gethen is a Balkanized, frozen planet whose people, at the peak of their sexual cycle, can manifest as either male or female. A diplomat from Earth and a native politician work together to bring Gethen into the galactic community; and they develop a mutual affection, causing each to reconsider his or her definition of love, sexuality, and gender.

Awards: James Tiptree, Jr. Memorial Retrospective Award, 1995; Gaylactic Spectrum Hall of Fame, 2003.

Subjects: Couples • Love • Politics • Sex change

Read-Alikes: Jacqueline Carey's <u>Kushiel's Legacy</u> has ample court intrigue, and an arduous journey in its first book, *Kushiel's Dart*, brings together two unlikely lovers. The ansible, a literary invention of Le Guin that allows simultaneous communication over any distance (thus allowing her interstellar community to exist), has been picked up by several writers, most notably Orson Scott Card in *Ender's Game.*

The Telling. New York: Harcourt, 2000. **G** **L**

Aka was once a cultural treasure, but contamination from extremists on Earth created a corporate state disdainful of the customs of its people. Book burnings and suppression of the native culture have not succeeded in totally destroying the traditions, discovers Sutty, Observer for the Ekumen. The traditions are preserved through oral tellings—and a hidden library holds the stories for future generations.

Subjects: Anthropology • Censorship • Economics • Libraries • Religion

Read-Alikes: In Margaret Atwood's *Handmaid's Tale*, a corporate theocracy seeks to impose a militant and intolerant, religiously based patriarchy on the ruins of the old culture.

Leigh, Stephen.

Mictlan Series. L B T

The harsh planet Mictlan was settled by the survivors of a starship explosion; the inbreeding that results is both genetic and cultural. The planet shapes both the Earthlings and the native Miccail into forms that can survive. Over time the two races develop into political and cultural rivals.

Subjects: Archaeology • Ecology • Hermaphrodites • Infertility • Religion

Read-Alikes: In Carole Ives Gilman's *Halfway Human*, blands are a third option to male and female genders among aliens.

Dark Water's Embrace. New York: Avon, 1998.

The planet Mictlan is not kind to the human colony abandoned there. Rising infertility and strange birth defects threaten its very survival, and among the women, only the fertile are truly valued. Anais, one of the infertile and also born with a birth defect, discovers that the humans are not the first species the planet has changed—and that her birth defects are the key to the future.

Speaking Stones. New York: Avon, 1999. L, B, T

A century later, the uneasy peace between the humans and the Miccail is threatened when a human hermaphrodite is kidnapped. A cryptic carved stone telling the secrets of the ancient Miccail faith holds the key to why the child was taken, as well as to a slim chance to save the planet from devastation.

McHugh, Maureen.

Mission Child. New York: Avon Books, 1998. T

On a colony planet only recently recontacted by Earth, a young clanswoman sees her village wiped out by marauders. A kinless refugee, she poses as a boy for safety, awakening her true self.

Subjects: Cross-dressing • Culture shock • Race relations • War

Read-Alikes: Delia Sherman's *Through a Brazen Mirror* has a young woman escape a violent death by posing as a man in the king's kitchens.

Scott, Melissa.

🌑 *Shadow Man.* New York: TOR, 1995. T

Side effects of the drug that makes faster-than-light travel possible have resulted in humanity dividing into five distinct genders. One planet, Hara, refuses to recognize this and forces its citizens to declare themselves male or female, regardless of actual gender. When Hara moves to rejoin the Concorde of human worlds, Warreven, one of the intersexed, leads a rebellion to demand equality.

Subjects: Culture shock • Gender roles • Hermaphrodites • Politics • Sex workers

Awards: Lambda Literary Award, 1996; Gaylactic Spectrum People's Choice Award, 1999; Gaylactic Spectrum Hall of Fame, 2003.

Read-Alikes: In Storm Constantine's <u>Wraeththu Trilogy</u>, radical evolutionary change creates the Wraethu (and a great deal of human tumult).

Computers and Artificial Intelligence (AI)

What constitutes identity? Is intelligence enough to warrant defining its possessor as a distinct entity worthy of respect—and, if so, what happens when that intelligence dwells in a body not made of flesh and blood, or one augmented by computer technologies such as implants? Can a human love another being that has been artificially created and thus lies outside the accepted definition of humanity, but still expresses emotions? And how can the wired world of computer nets help their human users in their search for memory and being and a definable society? These are the questions that GLBT characters in tales using computer science and AI as dominant elements explore.

Carter, Raphael.

The Fortunate Fall. New York: Tor, 1996. **L**

Popular reporter Maya Andreyeva broadcasts her stories, including her sensory impressions, over the Net through chipsets hardwired into her brain. Supported by Keishi, her new (and possibly not human) technician, she sets out in pursuit of a story that holds clues to her hidden past but implicates the government in genocide.

Subjects: Authors • Computers • Genocide • Memory

Read-Alikes: Another good cyberpunk story with a mystery at its core is Pat Cadigan's *Tea from an Empty Cup.*

Forbes, Edith.

Exit to Reality. Seattle: Seal Press, 1997. **T**

In AD 3000, many of humankind's problems have been solved—war, poverty, disease, and even ugliness are things of the past—but at the price of a stultifying conformity. In the midst of her ennui, Lydian trolls the message boards and finds Merle, a nonconformist who can teach her how to shape reality to her own needs.

Subjects: Computers

Read-Alikes: Geoff Ryman's *Lust* finds the main character adjusting his life by interaction with his own or others' doppelgängers.

Nader, George.

Chrome. Los Angeles: Alyson Books, 1995 (1978). **G**

Death awaits those who consort with robots, but the love between King Vortex and Chrome will not admit any obstacles.

Subjects: Artificial intelligence • Soldiers and sailors

Read-Alikes: The analogous human–elf relationship in David Pierce's *Elf Child* causes consternation in both societies.

Park, Severna.

The Annunciate. New York: Avon Eos, 1999. **L**

Only a few years ago, the Meshed, neurally linked into the sensory/computer network, ruled over the eleven worlds of ThreeSys. When the rebellion came, the social order crumbled. Now, the few remaining Meshed support themselves through selling a highly addictive drug to both sides of the continuing battle between Jacked (who use standard computer interfaces) and Jackless (who only trust the world as directly perceived). A wandering planet enters local space, bearing with it an AI emissary promising the solution to all the violence.

Subjects: Artificial intelligence • Computers • Nanotechnology • Substance abuse • Violence

Read-Alikes: In Laurie Marks's <u>Elemental Logic Saga</u>, pushing an addictive drug to control the masses is a strategy also used by the Sainnite invaders.

Picano, Felice.

Dryland's End. Binghamton, NY: Haworth, 2004 (1995). **G** **L** **B**

Cyberintelligences rebel against their makers and unleash a virus that could be the doom of three species of organic life. The long-established Matriarchy fights to remain in power, while its enemies try to use the crisis to overthrow its despotism. And on the isolated water planet Pelagia, a new hope for all life is stirring.

Subjects: Artificial intelligence • Religion • War

Read-Alikes: The <u>Hadra Series</u>, by Diana Rivers, and Monique Wittig's *Les Guérillères,* have at their core the war between the sexes.

Scott, Melissa.

Jazz. New York: Tor, 2000. **L**

The twenty-first century has a new art form and business opportunity: jazz, the intentional spread of misinformation on the Internet. Tin Lizzy left her adolescent brushes with the law behind to become a top jazz artist. She takes on an apparently clean job backing up a teen boy's clever new work, not realizing he was using software stolen from a Hollywood studio.

Subjects: Computers • Film industry

Read-Alikes: Lisa Mason's *Cyberweb* stars a tough hacker ex-lawyer fighting against a conspiracy to control cyberspace.

Night Sky Mine. New York: Tor, 1996. **G** **L**

Computer programs are bred, not written, in the far future; the best programs evolve in the wild. Ista lives undocumented on the fringes of society, learning to trap and tame these programs. In exchange for identity papers, she agrees to help a police officer and his contracted partner investigate some recent mineship disasters. They find themselves track-ing—and being tracked by—a lethally aware program cultivated by the Night Sky Mine Corporation.

Subjects: Artificial intelligence • Class conflict • Corporations • Virtual reality

Read-Alikes: Mark del Franco's *Unshapely Things* has the ex-druid main character working with the police to crack a conspiracy and avert a cataclysm.

❦ *Trouble and Her Friends.* New York: TOR, 1994. **L**

Hackers Cerise and Trouble go legit when the government starts cracking down on the freewheeling Net culture. When, years later, someone starts impersonating Trouble while invading and trashing corporate networks, the ex-lovers reunite to clear Trouble's name, setting up a deadly showdown in cyberspace.

Subjects: Computers

Awards: Lambda Literary Award, 1994.

Read-Alikes: William Gibson's *Neuromancer* is also an early and influential look at cyberspace, from the point of view of a hot ex-hacker recruited back into the business.

Winterson, Jeannette.

The Powerbook. New York: Alfred Knopf, 2000. **L** **T**

A cyberspace love story between a gender-neutral narrator, Ali (alias Alix) and an unnamed reader intended to be you. Moving between space, time, and place, the borders among fiction, reality, and gender shift constantly in a deliberately ambiguous story.

Subjects: Authors • Computers • Relationships

Genetic Modification

The idea of manipulating the basic genetic pattern of the human species to pro-duce an enhanced version with different abilities has been long used in science fiction tales. Its logic is sometimes cited in arguments about the precise causes of homosexual-ity. Usually present as a thread supporting a more central plot, as in Peter Hamilton's Night's Dawn trilogy, the few GLBT books that use it as a major plot structure either in-volve characters coping with the consequences of social engineering, as in *Teranesia*, or whose members have been touched by runaway applications of genetic manipulation.

Egan, Greg.

Teranesia. New York: HarperPrism, 1999. **G**

Prabir lived on an island paradise until civil war swept in, killing his parents and leaving their science compound in ruins. Prabir flees with his baby sister. Years later, Prabir has settled into a home with his boyfriend; his sister has followed her parents into the study of genetics. But a wave of mutations spreading out from their childhood home calls them back to face their fears.

Subjects: Death and dying • Evolution • Genetic modification • War

Read-Alikes: *Sacrament*, by Clive Barker, is another story of one man's stand against a wave of biological devastation.

Harris, Anne.

Accidental Creatures. New York: Tor, 1998. **L**

GeneSys pretty much rules Detroit. If you pass the tests, you can work in GeneSys offices; otherwise, you can dive into the mutagenic vats and harvest the biopolymers GeneSys grows. Helix, a four-armed mutant running away from home, ends up vat diving, to the horror of her new lover, Chango, whose sister died trying to organize the divers.

Subjects: Art and artists • Artificial intelligence • Class conflict • Genetic modification

Read-Alikes: A good collection of short fiction about the gay working class is *Everything I Have Is Blue*, edited by Wendell Ricketts.

Kress, Nancy.

Maximum Light. New York: TOR, 1998. **G**

Earth is so heavily polluted that most animal species are suffering a precipitous drop in their fertility; children are a precious commodity. Two young people—Cameron, a gay ballet dancer who has agreed to a memory wipe, and Shana, a streetwise teen finishing up her National Service—stumble onto a bizarre plan to create human/animal child substitutes. A seventy-year-old scientist, Nick Clementi, discovers that the roots of the conspiracy run deep into the government—and Cameron's lost memories are the key to exposing it.

Subjects: Conspiracy • Ecology • Genetic modification • Infertility • Memory

Read-Alikes: In Stephanie Smith's *Other Nature*, environmental collapse has nearly wiped out humans; the few children still being born seem hopelessly deformed but may be our last hope.

Ryman, Geoff.

Child Garden: A Low Comedy. London: Unwin Hyman, 1989. **L**

Milena is allergic to the viruses that the rest of humanity uses to transmit knowledge. To learn something, she must do it the old-fashioned way, from books and experience. Her allergies keep the state from infecting her to make her straight, and she finds some happiness with Rolfa, a lesbian engineered into the shape of a polar bear. When Rolfa is ripped away from her, Milena devotes her life to creating a monument in her honor.

Subjects: Art and artistis • Genetic modification • Music • Theater

Read-Alikes: In Gael Baudino's *Gossamer Axe*, music is key to the magic that reunites lovers.

Alternate Worlds and Time Travel

The idea of traveling through time and into alternate dimensions of reality fits well with the theme of GLBT identity, whose members often find themselves living in a de facto parallel social and spiritual universe to that of mainstream culture. This staple of SF (most famously used by H. G. Wells in *The*

Time Machine) has been given new features, with openly gay and lesbian characters who move within the fabric of space and the flows of time to pursue everything from love to the salvation of their worlds and our own.

Christian, Deborah.

Mainline. New York: Tor, 1996. **L B**

Reva, a hired killer, has the ability to see and move between worlds parallel to her own. By shifting in and out of her target's universe, she safely attacks and then disappears. When she assassinates a powerful politician with an implacable bodyguard, her natural instinct is to flee across the time lines—but the line where she made the hit is also the line where she fell in love.

Subjects: Alternate history • Assassins • Gangs • Psychics

Dedman, Stephen.

Foreign Bodies. New York: TOR, 1999. **L T**

Mike is one of the lucky ones in mid-twenty-first-century San Francisco—he has a home and a secure income. Aware of his own good fortune, he tries to help those less well-off, even assisting a homeless woman in publishing her fantastic tale of time-traveling body snatchers. But when he invites her in out of the rain one night, she takes advantage of the opportunity to swap bodies with him. As Mike tries to find his body again, he uncovers a fascist plot to overthrow the government.

Subjects: Alternate history • California • Homeless • Possession • Time travel

Read-Alikes: The criminal in Tanya Huff's *Fifth Quarter* escapes justice by taking over the body of a young assassin, forcing him to share a body with his sister.

Gerrold, David.

The Man Who Folded Himself. Dallas: Benbella Books, 2003 (1973). **G B**

A young gay man inherits a belt that allows him to travel across time, meeting and learning from other versions of himself—including a female variant. Told mostly from the point of view of one of the versions, this SF classic explores both the science and the psychology of time travel.

Subjects: Alternate history • Time travel

Read-Alikes: *Angel Lust,* by Perry Brass, is another imaginative gay time travel romance.

Johnson, Edwin Clark.

🏵 *Secret Matter.* South Norwalk, CT: Lavender Press, 1990. **G**

Kevin Anderson landed a dream job right out of college—helping to rebuild San Francisco, damaged in the Great Earthquake. Meanwhile, aliens arrive on Earth; Kevin and one of the Visitors fall in love. As the romance unfolds, Kevin slowly learns the secrets of the aliens—and why they really aren't so alien after all—on the way to saving two planets from destruction.

Awards: Lambda Literary Award, 1990.

Subjects: Alternate history • California • Coming out • Homophobia • Religion

Read-Alikes: In David Pierce's *Elf Child,* an elf and a human fall in love.

Piercy, Marge.

Woman on the Edge of Time. London: Women's Press, 2002 (1976) **G L T**

Consuela, committed to a mental institution, is visited by inhabitants of a wonderful future she must help create.

Subjects: Mental health • Sex workers • Time travel

Read-Alikes: *Bird-Eyes,* by Madelyn Arnold, is another story of the power of compassion set in a mental institution.

Russ, Joanna.

The Female Man. London: Women's Press, 2002 (1975) **L B**

Visiting across the time lines, four women from four parallel Earths (one where the United States never emerges from the Great Depression, another much like our own world in the late 1960s, a near-future variant where Manland and Womanland are at war, and a feminist separatist utopia) realize that they are the same woman, shaped by the gender and other social constructs of their worlds.

Subjects: Alternate history • Feminism • War

Read-Alikes: Michael Cunningham's *The Hours* has a similar scheme, following three people through a parallel day in their lives.

Sawyer, Robert.

The Neanderthal Parallax. **B**

Two Earths, ours and an alternate in which Neanderthals remained the dominant hominids, come into contact through a physics experiment that inadvertently captures a scientist from the Neanderthal world. The books explore the cultural and technological differences between the two alternates; most interesting is that the Neanderthals all seem to be bisexual, with interesting implications for their family structures.

Subjects: Alternate history • Diplomacy • Genetic modification • Love • Murder • Neanderthals

Read-Alikes: *Primal Skin,* by Leona Benkt Rhys, introduces Skin, a bisexual human-Neanderthal hybrid who is also a female shaman investigating a murder.

Hominids. New York: Tor, 2002.

Ponter, a Neanderthal scientist from an alternate universe, is pulled into our world, leaving behind his male lover to face trial for his murder.

Humans. New York: Tor, 2003.

Ponter leads an ambassadorial delegation to our Earth and invites his Homo sapiens friend, Mary, to cross back to his world.

Hybrids. New York: Tor, 2003.

Mary and Ponter decide to have a child together, with the help of the advanced science of the Neanderthals.

Psychic Powers

Like time travel and contact with alien species, the hidden powers of the mind (ranging from telekinesis to the more intimate touches of telepathy) have long appeared in SF writing. Blending these powers with same-sex bonds illuminates such linkages from the inside out, and they are used as the basis of the construction of social orders. While the most colorful of these is arguably Marion Zimmer Bradley's Order of Renunciates in the Darkover Series, the worlds of Menvannen and the Silents, created by Stephen Harper and Liz Williams, also offer options in the use of silent communication. Gays and lesbians of all ages experience a form of this during their periods of self-acceptance and coming out, as they learn to identify others like themselves.

Bradley, Marion Zimmer (selected titles from each series).

Darkover Series.

Darkover is a planet settled from Earth, then cut off from humanity for centuries. Technology has receded, but many of the inhabitants develop psychic powers in compensation. Same-sex attraction and group marriages appear in many of the books in this lengthy series, but the ones with the strongest GLBT theme are highlighted here.

Subjects: Coming out • Politics • Psychics

The Heritage of Hastur. New York: Daw Books, 1975. **G**

Two childhood friends, Lew Alton and Regis Hastur, struggle against the Terran Empire's attempt to conquer the planet Darkover. To unblock the channels of the psychic power that will help his side prevail, Regis must stop fighting his feelings and accept his homosexuality.

Read-Alikes: Only by coming to terms with his own sexuality is the main character in Geoff Ryman's *Lust* able to have a healthy and happy sex life.

The Saga of the Renunciates. **L B**

The Renunciates are a group of Darkover women who have separated from the patriarchal and oppressive Darkover society. This saga is the story of Magda, a Darkover-born Terran spy who infiltrates the Renunciates in an attempt to rescue her husband—but finds more appeal in their society.

Subject: Feminism • Psychics • Slavery • War

Read-Alikes: The Hadra Series, by Diana Rivers, also finds psychic women standing apart from the men who have oppressed them.

Shattered Chain. New York: DAW Books, 1983.

A group of Renunciates goes into the Dry Towns, a desolate region where women are kept as slaves and breeding stock, and rescues a pregnant woman and her daughter, Jaelle. Jaelle watches her mother die in childbirth; embittered by the experience, she joins the Renunciates to seek vengeance against the Dry Towns. Meanwhile Magda, of Terran stock but raised on Darkover, disguises herself as a Free Amazon to find and free her husband from bandits. Her subterfuge is discovered, however, and she must join the Renunciates or abandon her search.

Thendara House. New York: DAW Books, 1983.

> The women of the Free Amazons require the Terran Magda to fulfill her oath to them and serve housebound time in their residence in the capital of Thendara. In the process, Magda learns much about herself and her relationship with Jaelle, who is working in an exchange program with the Terrans—and Magda's ex-husband.

City of Sorcery. New York: DAW Books, 1984.

> A Terran craft crashes, and Alexis, its pilot, staggers out of the wilderness with vague recollections of a city of dark power drawing her back. Terrans and Renunciates alike try to find Alexis before she finds the City of the Sisterhood and brings upon herself the wrath of its rulers.

Harper, Stephen.

The Silent Empire. **G**

The Silent are the psychic backbone of the Terran Empire, communicating across vast distances in the Dream. When the Dream is disrupted, Kendi, a powerful Silent youth, investigates and eliminates the problems.

Subjects: Coming-of-age • Murder • Psychics • Slavery

Read-Alikes: Tanya Huff's *Blood Books* and Marc Del Franco's *Unshapely Things* also have detectives with supernatural powers and friends.

Nightmare: A Novel of the Silent Empire. New York: Roc, 2002.

> When the colony ship carrying Kendi and his family is pirated en route, the family is sold as slaves. Kendi turns out to be a Silent—able to communicate telepathically—so he is rescued from a life of drudgery and sent for training on a planet of Silents. Unfortunately, there's a murderer in their midst. As Kendi helps investigate the murders —and becomes a target himself—he falls for Ben, the non-Silent teen son of his private instructor.

Dreamer: A Novel of the Silent Empire. New York: Roc, 2001.

> A series of storms is disrupting the Dream that allows the Silents to communicate across the empire they serve, leaving dead and severely hurt Silent in its wake. Kendi, seeking freedom for the Silent, must stop the storms so he can reach them; Sejal, a free but poor Silent, may have the power to help him—but may also be the source of the disturbance.

Trickster: A Novel of the Silent Empire. New York: Roc, 2003.

> Kendi leads a bare-bones space expedition to find missing family members of the Silent, against a backdrop of a collapsing economy and an amped-up slave trade.

Offspring: A Novel of the Silent Empire. New York: Roc, 2004.

> Again, the Dream is disrupted, and only a few strong Silent can enter it—triggering the end of the imperial economy, massive trade collapse, and the fall of governments. Kendi seeks a murderer, in hopes of expelling him from the Dream and restoring imperial communications.

Williams, Liz.

Ghost Sister. New York: Bantam Books, 2001. **G L B**

Menvannen's landblindness, her incapacitating inability to connect psychically with her world, makes her a burden to her family. When her brother and protector takes her deep into the wilderness in a desperate attempt to heal her, she meets an offworld anthropologist who offers her a real chance at a cure—if the rest of the exploring party can be kept from destroying the planet's delicate balance.

Subjects: Disability • Ecology • Genetic modification • Psychics • Religion

Read-Alikes: Anne Rice's *Interview with the Vampire* and *The Vampire Lestat* introduce characters much like the colonists when the change comes upon them.

Space Opera

Possibly the best known of all SF genres, and the most popular, as witnessed by the phenomenon of the *Star Wars* films, this subgenre has a public media history reaching back to the first science fiction radio program, *Buck Rogers*, which ran for fifteen years starting in 1932. Tales of this kind mirror the action-oriented, sword-and-sorcery plots common in fantasy tales, except that in many cases the "magic" is provided by high technology. Topics explored using different approaches to gender are culture shock, interspecies relationships, and the struggle for freedom and dignity.

Arnason, Eleanor.

Ring of Swords. New York: TOR, 1993. **G**

Humans and Hwarhath are each the first intelligent aliens the other has met. Each race considers the other a threat, but the key to peaceful coexistence may lie with Nicholas Sanders, a human traitor and the lover of the Hwarhath military's leader.

Subjects: Aliens • Diplomacy • Space stations

Read-Alikes: In Illian Osidian's *Cat Toy,* human pilot Yai crashes on a planet of felinoid aliens, is captured, and is enslaved.

Brojim, R. C.

Cognate. Burke, VA.: Women's Work Press, 2000. **L T**

Humanity's space force, Explora Command, isn't really comfortable with GLBT spacers, relegating them to serve in the second tier. But hard work and anger have lifted lesbian Dani Forrest to the command of one of Explora's Minority Fleet starships. Fighting off pirates, fascinated by the enigmatic and possibly murderous Captain Ki, Dani must deal with the mysterious emotional disintegration of her crew—and preserve the peace of the galaxy.

Subjects: Diplomacy • Pirates • Religion • Space flight

Read-Alikes: In Gun Brooke's *Protector of the Realm,* the commander of a space station captures a dangerous fugitive—and, once the dust settles, the two women have married and are exploring their feelings for each other.

Bujold, Lois McMaster.

Ethan of Athos. New York: Baen Books, 1986. **G**

> For centuries, the planet Athos has maintained an all-male human population by using artificial wombs. When the ovarian cultures they rely on begin giving out—and the replacement genetic material the Athos government purchases is sabotaged—Dr. Ethan Urquhart is sent off-planet to find a new supplier. Within minutes of his arrival on Klein Station, Ethan meets his first woman, Elli Quinn, and plunges into the world of interstellar intrigue.

> **Subjects:** Biology • Espionage • Humor • Medicine • Space stations

> **Read-Alikes:** This book is an adjunct to the main plotlines in Bujold's Miles Vorkosigan Adventures—so far off the main line Miles himself does not show up. This is the only book in that series with significant GLBT content, but readers who enjoy *Ethan of Athos* should be introduced to the whole series. In *Glory Season*, David Brin created an all-woman world thrown into turmoil by the visit of a male diplomat.

11

Clarke, Arthur C.

🏵 *Imperial Earth: A Fantasy of Love and Discord.* New York: Harcourt Brace Jovanovich, 1976. **B**

> Since its earliest days as an independent republic, Titan has been led by the Makenzie family. Duncan, the latest in this line, travels to Earth to celebrate the quincentennial of the Declaration of Independence and stumbles into a mystery that involves two of his former lovers.

> **Awards:** Gaylactic Spectrum Hall of Fame, 2001.

> **Subjects:** Cloning • Coming-of-age • Politics • Relationships

> **Read-Alikes:** *The Vintner's Luck*, by Elizabeth Knox, comes close to the same mood, perhaps because its pastoral French setting matches the parochialism of Makenzie's Titan.

Delany, Samuel.

Stars in My Pockets, Like Grains of Sand. Middletown, CT: Wesleyan University Press, 2004 (1984). **G** **B**

> In a galaxy of 6,000 world-cultures, the lone survivor of a ruined planet and the scion of an ancient human-alien family find in each other their ideal mate. This sensuous yet deeply philosophical work explores the many ways people bond and share knowledge.

> **Subjects:** Families • Ritual • Slavery

> **Read-Alikes:** *Waking Beauty*, by Paul Witcover, takes an intense look at the way people connect. Storm Constantine's *Thorn Boy* also looks at the intersection of love and slavery.

Gerrold, David.

Starsiders Trilogy (aka Dingilliad). G Teen

The dysfunctional Dingillian family escapes Earth just as its economy begins a final collapse. As they travel, first to the moon, then the stars, they bring their problems along, as well as a prize everyone is after.

Subjects: Artificial intelligence • Coming-of-age • Divorce • Economics • Families • Humor

🏅 *Jumping Off the Planet.* New York: Tor, 2000.

A divorced father suggests to his three boys a trip to the moon via the Ecuador Beanstalk. Their lesbian mother chases after them, claiming kidnapping and custodial interference; meanwhile, countless strangers (including Mickey, the new boyfriend of the oldest son) take an inordinate interest in the affairs of the dysfunctional Dingillian family—and in the toy monkey the youngest child carries.

Awards: Gaylactic Spectrum Award, 2001.

Bouncing off the Moon. New York: Tor, 2001.

Earth is in turmoil, its economy and governments splintering. The Dingillian boys, newly divorced from their parents, and Mickey make it to the moon with the assistance of the mysterious Alexei, only to find themselves and their mysterious monkey (which is revealed to be an advanced artificial intelligence) at the center of a massive manhunt.

Leaping to the Stars. New York: TOR, 2002.

The reunited and expanded Dingillian family books passage on one of the last outbound colony ships, escaping the clutches of both the Lunar Authority and the Free Luna movement. But the Lunatics aren't the only ones desperate for the powerful artificial intelligence resident in their toy monkey. War breaks out as the various Earth colonies vie to control it. And the monkey seems to have an agenda all its own.

Park, Severna.

Emirate Novels. L

In the star empire of the Emirate, slaves are controlled by a virus that provides them health and youth for twenty years, then an excruciating death. Slowly losing a war, the Emirate is collapsing, giving hope but no certain future to the slaves.

Subjects: Genetic modification • Medicine • Psychics • Slavery • War

Read-Alikes: Samuel Delany, in his <u>Return to Neveryon</u> series, has written about slavery and its lasting impact on the owner and the owned.

Hand of Prophecy. New York: Avon Eos, 1998.

Frenna, a slave, learns of a cure for the controlling virus as she watches her lover survive the viral attack. Then, during a raid on her planet, she escapes one slaver only to be taken by another and is pressed into service as a medic in a gladiatorial arena. Her fight for freedom merges with her research into the cure as she uses friends, foes, and family politics to advance her cause.

Speaking Dreams. Ithaca, NY: Firebrand Books, 1992.

> A young woman who can see the future is sold into servitude. Together with the diplomat who becomes her owner, she struggles against slavers and allied aliens, in a tale of galactic intrigue.

Perry, Steve.

The Matador Series. B

The Matadors are men and women of principle, first opposing a corrupt and oppressive Galactic Confederation and then protecting the Republic that takes its place. They succeed through the mental discipline taught by their spiritual leader, Pen.

Subjects: Martial arts • Politics • Soldiers and sailors• Spirituality

Read-Alikes: In Diane Duane's <u>The Tale of the Five</u>, a young magic user gathers friends and allies to help him drive out the evil usurper who has taken his lover's throne.

The 97th Step. New York: Ace Books, 1989.

> This is the story of Pen, the man who teaches mental discipline to Khadaji, and is a prequel to *The Man Who Never Missed*. Pen moves from poverty as a child through adolescent woes and into the wisdom that comes with survival.

The Man Who Never Missed. New York: Ace Books, 1985.

> During battle, Emile Khadaji realizes how wrong are the methods of the Galactic Confederation he serves. He goes to ground in a garrison town, running a bar that serves the occupying soldiers—and recruits a force to end the oppression with a minimum of violence.

Matadora. New York: Berkley Publishing, 1986.

> Khadaji is out of the picture, but his revolution lives on. His bouncer, Dirisha Zuri, has gone underground but remembers his leadership; she moves to train as an elite bodyguard, but when the Confed closes down the school, she takes on the new task of rescuing Pen, the movement's spiritual leader.

The Machiavelli Interface. New York: Ace Books, 1986.

> The Matadors have begun to directly fight the Galactic Confederation and its leader, Marcus Wall. Outlawed and harried, the Matadors are still the galaxy's last, best hope for peace and freedom.

The Albino Knife. New York: Berkley, 1991.

> Since the demise of the Confederation, peace has reigned in the galaxy—but suddenly the Republic's first president is assassinated, and the Matadors must again defend freedom.

Robinson, Frank M.

🐾 *The Dark Beyond the Stars.* New York: Tor, 1997 (1991). G B

> Exploring an alien world, Sparrow loses his memory in a near-fatal mishap. After his convalescence, he returns to work on the *Astron*, a deterio-

rating generation ship searching for extraterrestrial intelligence, and tries to recover his past. But his computer access is restricted, his crewmates won't talk—and all the accidents he's having convince Sparrow that someone is out to kill him.

Subjects: Amnesia • Exploration • Mental health

Awards: Lambda Literary Award, 1991.

Read-Alikes: Octavia Butler's *Fledgling* has as its main character a female vampire-human hybrid with amnesia, who works out that she is important enough that a band of rogue vampires wants to kill her.

Wolfe, Chris Anne.

Aggar Series. [L]

Amazons, elite women soldiers from another planet, find a home with the psychically gifted women of medieval Aggar, as the Terran Empire crumbles.

Subjects: Espionage • Psychics • Search and rescue • Soldiers and sailors

Read-Alikes: The Hadra Series, by Diana Rivers, has a society of psychics working to create and defend a woman-centric culture.

Shadows of Aggar. Norwich, VT: New Victoria Publishers, 1991.

> On her last mission before returning from a medieval planet to her woman-only Amazon world, Diana must find and rescue a crashed Terran pilot. To help her in this task, she is assigned Elana, a native guide with psychic powers. As the two struggle to find the downed pilot and prevent an intergalactic war, they become romantically entangled.

Fires of Aggar. Norwich, VT: New Victoria Publishers, 1994.

> Generations after the events in *Shadows of Aggar*, the Terran Empire has fallen. Just before its collapse, the Amazons established a colony on Aggar and still help protect it from the depredations of raiders. Gwyn, the leader of the Amazons, rides to the aid of the psychically gifted Llinolae, ruler of Khirla, and falls in love.

Futurecrime

Criminal activity in future societies has been depicted in SF writing for decades, with many famous works such as Isaac Asimov's 1954 classic *The Caves of Steel* taking the reader into the ongoing battle to define and defend the limits of society. This concept of criminality has been widely utilized as a plot framework to explore the moralities of future social orders based on everything from variants of the corporate state where the elite rule to mythical biographies of crime victims. Same-gender relationships are present as a given feature of the world and are used to discuss broader issues of freedom (both personal and human) and its preservation and defense.

Burroughs, William S.

🎗 *Wild Boys: A Book of the Dead.* New York: Grove Press 1992 (1971). **G**
Feral boys fight governmental and societal oppression and engage in repetitive, primitive sex.

Awards: Publishing Triangle's 100 Best Lesbian and Gay Novels, Reader's Choice

Subjects: Sadomasochism • Sex • War

Read-Alikes: *Dance of the Warriors,* by Kevin Esser, mixes religious fanaticism and sexual abuse.

Dorsey, Candas Jane.

A Paradigm of Earth. New York: Tor, 2001. **B**
In a near-future Canada taken over by social and sexual conservatives, Morgan converts the house her parents left her into a refuge for sexual, artistic, and political iconoclasts. Emotionally empty, she discovers a kindred spirit in Blue, an enigmatic, androgynous alien and information sponge constructed by his masters to learn about Earth by becoming human.

Subjects: Aliens • Canada and Canadians • Mental health • Murder

Read-Alikes: In Elizabeth Knox's *The Vintner's Luck,* an angel learns about humanity and, in so doing, helps a farmer discover himself.

Eskridge, Kelley.

Solitaire. New York: Eos, 2002. **L**
Ren "Jackal" Segura, born at the dawn of a new age and the Hope of her company/state, was given every advantage—the best teachers, the choice assignments, the deference of everyone around her. But her mother angrily reveals a secret that shatters Ren's self-confidence. When the friends who could help her recover are killed in a terrible accident for which Ren is blamed, she must suffer in a virtual world until her lover can come to her rescue.

Subjects: Class conflict • Corporations • Prison • Virtual reality

Read-Alikes: Ren is manipulated into her roles as savior and scapegoat, much like Ender, the main character in Orson Scott Card's *Ender's Game.*

Griffith, Nicola.

🎗 *Slow River.* New York: Ballantine Books, 1995. **L**
From one of the most powerful families on Earth, Lore Van Oesterling was used to deference and respect. But one morning she wakes, bleeding and naked, in a dank alley. Spanner walks in, patches her up, and teaches her how to survive on the streets—and to hide from her enemies. This new life of deception and crime eats at Lore; to really survive she has to be reborn one last time, leave Spanner, and integrate her old self with the woman she has become.

Subjects: Class conflict • Coming-of-age • Crime • Ecology

Awards: Lambda Literary Award, 1995; Gaylactic Spectrum Hall of Fame, 2000.

Read-Alikes: In Lynn Flewelling's <u>Nightrunners Series</u>, an elf takes in a young human and trains him as a thief, assassin, and spy.

Nissenson, Hugh.

Song of the Earth. Chapel Hill, NC: Algonquin Books of Chapel Hill, 2001. **G** **T**

Murdered in an artistic dispute at the height of his career, genetically engineered artist John Firth Baker is the subject of this near-future fictional biography, organized around his e-mails, letters, diary entries, and images of his work.

Subjects: Art and artists • Genetic modification • Murder • War

Utopia/Dystopia

The concept of a perfect social order in which all forces are in balance and every citizen possesses equal rights and standing has been a literary device since long before Thomas More coined the term "utopia" for his book by that name. The centrality of the struggle for civil rights by people with different sexual orientations and gender identification finds expression in the worlds of SF as well. Alternative societies are based on a range of reconfigurations of the status of male and female (examples being Gearhart's classic *Wanderground* and Suzy Charnas's *Holdfast Chronicles*), the dominant use of reproductive technologies, and even the challenge of contact with alien species, presenting the reader with thought-provoking options to consider. And while the favored group finds bliss in its ideal society, the excluded or downtrodden generally suffer a hellish dystopia.

Charnas, Suzy McKee.

🎗 The Holdfast Chronicles. **L**

Most of the world perished from pollution and war, but a few families held on in the bunkers of the Holdfast. This culture, cruel and domineering, is inherently unstable but still does a lot of damage to those in its clutches—particularly the women, enslaved as a breeding population. Outside the Holdfast, though, are its enemies—escaped slaves of the Holdfast and the Motherlines, women with no need of men.

Awards: Gaylactic Spectrum Hall of Fame, 2003

Subjects: Families • Feminism • Genetic modification • Slavery

Read-Alikes: Monique Wittig's *Les Guérillères* portrays the beginnings of the fight by women warriors against the patriarchy.

🎗 *Walk to the End of the World.* New York, Ballantine Books, 1974.

The Holdfast is a brutal, post-apocalyptic world based on subjugation, where women are slaves for breeding and labor, and where young men are dominated by their seniors. When the young men rise in revolt, Alldera, raped and pregnant, finds her way to freedom.

Awards: James Tiptree, Jr. Memorial Retrospective Award, 1995.

🌳 *Motherlines.* New York: Berkley Publishing, 1978.

> Rescued by the Motherlines, a tribe of women who reproduce through cloning, Alldera is nursed back to health and gives birth. Though she finds love among these women, she cannot adapt to their ways.

Awards: James Tiptree, Jr. Memorial Retrospective Award, 1995.

Furies. New York: Tor, 1994.

> Having left the Motherlines for the Free Fems, former slaves who have found their way to freedom in the wilderness, Alldera inspires them to return to the Holdfast to free their sisters.

🌳 *Conqueror's Child.* New York: Tor, 1999.

> Sorrel, the child Alldera abandoned with the Motherlines, rides for the Holdfast to claim her mother's love but must protect her own son from being enslaved by the victorious women.

Awards: James Tiptree, Jr. Memorial Award, 1999.

Delany, Samuel.

🌳 *Dhalgren.* New York: Bantam Books, 1975. **B**

The Kid, suffering from amnesia, crosses a river into the isolated, decaying city of Bellona. He becomes leader of one of the local tribes, finds himself in an intense three-way affair with a woman and a teen boy, explores the city, and writes a book that seems to be Dhalgren itself.

Awards: Gaylactic Spectrum Hall of Fame, 2002.

Subjects: Amnesia • Authors • Exploration

Read-Alikes: Nalo Hopkinson's *Brown Girl in the Ring* is set in a near-future Toronto whose inner core is in ruins.

Forrest, Katherine.

Daughters Novels. **L**

Women escape a disturbingly patriarchal society by hiding on the planet Maternas. But eventually they must emerge to protect their sisters from the tyrants.

Subjects: Ecology • War

Read-Alikes: In the <u>Hadra Series</u>, by Diana Rivers, the Hadra, too, flee an oppressive, male-dominated society and establish their own culture.

Daughters of a Coral Dawn. Los Angeles: Alyson Books, 2002 (1984).

> Women plot to flee near-slave conditions on a male-dominated future Earth. They establish themselves on their own world, Maternas, where they build a new, just culture without men. Eventually, a spaceship mostly crewed by men comes across Maternas; the women are faced with the unpalatable choice of killing the men or letting them reveal the existence of Maternas to a still-tyrannical Earth.

9

10

12

13

14

15

16

Daughters of an Amber Noon. Los Angeles: Alyson Books, 2002.

> Women left behind form Unity, a colony in Death Valley, where they hide underground from an evil dictator determined upon their elimination. Shifting points of view tell a desperate story of survival.

Daughters of an Emerald Dusk. Los Angeles: Alyson Books, 2005.

> The women of Unity rejoin their children on Maternas but find that fifty years of separation means they have different visions for the future.

Livia, Anna.

Bulldozer Rising. London: Onlywomen, 1988. **L**

> In a future run by the young, it is a serious breach of the law to live past forty. But several women band together to find an alternative to the required suicide: For some, love is the answer.

Subjects: Age differences • Love

Read-Alikes: Doug Guinan's *California Screaming* takes a somewhat lighter but still satirical look at youth culture.

Marley, Louise.

The Terrorists of Irustan. New York: Ace Books, 1999. **L T**

> By the code of the Second Prophet, the women of Irustan are kept secluded, veiled, and controlled by the men. The mendicant Zahra, using cast-off medical technology from Earth, treats the women and children of her community. Appalled by case after case of brutal abuse and neglect, she rebels, but her vigilante justice draws down on her the full weight of outraged tradition.

Subjects: Class conflict • Feminism • Healhcare workers • Religion

Read-Alikes: Rachel Pollack's *Godmother Night* has as its eponymous character a fierce protector of women.

McHugh, Maureen.

🌳 *China Mountain Zhang.* New York: Tom Doherty Associates, 1992. **G**

> In a world dominated by Chinese Marxism, Engineer Zhang is marginalized by the circumstances of his birth, his homosexuality, and a basically passive nature. He finds himself, and love, sliding between the cracks of the rigid system. A second plotline deals with the colonization of Mars.

Awards: Lambda Literary Award, 1992; James Tiptree, Jr. Memorial Award, 1992; Gaylactic Spectrum Award Hall of Fame, 1999.

Subjects: Coming-of-age • Homophobia • Politics • Race relations

Read-Alikes: The alternate history *Fire on the Mountain*, by Terry Bisson, has a similar structure: people just trying to live, not do anything special. In one of the plot threads the socialist state of Nova Africa, product of John Brown's successful 1859 raid on Harper's Ferry, is sending an expedition to Mars.

Moffett, Judith.

Hefn Series. G T

9

The Hefn, masters of time, come back at the bidding of another race to teach humanity to live in harmony, with the earth and with each other. The books focus on the lives of a few people who meet the Hefn, rather than on the greater societal changes that result from their dominance.

Subjects: Aliens • Ecology • Kentucky • Religion • Time travel

Read-Alikes: Other strong statements about the importance of the balance of nature are *Oryx and Crake*, by Margaret Atwood, and *Sacrament*, by Clive Barker.

10

The Ragged World. New York: St. Martin's Press, 1991.

At the start of the twenty-first century, Earth's ecology is struggling to survive. Then the Hefn, gnomish galactic eco-enforcers, arrive to demand humanity restore the natural balance within nine years, or face extinction.

11

Time, Like an Ever-Rolling Stream. New York: St. Martin's Press, 1992.

The Hefn have occupied Earth, firmly but benevolently. One of the Hefn, Humphrey, has even begun training some of the brightest human teens in the intricate art of time travel. Hefn policies, though, particularly punishment by mind-wipe and a ban on procreation, have led to rebellion and are working against the restoration of Earth.

12

Starhawk.

The Fifth Sacred Thing. New York: Bantam Books, 1993. B

Transformed by peaceful revolution into a New Age paradise free of hunger and thirst, poverty, and prejudice, San Francisco provides an example to the rest of the world. When the Stewards, oppressive and intolerant rulers of the rest of what was the United States, send in a conquering army, the people of the city must find a way to resist without forsaking their souls.

13

Subjects: California • Nonviolence • Religion • War

Read-Alikes: A few centuries in the future, Ursula K. Le Guin's *Always Coming Home* shows a matriarchy in tune with nature, defending their Napa Valley civilization against a warlike, hierarchical, male-dominated tribe.

14

Womack, Jack.

Random Acts of Senseless Violence. London: HarperCollins, 1993. L

Twelve-year-old Lola is suddenly uprooted as the anarchy of the outside world invades her life of privilege. Her parents are unable to find decent work; the family descends into poverty. But with the help of friends in her new neighborhood, Lola learns to survive on the streets.

15

Subjects: Class conflict • Gangs • Martial law • New York City

Read-Alikes: In *Waking Beauty*, by Paul Witcover, a young woman is thrown into a grim life she never expected when, by chance, she loses her man to the wild wood. Nalo Hopkinson's *Brown Girl in the Ring* is set in a violent, partially abandoned future Toronto.

16

Short Stories

GLBT characters are also in the predominant form of SF, the short story. The first major anthology to collect this genre was *Kindred Spirits*, issued in 1984 by gay-owned Alyson Publications, followed in 1986 by *Worlds Apart: An Anthology of Lesbian and Gay Science Fiction and Fantasy.* The growth in recognition of GLBT threads in science fiction can be seen in the pages of the third major collection, *Flying Cups and Saucers*, issued twelve years later in 1998 and containing many of the winners of the first five years of the James Tiptree, Jr. Award, established in 1991 as an annual literary prize for science fiction or fantasy that expands or explores our understanding of gender. Readers can use this and its most recent successor, one of the two *Bending the Landscape* anthologies, as guides to identifying authors.

Short Story Collections (Single Author)

Gearheart, Sally Miller.

Wanderground: Stories of the Hill Women. Watertown, MA: Persephone Press, 1978. **L**

> In a series of connected stories, women have left the cities (and men) behind and developed psychic powers of communication and healing. In the lesbian utopia of Wanderground, consensus, not conflict, is valued. But as men move out from the cities, the women prepare to defend themselves.
>
> **Subjects:** Anthologies • Ecology • Psychics • War
>
> **Read-Alikes:** In the <u>Hadra Series</u>, by Diana Rivers, women flee the cities of men and establish their own society, developing psychic powers that help them defend it.

Short Story Anthologies (Multiple Authors)

DeCarnin, Camilla, Eric Garber, and Lyn Paleo, eds.

Worlds Apart: An Anthology of Lesbian and Gay Science Fiction and Fantasy. Boston: Alyson Publications, 1986. **G L**

> This group of eleven lesbian and gay short stories includes offerings from prominent authors Samuel Delany, Joanna Russ, James Tiptree Jr., and Jewelle Gomez. The anthology is mostly science fiction, with a few fantasy stories.
>
> **Subjects:** Anthologies • Cloning • Homophobia • Love
>
> **Read-Alikes:** Readers will find some of the same authors in *Swords of the Rainbow*. Readers seeking more fantasy may want to explore *Bending the Landscape: Fantasy.*

Elliot, Jeffrey M, ed.

Kindred Spirits. An Anthology of Gay and Lesbian Science Fiction Stories. Boston: Alyson Publications, 1984. **G L** ⏚

> These gay and lesbian science fiction and fantasy stories include several that have been anthologized elsewhere. Still, it is an interesting early compilation of speculative GLBT fiction.
>
> **Subjects:** Anthologies • Feminism • Homophobia • Love • Relationships

Read-Alikes: The comics collection *Prime Cuts*, by Howard Stangroom and Stephen Lowther, contains several SF stories. *The Future Is Queer*, edited by Richard Labonte and Lawrence Schimel, is a more recent GLBT SF anthology that looks at many of the same themes.

Griffith, Nicola, and Stephen Pagel, eds.

Bending the Landscape: Science Fiction. Woodstock, NY: Overlook Press, 1998. **G L**

This collection of twenty-one stories by straight and queer authors explores science fiction with a GLBT theme.

Awards: Lambda Literary Award, 1998; Gaylactic Spectrum Award, 1999

Subjects: Aliens • Anthologies • Love • Relationships

Read-Alikes: Readers may also want to look at Griffith and Pagel's other two anthologies, *Bending the Landscape: Fantasy* and *Bending the Landscape: Horror*.

Notkin, Debbie, ed.

Flying Cups and Saucers: Gender Explorations in Science Fiction and Fantasy. Cambridge, MA: Edgewood Press, 1998. **G L T**

Each story in this collection of winners and finalists from the first five years of the James Tiptree, Jr. Award expands the concept of gender identity and sex roles. Nearly all do so with GLBT characters or major themes, but even the few that do not are definitely gender-bending. The 1991–1997 and retrospective winners and finalists are listed in an appendix.

Subjects: Anthologies • Couples • Gender identity • Gender roles • Love

Read-Alikes: In the James Tiptree, Jr. Award Anthology Series (three volumes so far, with a fourth promised for 2008), winners, runners-up, and other authors pay tribute to Alice Sheldon, who wrote as James Tiptree Jr. for a decade before her identity was revealed.

Chapter 12

Horror Fiction

Definition

Horror fiction is best defined as those stories and tales designed to deliciously and deliberately frighten and terrify their readers through the portrayal of beings and situations that challenge accepted and known limits of reality.

Description and Characteristics

The diverse genre of horror fiction has long been home to a variety of behaviors and beings considered by mainstream society to be beyond acceptability. The beings that inhabit the pages of horror embody fear in natures that both allure and terrify. Familiar boundaries are either nonexistent or seen to be just one possibility in a wider universe. The objects of fear and their relationships to other inhabitants of the story and to the living provide opportunities to explore questions of identity, social roles, limitations, and issues of belief and emotion in an environment defined from the first page as different. The dubious reputation of horror stems partly from its subject matter (disapproval of serious belief in such creatures as vampires or the power of curses and possession has long been a part of public and religious education) and its use as the source of plots for comic books, often associated with sensational art. A basic pattern of the horror story is the collision of a familiar world with an entire realm where basic assumptions no longer apply—whether trust, sexual orientation, appropriate behavior, or even life and death.

History and Development

Deriving enjoyment from being terrified became a prominent effect of modern fiction in the late eighteenth century, with authors using creatures drawn from European folklore (e.g., vampires, werewolves, goblins, and fairy folk) or from the Christian spiritual universe (e.g., angels and demons). The earliest works of horror to incorporate themes of homosexuality were gothic novels, in which the GLBT subject appears as a secondary or minor character within the larger context of the story, rather than as its protagonist.

The nineteenth century, with its ambivalent attitude toward sexuality in general, and women's sexuality in particular, witnessed a continued fascination with the forbidden and a more open framing of same-gender relationships. Examples of the trend are John Polidori's 1819 work *The Vampyre*, Sheridan Le Fanu's 1872 *Carmilla* (in which the heroine shares a roof with the title vampiric character), and Oscar Wilde's famed *The Picture of Dorian Grey*, published in 1891. Although not as heavy in style as its Victorian predecessors, horror fiction of the first four decades of the twentieth century was shaped by the existence of magazines devoted to mass audiences. Among the better known is *Weird Tales*, which began publication in 1923. These inexpensive and widely read publications greatly expanded public awareness of horror as a literary genre and laid the groundwork for the later popularity of sinister plots. Appearing during this time were such works as Isidore Ducasse's *Lay of Maldoror* (1924), Natalie Barney's *The One Who Is Legion* (1930), and George Viereck's *Gloria* (1952). Contemporary work also augmented the relative lack of tales by mainstream authors that could be adapted into popular film scripts. A notable and enduring example is the 1963 film adaptation of Shirley Jackson's 1959 novel *The Haunting of Hill House* (redone in color in 1999 as *The Haunting*), which featured a frankly bisexual character who attempts to establish a relationship with the protagonist. During the homophile era of the 1960s, with its relatively more receptive public atmosphere, novels of horror reflected more closely lesbian and gay realities. An example is Maureen Duffy's thoughtful 1966 work *Microcosm*, among whose subjects are the ghosts of women who patronized a certain bar.

The Stonewall Riots in 1969 set the stage for the appearance of works in which gay and lesbian beings (human and inhuman) would be frankly depicted as fully realized characters, rather than as one-dimensional plot elements or stereotyped figures. Following the explosive popularity of Anne Rice's pair of male vampires, Louis and Lestat, in *Interview with the Vampire* (1976), came novels by writers such as Chelsea Quinn Yarbro, Jewelle Gomez, Poppy Z. Brite, and Clive Barker. This dynamic mixture of GLBT life with the classic forms of horror presents a delightful challenge to both readers and librarians.

Issues for the Readers' Advisor

Given the broad spectrum of this genre, the best approach for the readers' advisor may be to offer patrons unfamiliar with the genre, a particular author, a collection, or an anthology. This will allow them to acquire an idea of the limits and content of the genre and help them decide which type most appeals to them. A useful beginning can be made by introducing the subject of GLBT horror through the category of ghost stories, a section of horror that has become more familiar. Gothic romances are often flavored with the atmosphere of unseen menace and can serve to introduce the reader to broader aspects of horror literature. By acquiring background on earlier works and writers, motivated readers can move beyond the authors whose work first attracted them.

Chapter Organization

The chapter has been grouped into sections according to the central types of characters from the realms of night. It will come as no surprise that most of the works deal with the oldest of these, vampires (and their cousins among the undead) and werewolves, and ghosts, demons, and possessions. The idea of curses possessing the power to bring harm to a person or clan across the years is also present. The last section is story collections of GLBT horror, which first appeared in the late 1980s, although as this genre receives more attention, older examples may be unearthed, a project the readers' advisor can suggest to patrons.

Sources

"Ghosts and Horror Fiction." In *glbtq: An Encyclopedia of Gay, Lesbian, Bisexual, Transgender and Queer Culture*. Available at http://www.glbtq.com/literature/ghost_horror.html.

"Gothicism." In *glbtq: An Encyclopedia of Gay, Lesbian, Bisexual, Transgender and Queer Culture*. Available at http://www. glbtq.com/literature/ghost_horror.html.

Queer Horror, http://www.queerhorror. com/.

Vampires and Werewolves

From the time when Bram Stoker wrote the first words of *Dracula* to the twentieth-century tales of Anne Rice and her infamous creation Lestat, the concept of beings who must feed on the blood of the living to survive has been a popular one in fiction around the world. Writers utilizing GLBT themes and characters have continued to add to this tradition in a number of innovative and colorful ways, setting their stories in unconventional locations (e.g., the urbane vampire Desmond's New York and the extremely busy undead community in Toronto), and by exploring the emotional bonds and relationships formed by same-gender pairings, both among vampires and between them and humans.

The idea of gay and lesbian vampires and the concept that one may be recruited into their world by deliberate choice inverts the belief that one's sexual orientation can be determined by personal choice. Of particular interest are the GLBT works that speak for the female ranks of the vampire world, as this species has traditionally been portrayed almost exclusively as male. Their cousin the werewolf also appears, although not as frequently and seldom as a major character, possibly due to the exhaustion of this image by the horror films of the 1950s and 1960s.

See the short stories section of this chapter for collections and anthologies of stories on vampires or werewolves.

Cooke, John Peyton.

Out for Blood. New York: Avon, 1991. **G**

Dying from leukemia, twenty-three-year-old Chris jumped at the chance to join the ranks of the undead. Sent to train with a vampire master, he falls into the middle of a centuries-long struggle between his mentor and a crazed vampire hunter.

Subjects: Conspiracy • Revenge • Vampires

Read-Alikes: In David Thomas Lord's *Bound in Blood,* mother and son vampires battle through the centuries, and the son finds an ally in a man he made undead.

Dietz, Ulysses G.

Desmond: A Novel of Love and the Modern Vampire. Los Angeles: Alyson Books, 1998. **G**

Desmond Beckwith is a nice guy, for a vampire (he leaves his victims alive, if a little depleted), and—even as he faces undead eternity without a partner—he resists converting Roger, the man he loves. Desmond and Roger team up to solve a series of murders that have all the hallmarks of vampiric attack.

Subjects: Murder • New York City • Vampires

Read-Alikes: In Rebecca York's *Killing Moon,* werewolf/private investigator Ross Marshall hunts down a serial killer, assisted by his mortal lover Megan Sheridan.

Edmonson, Roger.

Silverwolf. Austin, TX: Banned Books, 1990. **G**

A series of bloody murders rocks Seattle's gay community. Gay private detective and ex-cop Cliff Davidson finds that the evidence points to a killer who is more than human.

Subjects: Law enforcement personnel • Washington State • Werewolves

Read-Alikes: *Torsos,* by John Peyton Cooke, features a gay detective on the trail of a savage killer that preys on young male prostitutes.

Huff, Tanya.

Blood Books. **G** **B**

Ex-cop P.I. Vicki Nelson teams up with bisexual vampire Henry Fitzroy to solve a series of monstrous mysteries in Toronto. Henry's mortal boyfriend, Tony Foster, and Vicki's ex-partner on the police force, Mike Celluci, jump in at crucial moments of the duo's struggles against werewolves, mummies, and other supernatural bad guys. These books were adapted as the Lifetime TV series *Blood Ties.*

Subjects: Books to film • Canada and Canadians • Magic • Murder • Vampires

Read-Alikes: Marc Del Franco's *Unshapely Things* brings age-old enmities to light as an ex-druid private detective tries to learn who is killing male prostitute fairies. Also, this series has a sequel, Tanya Huff's Smoke Trilogy, which follows Henry and Tony as they move to Vancouver.

Blood Price. New York: DAW Books, 1991.

Ex-cop Vicki Nelson teams up with bisexual vampire Henry Fitzroy and Detective Mike Cellucci to solve a series of supernatural killings in Toronto.

Blood Trail. New York: DAW Books, 1992.

Vicki Nelson, Mike Cellucci, and Henry Fitzroy work together again, to protect a family of werewolves from a fanatical assassin.

Blood Lines. New York: DAW Books, 1992.

A dark power from ancient Egypt rises from the crypt to threaten Toronto; Mike Cellucci calls on Vicki and Henry to help return the mummy to his tomb.

Blood Pact. New York: DAW Books, 1993

Vicki's mother dies, and her body disappears from the funeral home. When her mother's reanimated body comes visiting, Vicki seeks help from her boyfriend, Mike Cellucci, and vampire Henry Fitzroy. Henry's help, though, may come at too great a price.

Blood Debt. New York: DAW Books, 1997.

Now a vampire, Vicki has stayed in Toronto with Mike. Henry has moved to Vancouver, where he is plagued by visits from a handless ghost demanding vengeance. And each time the ghost appears, a murder takes place in the city.

McMahan, Jeffrey N.

Vampires Anonymous: A Novel. Boston: Alyson Publications, 1991.

An experienced vampire, Andrew feels amused contempt for the members of Vampires Anonymous, a twelve-step group dedicated to helping its members fight the urges to drink human blood. The leaders of the group, though, have a hidden agenda—the extermination of the vampires and their way of life.

Subjects: Conspiracy • Politics • Twelve-step programs • Vampires

Read-Alikes: In Jonathan Nasaw's *The World on Blood*, the vampire's thirst is also an addiction that can be solved by a twelve-step program.

Rice, Anne.

The Vampire Chronicles. G B

Lestat de Lioncourt dominates this series. Imperious, sometimes cruel, Lestat is a self-taught vampire, seeking after his origins and thus bringing to life a secret history of vampirism reaching back to the dawn of civilization. There is a strong sensual quality to these works, and the main characters, whether vampires or humans, are mostly bisexual.

The first five books, all starring Lestat in a major role, are by far the best of the series. Once Lestat goes into a multibook coma at the end of *Memnoch the Devil*, the series falters.

Subjects: Books to film • Music • Religion • Revenge • Sadomasochism • Vampires

Read-Alikes: Elizabeth Knox's *Daylight* presents a similarly complex and lush world, in which the head vampire resents his maker.

Interview with the Vampire. New York: Ballantine, 2004 (1976).

Louis, a vampire, tells the story of his life and undeath to a young journalist in San Francisco. Seduced by Lestat into undeath in antebellum New Orleans, Louis in his turn recruits the young Claudia. Louis and Claudia, chafing under Lestat's rule, fight to free themselves of his influence and flee to Paris to seek the knowledge and protection of an ancient vampiric coven. Claudia meets her doom, but Louis finds new strength. *Interview with the Vampire* was released as a movie in 1994.

The Vampire Lestat. New York: Ballantine, 2004 (1985).

The violent departure of his vampire offspring Louis and Claudia leaves Lestat weakened and near extinction; he finds refuge in a New Orleans crypt and reemerges during the 1980s to lead a struggling rock band to success, along the way telling the story of his recruitment into the ranks of the undead and his search for the origins of vampirism. Elements of this book appeared with its sequel in the 2002 movie *Queen of the Damned*. *Lestat: The Musical*, based on this book, with music by Elton John and lyrics by Bernie Taupin, premiered in San Francisco in December 2005. *Anne Rice's The Vampire Lestat: The Graphic Novel*, by Faye Perozich, unfortunately no longer in print, collects the twelve issues of her limited-edition comic book.

The Queen of the Damned. New York: Ballantine, 1997 (1988).

Lestat's music has awakened Akasha, the very first vampire. She has plans for a new world order run by her—and all other vampires are told to submit or perish. Merged with Lestat's emergence and musical career from *The Vampire Lestat*, this book was made into the 2002 movie *Queen of the Damned*.

The Tale of the Body Thief. New York: Ballantine, 1997 (1992).

Depressed and looking for a change, Lestat foolishly agrees to swap bodies with a psychic con man, Raglan James. When Raglan disappears with the vampire body, Lestat is forced to deal with human inconveniences—hunger, sleep, even a brush with death from pneumonia. The only person who helps Lestat regain his body is his human friend David Talbot—but after regaining his vampiric abilities, Lestat forces undeath upon David and loses his friendship.

Memnoch the Devil. New York: Ballantine, 1997 (1995).

Although this book fits into the chronology of <u>The Vampire Chronicles</u>, most of the text is taken up with Lestat's tour of heaven, hell, and Earth, led by Memnoch, who also explains the true cosmology. Memnoch was always God's best angel, constantly challenging him to do right by his creation and even now working to improve souls so they can enter heaven. After this tour, Lestat learns he may have been manipulated by Memnoch, goes into a rage, and is restrained by the other vampires. He sinks into a coma, where he stays for the next few books.

The Vampire Armand. New York: Knopf, 1998.

Vampires from around the world, gathered around the comatose Lestat, listen as Armand tells the story of his short life and long undeath—and the powerful, sensual relationship he forged with his vampire mentor, Marius.

Merrick. New York: Knopf, 2000.

> David asks the voodoo queen Merrick (from Rice's <u>Mayfair Witches Series</u>) to raise the ghost of Claudia so Louis can seek absolution for her death. Merrick seeks a price David is reluctant to grant—and Louis may pay a high price as well.

Blood and Gold. New York: Knopf, 2001.

> This is the 2,000-year-long story of the vampire Marius, recruited into the ranks of the undead from the streets of Imperial Rome and assigned to be caretaker of the powerful but slumbering king and queen of the vampires. He later mentors both Armand and Lestat in the ways of the vampire world.

Blackwood Farm. New York: Knopf, 2002.

> Quinn Blackwood seeks help from Lestat in ridding himself of evil spirits, including Goblin, who feeds from Quinn's energy, and Petronilla, the ghost who turned Quinn into a vampire and who is jealous of his mortal lover, Mona Mayfair.

Blood Canticle. New York: Knopf, 2003.

> Mona finds safety only when Quinn and Lestat bring her into the ranks of the undead. The three hunt together, choosing only deserving victims, and Rice pulls together her <u>Vampire Chronicles</u> and <u>Mayfair Witches</u> series.

Schiefelbein, Michael.

The Vampire Series. G B

As a Roman centurion, Victor wanted more than the platonic love offered him by a young Jewish man. His advances rejected, Victor kills and rapes his way through Jerusalem, but escapes justice by becoming a vampire. Rampaging through the centuries, he still longs for love but believes he will never again find it.

Subjects: AIDS • Clergy • Religion • Revenge • Sadomasochism • Vampires

Read-Alikes: John Michael Curlovich's *The Blood of Kings* pits a newly made vampire and his allies against a rival party of undead bent on taking over a fundamentalist Christian group.

Vampire Vow. Los Angeles: Alyson Books, 2001.

> Implacable in his hatred of Christianity, the new religion founded by the man he loved, Victor journeys through the centuries undermining the faith of others, fetching up at last in a Tennessee monastery at the turn of the twenty-first century.

Vampire Thrall. Los Angeles: Alyson Books, 2003.

> Victor continues his lonely mission of undermining Christianity, now in an Italian monastery, where he meets and falls in mutual love with Paul, a visionary artist infected with HIV. Victor resists this attraction until Paul witnesses him taking a victim's blood; Victor is then forced to make Paul his thrall, a completely dependent half-vampire.

Vampire Transgression. New York: St. Martin's Press, 2007.

Paul and Victor live together in Georgetown in violation of the vampire code, which forbids vampires to associate with each other. Both the Dark Kingdom and the Jesuits come after them, but their passions give them strength to resist.

Ghosts, Demons, and Possession

Spirits of the dead who walk the night, or beings who dwell in the shadows at the edges of our daily world, bringing terror and confrontation to the living, often serve as the catalysts for the resolution of ancient conflicts between light and darkness. They also act as messengers, forcing mortals to deal with realities they have striven to avoid or been unaware of until that time. Their casting as partners with GLBT characters focuses on the challenges individuals face in confronting crises of growth. This may be through the offering of ghostly affection, as in *The House at Pelham Falls*; through their desire to train humans in the use of their own dark sides (ultimately making them whole and stronger); or even sometimes through the return of souls from centuries past with unfinished emotional and physical business in the world of light.

Barker, Clive.

🌳 *Sacrament.* New York: HarperCollins, 1997 (1996). **G**

Gay environmentalist Will tries to raise world awareness of the plight of endangered species by writing their stories. An animal attack leaves him in a coma and forced to deal with a demon he met as a child, a creature whose role was to take the lives of the last members of each species.

Awards: Lambda Literary Award, 1996

Subjects: Authors • Coma • Demons • Ecology • Extinction

Read-Alikes: Nancy Kress's *Maximum Light* and Greg Egan's *Teranesia* both deal with the horrible, creeping destruction of the environment.

Bowes, Richard.

🌳 *Minions of the Moon.* New York: Tor, 1999. **G**

Growing up in Hell's Kitchen, gay youth Kevin Grierson survived by allowing his dark side to lead him. As an adult and the proprietor of an antique shop, Kevin finds terror and redemption as his Shadow comes back with a life of its own.

Awards: Lambda Literary Award, 1999

Subjects: Doppelgängers • Murder • New York City • Possession • Substance abuse

Read-Alikes: *Madrugada*, by David May, follows several San Francisco leathermen as they come to terms with the shadows they carry into and out of their relationships.

Brass, Perry.

Warlock: A Novel of Possession. New York: Belhue Press, 2001. **G**

Allen Barrow is a weak, conflicted man. Moving through a New York bathhouse, he is singled out for attention by the brutal but charismatic Destry Powars, who trains him in the dark secrets of his power.

Subjects: Occult • Possession • Sadomasochism

Read-Alikes: Aaron Travis's *Slaves of the Empire* tells another story of erotic dominance, set in ancient Rome.

Chambers, Jane.

Burning. New York: Jove, 1978. **L**

On vacation in New England, two women are possessed by the ghosts of Abigail and Martha, lovers burned as witches by eighteenth-century Puritans.

Subjects: Ghosts • Possession • Supernatural

Read-Alikes: In Lauren Maddison's *Witchfire,* Connor and her lover travel to England to find out who desecrated her grandmother's grave—and learn that current events are tied to their past lives, centuries before.

Huff, Tanya.

Smoke Trilogy. **G** **L** **B**

Vampire Henry Fitzroy and his ex-lover, former hustler Tony Foster, move to Vancouver; Tony gets work as production assistant on a contemporary gothic TV show, *Darkest Night.* In the process, Tony finds he has supernatural powers of his own and sets out to defend his show from otherworldly intruders.

Subjects: Canada and Canadians • Magic • Murder • Television • Vampires

Read-Alikes: Readers will enjoy *Falling,* by M. L. Rhodes, with its evil mage murderer. Also, this trilogy has a prequel, Tanya Huff's Blood Books, in which Henry plays a much larger role.

Smoke and Shadows. New York: DAW Books, 2004.

One of the actresses from the show dies at the hands of a Shadowlord from another universe, bent on infiltrating and seizing our own. Tony, Henry, and Arra Pelindrake, a wizard refugee from the Shadowlord's latest conquest, are Earth's last, best hope.

Smoke and Mirrors. New York: DAW Books, 2005.

Tony uses his nascent wizardly powers to fend off ghosts in the real haunted mansion *Darkest Night* is using as a set. Then he discovers the ghosts were fending off the truly malevolent power based in the house.

Smoke and Ashes. New York: DAW Books, 2006.

Wizard-in-training Tony wards off an approaching Demonic Convergence. Henry steps in to help, but it is the spells Arra left on Tony's laptop that prove crucial.

Martinac, Paula.

🌿 *Out of Time.* Seattle: Seal Press, 1999 (1990). **L**

Susan finds an old photo album filled with pictures of four women who lived and loved each other in the 1920s. These women haunt her dreams and quiet moments, seducing her into a quest for their pasts—and away from her own lover.

Awards: Lambda Literary Award, 1990

Subjects: 1920s • Ghosts

Read-Alikes: The theme of centuries-separated lovers is also found in Laura Adams's Tunnel of Light Series and Ellen Galford's *The Dyke and the Dybbuk.*

Pollack, Rachel.

Temporary Agency. New York: St. Martin's Press, 1994. **L**

In a late-twentieth-century world transformed by a shamanistic revolution, a corrupt government is willing to sacrifice its citizens to ensure its dominance. As a teen, Ellen enlists the aid of lawyer Alison Birkett in the struggle to save her cousin from the dark side. When the same malignant forces resurface ten years later, Ellen and Alison are thrown back together, discovering love as they stave off disaster.

Subjects: Demons • Love • Magic • Politics • Supernatural

Read-Alikes: Readers will also enjoy *Falling*, by M. L. Rhodes, the story of two men investigating murders that may have been performed by an evil wizard.

Weathers, Brenda.

The House at Pelham Falls. Tallahassee, FL: Naiad, 1986. **L B**

Confused but thrilled by her attraction to another woman, an archaeologist goes on sabbatical to write her next book. The house she rents, though, is haunted by a possessive, deadly poltergeist from whom even her new love may not be able to save her.

Subjects: Archaeology • Coming out • Ghosts

Read-Alikes: In *Dark Dreamer*, by Jenifer Fulton, a best-selling lesbian author moves from Manhattan to a haunted house in Maine.

Curses

The dark power of words to harm and heal, and the consequences they set in motion across years and lives, are a stock theme of world mythologies and horrific tales from every continent. Given the widespread use of words to attack GLBT persons (or those perceived to be such), the view of homosexuality as an abnormality, and the mystical status ascribed to gays and lesbians as "two-spirit people" with special spiritual gifts by many cultures, the presence of curses in GLBT horror takes on added dimensions. These range from the price of being made normal, as in *Shadowdance*, to attempting to become perfect, to the growth that comes with accepting one's nature and growing through it. Interwoven into all these stories is the power that lies in the spoken (and in horror, often the unspoken) word and the strength in naming, a process ultimately done by each individual.

Bailey, Robin White.

Shadowdance. Clarkston, GA: White Wolf Publishing, 1996. **G** **B**

Paralyzed since birth, Innowen receives from a passing witch the use of his legs. But this gift comes with a terrible price—each night he must dance, and anyone watching him dance must fulfill his or her darkest desire.

Subjects: Dancing • Love • Magic • War

Read-Alikes: Jaqueline Carey's <u>Kushiel's Legacy</u> series involves a similarly intricate world, with occasional dark magic making life difficult.

Duffy, Stella.

Singling Out the Couples. London: Sceptre, 1998. **G** **L** **T**

A princess without compassion magically transforms herself into the perfect woman to break up three couples, but loses her way when she starts feeling affection for one of her victims.

Subjects: Couples • Love

Read-Alikes: A similar comic edge is found in Henry Cantenacci's *A Deed with No Name* and Ellen Galford's *The Dyke and the Dybbuk.*

Knox, Elizabeth.

The Vintner's Luck. New York: Farrar, Straus & Giroux, 1998. **G** **B**

The young vintner Jobran has the first of his annual meetings with the angel Xas in his father's vineyard. As the nineteenth century progresses, they both learn something about heaven and hell, as Jobran loves and is loved by the male angel and by the Countess de Valday, his friend and patron. But all the while, a killer is on the loose.

Subjects: Angels • Farmers • France • Murder • Religion

Read-Alikes: Anne Rice's *Memnoch the Devil* also shows heaven and hell working together, with occasionally disastrous results.

Reed, Rick.

A Face Without a Heart. Darien, IL: DesignImage Group, 2000. **G** **B**

Beautiful and innocent Chicagoan Gary Adrion sits for a special portrait before setting out on a dissolute, selfish life. He remains young and unaffected by his choices, but his holographic portrait shows the consequences of his acts.

Subjects: Friendship • Holograms • Immortality

Read-Alikes: Another gay modern retelling of *The Picture of Dorian Gray* is Will Self's *Dorian*, which shares black humor with Oscar Wilde's original.

Witcover, Paul.

Waking Beauty. New York: HarperPrism, 1997. **L**

Women who lose their men to Beauty, the seductive scent wafting out from the untamed forest of Herwood, have everything taken from them—their families, their names, their dignity, even their hair. Sold as slaves, generally as prostitutes, these women find salvation in the form of a reincarnated saint of the wildwood and her female lover, who lead a rebellion against the rigid patriarchy. Many familiar fairy tales, slightly skewed, crop up in the intricate background of this crumbling world.

Subjects: Class conflict • Feminism • Politics • Religion • Supernatural

Read-Alikes: The sensual, intricate world built here rivals that of Jacqueline Carey's <u>Kushiel's Legacy</u> series.

Short Stories

Although the visibility of horror novels in recent years may give the reader the impression that the novel is the chief form of fiction designed to frighten, an equally predominant form among writers using GLBT themes has been the short story. Anthologies offer a historical introduction to the long pedigree of lesbian terror tales and explore the contributions to the dark world of gothic writing by gay men. Some anthologies reach back to the nineteenth century (*What Did Miss Darrington See?*), and others show the international, contemporary reach of this genre, with Canadian as well as American authors. Anthologies give the reader an opportunity to sample diverse offerings in the genre, and demonstrate authors' range. Many have been recognized with literary prizes established to encourage and promote quality GLBT writing in all genres, such as the Lambda Literary Award, ensuring that the future of dark tales populated by characters with a variety of sexual orientations will be secure.

Short Story Collections (Single Author)

Gomez, Jewelle.

🐾 *The Gilda Stories.* Ithaca, NY: Firebrand Books, 2005 (1991). **L**

A desperate runaway slave girl is adopted by the vampire Gilda. She joins the ranks of the undead and observes the changing social landscape of America across two centuries.

Awards: Lambda Literary Award, 1991

Subjects: African Americans • Anthologies • Race relations • Vampires

Read-Alikes: Octavia Butler's *Kindred* has an immortal woman protecting her family over the millennia, letting the reader see the culture change.

McMahan, Jeffrey N.

🐾 *Somewhere in the Night: Stories of Suspense.* Boston: Alyson Publications, 1989. **G**

Vampires, vengeance, hauntings, and Halloween all have their place in this set of stories about the macabre.

Awards: Lambda Literary Award, 1989

Subjects: Anthologies • Supernatural • Vampires

Read-Alikes: *Trysts*, by Steve Berman, is another original collection of queer horror and supernatural suspense.

Short Story Anthologies (Multiple Authors)

Brownworth, Victoria A., ed.

Night Bites: Vampire Stories by Women. Seattle: Seal Press, 1996. **L** **B**

Sixteen lesbian, bi, and straight tales give a chilling, lusty, feminist look into the world of vampires.

Subjects: Anthologies • Feminism • Vampires

Read-Alikes: *Dark Angels,* edited by Pam Keesey, contains more stories of feminist and lesbian vampires.

Night Shade: Gothic Tales by Women. Seattle: Seal Press, 1999. **L** **B**

These seventeen straight, bi, and lesbian stories by women focus on transformation—of the everyday into the eerie, the helpless into the hunter, the mythical into the mundane. Only one of the stories was previously published.

Subjects: Anthologies • Feminism • Shapeshifters • Supernatural

Read-Alikes: *Call of the Dark,* edited by Therese Szymanski, presents twenty-three lesbian stories of sensual but supernatural possession or seduction.

Burton, Peter, ed.

Bend Sinister: The Gay Times Book of Disturbing Stories. London: Gay Men's Press, 2002 **G**

Twenty-seven unsettling stories and a poem—psychological thrillers, dark fantasies, and horror— provide a spooky introduction to the genre. Established authors, such as Christopher Bram and Neil Bartlett, as well as newcomers have penned these literary, spine-tingling tales. The introduction, by editor Peter Burton, discusses how gothic literature benefited from the contributions of gay men.

Subjects: Anthologies • Supernatural • Vampires • Werewolves

Read-Alikes: *Bending the Landscape: Fantasy* contains a good leavening of GLBT horror and dark fantasy. Readers may want to look at *Bending the Landscape: Science Fiction* for additional GLBT speculative fiction.

Ford, Michael Thomas, William J. Mann, Sean Wolfe, and Jeff Mann.

Masters of Midnight. New York: Kensington, 2003. **G**

Four authors each contribute an erotically charged novella of gay vampires to this anthology.

Subjects: Anthologies • Erotica • Vampires

Read-Alikes: Find more gay vampires in the anthologies *Brothers of the Night,* edited by Michael Rowe and Thomas Roche, and *Blood Lust,* edited by M. Christian and Todd Gregory.

Griffith, Nicola, and Stephen Pagel, eds.

🎗 *Bending the Landscape: Horror.* Woodstock, NY: Overlook Press, 2001. **G** **L** **B** **T**
Eighteen tales of horror from a GLBT perspective make up this entertaining collection.

Awards: Gaylactic Spectrum Award, 2002

Subjects: Anthologies • Homophobia • Supernatural

Read-Alikes: *Bending the Landscape: Fantasy* contains several pieces of GLBT horror or dark fantasy. Readers may look at *Bending the Landscape: Science Fiction* for additional GLBT speculative fiction.

Keesey, Pam, ed.

Daughters of Darkness: Lesbian Vampire Stories. Pittsburgh: Cleis Press, 1993. **L**
Though female vampires dominated the folklore and early fiction of the genre, readers are hard pressed to find them in most current anthologies. In this anthology, ten established authors help lesbian vampires take back the night.

Subjects: Anthologies • Erotica • Vampires

Read-Alikes: *Blood Sisters,* edited by Bianca de Moss, contains eighteen more stories of lesbian vampires.

Mann, William J., ed.

Grave Passions. Tales of the Gay Supernatural. New York: Masquerade Books, 1997. **G**
These eighteen tales of supernatural obsession, lust, and love, written by prominent gay authors, include quite a bit of humor amid the horror.

Subjects: Anthologies • Ghosts • Humor • Supernatural • Vampires • Werewolves

Read-Alikes: *The Ghost of Carmen Miranda,* edited by Scott Brassart and Julie Trevelyan, is another spooky but ultimately humorous GLBT anthology.

Rowe, Michael, ed.

Queer Fear Anthologies. **G** **L**
These anthologies of gay-themed terror contain offerings from established Canadian and U.S. writers, such as Gemma Files, Michael Thomas Ford, and Robert J. Sawyer, as well as newer talents, like Sèphera Girón and C. Mark Umland.

Subjects: Anthologies • Mental health • Mythology • Supernatural

Read-Alikes: *Shadows of the Night,* edited by Greg Herren, collects queer horror from noted authors such as Therese Szmanski, William Mann, and Lawrence Schimel.

Queer Fear: Gay Horror Fiction. Vancouver, BC: Arsenal Pulp Press, 2000.
These eighteen tales of urban terror and strange creatures are made darker and more disturbing by the alienation from society of the gay protagonists. Only one story, Caitlin Kiernan's "Spindleshanks" is lesbian-themed.

🎗 *Queer Fear II: Gay Horror Fiction.* Vancouver, BC: Arsenal Pulp Press, 2002.

> The series continues with these twenty-two stories of gay horror by Canadian and U.S. authors, including many of the same authors who contributed to *Queer Fear*.

> **Awards:** Lambda Literary Award, 2002; Gaylactic Spectrum Award, 2003

Salmonson, Jessica Amanda, ed.

🎗 *What Did Miss Darrington See? An Anthology of Feminist Supernatural Fiction.* New York: Feminist Press at the City University of New York, 1989. **L**

> Most of the stories in this collection of feminist stories are from literary magazines of the nineteenth and early twentieth centuries. The book is interesting as a precursor to lesbian anthologies such as *Daughters of Darkness*.

> **Awards:** Lambda Literary Award, 1989

> **Subjects:** Anthologies • Feminism • Ghosts • Psychics

> **Read-Alikes:** *Haunted Women*, edited by Alfred Bendixen, covers the same period and subject, but repeats only one story ("Luella Miller") .

Sandler, Helen, ed.

Necrologue. London: Diva, 2003. **L**

> Thirty stories by British lesbian authors look at death, dying, the undead, and the occult.

> **Subjects:** Anthologies • Death and dying • Ghosts • Occult

> **Read-Alikes:** *Bend Sinister*, edited by Peter Burton, looks at the same subjects but from the British gay male point of view.

Chapter 13

Mystery and Crime

Definition

A mystery is a work of literature that presents one or more crimes or curious events (most often a murder) whose causes are unclear or hidden and that offers the opportunity of deducing the solution from clues provided by the author.

Description and Characteristics

Mystery writing is characterized by events that lie outside the limits of acceptable behavior—usually a murder or disappearance—that also seem to defy explanation. One or more of the characters tries to piece together an account of the event and uncover the responsible party, either as part of a law enforcement organization (police procedurals) or independently (private detectives and amateur sleuths). Emotions often run high in such works, with extremes of passion recalling the more excessive romances and providing an opportunity for readers to explore situations they may never encounter. This quality of testing limits makes the genre a natural home for GLBT themes.

History and Development

Homosexuals have long figured as characters in mystery writing, with the degree of representation varying according to the sexual orientation of the author, cultural attitudes toward GLBT people at the time of writing, and the demands of plot and theme. The male homosexual appeared sporadically in American and British mysteries published between the Great Depression and the Stonewall Riots of 1969, most commonly as either victims or villains, seldom as whole and successful individuals. Examples from this period are Dashiell Hammett's *The Maltese Falcon* (1930), with its evil and highly effeminate criminal Joel Cairo; the blackmailer Arthur Geiger in Raymond Chandler's *The Big Sleep* (1939); and the attractive but amoral bisexual title character of *The Talented Mr. Ripley*, by Patricia Highsmith (1955). Less stereotyped images of gay men are presented in Gore Vidal's first mystery, *Death in the Fifth Position*, published in 1952, which laid the foundation for the appearance of an openly gay detective in George Baxt's *A Queer Kind of Death* (1966).

The aftermath of the Stonewall Riots further developed the type of writing initiated by Vidal and Baxt, resulting in a proliferation of works featuring openly gay police officers, detectives, and lawyers involved in criminal investigations, a phenomenon begun with the appearance of *Fadeout* by Joseph Hansen in 1970. Hansen's writing was followed by the works of Nathan Aldyne, Richard Stevenson, Samuel Steward, Michael Nava, and Mark Richard Zubro. These last two have continued the tradition of the Brandstetter novels, with continuing characters and portrayals of gay men as believable human beings coping with both crime and a variety of subjects, ranging from AIDS and homophobia to class conflicts. A notable contrast in writing featuring lesbians is that, whereas most of the works written by or depicting gay men were issued by mainstream houses, women's works were often first issued in smaller numbers by women-owned publishing houses in the alternative press.

Lesbian mysteries had their birth in the lesbian pulp fiction novels of the 1950s and 1960s, intended for heterosexual men but adopted by the lesbians of the time as their own. Full of suspense, deception, and intrigue, they depicted a hidden realm, mirroring the condition of many of the women who read them. The culture created by the women's movement and the immediate post-Stonewall years produced important feminist writing but did not emphasize the development of new and accurate models of lesbians in mysteries, with the notable exception of Monique Wittig's 1969 novel *Les Guerillieres,* which invented the figure of the lesbian as militant worker for change, reflecting the political culture wars underway at the time. Something of Wittig's model carries over into the first lesbian crime novel with feminist themes, M. F. Beal's *Angel Dance,* whose feisty Chicana detective Kat Guerrera debuted in 1977.

The use of feminist dialogues and women's issues is an ongoing plot presence in all lesbian mysteries to some degree, with applications as varied as satire, the range of urban lesbian identities, and the reexamination of the butch–femme continuum. Most of the mysteries in this class have appeared since the 1980s, with a wide range of form and content used by a diverse group of major new writers such as Nicola Griffith, Ellen Hart, Claire McNab, Barbara Wilson, and Mary Wings.

Issues for the Readers' Advisor

Mystery fiction is a solidly established genre widely found in many public, college, and university library collections, with a high level of awareness among readers of all ages. The demand for titles will be constant and highly varied, with some patrons active fans of a particular author or series and others simply seeking any crime novels with GLBT protagonists. Well-written GLBT mysteries have a strong following in the straight community as well as the GLBT community, so mysteries may be the best-developed GLBT section of many libraries. Anthologies of GLBT writing should also be examined for mystery stories and as a guide to new and emerging writers.

Chapter Organization

The entries in this chapter have been arranged by the type of detective in the story. Police and other official governmental investigators are the first considered, followed by the stories of licensed private investigators, then works on amateur detectives. Closing the chapter is a section on short stories, both collections of the work of one person and anthologies featuring several authors.

Mysteries with significant fantasy or science fiction or horror elements are covered in those chapters. The science fiction mysteries (chapter 11) are gathered into a section titled "Futurecrime"; fantasy mysteries and thrillers did not divide as neatly into their own section but can be found predominantly in the "Renaissance" and "Contemporary Magic" sections of chapter 10. Only a very few horror books contained elements of mystery, and those were put into the section in chapter 12 denoting the predominant horror theme, such as "Vampires and Werewolves" or "Ghosts, Demons, and Possession."

Sources

Betz, Phyllis M. *Lesbian Detective Fiction: Woman as Author, Subject and Reader.* Jefferson, NC: McFarland, 2006.

Gosselin, Adrienne Johnson, ed. *Multicultural Detective Fiction: Murder from the "Other" Side.* New York: Garland, 1999.

Gunn, Drewey Wayne. *The Gay Male Sleuth in Print and Film: A History and Annotated Bibliography.* Lanham, MD: Scarecrow Press, 2005.

Kelley, James. "Mystery and Detective Fiction." In *Gay Histories and Cultures,* edited by George E. Haggerty, 624–25. New York: Garland, 2000.

Markowitz, Judith A. *The Gay Detective Novel: Lesbian and Gay Main Characters and Themes in Mystery Fiction.* Jefferson, NC: McFarland, 2004.

Munt, Sally R. "Mystery Fiction, Lesbian." In *Gay and Lesbian Literary Heritage,* edited by Claude Summers, 504–8. New York: Holt, 1995.

Munt, Sally R. "Mystery and Detective Fiction." In *Lesbian Histories and Cultures,* edited by Bonnie Zimmerman, 524–25. New York: Garland, 2000.

Pebworth, Ted-Larry. "Mystery Fiction, Gay Male." In *Gay and Lesbian Literary Heritage,* edited by Claude Summers, 500–504. New York: Holt, 1995.

Police Procedurals

Those mysteries in which crimes are solved by detectives on a police force are known as police procedurals. GLBT communities have long had difficult relationships with the police. Katherine Forrest's closeted Kate Delafield, first appearing in 1984, stars in the first major GLBT police procedurals. Claire McNab's Australian detective, Carol Ashton, also began her series closeted in 1988, but was completely out by 1991.

Boyd, Randy.

Uprising. Indianapolis, IN: West Beach Books, 1998. **G**

A conservative U.S. senator becomes the target of a conspiracy by three deeply closeted celebrities. In response, the FBI assigns a heterosexual agent to expose the plot while serving as bait for one of the conspirators' affections.

Subjects: African Americans • Homophobia • Law enforcement personnel • Murder • Politics

Read-Alikes: In Suzanne Brockmann's *Hot Target,* Jules Cassidy is a gay FBI agent assigned to protect a Hollywood producer from homopobes.

Clare, Baxter.

L.A. Franco Mysteries. **L**

Lesbian hardboiled LAPD detective L. A. Franco heads an investigative team in the city's roughest district.

Subjects: California • Law enforcement personnel • Murder • Relationships

Read-Alikes: Sara Paretsky's <u>V.I. Warshawski Novels</u> present a hardboiled female private eye working through relationship and abandonment issues.

Bleeding Out. Tallahassee, FL: Bella Books, 2000.

Fresh out of the police academy, Franco is assigned to Figueroa, the grittiest part of Los Angeles. Almost immediately she has to prove herself by tracking down a serial killer.

Street Rules. Tallahassee, FL: Bella Books, 2003.

The murder of an entire barrio family seems open and shut until a chance remark over dinner leads Franco to suspect police involvement. Slowly coming out of the closet, she might find romance, too, if the job doesn't get in the way.

Cry Havoc. Tallahassee, FL: Bella Books, 2003.

Franco and her oddly assorted team tackle the riddle of a naked, dead body found sitting in a car accompanied by a headless chicken. The available clues point into the shadowed world of voodoo magic. An unfolding love affair pulls at Franco as she tries to focus on unraveling this complicated plot.

Last Call. Tallahassee, FL: Bella Books, 2004.

Devastated by the loss of her right-hand man, Franco tries to get over her grief and growing dependence on alcohol by pursuing one of his cold cases. But her obsession with the case is threatening her burgeoning romance—and her life.

End of Watch. Tallahassee, FL: Bella Books, 2006.

Forced at last to deal with her demons, Franco returns to New York's Lower East Side, where she grew up. Unexpectedly, she discovers a lead in the murder of her father, which she witnessed at the tender age of ten.

Cooke, John Peyton.

Chimney Sweeper. New York: Mysterious Press, 1996. **G**

> One-time drifter Jesse Colson is assigned to assist a detective working on a murder Jesse committed before joining the force.
>
> **Subjects:** Homophobia • Law enforcement personnel • Murder • Sex workers • Wisconsin
>
> **Read-Alikes:** In Scott Turow's *Presumed Innocent*, after a prosecutor's ex-mistress is found raped and murdered, he is given the case—but develops into the prime suspect.

Torsos. New York: Mysterious Press, 1993. **G** **B**

> A serial killer targets gay men who work the streets in Depression-era Cleveland, leaving pieces of them as clues in the seedy Kingsbury Run District. Bisexual city cop Hank Lambert and Eliot Ness assemble possible culprits while Lambert secretly uses his contacts inside the gay world, among them a young hustler who suspects he knows who the killer is. Based on an actual series of murders, this is a gritty and realistic portrayal of a gay community not previously represented in mystery fiction.
>
> **Subjects:** 1930s • Families • Law enforcement personnel • Love • Murder • Ohio
>
> **Read-Alikes:** In *Choice of Evil*, by Andrew Vachss, bemoaning the death of his bisexual girlfriend, a contemporary gun-for-hire protects a serial killer who exacts revenge on homophobes.

Forrest, Katherine.

Kate Delafield Series. **L**

> Los Angeles police officer Kate Delafield solves crimes while struggling with professional homophobia and personal demons. She grows and gradually emerges from the closet over the course of the series.
>
> **Subjects:** California • Hate crimes • Homophobia • Law enforcement personnel • Murder
>
> **Read-Alikes:** Similar themes of professional homophobia and personal integrity drive Gerri Hill's *Hunter's Way* and *In the Name of the Father*.

Amateur City. Los Angeles: Alyson Books, 2003 (1984).

> Kate starts the series mourning the accidental death of her long-time lover. Unable to grieve publicly, she plunges into her work when she and her homophobic partner are assigned to investigate the death of a prominent businessman. The obvious suspects are the victim's co-workers—and one of them is a woman who helps Kate start healing.

Murder at the Nightwood Bar. Los Angeles: Alyson Books, 2003 (1987).

> A homeless teen prostitute is beaten and left dead outside a lesbian bar; a still-closeted Kate investigates but finds herself suspected and resented by the women who frequent the establishment.

🌲 *Beverly Malibu.* Los Angeles: Alyson Books, 2003 (1989).

> Kate is assigned to investigate the death of Owen Sinclair, a retired producer. As his connections to the notorious House Un-American Activities Committee of the 1950s and its witch hunt of the Hollywood community emerge, she wonders if the motive for the murder lies in the present or the past.

> **Awards:** Lambda Literary Award, 1990

🌲 *Murder by Tradition.* Los Angeles: Alyson Books, 2003 (1991).

> The murder of a gay restaurant owner places Kate in an awkward position—the defense attorney for the perpetrator is the only heterosexual man who knows she is a lesbian.

> **Awards:** Lambda Literary Award, 1991

Liberty Square. New York: Berkley, 2000 (1996).

> Kate and her lover go to Washington, D.C., for a reunion of the Marines Delafield served with in Vietnam. Reminisces are cut short when a hail of bullets cuts down an attendee and the rest of the veterans are suspects.

Apparition Alley. New York: Berkley, 2000 (1997).

> A drug bust goes bad in a hail of gunfire, and Kate is winged by another cop—but no one will admit to shooting. Soon Kate realizes her cover might be blown; a murdered officer was rumored to have compiled a list of gay and lesbian police officers.

Sleeping Bones. New York: Berkley Prime Crime, 2000 (1999).

> Paired with a new, more sympathetic partner, Kate investigates the death of a famous anthropologist. CIA black ops, scientific rivalries, and the victim's attractive daughter obscure the trail.

🌲 *Hancock Park.* New York: Berkley, 2005 (2004).

> Affluent Hancock Park is rocked by the slaying of Victoria Talbot, and her philandering husband is quickly picked up as the obvious perpetrator. Kate, upset because her lover walked out, still has enough poise to see the shakiness of the state's case.

> **Awards:** Lambda Literary Award, 2004

Macadam, Heather Dune.

Weeping Buddha. New York: Akashic Books, 2002. **L**

> Two Long Island detectives contend with an apparent murder-suicide. The trail of clues leads to a Buddhist retreat house, where the murdered woman left an offering of her hair as a sign of grief.

> **Subjects:** Friendship • Law enforcement personnel • Murder • New York State • Religion

> **Read-Alikes:** Cynthia Tyler's mysteries, *Descanso* and *Shadow Work*, star Chris Cameron, a psychotherapist with Buddhist leanings.

Mackle, Elliott.

It Takes Two. Los Angeles: Alyson Books, 2003. ▣ G

Two dead bodies lie in a Fort *Myers* motel parking lot, in 1949. The local sheriff seems intent on keeping detective Bud Wright from making any significant headway—but Wright's lover is the prime suspect.

Subjects: 1940s • Florida • Law enforcement personnel • Murder • Race relations • Relationships

Read-Alikes: An equally intense and steamy novel, set in the same time, is Christopher Bram's *The Father of Frankenstein*. Look also at Curt Colbert's *Queer Street*, set in post–World War II Seattle.

McNab, Claire.

Carol Ashton Series. ▣ L

Australian Detective Inspector Carol Ashton takes her work seriously, frequently to the detriment of her personal life. She starts the series deeply closeted, afraid of the rampant homophobia of the Sydney police force, but is fully out by the fourth book.

Subjects: Australia • Homophobia • Law enforcement personnel • Murder • Relationships

Read-Alikes: Another Australian mystery series is the <u>Marc and Paul Mysteries</u>, by Phillip Scott.

Lessons in Murder. Ferndale, MI: Bella, 2004 (1988).

A bizarre murder at a Sydney high school reveals a web of jealousies and relationships that provide ample motives. Carol and the prime suspect, Sybil Quade, fight their instant attraction to each other as they face off on opposite sides of the investigation.

Fatal Reunion. Tallahassee, FL: Naiad, 1991 (1989).

Christine, Carol's ex-lover, is accused of killing her husband. As she works the case, Carol realizes she still has feelings for Christine, jeopardizing her relationship with Sybil.

Death Down Under. Tallahassee, FL: Naiad, 2003 (1990).

On the trail of a serial killer, Carol is surprised to find connections to the movie her lover is working on.

Cop Out. Tallahassee, FL: Bella, 2003 (1991).

A wealthy heiress is found with the murder weapon next to the dead body of her closeted brother—but Carol turns up other suspects: the victim's combative wife and the abusive husband of the heiress.

Dead Certain. Tallahassee, FL: Bella, 2003 (1992).

Australia's top male opera star apparently committed suicide, but Carol thinks the hotel room crime scene looks staged. Even with her personal life in turmoil, Carol works through the tangled motives of the victim's associates to find his murderer. First published in 1992, the Australian edition was titled *Off Key*.

Body Guard. Tallahassee, FL: Naiad Press, 1995 (1994).

Wounded during an earlier investigation, Carol is assigned to light duty as bodyguard to an abrasive but attractive visiting American feminist.

Double Bluff. Tallahassee, FL: Naiad Press, 1995.

Carol investigates the apparent suicide of a wealthy businessman. Powerful interests want the case closed, which may be why someone is stalking her girlfriend.

Inner Circle. Tallahassee, FL: Naiad, 1996.

Carol ties some execution-style murders and the bombing of a police station to a group of right-wing extremists, putting her life in danger.

Chain Letter. Tallahassee, FL: Naiad, 1997.

A serial killer seems to be using an odd and threatening chain letter to choose his victims; Carol is tapped to investigate.

Past Due. Tallahassee, FL: Naiad, 1998.

Carol uncovers a tangle of corruption and avarice behind the murder of a reproductive specialist.

Set Up. Tallahassee, FL: Naiad, 1999.

Carol trails both a killer for hire and a mysterious, darkly seductive woman who may take her down the wrong path.

Under Suspicion. Tallahassee, FL: Naiad, 2000.

Training in Los Angeles, Carol gets in an argument with an instructor, who shortly afterward is found murdered. To prove her innocence, she needs to find the real killer.

Death Club. Tallahassee, FL: Naiad, 2001.

Carol investigates a women's golf tournament thrown into disarray when one of the leaders, the homophobic, hard-driving Fiona Hawk, is murdered on the course.

Accidental Murder. Tallahassee, FL: Bella Books, 2002.

Carol is called in to investigate an accidental death in Sydney. When she discovers a string of similar deaths across the country, she realizes there is a fiendishly clever killer on the loose.

Blood Link. Tallahassee, FL: Bella, 2003.

Until the sudden death of the reclusive billionaire Thurmond Rule, no one had been able to figure out a pattern to a wave of murders. Carol soon realizes that the dead were all potential heirs—and the likely murderer has to be one of the few remaining.

Fall Guy. Ferndale, MI: Bella, 2005 (2004).

A murdered millionaire was almost universally hated, because of his penchant for publicly embarrassing people with his practical jokes. When he plunges to his death after someone cut his parachute cords, Carol finds it difficult to narrow the list of suspects—until an elaborate practical joke at the funeral casts suspicion on the victim's son.

Denise Cleever Thrillers. L

Australian Security Intelligence Organization secret agent Denise Cleever uses her good looks, charisma, and cleverness to investigate and infiltrate suspect organizations.

Subjects: Australia • Conspiracy • Law enforcement personnel • Terrorism

Read-Alikes: Neil S. Plakcy's *Mahu* introduces gay Hawaiian police detective Kimo Kanapa'aka; in *Mahu Surfer*, he goes undercover to track down a killer.

Murder Undercover. Tallahassee, FL: Naiad, 1999.

Denise is sent to an island resort off the Great Barrier Reef following rumors of a planned coup against the government. Her task becomes more challenging when the daughter of the implicated family becomes attracted to her.

Death Understood. Tallahassee, FL: Naiad, 2000.

Denise goes undercover at a conservative political think tank but is threatened when a member of the family that operates the think tank recognizes her and another is attracted to her.

Out of Sight. Tallahassee, FL: Naiad, 2003 (2001).

A brutal terrorist group has thus far escaped infiltration, so Denise is called in to do the job—but the woman whose identity she assumes has a brother bent on killing her.

Recognition Factor. Tallahassee, FL: Bella, 2003 (2002).

Denise's expertise is requested by the U.S. government when an international terrorist threatens Los Angeles. Denise has dealt with him before; in fact she is the only agent to do so and live.

Death by Death. Tallahassee, FL: Bella, 2003.

Security forces realize there is a connection between the assassinations of a statesman and an intellectual: Both had been patients at a clinic run by a secretive but charismatic psychiatrist. Denise is sent to join his staff, putting both mind and body at risk.

Murder at Random. Ferndale, MI: Bella, 2006 (2005).

Random murder by contract killers is the new method of terror devised by Australian terrorist group Righteous Scourge. Denise goes undercover at a newspaper that seems to get early notice of the killings and discovers ties among the paper, the terrorists, and a shadowy religious cult.

Radclyffe.

Justice Series. L

Special Crimes Unit Sergeant Detective Rebecca Frye struggles to create a personal life amid her dangerous and dramatic life as a police officer.

Subjects: Law enforcement personnel • Murder • Pornography • Sexual abuse

Read-Alikes: In Mark Del Franco's *Unshapely Things*, ex-druid Connor Grey works with the police to hunt the man killing gay prostitutes.

A Matter of Trust. [2nd ed.] Philadelphia: Bold Strokes Books, 2006.

> Preparing for divorce, Michael Lassiter hires cyberspecialist JT Sloane to protect her company from her husband, but JT and Michael soon realize they want more than just a business relationship. Originally written as a romance in 2003, this book was revised into a prequel to the Justice Series.

Shield of Justice. Philadelphia: Bold Strokes Books, 2005 (2002).

> Rebecca might be able to end a series of rapes and assaults on female prostitutes, now that a victim has survived. However, that victim is deeply traumatized, and Rebecca turns to Dr. Catherine Rawlings, who had been the victim's psychiatrist. Rebecca and Catherine struggle with ethics and the need to prevent more attacks, and their growing need for each other.

In Pursuit of Justice. Port Arthur, TX: Quest, 2006 (2003).

> Recovered from a nasty gunshot wound and the loss of her partner, Officer Jeff Cruz, Rebecca returns to work and is assigned to work with JT to crack an online child pornography ring. Drawing on support from prostitute Sandy and police officer Dellon Mitchell, they form an unofficial task force.

🎗 *Justice in the Shadows.* Philadelphia: Bold Strokes Books, 2005.

> Rebecca attempts to uncover a local ring dealing in child pornography that has already killed several people and wounded others—only to have the official investigation shut down. Assembling an unlikely team, ranging from a vengeful computer expert to a prostitute turned police informant, Rebecca pursues her elusive foes.

> **Awards:** Goldie Award, 2005

🎗 *Justice Served.* Philadelphia: Bold Strokes Books, 2005.

> JT uncovers the mole in the police force, but he is murdered before the team can expose the mole. Rebecca discovers that the conspiracy and the child pornography ring extend far outside the police force, but her task force is determined to bring the criminals to justice.

> **Awards:** Goldie Award, 2006

Zubro, Mark.

Paul Turner Series. G

Openly gay detective Paul Turner juggles his duties to his two boys and his work as a Chicago policeman. Straight partner Buck Fenwick provides backup and a constant stream of wisecracks as they solve politically sensitive cases.

Subjects: Illinois • Law enforcement personnel • Murder • Politics

Read-Alikes: In Curt Colbert's *Queer Street*, corruption and city politics also muddy trails.

Sorry Now? New York: St. Martin's Press, 1991.

> Paul reluctantly looks into the possibility that gay activists are behind the vengeance slayings of people connected to conservative causes. His sources in the gay community lead him to the killers.

Political Poison. New York: St. Martin's Press, 1993.

> Investigating the killing of a popular alderman, Paul and Buck search for motives in the murky world of Chicago politics.

Another Dead Teenager. New York: St. Martin's Press, 1995.

> Two suburban teens, from politically connected families, are found dead in Chicago, and Paul and Buck can find no apparent motive for the killings. But Paul slowly comes to fear his family is the real target.

Truth Can Get You Killed. New York: St. Martin's Press, 1997.

> A homophobic judge is killed, and Paul's search for the culprit is complicated by the overwhelming joy in the GLBT community—and the murders of two of his sources.

Drop Dead. New York: St. Martin's Press, 1999.

> A prominent fashion model plunges to his death from a skyscraper in the Loop. The search for the truth leads Paul and Buck into the boardrooms of the wealthy, glittering world of high fashion, and Chicago's back streets.

Sex and Murder.com. New York: St. Martin's Press, 2001.

> Two wealthy Chicago software mavens, one gay and one straight, are murdered. Paul and Buck discover the victims had an odd rivalry: They competed for who could bed the most partners, paying their pawns handsomely. Then, policemen around the country are being targeted by assassins—which just might be related to the deaths of the programmers.

Dead Egotistical Morons. New York: St. Martin's Press, 2003.

> After their final concert, a member of a popular boy band is found murdered in the shower. Paul and Buck unravel stories of exploitation, artistic conflicts, and dueling egos.

Nerds Who Kill. New York: St. Martin's Press, 2005.

> Paul takes his family to a science fiction convention, but it is a busman's holiday for him, as several attendees (and one policeman) are murdered.

Hook, Line, and Homicide. New York: St. Martin's Press, 2007.

> Paul's hope for a quiet vacation fishing with family and friends is dashed when he breaks up a fight between a group of Native Americans and some local thugs. Petty vandalism, burglaries, and general harassment follow—and then the leader of the thugs is found dead near Paul's houseboat.

Private Investigators

These are novels in which the detective is not officially a member of a police force but has been trained and licensed and takes cases for hire. Former police officers, journalists, and insurance investigators are all skilled at finding clues and researching crimes that aid in a career as a private detective. The archetypal gay P.I. is Joseph Hansen's Dave Brandstetter, who first appeared in print in 1970.

Bidulka, Anthony.

Russell Quant Mysteries. G

Gay former policeman Russell Quant used an unexpected bequest to set himself up as a private detective in bucolic Saskatchewan—a risky move, considering the low crime rate. The action often moves from the Canadian prairie to exotic locales as Quant travels in pursuit of the truth.

Subjects: Canada and Canadians • Computers • Travel

Read-Alikes: Another series set in the Canadian West is the Detective Lane Mysteries, by Gary Ryan.

Amuse Boche. Toronto: Insomniac Press, 2003.

> A year into his career as a private detective, Russell stumbles into a compelling murder case, with a wide range of suspects (including his client) and the chance to escape Saskatoon for Paris.

🏵 *Flight of Aquavit.* Toronto: Insomniac Press, 2004.

> Unsure whom he can trust, Russell searches for the blackmailer "Loverboy" in Saskatoon, then in the treacherous canyons of New York City.

> **Awards:** Lambda Literary Award, 2004

Tapas on the Ramblas. Toronto: Insomniac Press, 2005.

> Russell takes a Mediterranean cruise with the wealthy Wiser family, hoping to ferret out which relative is intent on killing his client, their matriarch.

Stain of the Berry. Toronto: Insomniac Press, 2006.

> Russell's name and number show up in the effects of a young woman who has just jumped from her apartment. Whether this is murder or suicide depends on whether the boogeyman is real.

Sundowner Ubuntu. Toronto: Insomniac Press, 2007.

> A mother hires Russell to track down her son, estranged from her for decades, and Russell heads off to Africa in pursuit.

Douglas, Lauren Wright.

Caitlin Reece Mysteries Series. L

Former crown prosecutor Caitlin Reece now supports herself as a freelance private investigator in Victoria, the temperate capital city of British Columbia. Somewhat tenderhearted, she still never leaves home without her .357 Magnum.

Subjects: Canada and Canadians • Conspiracy • Relationships

Read-Alikes: Jennifer Jordan's Kristin Ashe Mysteries involves another detective with a strong sense of social responsibility and drive for justice.

The Always Anonymous Beast. Tallahassee, FL: Naiad, 1987.

> Closeted TV anchorwoman Val Frazier is threatened with exposure, and her lover, Professor Tonia Konig, reluctantly calls on Caitlin for help. Caitlin finds a dangerous group behind the blackmail—and a deepening passion for her employer.

🌺 *Ninth Life.* Tallahassee, FL: Naiad, 1990.

Caitlin sets up a meeting, but her potential employer is being chased by unknown assailants. The meeting is cut short, and the only evidence is a mutilated cat. When this woman turns up dead, Caitlin plunges into a nasty struggle between activists and animal experimenters.

Awards: Lambda Literary Award, 1991

The Daughters of Artemis. Tallahassee, FL: Naiad, 1991.

Sean Macklin was just released from prison, still harboring a grudge against Caitlin. While the Full Moon Rapist terrorizes Victoria, Caitlin tracks a missing heir to a commune and finds both romance and peril.

A Tiger's Heart. Tallahassee, FL: Naiad, 1992.

Jory, the ten-year-old daughter of Caitlin's ex-lover Jonna, tells Caitlin she witnessed her own father kill Jonna. The police dismiss the story, so Jory asks for Caitlin's help.

Goblin Market. Tallahassee, FL: Naiad, 1993.

Laura Neal is receiving odd puzzles, created from her old photos, and hires Caitlin to solve the mystery. Caitlin gathers a motley crew of helpers to track down the most likely suspects.

A Rage of Maidens. Tallahassee, FL: Naiad, 1994.

A rape a few years before destroyed a family, and now the perpetrator is about to go free. Increasingly isolated, Caitlin is determined to prevent him from hurting anyone else.

Grey, Dorien.

Dick Hardesty Series. 🄶 🄱

Forced from his public relations position upon learning some unsavory truths about his top client, Dick Hardesty launches a new career as a private investigator. This entire series is self-published and was first released as e-books.

Subjects: 1980s • Homophobia • Law enforcement personnel • Murder

Read-Alikes: Lori L. Lake's <u>Gun Series</u> is a similarly intense group of mysteries, starring two lesbian police officers from St. Paul, Minnesota.

The Butcher's Son. San Francisco: GLB Publishers, 2001.

The police chief (aka "The Butcher") is curiously unconcerned when someone starts torching gay bars. Dick, working for the chief in his bid for public office, uncovers his connections to radical right-wingers.

The 9th Man. San Francisco: GLB Publishers, 2001.

Dick investigates a string of murders ignored by the police because the victims are queer. This is his first outing as an official P.I.

The Bar Watcher. San Francisco: GLB Publishers, 2001.

> The search for the killer of several members of the community becomes complicated as Dick realizes he may be sleeping with the culprit.

Hired Man. San Francisco: GLB, 2002.

> Dick is working on a job when the client turns up dead—and turns out also to be a client of a gay and bisexual escort service.

The Good Cop. San Francisco: GLB, 2002.

> A new chief of police replaces the old, bigoted one, and his first priority is improving police service to the queer community.

The Bottle Ghosts. San Francisco: GLB, 2005.

> Dick is asked to look for a man's alcoholic partner but soon finds evidence that gay alcoholics have been disappearing for years in his city—and the police force puts searching for missing gay alcoholics at the very bottom of its to-do list.

The Dirt Peddler. San Francisco: GLB, 2003.

> A loud, obnoxious, homophobic author hires Dick to find out who is threatening him with blackmail. Soon thereafter, the client is found dead with a hustler who'd been staying with Dick and his lover, Jonathan Quinlan.

The Role Players. San Francisco: GLB, 2004.

> On vacation with his lover in New York, Dick is asked to investigate the murder of the male lead in a play.

The Popsicle Tree. San Francisco: GLB, 2005.

> Dick and Jonathan return from vacation to find new upstairs neighbors, single mother Carlene and her young son, Kelly. While Carlene, worried about threats from an ex-girlfriend, takes a break from parenting, she leaves Kelly with Jonathan—then gets killed in a suspicious hit-and-run.

The Paper Mirror. San Francisco: GLB, 2005.

> Just before a new GLBT library and research center opens, the cataloger dies in an apparent accident. Although the coroner rules the death accidental, the board of the library foundation asks Dick to make sure there was no foul play.

The Dream Ender. San Francisco: GLB, 2007.

> A man suspected of deliberately spreading AIDS is found killed. When a couple of Dick's friends become the prime suspects, he starts looking a little deeper than the police are willing to do.

Griffith, Nicola.

Aud Torvingen Series. **L** **B**

Aud is many things: an independently wealthy adrenaline junky; a Norwegian-born former Atlanta police officer; and a smart, sexy lesbian bodyguard/private detective who's been hurt a few times.

Subjects: Art and artists • Law enforcement personnel • Murder

Read-Alikes: *Painted Moon,* by Karin Kallmaker, features a main character who must decide if life and love are still possible after a partner's death.

🎗 *Blue Place.* New York: Avon, 1998.

> Contracted to investigate an art forgery, Aud uncovers money laundering, drugs, murder, and love, in this fast-paced page-turner.

Awards: Lambda Literary Award, 1998

Stay: A Novel. New York: Nan A. Talese • Doubleday, 2002.

> The disappearance of a friend's fiancé lures Aud from self-imposed exile into an evil underworld, where solving the case may relieve her guilt and grief.

Always. New York: Riverhead, 2007.

> Still missing Julia, Aud and her friend Matthew Dornan visit her mother in Seattle, where they get pulled into an investigation of sabotage—and both Aud and Matthew fall for the same woman.

Hansen, Joseph.

Dave Brandstetter Series. G

Gay hard-boiled detective Dave Brandstetter investigates suspicious deaths for insurance companies, first for his father's company and then freelance. Brandstetter was the first major gay detective in print and aged naturally over the course of the series.

Subjects: California • Law enforcement personnel • Murder • Music

Read-Alikes: Dave Brandstetter was purposely modeled after Mickey Spillane's Mike Hammer, whose first book was *I, the Jury.* Like Dave, the protagonist in Bill Pronzini's <u>Nameless Detective</u> series aged over time; one of the later books in the series, *Nightcrawlers,* has a definitely gay theme.

Fadeout. Madison: University of Wisconsin Press, 2004 (1970).

> Grieving after the death of his longtime lover, Dave is sent to investigate the apparent death of a local celebrity whose car (but not his body) turns up in a flooded arroyo after a sudden storm. Dave's investigation turns up some twists in the town that make him think the celebrity is not dead—but his marriage and life were not happy, either. This work, written in 1967, was first published in 1970, after Hansen searched for three years for a publisher that would not sensationalize the homosexuality of the detective.

Death Claims. Madison: University of Wisconsin Press, 2004 (1973).

> Dave investigates the murder of John Oats, whose drugged body is discovered washed up on the beach. His son, the beneficiary of his life insurance policy, is missing.

Troublemaker. New York: Alyson Books, 2002 (1975).

> The obvious suspect in the murder of a gay bar owner is the naked man who was wiping fingerprints off the gun when the body was discovered—but Dave finds a few loose threads that point to someone else.

The Man Everybody Was Afraid Of. New York: Holt, Rinehart & Winston, 1978.

A gay activist is charged with the murder of a police chief, but Dave finds out that the chief had many enemies. Helping Dave with the case is Cliff Harris, who becomes his new love interest.

Skinflick. New York: Holt, Rinehart & Winston, 1980.

A fundamentalist with a double life trashes a Hollywood porn shop, then turns up dead. Police suspect the owner of the shop and leave Dave to run down the loose ends.

Gravedigger. New York: Holt, Rinehart & Winston, 1985 (1982).

A young woman whose father took out an expensive insurance policy on her disappears, apparently murdered by her cult's guru. But the father has disappeared, too, so Dave can't close the case.

Nightwork. New York: Holt, Rinehart & Winston, 1985.

Dave is called in to investigate the death of a truck driver murdered through the sabotage of his vehicle and finds many people with a motive to kill him—from his abused wife to the people objecting to what he hauled.

The Little Dog Laughed. New York: Henry Holt, 1987.

When a foreign correspondent is found shot dead in his home, the police and his daughter both suspect suicide. His insurance company, though, sends Dave in to investigate—and his search for answers puts him in the middle of a life-threatening Central American political struggle.

Early Graves. New York: Mysterious Press, 1987.

In this powerful evocation of AIDS hysteria, the body of the latest victim of a serial killer targeting gay men with AIDS is left at the detective's door. Dave is determined to bring the perpetrator to justice.

Obedience. New York: Mysterious Press, 1989.

When a Vietnamese marina owner is murdered, suspicion falls on a man he was about to evict from his berth. The suspect's insurance company sends Dave in to check this out, and he finds there have been several other suspicious deaths in the Vietnamese community.

The Boy Who Was Buried This Morning. New York: Plume, 1991.

A young man is killed while playing a combat war game. Dave, called in to work out how this happened, finds himself pursuing leads to a secretive neofascist movement.

🎗 *A Country of Old Men: The Last Dave Brandstetter Mystery.* New York: Viking, 1991.

A wild story of abduction and abuse told by an injured child found wandering on the beach brings Dave out of retirement. When a prominent guitarist is killed, the child's story suddenly seems credible, setting off a search through the underworlds of politics, the record industry, and the issues of child exploitation.

Awards: Lambda Literary Award, 1991

Herren, Greg.

Murder in the Rue Dauphine. Los Angeles: Alyson Books, 2002. **G** **L**

A potential client of Chanse MacLeod is murdered before he can explain why he wishes to hire the detective. Attempts to find the killer lead Chanse down Bourbon Street, through the mansions of the wealthy, and into the heart of the gay activist movement in the city.

Subjects: Authors • Homophobia • Louisiana • Sex workers

Read-Alikes: Louisiana is the setting for W. Randy Haynes's *Cajun Snuff,* featuring FBI agent Adam Tyler Stephen.

Lordon, Randye.

Sydney Sloane Mysteries. **L**

Sydney Sloane and her straight male partner Max work well personally and professionally, sharing an easy familiarity. Sydney is estranged from most members of her family but is constantly working to put it back together and is often at odds with her long-suffering life partner, too.

Subjects: Murder • New York City • Relationships

Read-Alikes: Another tough feminist private eye in a big city is featured in Sara Paretsky's V. I. Warshawski Mysteries. Sarah Schulman's *Rat Bohemia* is another look at the estrangement of families from their queer children.

Brotherly Love. New York: St. Martin's Press, 1994.

When an escaped murderer resembles Sydney's brother, thought to be long dead, she sets off to see if his apparent death was another in his long line of cons—but there are more sinister people looking for him, too.

Sister's Keeper. New York: St. Martin's Press, 1996.

Sydney's childhood friend, Zoe, is killed in what looks to be an accident. But Zoe's trashed apartment, her abusive ex-husband, and the murder of Zoe's best friend all lead Sydney to believe otherwise.

🎗 *Father Forgive Me.* New York: Avon Books, 1997.

A woman hires Sydney to find out how her brother, who never did drugs, was found dead of a heroin overdose on a gritty Hudson River pier.

Awards: Lambda Literary Award, 1998

Mother May I. New York: Avon Books, 1998.

A prominent doctor is accused of murdering his wife. Before Sydney can interview him, he vanishes, leading her on a hunt through some of New York City's grittier places.

Say Uncle. New York: Avon Books, 1999.

Sydney's uncle insists he was framed for arson and murder. Though she hasn't talked to him in years—he couldn't handle her being a lesbian—they had once been very close.

East of Niece. New York: St. Martin's Press, 2002.

Sydney swore off ever helping her family with her investigative skills again and headed to the Riviera for a much-needed vacation. Still, her favorite niece has nowhere else to turn in her search for her missing (and possibly murderous) husband, so Sydney makes an exception.

Son of a Gun. New York: St. Martin's Press, 2005.

When an old police friend is shot and hospitalized, Sydney stops by to give emotional support to his wife, Peggy. But Peggy is hiding secrets that imperil both her life and her child's.

Maiman, Jaye.

Robin Miller Mysteries Series. 🄻

Robin Miller is a famous and successful, but closeted, romance novelist who puts her research skills to work trying to solve the mystery of a friend's death in her first case. During this case she is outed, and she realizes that an openly lesbian author writing heterosexual romances is unlikely to fly. She felt she'd done well in this case, though, so she went professional as a private detective at a New York agency.

Subjects: Law enforcement personnel • Louisiana • Love • Murder • New York City

Read-Alikes: Another series with a strong emphasis on relationships is Kate Allen's Alison Kaine Mysteries.

I Left My Heart. Tallahassee, FL: Naiad, 1991.

Police rule the death of Robin's ex-lover accidental, but she isn't sure. Robin undertakes her own investigation and finds additional mysteries—and maybe a femme fatale. Along the way she is outed, ending her career as a romance novelist.

🌷 *Crazy for Loving.* Tallahassee, FL: Naiad, 1992.

Robin is in New York City taking over a detective agency when business suddenly picks up. A friend asks her to track down an old flame, a client's husband turns up dead in his classroom, and new love beckons at the worst possible time.

Awards: Lambda Literary Award, 1993

Under My Skin. Tallahassee, FL: Naiad, 1993.

Robin, on vacation in the Poconos, senses something's not right when a lesbian homeowner is murdered and the only suspect the police consider is the deceased's ex-girlfriend.

Someone to Watch. Tallahassee, FL: Naiad, 1995.

Robin's lover has a friend accused of a murder with political implications, so she takes on the case of proving his innocence. At the same time, Robin struggles with her guilt over past acts and how this affects all her relationships.

Baby, It's Cold. Tallahassee, FL: Naiad, 1996.

The child of Robin's new girlfriend is kidnapped, and the police seem too inept to help. As a cold winter blasts its way into the city, Robin fights a fever and her own emotional turmoil to save this child's life.

Old Black Magic. Tallahassee, FL: Naiad, 1997.

> A series of murders spreads fear from the Deep South to New York. Robin must locate the killer before the killer strikes again—and Robin herself may be one of the targets.

Every Time We Say Goodbye. Tallahassee, FL: Naiad, 1999.

> Stuck on a case, overwhelmed by her lover's visiting relatives (including a niece who disappeared), and hating the cold of another New York winter, Robin is not prepared for her ex to show up intent on winning her back. And it may be the last straw for her lover, too.

Marcy, Jean.

Meg Darcy Series. L

Meg Darcy works as an investigator for her uncle's firm in Saint Louis, often working alongside the object of her desire, police detective Sarah Lindstrom.

Subjects: Families • Law enforcement personnel • Missouri • Murder

Read-Alikes: Another good mix of suspense and romance is Jlee Meyer's *First Instinct.*

Cemetery Murders. Norwich, VT: New Victoria, 1997.

> The niece of a serial killer's fourth victim, disgusted with the inability of the police to crack the case, hires Meg. Her investigation leads her into conflict with the closeted but attractive policewoman Sarah Lindstrom, also looking for the culprit.

Dead and Blonde. Norwich, VT: New Victoria, 1998.

> Sarah's ex-lover is murdered in Sarah's bed, marking her as a likely perpetrator. Of course, there are other prospects—the dead woman's jealous ex-husband and her current lover among them—so Meg tries to sort things out, with the help of her best gay friend, Patrick.

🏵 *Mommy Deadest.* Norwich, VT: New Victoria, 2000.

> Meg receives a frantic call for help from an old friend, whose nephew is charged with murdering the school principal. Her attempts to unravel the puzzle are complicated by the presence of her niece, her lover, and a friend, who all want to help, and the strange death of one of her police officer father's colleagues.

> **Awards:** Lambda Literary Award, 2000

Cold Case of Murder. Norwich, VT: New Victoria, 2003.

> A simple adoption is complicated by the unsolved murder eight years before of the child's birth mother—and the fact that the policeman in charge of the murder investigation is the child's adoptive father. Meg and Sarah continue their hot-and-cold relationship while working together to solve this mystery.

Pincus, Elizabeth.

Nell Fury Mysteries. [L]

Nell Fury solves crimes—often with political implications—in San Francisco and dotes on the daughter she raises part-time with her ex-girlfriend.

Subjects: California • Insurance • Law enforcement personnel • Murder

Read-Alikes: Kate Allen's detective in the <u>Alison Kaine Mysteries</u> has the same adventurous outlook on life and sex and a strong connection to her community.

Two Bit Tango. Duluth, MN: Spinsters Ink, 1992.

Nell debuts in the case of a missing heiress, whose twin sister has hired her to locate her missing sibling. In the process, Nell uncovers more than she bargained for: A prominent local politician seems to be involved, and the sister turns up working in a strip club.

Awards: Lambda Literary Award, 1992

Solitary Twist. Duluth, MN: Spinsters Ink, 1992.

A chance meeting leads to work for Nell investigating the new fiancé of an acquaintance's ex-lover. While Nell investigates, the fiancé is disgraced and the ex-lover is kidnapped. As she makes headway on the case, suddenly she is summarily paid off and the job is terminated, but Nell's sense of justice won't let her quit.

Hangdog Hustle. Duluth, MN: Spinsters Ink, 1995.

Nell is hired to look into the circumstances of the murder of a young, gay Japanese American. While everyone speculates whether it was gay-bashing or racism, Fury turns up clues that point to quite different motives, as well as powerful enemies.

Redmann, J. M.

Micky Knight Mysteries. [L]

Tough lesbian private detective Mickey Knight calls on her network of strong women to solve crimes in New Orleans, often raking up painful elements of her own past along the way.

Subjects: AIDS • Louisiana • Murder • Pornography • Relationships, parent-child • Sex workers • Sexual abuse • Substance abuse

Read-Alikes: W. Randy Haynes's *Cajun Snuff* is another detective story that brings Louisiana alive.

Death by the Riverside. Ferndale, MI: Bella Books, 2001 (1990).

Mickey is played for a fool by a woman intent on swindling her gay brother out of their grandfather's will—and drug lords are also after the property in question. Meanwhile, all the family issues bring up parts of Mickey's past she'd rather keep buried.

Deaths of Jocasta. Ferndale, MI: Bella Books, 2002 (1992).

An easy gig for Mickey working security for a posh event is disrupted when the woman she is falling in love with is implicated in the murder of one of the guests. As Mickey works out how to get closer to this woman, so does the real killer.

🌲 *Intersection of Law and Desire.* Ferndale, MI: Bella Books, 2003 (1995).

> Mickey finds herself confronting her own past when she agrees to work on two cases, both involving child abuse. Now she must walk into some of the darker corners of New Orleans in an attempt to find the culprits, even if it means risking her relationship with her partner.

> **Awards:** Lambda Literary Award, 1996

Lost Daughters. Ann Arbor, MI: Bywater Books, 2005 (1999).

> Mickey has two missing person cases: a mother seeking her estranged lesbian daughter and an HIV-positive drag queen looking for his birth mother. The investigation unearths Mickey's desire to seek out her own long-absent mother, but before she can, a serial killer starts targeting lesbians.

Saylor, Steven.

Roma sub Rosa Series. G B

Gordianus the Finder, a man creating the role of the private investigator, is not himself gay or bisexual but moves freely in the company of powerful men who are—in fact, much of his work come from one such, the orator Cicero. The character and corruption of Rome, in the declining days of the Republic, come alive in Saylor's work.

Subjects: Antiquity • Italy • Murder • Politics

Read-Alikes: Ancient Rome also comes to life in Robert Graves's *I, Claudius* and *Claudius the God.* Additional Roman mysteries can be found in *The Mammoth Book of Roman Whodunnits,* edited by Mike Ashley. Also, don't miss two volumes of Saylor's Gordianus short stories, *The House of the Vestals* and *A Gladiator Dies Only Once,* listed in the "Short Story Collections" section of this chapter.

Roman Blood. New York: St. Martin's Press, 2000 (1991).

> Rising advocate Cicero earns the enmity of the dictator Sulla by accepting the defense of an accused murderer. Gordianus is hired to find the real killer.

Arms of Nemesis. New York: St. Martin's Press, 2001 (1992).

> While Spartacus leads a slave revolt, Gordianus and his adopted son Eco are sent to the Bay of Naples to investigate the murder of the cousin of Crassus, the richest man in Rome.

🌲 *Catilina's Riddle.* New York: St. Martin's Press, 2002 (1993).

> Gordianus is asked by his patron, Cicero, to investigate rumors of a coup. When a headless corpse turns up in his stable, Gordianus realizes the stakes may be even higher than he thought.

> **Awards:** Lambda Literary Award, 1993

The Venus Throw. New York: St. Martin's Press, 1996 (1995).

> After several envoys from the still-independent Egypt are killed, the pharaoh's ambassador asks Gordianus for help.

A Murder on the Appian Way. New York: St. Martin's Press, 1997 (1996).

> When a populist politician is waylaid on the road to Rome, his patrician rival, Milo, is suspected, and the Roman mob erupts in anger. Cicero takes on Milo's case and again hires Gordianus to investigate the crime, bringing Gordianus into contact with notables like Pompey, Julius Caesar, and Marc Anthony.

Rubicon. New York: St. Martin's Press, 2000 (1999).

> Julius Caesar brings legions across the Rubicon, and when Pompey's cousin is murdered in the garden of Gordianus, the Finder is pulled into the turmoil.

Last Seen in Massilia. New York: St. Martin's Press, 2001 (2000).

> Rumors have spread that Gordianus's adopted son, Meto, was executed for displeasing Julius Caesar while serving in his legions. Unwilling to accept this without seeing a body, Gordianus investigates the camp of Caesar's legions.

A Mist of Prophecies. New York: St. Martin's Press, 2003 (2002).

> As civil war rages, Rome's most influential women are suspects in the death of the prophetess Calpurnia, with whom Gordianus is having an affair.

The Judgment of Caesar. New York: St. Martin's Press, 2005 (2004).

> Gordianus arrives in turbulent Egypt to search for his missing wife just as Julius Caesar arrives to court the beautiful Cleopatra. Meto, Gordianus's adopted son, has come with Caesar, as legionary and occasional bedmate of the general.

Scoppettone, Sandra.

Lauren Laurano Mysteries Series. 🄻

Private investigator Lauren Laurano, with a little help from her psychotherapist partner Kip, works on cases from her Greenwich Village base.

Subjects: Computers • Couples • Families • New York City • Sexual abuse

Read-Alikes: Scoppetone also wrote under the pseudonym Jack Early, and those mysteries have the same genuine humor and intimate knowledge of neighborhoods and communities. *A Creative Kind of Murder*, also set in New York City, won a Shamus Award in 1985.

Everything You Have Is Mine. New York: Ballantine, 1992 (1991).

> Initially hired to track down a rapist, Lauren learns she is hunting the victim's murderer. Scattered clues lead back into social action networks of thirty years before and through the fluid spaces of computer dating services.

I'll Be Leaving You Always. New York: Ballantine, 1994 (1993).

> When Lauren's best friend Megan is murdered, the investigator doesn't trust the police to find all the facts. But once Lauren learns the secrets Megan was keeping, she finds it difficult to trust anyone.

My Sweet Untraceable You. New York: Ballantine, 1995 (1994).

> Lauren takes on the thirty-eight-year-old cold case of a mother's disappearance. Paternity issues and reluctant relatives complicate the case but Lauren knows she is on the right trail when a string of murders hits her close to home.

Let's Face the Music and Die. New York: Ballantine, 1997 (1996).

> While Lauren's lover is away at a lengthy conference, another friend needs help: The police suspect her of brutally killing her elderly aunt, and she has no alibi and a powerful motive. Lauren hits the streets and Internet to track down the real killer but finds a new romantic entanglement getting in the way.

Gonna Take a Homicidal Journey. New York: Ballantine, 1999 (1998).

> Relaxing in the countryside, Lauren is hired to investigate a suicide. Frustrated by the silence of the town's prominent citizens, Lauren keeps trying different angles—and knows she is on the right track when she receives a death threat.

Stevenson, Richard.

Donald Strachey Mysteries. G L

Donald Strachey is young, clever, and impulsive; steadied by his Jesuit-trained lover, Timmy Callahan, he makes his living as Albany's only gay private investigator.

Subjects: Books to film • Conspiracy • Homophobia • Law enforcemenr personnel • Murder • Relationships

Read-Alikes: Another gay small-town New York detective is Tom Wilder, in Jon Froscher's *The Woodstock Murders*.

Death Trick. New York: Harrington Park Press, 2003 (1981).

> The wealthy parents of a gay man suspected of murder hire Donald to find their son. As he investigates, the detective becomes convinced of the man's innocence but struggles to find him before the police do.

On the Other Hand, Death. New York: St. Martin's Press, 1995 (1984).

> An intense, anonymous campaign of intimidation leads a lesbian couple to ask for Donald's help.

Ice Blues. New York: Harrington Park Press, 2007 (1986).

> After a nasty snow, Donald's car is towed, and when he goes to pick it up, he finds a dead body in the back seat. Donald finds himself up against the political establishment, drug dealers, and a homophobic police force convinced he is the killer.

Third Man Out. New York: Harrington Park Press, 2007 (1992).

> Queer Nation provocateur John Rutka made enemies by outing closeted conservatives, so he asks Donald to protect him. Donald refuses, finding the man's methods appalling, but when the activist turns up dead, he feels obligated to locate his killers. First published in 1992, this was made into a TV movie in 2005.

A Shock to the System. New York: Harrington Park Press, 2007 (1995).

> The Albany police ruled the death of Paul Haig a suicide. But his mother insists his lover is the culprit, the lover points the finger at Haig's psychiatrist, and the psychiatrist has no alibi but insists he is innocent. All three pay Donald to find the real killer—and then all

three tell him to drop the case. First published in 1995, this was made into a TV movie in 2006.

Chain of Fools. New York: Harrington Park Press, 2007 (1996).

Donald's lover has connections to a newspaper family under attack. The attackers are willing to kill to get the liberal paper in the right hands—and the family is covering up an earlier murder, too.

Strachey's Folly. New York: St. Martin's Press, 1999 (1998).

On a visit to Washington, D.C., to view the NAMES Quilt, Donald and his lover search for the truth behind the presence of a fake panel and try to figure out why a conservative politician was visiting the Quilt in disguise.

Tongue-Tied. New York: St. Martin's Press, 2003.

Donald doesn't like Jay Plankton's politics or on-air personality, but the death threats the shock jock was receiving were apparently coming from a now-defunct radical gay group to which Donald once belonged.

Thomas, Jessica.

Alex Peres Mysteries. L

Provincetown photographer Alex Peres enjoys her life, taking long walks. Fargo, her black lab, drags her into a new job solving mysteries.

Subjects: Dating • Massachusetts • Murder • Pets

Read-Alikes: A good combination of romance and suspense is found in Gerri Hill's *The Target*.

Caught in the Net. Tallahassee, FL: Bella Books, 2004.

Just as Alex gets her life in order, the love of her life walks into the bar, and Fargo finds an important clue on the beach.

Awards: Goldie Award, 2005

Turning the Tables. Ferndale, MI: Bella Books, 2005.

There are many people with a motive to kill the houseboy at a GLBT bed and breakfast, but the police focus on one of the owners. Alex and Fargo take time out from their more mundane assignments to find out why.

Weekend Visitor. Ferndale, MI: Bella Books, 2006.

A lovely young woman living with a mousy local lesbian says she was raped on the way home from a night out. Alex investigates, but the DNA evidence is inconclusive. The pregnancy test came back positive, but it looks like she is a couple months along.

Murder Came Second. Ferndale, MI: Bella Books, 2007.

A Broadway genius re-creates Hamlet as a musical and decides to premiere it in Provincetown. A tabloid reporter, billeted next door to Alex, is the first to die, but the body count rises rapidly when the play opens.

Wings, Mary.

Emma Victor Series. 🄻

Emma Victor is burned out as an activist and a publicist. She finds, though, that she has a knack for sleuthing and trains to become a private investigator.

Subjects: California • Conspiracy • Feminism • Murder

Read-Alikes: Another great hardboiled California feminist is featured in Sue Grafton's <u>Kinsey Millhone Mysteries.</u>

She Came Too Late. Los Angeles: Alyson Books, 2000 (1986).

Emma takes a job staffing a hotline for abused women. After one of her clients is murdered, Emma goes looking for the killer and discovers a network of eminent Bostonians intent on thwarting her.

She Came in a Flash. Los Angeles: Alyson Books, 2001 (1988).

Recovering from a love affair gone bad, Emma moves to Los Angeles and helps publicize a Women's Benefit Concert. When a cultist is murdered and suspicion falls on one of the performers, Emma finds the clues lead to a mysterious commune that supported the concert.

She Came by the Book. New York: Berkley, 1997 (1995).

At the opening of the Gay & Lesbian Archives, the director is poisoned, and a prominent lesbian author has a motive. Hired to clear the woman's name, Emma is thwarted by two more murders before she realizes the killer's identity.

She Came to the Castro. New York: Berkley, 1998.

Emma, newly licensed to carry a concealed weapon, takes a job carrying cash for a blackmailer. Before she can collect the incriminating evidence, though, her employer is killed.

She Came in Drag. New York: Berkley, 1999.

Emma takes a job protecting a scientist who outed a prominent rock star on national TV. When her client is implicated in a murder, Emma wends her way through angry fans and a Halloween-crazed city to find the true killer.

Amateur Detectives

These detectives work cases they stumble into, often beginning by having to prove their own or a friend's innocence. They don't have formal training or a police badge; in fact, they are frequently at odds with the police, who want to close the book on a case as soon as they find a likely suspect. Because of the troubled relationship many GLBT communities historically had with police, amateur detectives still strike a chord with GLBT readers.

Arnott, Jake.

The Long Firm. New York: Soho Press, 1999. **G**

A prominent 1960s gay London gangster has his life story (based on that of the no-torious Kray Twins) told by several associates.

Subjects: 1960s • Books to film • England • Organized crime • Sexual abuse

Read-Alikes: An intense nonfiction look at the Kray Twins (and their organized crime "Firm" that controlled much of 1960s London) is *The Enforcer*, by Albert Donoghue and Martin Short. Claire Macquet's *Looking for Ammu* explores London's present-day criminal underworld.

Azolakov, Antoinette.

Cass Milam Mysteries. **L**

Middle-aged Austin butch lesbian Cass "Mama" Milam uses her network of lov-ers, friends, and contacts to learn the truth behind the deaths of friends.

Subjects: Love • Murder • Texas

Read-Alikes: Another series with a strong butch lesbian is Kate Allen's Alison Kaine Mys-teries.

Cass and the Stone Butch. Austin, TX: Banned Books, 1987.

A friend of Cass, driving back from an illicit rendezvous, dies in a crash. Cass joins with the dead woman's lover to discover if this was murder.

🏵 *Skiptrace.* Austin, TX: Banned Books, 1988.

Cass tracks down an old lover while solving the murder of an acquaintance.

Awards: Lambda Literary Award, 1989

Boyd, Randy.

Devil Inside. Indianapolis, IN: West Beach, 2002. **G**

Businessman Kordell Christie is delighted when an old childhood friend, Mario, reenters his life, but there have been changes. A day after their reunion, his friend is accused of child molestation, and Mario's memory problems lead the two on a wild chase to find the truth behind the weird fragments that keep surfacing.

Subjects: African Americans • California • Mental health • Parenting • Sexual abuse

Read-Alikes: In Joe R. Lansdale's *Bad Chili*, Gay P.I. Leonard Pine, falsely accused of mur-dering his ex-boyfriend, embarks on a quest to clear his name.

Bram, Christopher.

Gossip. New York: Dutton, 1997. **G**

A chance meeting in an online chat room leads a New York bookstore clerk into an affair with a right-wing journalist. When his new interest is murdered, a trail of e-mails lands the clerk in jail, struggling to prove his innocence.

Subjects: Authors • Computers • District of Columbia • Murder • Politics

Read-Alikes: Jon P. Bloch's *Best Murder of the Year* features a gay gossip columnist accused of committing murder at the Academy Awards.

Cathcart, Dwight.

*Ceremonie*s. Boston: Adriana Books, 2005. **G**

In 1984, three teenage boys beat Charles Howard and threw him into a river, where he drowned. The reader learns the details through first-person narratives from people of the small Maine town where the crime occurred.

Subjects: 1980s • Hate crimes • Homophobia • Maine • Murder

Read-Alikes: *The Laramie Project*, by Moisés Kaufman and the Tectonic Theater Project, takes a similar approach to the true story of Matthew Shephard's murder.

Craft, Michael.

Mark Manning Series. **G** **B**

Journalist Mark Manning looks into cases of missing persons, murders, and family secrets in Chicago and Wisconsin.

Subjects: Authors • Families• Illinois • Murder • Politics • Wisconsin

Read-Alikes: Some characters from this series also appear in Craft's straight female detective series, the <u>Claire Gray Series</u>. Claudia McKay's <u>Lynn Evans Mysteries</u> also feature a journalist with a knack for solving mysteries.

Flight Dreams. New York: Kensington Books, 1997.

Mark's publisher gives him a ninety-day deadline to prove that heiress Helena Carter, missing for seven years, is still alive. Tension builds between Mark and the Catholic Church, which stands to inherit Helena's millions if she is declared legally dead, and a religious sect based in the Southwest. Mark comes out in the course of this adventure.

Eye Contact. New York: Kensington Books, 1998.

Another reporter is killed while covering the sensational claims of a supposed astrophysicist, leading Mark to redouble his efforts to expose the charlatan.

Body Language. New York: Kensington Books, 1999.

Mark quits his Chicago newspaper job to take over a family newspaper in Dumont, Wisconsin. Family politics disturb the idyll of his homecoming, though, when his cousin is murdered and her emotionally disturbed son is accused of the crime.

Name Games. New York: St. Martin's Minotaur, 2000.

When a leading designer of dollhouse interiors is strangled on a visit to Dumont, Mark searches for leads in the depths of the toy industry

Boy Toy. New York: St. Martin's Minotaur, 2001.

Hunky high school athlete Jason Thrush is killed, and most of Dumont seems to have a motive—from his father, who had just taken out a life insurance policy on him, to his sister, also betting on his demise, to his rival in the theater. Mark sifts through the facts to find the true killer.

Hot Spot. New York: St. Martin's Minotaur, 2003.

> Mark and his partner attend the wedding of a friend to a major political hopeful. A chief contributor to the campaign dies at the ceremony under circumstances that implicate the bride. Fast-paced and complicated, this book keeps the reader guessing until the very last page.

Bitch Slap. New York: St. Martin's Minotaur, 2004.

> Mark is guiding the family newspaper to a friendly merger with a local paper company when an altercation and the discovery of some questionable accounting practices—and the death of the paper company manager—complicate the transaction.

Dreher, Sarah.

Stoner McTavish Series. L

Supernaturally gifted travel agent and sometime sleuth Stoner McTavish voyages widely, solving mysteries and fighting evil. There are elements of horror, fantasy, and science fiction in some of these stories, but always a mystery to be solved.

Subjects: Murder • Relationships • Supernatural • Travel

Read-Alikes: Ghosts and angels figure prominently in Mark A. Roeder's *Someone Is Killing the Gay Boys of Verona*.

Stoner McTavish. Norwich, VT: New Victoria, 1985

> Stoner visits the Grand Tetons to check out the husband of a friend's granddaughter. Her investigation into a threat against the woman is complicated when she realizes she is falling in love with her.

Something Shady. Norwich, VT: New Victoria, 1986.

> To solve the mysterious disappearance of a nurse, Stoner goes undercover at a "rest home" facility on the coast of Maine. Her cover as a mental patient exposes her to the machinations of the facilities director and places her in a terrifying environment.

Gray Magic. Norwich, VT: New Victoria, 1987.

> Stoner and her newly found lover Gwen vacation in Arizona, only to be drawn into an ancient struggle between light and darkness.

Captive in Time. Norwich, VT: New Victoria, 1990.

> Stoner finds herself transported back to 1871 and a small town in Colorado, which is under threat from a series of unexplained fires.

OtherWorld. Norwich, VT: New Victoria, 1993.

> Stoner travels with her family and business partner to the Disney World Resort for a holiday. When one of them is kidnapped, Stoner journeys into an alternative reality where the rides come to life and back into a shared past she thought was long over.

Bad Company. Norwich, VT: New Victoria, 1995.

> A feminist theater company finds itself the subject of sabotage, threatening notes, and a series of menacing accidents, which draw Stoner and her partner Gwen into the spiraling crisis.

Shaman's Moon. Norwich, VT: New Victoria, 1998.

> Dark spirits are stirring in the small town of Shelburne Falls. Stoner must solve the threat to her aunt before evil has its way.

Drury, Joan M.

Feminist Mystery Series. 🅛 🅑

Newspaper columnist Tyler Jones finds the clues to mysteries in the tangled relationships of family and friends.

Subjects: Authors • Murder • Relationships

Read-Alikes: Claudia McKay's series <u>Lynn Evans Mysteries</u> also features a journalist with a knack for solving mysteries.

The Other Side of Silence. Duluth, MN: Spinsters Ink, 1993.

> Tyler and her dog find a body in San Francisco's Golden Gate Park. The ensuing investigation leads to an abusive family with many secrets.

Silent Words. Duluth, MN: Spinsters Ink, 1996.

> Sent by her dying mother's command to "learn the truth," Tyler journeys to the family home on the shores of Lake Superior. Her quest uncovers a web of hidden agreements, and the discovery of a couple of corpses complicates things even further.

Closed in Silence. Duluth, MN: Spinsters Ink, 1996.

> The discovery of a dead body disrupts Tyler's twentieth college reunion. She doesn't recognize the deceased, but her five friends do—and any one of them could be the murderer.

Gummerson, Drew.

Lodger. London: Prowler/GMP, 2002. 🅖

An unsuccessful gay writer who needs a lodger to split expenses shares his home with a coarse straight man. The writer refuses to believe his lodger's drunken confession of murder until after the tenant unexpectedly disappears for a weekend—and comes back badly beaten.

Subjects: Authors • England • Families • Humor

Read-Alikes: A similar surreal, comic, occasionally menacing atmosphere is found in *The Summer They Came*, by William Storandt.

Hart, Ellen.

Jane Lawless Series. 🅛

Minneapolis restaurant owner Jane Lawless and her wisecracking close friend Cordelia Thorn stumble into and solve mysteries concerning their acquaintances.

Subjects: Couples • Families • Food • Minnesota • Murder • Substance abuse

Read-Alikes: Jane DiLucchio's *Relationships Can Be Murder* has a similar semi-cozy feel to it.

Hallowed Murder. New York: St. Martin's Press, 2003 (1989).

When a woman's death is dismissed as suicide but her sorority sisters insist it was not, Jane and Cordelia find fundamentalism, bigotry, and family troubles made the victim's lesbianism a motive for murder.

Vital Lies. New York: St. Martin's Press, 2004 (1991).

Celebrating the winter solstice at a friend's inn, Jane and Cordelia are asked to solve an old mystery. Before they can get started though, a series of spiteful pranks escalates to brutal murder.

Stage Fright. New York: St. Martin's Press, 2004 (1992).

Jane discovers the body of an actor impaled on part of a stage set and becomes a suspect. She and Cordelia seek the murderer among the victim's dramatic family.

A Killing Cure. New York: St. Martin's, 2005 (1993).

Two directors of the Gower Foundation are found dead; the police arrest a former employee for one slaying but rule the other an accidental death. The remaining directors disagree and ask Jane to get to the bottom of things—but then turn markedly uncooperative as she delves into old club business.

A Small Sacrifice. New York: Ballantine Books, 1996 (1994).

Cordelia goes to an alcoholic friend's new theater in Spring Green, Wisconsin, accompanied by four other friends, determined to stage an intervention. Old friendships give way to rancor and one friend dies; Cordelia asks Jane to come help sort things out.

Awards: Lambda Literary Award, 1994

Faint Praise. New York: Ballantine Books, 1997 (1995).

A famous TV personality, Arno Heywood, dresses in women's clothes before plunging to his death from a skyscraper. Jane is convinced to move into the dead man's apartment to put an end to an escalating series of crimes in his building, but before she can solve the case, a brutal murder raises the stakes.

Robber's Wine. New York: Ballantine Books, 1998 (1996).

Jane cancels a holiday when an old friend's mother is murdered just before she can confide family secrets to her children. As the case unfolds and more murders are committed, suspicion falls on virtually everyone connected with the family.

Awards: Lambda Literary Award, 1997

Wicked Games. New York: St. Martin's Press, 1999 (1998).

Jane takes a new tenant who claims to be having psychic visions of murder. After his sister moves nearby and a girl's bones are found in Jane's yard, she learns her house was once their home—and there are more deaths in their past.

Hunting the Witch. New York: St. Martin's Press, 2000 (1999).

Jane, recuperating from injuries, is asked by a friend to pose as a consultant to investigate the death of an opponent of a charity rehabilitation project. The widow of the deceased asks her to find out if her late husband had been gay, and Jane becomes involved with the primary suspect in his murder.

Awards: Lambda Literary Award, 2000

Merchant of Venus. New York: St. Martin's Press, 2002 (2001).

> Jane and Cordelia go east for the wedding of Cordelia's sister to a famous but reclusive director. The groom, and then the young filmmaker hired to record the event, are murdered. As Jane attempts to make sense of a wildly varied field of suspects, old Hollywood ghosts begin to stir.

Immaculate Midnight. New York: St. Martin's Press, 2003 (2002).

> Minneapolis attorney Raymond Lawless and his family find themselves under attack following the execution of a serial arsonist known as the Midnight Man. His daughter Jane attempts to find the culprit, with the aid of her lover, a Norwegian gypsy, and a flamboyant local actress friend.
>
> **Awards:** Lambda Literary Award, 2002

Intimate Ghost. New York: St. Martin's Press, 2005 (2004).

> Jane caters a wedding reception. She watches in horror as the entire group begins to act out under the influence of hallucinogens slipped into the food. This is only the beginning of the chaos; she and Cordelia turn up a kidnapping, bodies, and a decades-old legacy of deception.
>
> **Awards:** Goldie Award, 2005

Iron Girl. New York: St. Martin's Press, 2006 (2005).

> Finally dealing with the effects of her dead lover, Jane turns up evidence that a convicted murderer may not have committed the crime. A double of her dead lover appears and sweeps Jane off her feet—but Cordelia is suspicious.
>
> **Awards:** Goldie Award, 2006

Night Vision. New York: St. Martin's Press, 2006.

> Movie star Joanna Kasimir returns to Minneapolis to star in a production at Cordelia's theater and hires Jane to protect her from her abusive ex-husband. Joanna's brother also comes to town—and when the husband is killed, the brother is the likeliest suspect.

Herren, Greg.

Scott Bradley Series. G

> Scott Bradley starts training for his private investigator's license after he finds he has a talent for intrigue.
>
> **Subjects:** Bars • Homophobia • Louisiana • Religion • Spirituality
>
> **Read-Alikes:** The Australian Mardi Gras is the setting for Phillip Scott's *Mardi Gras Murders*, featuring Marc and Paul investigating a serial killer.

Bourbon Street Blues. New York: Kensington Books, 2003.

> Scott, a French Quarter–based personal trainer gifted in Tarot, finds himself in possession of information about a plot to destroy the city. Told with care for local color and atmosphere, his adventures in search of love include frying pan–wielding lesbians, the FBI, hungry alligators, and political scandal.

Jackson Square Jazz. New York: Kensington Books, 2004.

> Dealing with the rigors of a long-distance relationship, Scott goes out to the bars and returns home with Colin, a hot ice skater. Scott sets up a date with the athlete but trips over a body during the assignation, then works to prove Colin innocent of the murder.

Hunt, David.

🎗 *Magician's Tale.* New York: G.P. Putnam's Sons, 1997. **G** **L**

San Francisco photographer Kay Farrow is stunned when one of her subjects is killed. She determines to solve the case and winds up entering both the world of the city's male hustlers and that of professional magic.

Subjects: California • Murder • Photography • Sex workers

Awards: Lambda Literary Award, 1997

Read-Alikes: The brooding atmosphere of the city is reminiscent of Anne Rice's depiction of New Orleans in *Interview with a Vampire.*

Hunter, Fred.

Alex Reynolds Mysteries. **G**

Extreme campiness characterizes these ensemble cast pieces featuring graphic designer and amateur sleuth/spy Alex Reynolds, his husband Peter, and his British mother Jean, solving spy-related cases with the reluctant help of the CIA.

Subjects: Humor • Illinois • Law enforcement personnel • Murder

Read-Alikes: Rick Copps's Actors Guide Series is another action-packed, humorous gay mystery series.

Government Gay. New York: St. Martin's Press, 1998 (1997).

> In a comedy of errors, Alex lights the cigarette of a spy, convincing both the foreign agents trailing him and the CIA that Alex has acquired top-secret information. Jean and Peter are pulled into the comic mayhem.

Federal Fag. New York: St. Martin's Press, 1999. (1998)

> After recognizing his former lover in one of the films and finding him dead before they can meet, Alex is drawn into the world of gay pornography. Peter and Jean sort out a confusing sequence of events.

Capital Queers. New York: St. Martin's Press, 2000. (1999)

> Alex and Peter lose a dear friend, Mason, and his prized doll collection is shattered in pieces around his body. A week later, Mason's partner Ryan suffers the same fate—and the same doll pieces are present. With a hint from the CIA and more than a little help from Jean, Alex and Peter focus their investigation on a doll Mason had recently acquired.

National Nancys. New York: St. Martin's Press, 2000.

> Alex and Peter volunteer in the campaign of a liberal Senate candidate whose Chicago office is bombed. Immediate suspicion falls on the religious Right, and the FBI asks Alex and Peter to investigate.

Chicken Asylum. New York: St. Martin's Press, 2001.

> Alex, Peter, and Jean let a gay Iraqi stay with them while the CIA debriefs him. Not surprisingly, this brings the trio to the attention of the terrorists from whom he defected—which seems to have been the CIA's plan all along.

LaFavor, Carole.

Renee LaRoche Series. **L**

A schoolteacher turned amateur sleuth, Renee LaRoche seeks the truth while dealing with the problems of life as a two-spirit person both on and off her Ojibwa reservation.

Subjects: Minnesota • Native Americans • Sexual abuse

Read-Alikes: The solid presence of the Ojibwa culture is reminiscent of Tony Hillerman's treatment of the Navajo in the Joe Leaphorn Mysteries.

Along the Journey River. Ithaca, NY: Firebrand Books, 1996.

> Renee steps in when priceless tribal artifacts are stolen from the school where she teaches her fellow Ojibwas—and her chief is found dead with a bullet in his back.

Evil Dead Center. Ithaca, NY: Firebrand Books, 1997.

> When the death of an Ojibwa woman near the reservation is chalked up to alcoholism and the effects of unprotected exposure to the weather, Renee disagrees and pursues her own investigation.

Maddison, Lauren.

Connor Hawthorne Series. **L**

Connor Hawthorne, a former attorney turned mystery writer, uses her inborn psychic powers and the assistance of her Navajo companion's spiritual wisdom to work her way through real-life cases.

Subjects: Authors • Conspiracy • Relationships • Spirituality • Supernatural

Read-Alikes: In Steven Cooper's *With You in Spirit*, family relationships and the supernatural converge while Graydove Hoffenstein, a Native American Jew, employs a clairvoyant to prove his mother did not kill his father. In Mark Del Franco's *Unshapely Things*, an ex-druid tries to stop the supernatural murders of gay prostitutes—and stop the conspiracies of the Unseelie Court.

Deceptions. Los Angeles: Alyson Books, 1999.

> Connor's longtime companion Ariana is murdered, and political considerations force the case to be closed too quickly. With the help of her family's "second sight" and her Navajo guide Laura, Connor follows the trail across New Mexico to find the villain.

Witchfire. Los Angeles: Alyson Books, 2001.

> After her grandmother's grave is desecrated, Connor goes to England with Laura to find out why—and maybe learn something about her family's psychic powers at the same time.

Death by Prophecy. Los Angeles: Alyson Books, 2002.

Hawthorn and Laura tour California's mission country, where they become involved in violence, which may be either contemporary protest or the continuance of a centuries-old struggle within the Catholic Church.

Epitaph for an Angel. Los Angeles: Alyson Books, 2003.

In Boston at the funeral of Laura's mother, Connor is a horrified witness to the deaths of her own mother and the deceased's aunt. An amulet, "the thief of souls," long a legacy of the Hawthornes, may be the key to a centuries-old conspiracy.

Eleventh Hour. Los Angeles: Alyson Books, 2004.

Laura and Connor are relaxing in Palm Springs, but a chance poolside encounter soon has them flying to England to investigate Sister Sonia, a psychic healer who is channeling powers she does not understand.

McDermid, Val.

Lindsay Gordon Series. L

In this series out British lesbian and journalist Lindsay Gordon stumbles into mysterious situations featuring social and political elements.

Subjects: Authors • England • Murder

Read-Alikes: *Blind Curves,* by Diane Anderson-Minshall, is an intense mystery in which a lesbian journalist is suspected of killing her enemy.

Report for Murder. Ann Arbor, MI: Bywater Books, 2005 (1987).

Assigned to cover a fund-raiser at an all-girl's school, Lindsay is on hand when the headmistress is found garroted. An old friend is accused of the crime, and Lindsay and her new lover, Cordelia, set out to solve the mystery.

Common Murder. Ann Arbor, MI: Bywater Books, 2005 (1989).

An ex-girlfriend of Lindsay's is accused of attacking a lawyer trying to shut down a women's camp—and shortly after Deborah is released on bail, the lawyer is killed. Meanwhile, trouble is brewing between Lindsay and Cordelia.

Deadline for Murder. Ann Arbor, MI: Bywater Books, 2005 (1991).

A bisexual seductress is murdered, and Lindsay's determination to find the killer is intensified when another friend is accused of the crime. Blackmail, stolen evidence, and the darker side of journalism all complicate her search for the truth. First published as *Final Edition* in 1991.

Conferences Are Murder. Ann Arbor, MI: Bywater Books, 2006 (1993).

Lindsay, taking a break from her work in California, covers a trade union gathering in Sheffield. One of her enemies, labor organizer Tom Jack, falls to his death from the window of Lindsay's room on the hotel's tenth floor—so Lindsay needs to solve the case to clear her name. First published as *Union Jack* in 1993.

Booked for Murder. Ann Arbor, MI: Bywater Books, 2006 (1996).

> Lindsay travels to London to investigate the death of an old friend and popular author of teen books, who was killed by the method described in the friend's forthcoming novel.

Hostage to Murder. Ann Arbor, MI: Bywater Books, 2005 (2003).

> Returned to Scotland, Lindsay goes back to freelance journalism with her friend Rory McClaren. A local businessman's son is kidnapped, and Lindsay and Rory follow the trail to Russia on a desperate rescue mission that could cost Lindsay her life.

Michaels, Grant.

Stan Kraychik Series. G

Sassy, flamboyant hairdresser Stan Kraychik solves crimes at stereotypically gay destinations, such as Key West, the opera, and the ballet.

Subjects: Law enforcement personnel • Massachusetts • Murder • Urban renewal

Read-Alikes: Another fast-moving, funny group of mysteries is Rick Copps's <u>Actors Guide Series.</u>

Body to Dye For. New York: St. Martin's Press, 1991. (1990)

> Stan is suspected in the death of a National Park Ranger he'd been eying. With a quick wit, sharp tongue, and some unorthodox methods, Stan tries to prove his innocence.

Love You to Death. New York: St. Martin's Press, 1993. (1992)

> Without a date for Valentine's Day, Stan decides to attend a posh reception. When a guest is poisoned, Stan tries to clear his friend Lauren of suspicion.

Dead on Your Feet. New York: St. Martin's Press, 1993.

> When a ballet director is messily killed, Stan is asked to interview the entire self-absorbed ballet company, including new boyfriend Rafik, who may be just too good to be true.

Mask for a Diva. New York: St. Martin's Press, 1996. (1994)

> A special gig as wig assistant in an opera production takes Stan to Boston, where the lead soprano is silenced for good. Stan is again deputized to do the interrogations.

Time to Check Out. New York: St. Martin's Press, 1997. (1996)

> Mourning the accidental death of Rafik, which left him independently wealthy, Stan goes to Key West. There, less than a day after checking in, he is summarily evicted by the homophobic landlady, who is found dead soon thereafter. Since she was contesting her son's will—which left all his riches to his friends—Stan has a long list of motivated people to investigate.

Dead as a Doornail. New York: St. Martin's Press, 2000. (1998)

> Stan finds the contractor he hired to restore his brownstone in the house one morning, dead. Stan may have been the actual target, and a new love distracts him as he tries to solve the puzzle.

Miller, Carlene.

Lexy Hyatt Mysteries. [L]

Investigative reporter Lexy Hyatt finds her skill at working a story useful in solving crimes, to the chagrin of the professional crime-fighters.

Subjects: Authors • Murder

Read-Alikes: Another journalist who solves crimes is found in Claudia McKay's <u>Lynn Evans Mysteries</u>.

Killing at the Cat. Norwich, VT: New Victoria, 1998.

> Out for the evening at her favorite bar, Lexy's fun is brought to a swift end when another patron is killed. She uses the research for her story on the incident as the basis for her sleuthing. A homophobic skinhead gang that may have targeted the bar muddles the trail.

Mayhem at the Marina. Norwich, VT: New Victoria, 1998.

> A corpse is found in the lake from which a small Florida town derives its tourist income. Lexy looks for clues and finds the murder weapon in the possession of her new friend, Charlie.

Reporter on the Run. Norwich, VT: New Victoria, 2001.

> The feuding twin owners of the paper Lexy works for is putting on an orienteering competition for the staff, and Lexy is asked to enter to make sure no one cheats. A murder on the course turns up lots of people with a motive, but Lexy uses some inside information to catch the killer.

Nava, Michael.

Henry Rios Mysteries. [G] [L]

The mysteries in this series are almost secondary to the complex character of Henry Rios, a Mexican American attorney haunted by the deaths of friends and family yet compelled to solve crimes.

Subjects: AIDS • California • Civil rights • Hispanics • Lawyers • Murder

Read-Alikes: Steven Lewis's *Cowboy Blues* is another character-driven Los Angeles gay mystery.

A Little Death. Los Angeles: Alyson Books, 2003 (1986).

> Gay attorney Henry Rios is assigned to be the pubic defender of a man who turns out to be the heir of a wealthy family. They become friends, and his client warn Rios he fears for his life, but he is killed before he can explain. Unanswered questions create a trail that leads into the homes of the wealthy and deep into the past.

🎗 *Goldenboy.* Los Angeles: Alyson Books, 2004 (1988).

> The murder of a young man leads attorney Henry Rios into a complex network of deception and danger in the glittering night world of the film and theater set.
>
> **Awards:** Lambda Literary Award, 1988

🎗 *How Town.* New York: HarperTrade, 1990.

> Attorney Henry Rios receives a call from his estranged sister, who asks him to defend a friend's husband accused of murder. The case leads him back to his former hometown in California's Central Valley and into dark corners of the human mind.
>
> **Awards:** Lambda Literary Award, 1990

🎗 *Hidden Law.* Los Angeles: Alyson Books, 2004 (1992).

> Openly gay Latino attorney Henry Rios is caught in a web of conflicting duties to his community, his clients, and his HIV-positive lover when a prominent local politician is murdered.
>
> **Awards:** Lambda Literary Award, 1992

🎗 *Death of Friends.* Los Angeles: Alyson Books, 2004 (1996).

> Attorney Henry Rios is forced to revisit an old friendship when the lover of a closeted married friend shows up on his doorstep to report a murder. The trail leads through judicial chambers, a porn studio, and deep into the past.
>
> **Awards:** Lambda Literary Award, 1996

Burning Plain. Los Angeles: Alyson Books, 2004 (1997).

> Attorney Henry Rios is still recovering from the death of his partner when he begins a relationship with a young actor who was formerly one of his clients. When the young man is murdered after leaving Henry's house, the police suspect Henry—until other deaths hit the gay community. Henry sets out to track down those responsible.

🎗 *Rag and Bone.* New York: Putnam, 2001.

> The last in the group of novels following the career of openly gay attorney Henry Rios, this emotionally charged story takes the reader deep into the underworld of Los Angeles and into the complexities of beginning new relationships. Rios is faced with the challenge of rebuilding life with his sister and a new lover and helping his newly found niece face a murder charge.
>
> **Awards:** Lambda Literary Award, 2001

Nelson, Casey.

Nothing Gold Can Stay. New York: Dutton, 2000. **G**

> A summer graduate theater program and possible romance turn into a nightmare for Ray O'Brien when his love interest is implicated in the messy death of another student.
>
> **Subjects:** Authors • Couples • England • Students, college • Theater

Read-Alikes: The <u>Actors Guide Series</u>, by Jon D. Bloch, also takes an amusing look at dark doings among the theater set.

Raphael, Lev.

Nick Hoffman Mystery Series. 🄶 🄻 🄱

State University of Michigan professor of English Nick Hoffman and his lover Stefan Borowski solve crimes, in these amusing satires of academic life and politics.

Subjects: Jews • Literature • Michigan • Murder • Relationships • Teachers

Read-Alikes: Stefan first appears (and comes out) in Raphael's literary novel *Winter Eyes.* In C. S. Laurel's *B. Quick,* a small college in Colorado is the setting for murder.

Let's Get Criminal. New York: St. Martin's Press, 1997. (1996)

> When Nick's mysterious and annoying new officemate is killed, the police focus their attention on Stefan, and Nick determines to prove his innocence.

The Edith Wharton Murders. New York: St. Martin's Press, 1999. (1997)

> Warring schools of thought on Edith Wharton's work seem to take things too far as murder interrupts a symposium—and Nick, who organized the conference, is determined to find the culprits.

Death of a Constant Lover. New York: St. Martin's Press, 2000. (1999)

> Trying to get past the murders of the last few years, Nick accepts his destiny when he witnesses the death of one of his students during a campus demonstration—and another student is killed soon after.

Little Miss Evil. New York: Walker, 2000.

> Nick, who's always been gay, is confused by his attraction to fellow English professor Juno Dromgoole, who is seeking allies in her quest to become dean. Campus politics turns deadly when the controversial new professor Camille Cypriani is found strangled with a scarf belonging to Juno.

Burning Down the House. New York: Walker, 2001.

> Juno has been receiving harassing phone calls and asks Nick to find out who is involved. Both Nick and Juno are subjected to increasing intimidation but, to Nick's relief, no murder. A side plot deals with Nick's increasing fascination with and lust for Juno.

Tropic of Murder. McKinleyville, CA: John Daniel, 2004.

> Nick and Stefan flee winter and campus politics for a Caribbean resort. The holiday idyll vanishes when they discover the body of a resort employee.

Hot Rocks. McKinleyville, CA: John Daniel, 2007.

> Nick abruptly stops musing aloud about his midlife crisis when he realizes the man in the steam room with him is dead. Juno and Nick team up to solve the mystery.

Rice, Christopher.

Density of Souls. New York: Hyperion, 2000. **G**

A web of deceit centering on childhood friends Meredith, Brandon, Greg, and Stephen entangles four families. Peer pressure redefines the friendships, with consequences that reverberate for years to come.

Subjects: Coming out • Death and dying • Friendship • Homophobia • Louisiana

Read-Alikes: Bart Yates's *Leave Myself Behind* is another searing depiction of a gay teenager facing down discrimination.

🎗 *Snow Garden.* New York: Hyperion Press, 2003. **G** **L**

The lives and secret pasts of college students Tim, Randall, Jesse, and Kathryn interweave with those of one of their professors and the realities of being openly gay on a prestigious campus. Foul play is suspected when the professor, who is having an affair with Randall, is suddenly widowed.

Awards: Lambda Literary Award, 2003

Subjects: Authors • Murder • Students, college • Teachers

Read-Alikes: *The Lake of Dead Languages*, by Carol Goodman, is an equally taut thriller, about secrets and murder at an all-girls high school.

Schulman, Sarah.

🎗 *After Dolores.* New York: Dutton, 1988. **L**

An unnamed, heart-broken narrator wanders about New York City looking for her girlfriend, Dolores. Plotting ways to win Dolores back, the narrator stumbles onto a murder, obtains a gun, vows to find the murderer, and thus win back Dolores.

Awards: Stonewall Book Award, 1989

Subjects: Murder • New York City • Relationships

Read-Alikes: Claire Macquet's *Looking for Ammu* explores London's underworld as the heroine seeks the woman she idolizes.

Sims, Elizabeth.

Lillian Byrd Crime Stories. **L**

A reporter with a knack for making bad choices, Lillian Byrd uses her investigative skills (which include a hilarious talent for impersonation) to solve the crimes she stumbles onto. Her pet rabbit, Todd, is a well-loved sidekick.

Subjects: Michigan • Murder • Pets

Read-Alikes: Another mystery that effectively combines humor and suspense is Morgan Hunt's *Sticky Fingers*.

Holy Hell. Los Angeles: Alyson Books, 2002.

While researching her article on the murder of a lesbian bar DJ, Lillian fends off the amorous advances of her boss's son—and gets fired. Unwilling to let the story drop, she continues her investigation but tips the perpetrators to her interest.

🌳 *Damn Straight.* Los Angeles: Alyson Books, 2003.

> Lillian goes to the Dinah Shore Invitational Golf Championship to help a friend and ends up aiding an LPGA star who is being terrorized by a stalker.
>
> **Awards:** Lambda Literary Award, 2003

Lucky Stiff. Los Angeles: Alyson Books, 2004.

> An old friend reveals secrets that call into question the official report of the deaths of Lillian's parents when she was twelve. This story is markedly darker than the first two.

Easy Street. Los Angeles: Alyson Books, 2005.

> Helping an ex-police friend renovate her house, Lillian is surprised to find a cache of money hidden inside a wall they demolish—and connections between her friend and a dead street person.

Stukas, David.

Robert Wilsop Series. 🄶

Recovering Catholic and women's hygiene product ad writer Robert Wilsop is joined by two friends—the wealthy, hypersexual Michael Stark and the statuesque soccer star Monette O'Reilley—in solving crimes.

Subjects: Humor • Murder • Relationships

Read-Alikes: *The Summer They Came,* by William Storandt, has a similar campy humor.

Someone Killed His Boyfriend. New York: Kensington Books, 2001.

> Max's perfect boyfriend leaves him humiliated at the altar and then is found murdered. The police find Max an obvious suspect; Monette and Robert join with Max to hunt down the real killer.

Going Down for the Count. New York: Kensington Books, 2002.

> Count Siegfried von Schmidt has swept Robert off his feet and off to Germany. Michael is the prime suspect, though, when the count is found knifed in Berlin. Fortunately, Monette is present to head up the investigation.

Wearing Black to the White Party. New York: Kensington, 2003.

> Rex Gifford, the organizer of Palm Springs' Red Party, is found electrocuted in his pool. Robert and Michael, with the aid of Rex's formidable friend Monique, take on the task of solving this desert riddle.

Biceps of Death. New York: Kensington, 2004.

> Someone slips a DVD in Robert's gym bag, then falls to his death before retrieving it—and the DVD is filled with salacious images of prominent (and officially straight) men around town. Robert's life is at risk, and he turns to Monette for help in untangling this mystery.

Swearingen, Ida.

🌳 *Owl of the Desert.* Norwich, VT: New Victoria, 2003. 🄻

> Newly released from prison after turning state's evidence, Kate Porter is immediately drawn into working for the police against her radical militia father—only to find that the enemies are not who they appear to be.

Awards: *ForeWord Magazine*'s Book of the Year Award, 2003

Subjects: Conspiracy • Convicts • Kansas • Politics • Relationships, parent-child • Soldiers and sailors

Read-Alikes: *Sappho Rising*, by Mary Vasiliades, has a militia subplot.

Szymanski, Therese.

Motor City Thriller Series. L T

Butch nightclub owner Brett Higgins was involved in organized crime for years, until she met the policewoman who changed her life. The enemies she made in the underworld have long memories, though, and keep coming after her.

Subjects: Crime • Law enforcement personnel • Michigan • Murder

Read-Alikes: Patricia Highsmith's <u>Tom Ripley Series</u> presents another rogue the reader can't help but love.

When the Dancing Stops. Tallahassee, FL: Naiad, 1997.

Brett is respected in Detroit's underworld and is known to the cops as the owner of a shady nightclub that fronts for criminal activity. Smitten with a policewoman, though, Brett saves her from the mob and leaves her dark past behind.

When the Dead Speak. Tallahassee, FL: Naiad, 1998.

Brett and Allie have moved to California to escape the enemies Brett made in Detroit—but someone has followed them and leaves a chilling calling card—bloody clothes and a butcher's knife.

When Some Body Disappears. Tallahassee, FL: Naiad, 1999.

Back in Michigan, police again investigate Brett for murder—and her old enemies are again on her trail. Brett's only chance for survival is to find the killers herself.

When Evil Changes Face. Ferndale, MI: Bella Books, 2000.

Brett Higgins and her lover, Allie Sullivan, return to the world of high school, posing as brother and sister to investigate a suspected drug operation. They become targets for both an unknown killer and the affections of their unsuspecting classmates.

When Good Girls Go Bad. Tallahassee, FL: Bella Books, 2003.

A serial killer takes down one of Brett's dancers, and the police see Brett as the most likely suspect. Allie goes undercover as a dancer to trap the murderer.

When the Corpse Lies. Tallahassee, FL: Bella Books, 2004.

Brett's business is now completely legit, but she still has a hankering for the wild side—which she appeases through cybersex. Her online experiences lead underworld enemies to her; when she tries to hide, the police think she is running because she killed someone she picked up.

When First We Practice. Tallahassee, FL: Bella Books, 2005.

> Allie's ex-partner Jill pulls a gun at a club, and Brett steps in to defuse the situation. The next morning, though, Jill is defending herself against a murder rap, and Allie asks Brett to investigate.

Van Adler, T. C.

Father Brocard Mysteries Series. ⓖ ⓑ ⓣ

> Gay Father Brocard investigates international art thefts and ancillary crimes, with the assistance of Zinka Pavlic, a Serbo-Croatian transsexual art historian.

Subjects: Art and artists • Crime • Murder • Pennsylvania • Prisons • Religion

Read-Alikes: *Death Goes on Retreat,* by Carol Anne O'Marie, takes a gentler look at official and unofficial Catholic responses to homosexuality.

St. Agatha's Breast. Los Angeles: Alyson Books, 2001 (1999)..

> Several paintings were taken from San Redempto Monastery; the single remaining painting is revealed to be a previously unknown treasure. While Father Brocard and Zinka search for clues, the enemies of his order gather and start picking off his brethren.

Evil That Boys Do. Los Angeles: Alyson Books, 2003.

> A murder at the Pennsylvania penitentiary where he is chaplain sets Father Brocard on the trail of a long-vanished Caravaggio painting, aided by his unlikely transsexual art historian colleague, Zinka. Their search leads to Paris and Palermo, and to meetings with memorable characters such as Dean the Nose, before the riddle is finally resolved.

Webb, Cynthia.

No Daughter of the South. Norwich, VT: New Victoria, 1997. ⓛ

> Struggling New York journalist Laurie Coldwater returns to her hometown in Florida to investigate the death of her African American lover's father, only to find that her ex-husband is now the local sheriff and her own family are anything but welcoming.

Subjects: African Americans • Authors • Families • Florida • Homophobia • Race relations

Read-Alikes: Claudia McKay's <u>Lynn Evans Mysteries</u> also feature a lesbian reporter and amateur sleuth. Christopher Bram's *Gossip* does a good job depicting life in the conservative South.

Welsh, Louise.

Cutting Room. Edinburgh: Canongate Books, 2002. ⓖ

> Gay auctioneer Rilke finds a horrifying cache of pornography centering on deliberate killing for its sexual overtones. His search to learn if the murder was fake or real leads him—and the reader—into some of the city's darker corners.

Subjects: Auctions • Murder • Pornography • Scotland

Read-Alikes: Reginald Hill's *A Pinch of Snuff* also looks at a snuff film ring.

Wilson, Barbara.

Cassandra Reilly Series. G L B T

9

Cassandra Reilly is a publisher's translator who loves to travel. With her knack for languages, she is a natural for jumping into foreign investigations.

Subjects: Authors • Books to film • Relationships • Travel

Read-Alikes: *Love's Last Chance*, by Krandall Kraus, is a mystery set in a series of exotic locations. Don't miss the collection of Cassandra's exploits, *Death of a Well-Travelled Woman*, listed in the "Short Story Collections" section of this chapter.

10

🎗 *Gaudi Afternoon.* Seattle: Seal Press, 2001 (1990).

Cassandra, a lesbian expatriate writer in Barcelona, is asked to find a stranger's husband to resolve a legal settlement. When the husband turns out to be female, the issue of child custody rears its head. This book was made into a movie in 2001.

11

Awards: Lambda Literary Award, 1990

Trouble in Transylvania. Seattle: Seal Press, 1993.

On her way to China by train via Budapest, Cassandra steps in to help a new friend defend herself against accusations of murdering a Romanian spa owner.

12

Case of the Orphaned Bassoonists. Seattle: Seal Press, 2000.

A friend accused of stealing a valuable antique bassoon asks Cassandra for help. The retrieval of the lost instrument is soon overshadowed by a murder.

13

Wilson, John Morgan.

Benjamin Justice Mysteries Series. G

Fired from his newspaper for an ethical lapse, middle-aged Ben Justice finds a new life investigating crimes freelance.

Subjects: AIDS • Authors • California • Homophobia • Law enforcement personnel • Murder

14

Read-Alikes: Curt Colbert's *Queer Street* is a hardboiled novel set in 1940s Seattle that has a similar noir edge.

Simple Justice. New York: Bantam, 1997. (1996)

Called in by his ex-boss to get to the bottom of the murder of a young gay man, Ben doubts the police assertion that their collar, a young gay Hispanic, committed the crime.

15

Revision of Justice. New York: Bantam, 1999. (1997)

A regular monthly party for Hollywood gay screenwriters turns ugly when one is killed. After a second murder is committed, Ben turns up a hidden Hollywood scandal that ties some of the partygoers together.

16

🌑 *Justice at Risk.* New York: Bantam, 2000. (1999)

> Ben is hired to take over the writing of a series on AIDS for public television, but the director soon turns up dead in a notorious cruising area. Ben and his coproducer follow clues into the S/M subculture of the city and a possible cover-up by the police.
>
> **Awards:** Lambda Literary Award, 1999

🌑 *Limits of Justice.* New York: Bantam, 2001. (2000)

> Ben receives an advance from an heiress who wants to counter charges that her late celebrity father engaged in sexual abuse. The next day, the woman is dead. Ben exposes some of the darker levels of the Los Angeles' underworld as he works to find her killer.
>
> **Awards:** Lambda Literary Award, 2000

🌑 *Blind Eye: A Benjamin Justice Novel.* New York: St. Martin's Press, 2003.

> A friend's fiancée is murdered in a drive-by shooting, which may or may not be related to Ben's search for a clergyman from his past. Threats from the underworld and local religious leaders only make him more determined to succeed.
>
> **Awards:** Lambda Literary Award, 2003

Moth and Flame. New York: St. Martin's Press, 2004.

> When the original author is brutally slain, Ben accepts a commission to finish some publicity for the twentieth anniversary of West Hollywood. Ben's research connects his predecessor's death with the disappearance decades ago of a bisexual handyman.

Rhapsody in Blood. New York: St. Martin's Press, 2006.

> Ben is in the resort town of Haunted Springs, where a movie is being filmed about the murder of a starlet there fifty years ago and the lynching of a black man that followed soon after. A gossip columnist is also there, ferreting out personal information about the cast; when she is killed, Ben is faced with many suspects who wanted her dead.

Wings, Mary.

🌑 *Divine Victim.* New York: Dutton Adult, 1993. 🇱

> The narrator's lover inherits a house full of religious art in Billings, Montana, from her deceased great-aunt, on the condition that she live there for one year. The couple leave the Bay Area to take up residence, only to find unraveling the past of the house as complicated as the valuable paintings.
>
> **Awards:** Lambda Literary Award, 1993
>
> **Subjects:** Art and artists • Montana • Relationships • Religion
>
> **Read-Alikes:** Barbara Wilson's *If You Had a Family* looks at the effects of a Christian Scientist background and family dysfunction on future relationships.

Woodcraft, Elizabeth.

Frankie Richmond Series. 🇱

A streetwise, Motown-loving London family attorney's chaotic private life interferes with her career in this amateur sleuth series.

Subjects: England • Lawyers • Murder • Music

Read-Alikes: In his <u>Tom Thorne Mysteries</u>, Mark Billingham often sends his Detective Inspector plunging into London's criminal underworld. Thorne is accompanied by a gay housemate on his excursions in *The Burning Girl*.

🎗 *Good Bad Woman.* New York: Kensington Publishing, 2003 (2000).

> Frankie's client skips town after the preliminary hearing, and Frankie soon finds herself charged with the murder of a mysterious stranger. She plunges into the streets to prove her innocence.

> **Awards:** Lambda Literary Award, 2003

Babyface. London: HarperCollins, 2003. (2002)

> When Frankie agrees to a woman's plea to prove her boyfriend innocent of murder, Frankie freely admits she has accepted largely because she likes the way the girlfriend looks. Birmingham's underworld pulls her in, and soon Frankie is dodging bullets on her way to the truth.

Zimmerman, R. D.

Todd Mills Mysteries Series. G

Award-winning television journalist Todd Mills uses his investigative reporting skills to solve crimes.

Subjects: Authors • Homophobia • Minnesota • Murder

Read-Alikes: Another journalist who solves crimes is found in Claudia McKay's <u>Lynn Evans Mysteries</u>. In *Blind Curves*, by Diane Anderson-Minshall, a lesbian journalist has to prove her innocence.

Closet. New York: Delta, 1997. (1995)

> The brutal murder of his secret lover, Michael, forcibly outs Todd, who finds his career and his identity both in question as he attempts to track the killer through gay Minneapolis.

> **Awards:** Lambda Literary Award, 1995

Tribe. New York: Delta, 1997. (1996)

> Past sexual history comes back to surprise Todd when Zeb—son of either Todd or his male college lover and the woman they both dated—arrives on the run from religious fundamentalists led by his stepfather

Hostage. New York: Delta, 1998. (1997)

> A prominent member of Congress is snatched by a three AIDS victims intent on punishing his indifference to the epidemic by infecting him as well. Todd uses his knowledge of AIDS to track the kidnappers.

🎗 *Outburst.* New York: Delta, 1999. (1998)

> Todd witnesses the murder of a gay police officer on a Minneapolis bridge. While Todd and his police officer partner dodge thunderstorms and gather evidence, another killing takes place—and they realize the conspiracy goes deeper than they thought.

> **Awards:** Lambda Literary Award, 1999

Innuendo. New York: Dell, 2000. (1999)

>   Todd is offered the chance of a lifetime when a major Hollywood star arrives in the Twin Cities and grants him an interview. The celebrity, though, may be linked with the death of a young man mentored by Todd's police officer partner.

Zubro, Mark.

Tom Mason and Scott Carpenter Series. G

Lovers Tom Mason, a suburban high school English teacher, and Scott Carpenter, a professional baseball player, solve Chicago-based crimes arising from their careers.

Subjects: Coming out • Homophobia • Illinois • Murder • Students, high school • Teachers

Read-Alikes: Rick Copp's Actors Guide Series brings the same pace and excitement to London, but adds a little more humor.

🎗 *A Simple Suburban Murder.* New York: St. Martin's Press, 1989.

>   Tom and Scott solve the murder of one of Tom's highly unpopular colleagues.

>   **Awards:** Lambda Literary Award, 1990

Why Isn't Becky Twitchell Dead? New York: St. Martin's Press, 1991 (1990).

>   A student is accused of killing his girlfriend, but his mother asks Tom to investigate. Scott uses his fame to open doors in the investigation, which leads them to a deadly drug ring operating in the high school.

The Only Good Priest. New York: St. Martin's Press, 1992 (1991).

>   Friends of Tom and Scott ask them to look into the murder of Father Sebastian, who was devoted to his outreach to Chicago's GLBT community. The church hierarchy and police collaborate to block the investigation.

The Principal Cause of Death. New York: St. Martin's, 1992. (1991)

>   Tom's principal is killed, and several people on the faculty and staff have a motive. Tom uses his knowledge of school politics to solve the crime, but not before he and Scott are nearly burned alive.

An Echo of Death. New York: St. Martin's Press, 1995. (1994)

>   Scott's former teammate, Glen Proctor, who'd been involved in smuggling, turns up dead in Scott's living room. As Scott and Tom hunt for clues, drug lords and grave robbers are after them.

Rust on the Razor. New York: St. Martin's Press, 1996.

>   Tom and Scott go south to be with Scott's father, who was hospitalized. A homophobic sheriff's body is found in Tom's car and, being gay, he is the prime suspect. Scott, still dealing with the aftershocks of having just come out, must find the real killer.

Are You Nuts? New York: St. Martin's Press, 1999. (1998)

>   Tom finds a body in the high school library, and one of his friends is accused of committing the murder. Scott rouses himself from his depression to help Tom crack the case.

One Dead Drag Queen. New York: St. Martin's Press, 2000.

> Tom narrowly survives the bombing of a clinic; as he recuperates in the hospital, Scott starts an investigation into who wanted the Tom silenced.

9

Here Comes the Corpse. New York: St. Martin's Press, 2002.

> Plans for Tom and Scott's wedding go amiss when Tom's ex-lover is killed before he can pass along important information. Then Scott's nephew disappears, and the two kick the investigation into high gear.

10

File Under Dead. New York: St. Martin's Press, 2004.

> Tom mostly enjoys his time at the GLBT teen center, except for dealing with the annoying director. Many people feel the same way, so when the director is killed, Tom thinks the police moved too fast in naming their prime suspect. Scott is on the road, so he hardly appears in this adventure.

11

Everyone's Dead But Us. New York: St. Martin's Press, 2006.

> The owner of a Greek island gay resort is found dead while Tom and Scott are vacationing there. Then an explosion kills several resort staff, a winter storm cuts the island off from the mainland, and corpses start piling up. Out of a sense of self-preservation, Tom and Scott start investigating.

12

Short Story Collections (Single Author)

13

Saylor, Steven.

Mysteries of Ancient Rome. G

> Saylor has accompanied his Roma Sub Rosa Series with two collections of short stories starring Gordianus.
>
> **Subjects:** Anthologies • Antiquity • Italy • Murder • Politics
>
> **Read-Alikes:** Additional Roman short stories can be found in *The Mammoth Book of Roman Whodunnits*, edited by Mike Ashley.

14

The House of the Vestals. New York: St. Martin's Press, 1998.

> Gordianus shines in nine short stories; all take place in the period between the novels *Roman Blood* and *Arms of Nemesis*.

A Gladiator Dies Only Once. New York: St. Martin's Press, 2005.

> Gordianus hones his investigative skills at gladiator matches and chariot races in this collection of nine cases from his early career.

15

16

Wilson, Barbara.

Cassandra Reilly Series. **L**

Death of a Much-Travelled Woman. Chicago: Third Side Press, 1998.

In this collection of nine stories, translator Cassandra Reilly continues her peripatetic crime solving.

Subjects: Anthologies • Murder • Travel

Read-Alikes: Lucy Jane Bledsoe has edited two stellar collections of literary essays, *Gay Travels* and *Lesbian Travels*.

Short Story Anthologies (Multiple Authors)

Burton, Peter, ed.

Death Comes Easy: The Gay Times Book of Murder Stories. London: Prowler/GMP, 2004. **G**

This collection of twenty-nine stories is a useful introduction to both established (Steven Saylor, Perry Brass, Patrick Gale) and emerging writers in the genre. The focus in all these tales is an examination of the varied motivations for murder.

Subjects: Anthologies • England • Murder

Read-Alikes: Another good collection of short mysteries is *Finale*, edited by Michael Nava.

Forrest, Katherine F., ed.

Women of Mystery. New York: Harrington Park Press, 2006. **L**

This anthology of lesbian suspense and mystery short stories contains a tantalizing mix of old and new: Established authors such as Ellen Hart, Victoria Brownworth, and Joan Drury all provided new stories, commissioned for this volume.

Subjects: Anthologies • Murder

Read-Alikes: *They Wrote the Book*, edited by Helen Widrath, is a collection of essays on writing mysteries, including contributions from lesbian and bisexual authors.

Meriwether, Sean, and Greg Wharton, eds.

Men of Mystery. New York: Harrington Park Press, 2007. **G**

This is a solid collection of sixteen stories of suspense, mystery, and intrigue by well-known authors such as Simon Sheppard, Jeff Mann, and Patrick Califa—and several who are not so well known. The stories were commissioned specifically for this book.

Subjects: Anthologies • Erotica • Murder

Read-Alikes: *Bend Sinister*, edited by Peter Burton, is more horror than mystery but maintains the suspense and erotic elements of mystery.

Chapter **14**

Comics and Graphic Novels

Definition

Cartoons, comic strips, and graphic novels use small drawings to tell a story succinctly. Cartoons are one- or two-panel works and generally do not have a continuing story line. Comic strips and comic books usually do tell a continuing story, but in installments. Graphic novels tell complete stories, conceived of and published as books.

Description and Characteristics

In a typical novel written for adult readers, the author does not include pictures to help the reader imagine the people and places described. When an occasional illustration is shown, it gives pause and breaks the flow of the written narrative. In comics and graphic novels, however, illustrations and text interact to deliver the story, each affecting the reader's perception of the other. Generally, in fact, the author of a comic or graphic novel is also its illustrator, and the story and art develop in tandem. (When there is a separate illustrator, that fact is noted in the entries in this chapter.)

The illustrations in comics and graphic novels vary widely in style and quality. Some feature primitive drawings or sketches; others have finely detailed illustrations. Further, depending on what the artist wants the reader to focus on most, some books will have both simple and detailed art within the same panel. In *The Importance of Being Earnest*, Tom Bouden uses simply drawn characters but exquisite backgrounds. Tim Barela, in his Leonard and Larry series, concentrates his illustrations on his characters more than their setting.

Comics and graphic novels also vary greatly in length. Many cartoons are single panels. Other artists find they need a larger canvas, from several panels up to a book-length treatment. Some artists express themselves with only occasional work; others establish themselves through periodic publication in newspapers, magazines, or comic book series.

History and Development

GLBT sequential art started in the 1950s with Tom of Finland, who produced several eight-panel erotic chapbooks, frequently with a humorous twist. Physique magazines, which displayed photographs of artfully depicted, nearly nude athletic men, featured illustrations by Tom and his emulators; starting in the late 1960s, as physique magazines were supplanted by forthrightly erotic magazines, artists like The Hun or Etienne provided more sexually explicit cartoons.

Gay cartoons did not receive much encouragement from the underground comics of the 1960s and 1970s counterculture. Female artists, though largely ignored by the mainstream comics industry, found some opportunity and inspiration in the underground press. Lesbian Roberta Gregory sold her first story to *Wimmin's Comix* in 1974 and followed up this success by self-publishing *Dynamite Damsels* in 1976. In the 1980s and 1990s, gay male artists like Robert Kirby and Belasco and bi-dyke Leanne Franson all used self-published chapbooks or zines to make their work available.

The development of news and literary magazines in the 1970s allowed a further evolution in GLBT cartoons. Soon, cartoons illustrating the lighter side of GLBT life appeared within their pages. *Christopher Street* set out to be a gay *New Yorker* magazine, complete with clever comics based on the gay scene in New York's Greenwich Village. GLBT newsmagazine *The Advocate* has featured such artists as Donelan, Howard Cruse, Tim Barela, and Andrea Natalie. *Frontiers Newsmagazine* has run strips by Tim Barela and Glen Hanson and Allan Neuwirth.

GLBT newspapers, such as the *Los Angeles Advocate*, Boston's *Gay Community News*, or DC's *Washington Blade*, were available at first only in major metropolitan areas but became increasingly present in smaller communities across the country, providing another avenue for cartoonists to reach the public. Alison Bechdel, with her series Dykes to Watch Out For, began publishing unconnected vignettes of lesbian life in 1983 in the feminist monthly *Womannews* but soon moved on to a serial soap opera with an ever-expanding cast of characters. Other cartoonists who have found success with serials in GLBT publications include Eric Orner, Glen Hanson, Allan Neuwirth, and Robert Kirby. As GLBT periodicals such as Chicago's *Windy City Times*, Minneapolis/Saint Paul's *Lavender Magazine*, and the *Seattle Gay News* moved online, the cartoons moved with them.

The online environment has allowed GLBT cartoonists to reach even more readers. Besides the sites of GLBT newspapers and magazines, there are a few noteworthy places on the Web to access GLBT comics. PlanetOut (http://www.planetout.com/entertainment/) gives access to several continuing comic series, including Dykes to Watch Out For and The Mostly Unfabulous Social Life of Ethan Green. Online aficionados should check out Gay League, a fan site for gay comic readers and creators (http://www.gayleague.com/home.php) and Prism Comics (http://www.prismcomics.org/), a nonprofit organization that supports queer comics, creators, and readers and also annually produces *Prism: Your LGBT Guide to Comics*.

As the GLBT community has become more open and accepted, supporting characters in mainstream cartoons such as *For Better or For Worse*, *The X-Men*, and *Green Lantern* have come out. These works are beyond the scope of this book, however, as the GLBT content provides only a minor, and often muted, theme in these comics; also, the flimsy comic book format of the Marvel and DC comics doesn't hold up well to library use. As these mainstream comics are anthologized into book format, though, they will provide a useful adjunct to a library's collection of GLBT comics and graphic novels.

Manga, a Japanese comic-style art form, has become very popular in the United States. Shounen-ai manga has gay male characters and plots, and shujo-ai manga has lesbian characters and plots, but much of this manga has not yet been translated. Yaio and yuri (gay and lesbian erotic manga) is more often translated. As manga becomes more available in English, U.S. libraries will gain an important way of providing more diversity within their GLBT collections.

Issues for the Readers' Advisor

Librarians wishing to collect GLBT comics and graphic novels should expect to deal with disdain from some of their patrons, as well as administrators and staff members. In fact, you may first have to fight a battle to have comics in your library at all before you can even deal with the issue of bringing in GLBT materials in graphic form. The quality of the artwork or the strength of the story may help convince some patrons that comics and graphic novels are worth having in the library. Other detractors may be mollified by the popularity of the general collection of comics and graphic novels provided and the way graphic novels help build circulation statistics.

The popularity of graphic novels and comics, particularly among teens, means that some teens and even children could stumble across the GLBT materials. This is not necessarily a bad thing; GLBT teens, friends, or family of GLBT people may well be grateful to find them. Because some patrons might object to children having easy access to these materials, however, you may find it expedient to shelve adult-level or adult-themed comics and graphic novels in the adult services area.

Be aware, too, that some of the graphic works are indeed graphic. The books in this section that carry the subject heading "erotica" will contain sexual images that could offend some library patrons. Again, you may find it wise to shelve these items in the adult services collection.

Chapter Organization

The entries in this chapter focus first on collections of single-panel comics and comic strips, continuing stories in which developing plots and characters emerge over time. The second section covers collections (both graphic short stories and single-panel cartoons by individual authors) and anthologies of the work of several authors. A look at graphic novels, both fiction and nonfiction, concludes this chapter.

Sources

"Comics and Cartoons." In *Completely Queer: The Gay and Lesbian Encyclopedia*, edited by Steve Hogan and Lee Hudson, 145–48. New York: Henry Holt, 1998.

"Comics and Graphic Novels." *In glbtq: An Encyclopedia of Gay, Lesbian, Bisexual, Transgender and Queer Culture.* Available at http://www.glbtq.com/arts/comic_strips_cartoons.html.

Donovan, James M. "Comics Strips and Books." In *Gay Histories and Cultures*, edited by George E. Haggerty, 208–9. New York: Garland, 2000.

Gay League, http://www.gayleague.com/home.php.

Prism: Your LGBT Guide to the Comics. Atlanta, GA: Prism Comics 2003– . Available at http://www.prismcomics.org.

Thalheimer, Anne H. "Comics and Comic Books." In *lgbt: Encyclopedia of Lesbian, Gay, Bisexual, and Transgender History in America*, edited by Marc Stein, 249–52. New York: Thomson/Gale, 2004.

Cartoon and Comic Strip Collections

Single-panel cartoons and comic strips are typically first published in mini-books, magazines, and newspapers. Though each cartoon or strip might be part of an ongoing story, they are, at least at first, published periodically. Each cartoon or strip then constitutes an episode, which could stand alone for the benefit of the reader who only occasionally picked up the periodical. Fans of GLBT comics have welcomed collections of single-panel and comic strips, both in books and in two serials, *Meatmen* and *Gay Comics*.

Other authors publish in serial comic books, a few dozen pages in length. This format allows the author to present a longer segment of the story at one time but makes it more difficult for the occasional reader to follow the plot. Considering the ephemeral nature of the monthly comic book, we have not included these serials, unless they have been collected and published in book format.

Collections are compilations of the work of a single artist or a pair of artists working together. Most are comic strips with continuing characters and plots; a few, though, are single-panel works (simple quips, like in a *New Yorker* cartoon). Still others are collections of an author's short fiction work from several periodicals.

Continuing Stories

These are the comic collections that most resemble graphic novels: Continuing characters and plotlines give the illusion of a planned whole. These comic strips evolved over the years, released a strip at a time into the weekly or monthly periodicals that carried them.

9

Barela, Tim.

Leonard & Larry Series. G

Friends, relatives, ex-wives, coworkers, hangers-on, stalkers, and the occasional pair of ghosts make life interesting for leatherman Larry Evans and photographer Leonard Goldman, the gay couple at the heart of this comic series. Each volume contains an introduction and recap of previous action. Because of Barela's deft touch in detailing body and facial hair and his determination that his characters will age, this series is particularly well loved by members of the bear community: men who like furry men and aren't too concerned about age and beauty.

10

Subjects: California • Couples • Families • Humor • Leather • Politics

Read-Alikes: *Tales of the City*, by Armistead Maupin, is another long-running serial with many interconnected characters. Readers who are interested in the bear culture may enjoy Ron Suresha's *Bears on Bears*, a collection of interviews and discussions.

11

Domesticity Isn't Pretty. Minneapolis, MN: Palliard Press, 1993.

Meet long-term partners Larry and Leonard, assorted family members, and friends. Larry's fear of aging intensifies when he becomes a grandfather and his youngest son comes out. Leonard demands recognition of Larry from his traditional Jewish mother. Larry's lovelorn employee, Jim, falls for Merle, while friend Bob finds himself a stalking victim. The introduction recounts Barela's cartooning career.

12

Kurt Cobain and Mozart Are Both Dead. Minneapolis, MN: Palliard Press, 1996.

Larry enjoys being a grandparent until he finds himself the Lamaze coach for his second grandchild. Without Larry's blessing, Leonard plans their wedding. Merle and Jim's relationship is tested by Merle's success as a soap opera hunk. Bob's partner Frank develops his uniform fetish. A gay bashing brings everyone closer.

13

Excerpts from the Ring Cycle in Royal Albert Hall. Minneapolis, MN: Palliard Press, 2000.

Leonard grows a goatee, and a love affair ensues. Larry struggles with his ex-wife dating an acquaintance, but becomes distracted when he learns he will be a grandfather again, or will he? Merle supports Jim through a difficult situation. Bob's stalker finds a new target.

15

How Real Men Do It. Minneapolis, MN: Palliard Press, 2003.

Leonard and Larry remodel their home and deal with new neighbors. Larry's fear of aging increases as he nears his fiftieth birthday, and indulging the grandchildren lands him in trouble. Merle's career is in danger until he finds a creative way to salvage the situation, while partner Jim finds himself targeted for a new romance.

16

Bechdel, Alison.

Dykes to Watch Out For Series. L B T Teen

In this long-running, nationally syndicated serial and humorous soap opera with a social conscience, Alison Bechdel portrays Mo and her extended group of friends—Audrey, Clarice, Ginger, Harriet, Jezanna, Lois, Sidney, Sparrow, and Toni chief among them—facing lesbian life and love. Starting with her fourth book, Bechdel gives her readers bonus chapters, which contain extra material that never made it into the newspapers.

Subjects: Business • Couples • Families • Humor • Politics

Read-Alikes: In *Go Fish*, by Guinevere Turner and Lea Delaria, a group of Chicago lesbians explore life and love. The soap opera aspect of Dykes to Watch Out For is better captured by Armistead Maupin's epic *Tales of the City* or his shorter work, *Maybe the Moon*. Also, look at Bechdel's autobiographical work, *The Indelible Alison Bechdel* and *Fun Home*, annotated later in this chapter.

Dykes to Watch Out For. Ithaca, NY: Firebrand, 1986.

As this popular series begins, there are no established characters or continuing plotlines, just keen insights on lesbian culture, like how to choose Ms. Right, lesbian etiquette, and cats.

More Dykes to Watch Out For. Ithaca, NY: Firebrand, 1988.

The lives of Mo and her pals now take center stage. Mo starts her job at Madwimmin Books, marches on Washington, and falls in love with Harriet. Among the other continuing characters, we meet Mo's sex-positive best friend Lois, karate chum/law student Clarice and her partner Toni, and Madwimmin Books owner Jezanna.

🌸 *New Improved! Dykes to Watch Out For.* Ithaca, NY: Firebrand, 1990.

Milkweed moves in with Lois and her roommates, Ginger and Sparrow. Clarice has a fling with Ginger, but Toni eventually forgives her. Lois continues her wanton ways; Mo starts therapy.

Awards: Lambda Literary Award, 1990

🌸 *Dykes to Watch Out For: The Sequel.* Ithaca, NY: Firebrand, 1992.

As protests against the patriarchy merge with opposition to the first Gulf War, Toni and Clarice plan their commitment ceremony. Mo and Harriet meet, date, and move in together. Jezanna hires Thea as the buyer at Madwimmin Books. In "Serial Monogamy," a twenty-eight-page end-of-book bonus, Alison Bechdel depicts her ongoing search for Ms. Right.

Awards: Lambda Literary Award, 1992

🌸 *Spawn of Dykes to Watch Out For.* Ithaca, NY: Firebrand, 1993.

Harriet breaks up with Mo, Lois turns thirty, and the whole gang of dykes to watch out for marches on Washington. Toni and Clarice decide to have a baby; the bonus at the end of this book is Toni giving birth to son Raffi, with all her friends gathered around.

Awards: Lambda Literary Award, 1993

Unnatural Dykes to Watch Out For. Ithaca, NY: Firebrand, 1995.

Harriet's new girlfriend runs for city council and wins the race but loses Harriet. Jezanna's mother is diagnosed with cancer, and her nurse, Audrey, falls for Jezanna. In the extra material at the end of this book, Mo gives her perspective on lesbian history.

Hot Throbbing Dykes to Watch Out For. Ithaca, NY: Firebrand, 1997.

To compete with the book superstores, Madwimmin Books starts selling sex toys. Clarice adopts Raffi, Toni's son, and Carlos starts babysitting. Mo meets the maddening Sydney. The added chapter shows a week in the life of Mo's crowd.

Split-Level Dykes to Watch Out For. Ithaca, NY: Firebrand, 1998.

After Ginger gets her PhD, she starts teaching at a small college. The house Lois, Sparrow and Ginger rent together goes on the market, so Sparrow and Ginger scrape together a down payment. Sparrow breaks up with girlfriend June and asks boyfriend Stuart to move in. Clarice, Toni, and Raffi move to the suburbs, and Mo and Sydney move in together. When Jezanna's mother dies, her father moves in with her and Audrey. The bonus chapter details the day everybody moves.

Post-Dykes to Watch Out For. Ithaca, NY: Firebrand, 2000.

Sydney lives large, and her credit card debts mount. Harriet becomes a single mom. Jezanna enters menopause as her father starts dating again. Lois—or is it Louis?—explores a masculine side. The political front is busy, too, with Kosovo, Y2K, the Millennium March on Washington, and the run-up to the 2000 election. In the bonus material at the end of the book, Sydney gets tenure, Clarice and Toni agree to open up their relationship, and Lois starts dating Jerry, an FTM transsexual.

Dykes and Sundry Other Carbon-Based Life Forms to Look Out For. Los Angeles: Alyson Books, 2003.

When civil unions hit Vermont, Clarice and Toni get hitched. Against the political background of the contested 2000 presidential election and the 9/11 terrorist attacks, Madwimmin Books, still losing business to the chain bookstores, closes its doors. Mo starts library school. In the extra chapter, family visits give the characters some background.

Awards: Lambda Literary Award, 2003

Invasion of the Dykes to Watch Out For. Los Angeles: Alyson Books, 2005.

As Mo supports herself pitching books at Bounders, Sydney fights cancer. Stuart and Sparrow face parenthood with trepidation and a major rehab project; Toni and Clarice deal with teen Raffi and the fight for same-sex marriage. The extra chapter has Sydney and Ginger heading off to an academic conference, Clarice and Ana taking Raffi and Stella to Chicago, and Toni and Gloria staying at home working on marriage rights and wrongs.

Belasco.

The Brothers of New Essex: Afro-Erotic Adventures. San Francisco: Cleis Press, 2000. **G**

This collection of loosely related stories from artist Belasco's self-published zine features the explicitly drawn sexual adventures of Boo and his friends in the city of New Essex.

Subjects: African Americans • Erotica • Race relations • Sex

Read-Alikes: James Earl Hardy's B-Boy Blues Series has the same sultry urban background. The cartoons in Brad Parker's *Oh Boy!* contain frankly sexual content.

Braddock, Paige.

Jane's World: Collection 1. Sebastopol, CA: Girl Twirl Comics, 2007. **L** **B**

As she moves through wacky adventures both real and imagined, Jane falls for bad girl Chelle. Alien abductions, the wrath of God, and secret agents combine to make Jane's world complicated but fun.

Subjects: Humor • Relationships

Read-Alikes: *Love & Rockets*, by Gilbert Hernandez and Jaime Hernandez, has a similar twisted logic, humor, and world of adventure.

Cruse, Howard.

Wendel All Together. Milford, CT: Olmstead Press, 2001. **G**

Mailroom clerk Wendel, his partner Ollie, an aspiring actor, and assorted friends make their way through 1980s America with humor and panache. This compilation includes all the Wendel strips published in the *Advocate,* including those previously published in the collections *Wendel* (1986) and *Wendel on the Rebound* (1989), both now out of print.

Subjects: Couples • Parenting • Politics • Theater

Read-Alikes: Jeff Krell's *Jayson* has the same optimistic attitude but depends more on satire and stereotypes for its humor.

DiMassa, Diane.

The Complete Hothead Paisan: Homicidal Lesbian Terrorist. San Francisco: Cleis Press, 1999. **L**

To Hothead, everything wrong in the world is the fault of oppressive straight white males. Well-armed, caffeinated, and full of righteous indignation, she's out to even the score. This omnibus volume combines two earlier books, *Hothead Paisan* (1993) and *The Revenge of Hothead Paisan* (1999), both now out of print.

Subjects: Anger • Homophobia • Humor • Revenge

Read-Alikes: In *The Terrorists of Irustan*, by Louise Marley, the main character takes vigilante justice against a patriarchal society.

Franson, Leanne.

Bi-Dyke Liliane Collections. **B**

Canadian children's book illustrator and bisexual Leanne Franson uses alter ego Liliane to explore issues of life, love, and society with incisive humor.

Subjects: Couples • Dating • Humor

Read-Alikes: The same gentle humor is found in *The Bisexual's Guide to the Universe*, by Nicole Kristal and Mike Szymanski.

Assume Nothing: The Evolution of a Bi-Dyke. Brighton and Hove, Sussex, UK: Slab-O-Concrete Publications, 1997.

> Canadian children's book illustrator Leanne Franson collects several of her mini-comics, starring bi-dyke Liliane as she wanders in and out of relationships.

Teaching Through Trauma. Brighton and Hove, Sussex, UK: Slab-O-Concrete Publications, 1999.

> In Franson's second collection, Liliane learns life lessons from lovers, family, sperm donors, and even hamsters.

Don't Be a Crotte. Toronto: Dansereau Editeur, 2004.

> As Liliane continues to explore life, she deals with untruthful lovers, uncaring landlords, and biphobia from both the straight and gay communities.

Gregory, Roberta.

Bitchy Butch: World's Angriest Dyke! Seattle: Fantagraphics, 1999. **L**

> Bitchy Butch is an irritable, middle-aged lesbian with a grudge against almost everyone, including (but not limited to) straight men and women, bisexual women, lipstick lesbians, gay men, and the religious Right. Raging at the cultural dominance of straight men, she yearns for the days of her youth in the seventies, when lesbian culture began to bloom. This collection brings together material published in *Gay Comix* and other alternative comics during the 1990s as well as original material created just for this book.

Subjects: Anger • Homophobia • Humor

Read-Alikes: Bitchy Butch's straight kindred spirit, Bitchy Bitch, starred in *Naughty Bits*, Roberta Gregory's 1991–2004 solo magazine.

Hanson, Glen. Illustrated by Allan Neuwirth.

Chelsea Boys. Los Angeles: Alyson Books, 2003. **G**

> Dumpy Nathan, hunky Sky, and fabulous Soiree share an apartment in New York's fashionable Chelsea District, in this widely syndicated strip.

Subjects: Friendship • Humor • New York City • Roommates

Read-Alikes: *A Couple of Guys*, a weekly comic strip by Dave Brousseau, tells the story of New York couple Joey and Eric and their circle of friends.

Hernandez, Jaime.

Locas: The Maggie and Hopey Stories. Seattle: Fantagraphics, 2004. **L B**

> In the twenty-year run of *Love & Rockets*, Hopey and Maggie are occasionally a couple. Always touring, Hopey wants to make it big in the music scene; Maggie just wants Hopey. They drift apart over the years, never

losing the core of their friendship. A wide cast of memorable characters, from an insane dictator to a sexpot woman wrestler, people this strip.

Subjects: Friendship • Hispanics • Music • Relationships

Read-Alikes: Pair this with Gilbert Hernandez's *Palomar*, also drawn from *Love & Rockets*.

Kinnard, Rupert.

B.B. and the Diva. Boston: Alyson Publications, 1992. G

Superhero Brown Bomber and his best friend, the Diva Touché Flambé, slap down oppressors like the first President Bush, the Pope, and Jesse Helms. First appearing in 1977 as *Cathartic Comics* in the Cornell University student paper, these two were the first gay black superheroes.

Subjects: African Americans • Humor • Politics • Race relations • Superheroes

Read-Alikes: Similar campy humor is found in A. Jay's *The Amazing Adventures of Harry Chest*, which details the escapades of a gay secret agent.

Kirby, Robert.

Curbside. G Teen

Robert Kirby follows the adventures and misadventures, trials and tribulations, loves and losses of a group of gay friends. Each book focuses on a new pair: Rob (loosely based on the author) and Tony in Minneapolis in the first volume; Nathan and Drew in New York in the second.

Subjects: Couples • Friendship • Humor • Infidelity

Read-Alikes: Dave Brousseau's *A Couple of Guys* takes a lighthearted look at life as a gay couple in New York City; *Kyle's Bed And Breakfast*, by Greg Fox, is set in suburban Long Island but has a more serious tone.

Curbside. New York: Hobnob Press, 1998.

Kirby relates the life and relationships of Rob and his boyfriend Tony in this collection of the first four and one-half years of this strip. This is the most autobiographical of Kirby's books. Issued in a small press run, this book can be a challenge to find but provides valuable background for Kirby's later work.

Curbside Boys: The New York Years. San Francisco: Cleis Press, 2002.

In this second collection of Curbside strips, the action switches to follow the bittersweet course of the relationship between Nathan and Drew.

König, Ralf.

Roy & Al. Vancouver, BC: Arsenal Pulp, 2006. G

This is the erotic and amusing story of a gay couple, as told by their dogs. Roy is a slightly rotund mongrel with an easygoing outlook; Al is a highly strung purebred with an attitude.

Subjects: Erotica • Humor • Pets • Relationships

Read-Alikes: May Sarton's *The Fur Person* tells the story of cat Tom Jones, who after a life on the street goes looking for an old maid to take him in—and finds a lesbian couple instead.

Moore, Terry.

Complete Strangers in Paradise Treasury Edition. New York: HarperCollins, 2004. **L** **B** **Teen**

Strangers in Paradise tells the complex story of the lives and loves of two women, Francine and Katchoo, and their friend David, all against the backdrop of a shadowy conspiracy to control the U.S. government. First published as a three-issue serial in 1993, the series had special appeal to women, and *Strangers in Paradise* continued to be published as a comic book until June 2007. Both softcover and hardcover compilations have been issued over the years, but the Treasury Edition pulls together the highlights of the first ten years.

Subjects: Anger • Crime • Dating • Homophobia • Sexual abuse

Read-Alikes: Melissa Scott's *Trouble and Her Friends* and *Jazz* both share with *Strangers in Paradise* the shadowy conspiracy and the network of friends and lovers used to thwart it.

Orner, Eric.

The Mostly Unfabulous Social Life of Ethan Green. **G**

Average gay man Ethan Green deals with love, dating, politics, work, and fun, with the assistance and occasional obstruction of his circle of friends (which includes the Hat Sisters, Leo, Doug, and Bucky) in these collections of his widely syndicated strips. This comic series was made into a live-action movie of the same name in 2006.

Subjects: Books to film • Dating • Humor

Read-Alikes: Michael Thomas Ford's *My Big Fat Queer Life* has the same dry, snarky humor.

The Mostly Unfabulous Social Life of Ethan Green. New York: St. Martin's Press, 1992.

> Insecure Ethan worries about his looks, a lackluster dating life, and the state of the world, often consulting his psychic for advice. The Hat Sisters, a pair of cross-dressing divas, save the world from homophobia, and The Midwestern Guy, an infomercial relationship therapist, serves as a Greek chorus, constantly reminding Ethan of his mediocrity. Life improves when Leo enters the picture.

The Seven Deadly Sins of Love: The Still Unfabulous Social Life of Ethan Green. New York: St. Martin's Press, 1994.

> Ethan finds himself attracted to coworker Doug and begins a romance, but there is a surprising twist. When the AIDS plague hits hard, the only hope seems to be in taking political action in the 1992 Democratic election victory and the 1993 March on Washington.

The Ethan Green Chronicles: More Stories from His Unfabulous Social Life. New York: St. Martin's Press, 1997.

> Doug and Ethan are on the rocks, and Ethan is depressed, so friends Charlotte and Bucky drag him out of the house. On a trip to Montreal,

9

10

11

12

13

15

16

Etienne makes Ethan forget the past, but Etienne himself has a secret past. The Hat Sisters go back in time to prevent the AIDS epidemic.

Ethan Exposed: Further Adventures from Ethan Green's Unfabulous Social Life. New York: St. Martin's Press, 1999.

Ethan gets a job as an assistant to a closeted TV weatherman, and Etienne's sordid secrets sideline their relationship. Doug returns, and he and Ethan struggle for a level of commitment acceptable to both. Bucky becomes foster father to Moon, a lesbian teen, and The Hat Sisters attempt to save President Clinton from political ruin.

Short Story Collections (Single Author)

Artists who write graphic short stories without a continuing plotline may find their work published in a variety of periodicals. These collections help pull the artist's work together for the reader.

Cruse, Howard.

Dancin' Nekkid with the Angels: Comic Strips & Stories for Grownups. New York: St. Martin's Press, 1987. **G**

This collection of Cruse's early work, mostly drawn from the underground press, shows an incredible range of style, story, and mood, as he considers the subjects of safe sex, homophobia, coming-of-age, LSD, and UFOs. The comics are organized by theme, not chronologically, but a determined reader can trace the development of Cruse's unique style from 1972 to 1987.

Subjects: Anthologies • Homophobia • Humor

Read-Alikes: These diverse and sometimes serious stories are matched in tone by Michael Thomas Ford's *My Big Fat Queer Life.*

Stangroom, Howard, and Stephen Lowther.

Prime Cuts: All-Male Strips from Gay Comix, Meatmen, and Elsewhere. Berlin: Bruno Gmünder, 2005. **G**

In the 1980s and 1990s, the cartooning team of Howard Stangroom and Stephen Lowther produced often amusing, often science fiction, generally erotic adventures for GLBT serials, including *Gay Comix* and *Meatmen.* Their entire body of work together, as well as strips created entirely by Stephen Lowther, is included in this collection.

Subjects: Anthologies • Erotica • Humor

Read-Alikes: The serials *Gay Comix* and *Meatmen* will have many similar cartoon stories. For more of the SF elements of many of these stories, look to *Bending the Landscape: Science Fiction,* edited by Nicola Griffith and Steven Pagel.

Single-Panel Cartoons

These are one-line gags or quips; generally, the artwork is subordinate to the joke.

Lake, Julian.

Gay Cartoons Collections. G L

The creator of the Web-based Gay Cartoons Site (now defunct) presents coming out, business, travel, and relationships from a gay perspective. The cartoons themselves are simplistic: talking heads telling jokes.

Subjects: Business • Coming out • Couples • Humor • Relationships, long-term couples • Travel

Read-Alikes: Campy but sophisticated humor, these cartoons invite comparison to the wit of Oscar Wilde in *Lady Windermere's Fan* and of Quentin Crisp in *The Naked Civil Servant*.

> *Guess Who's Coming Out at Dinner?* Boston: Rubicon Media, 1998.
>
> *Please Don't Come Out While We're Eating.* Boston: Rubicon Media, 2000.
>
> *From Provincetown with Love.* Boston: Rubicon Media, 2002.
>
> *Domestic Partners, Inc.* Boston: Rubicon Media, 2003.

Natalie, Andrea.

Stonewall Riots Collections. L

These three books collect the popular single-panel comic *Stonewall Riots*, syndicated nationally in the late 1980s and early 1990s in the GLBT press. The cartoons take an ironic look at gay life and customs and raise an early warning flag about the perils of the politically correct.

Subjects: Humor

Read-Alikes: The *Gay Comics* anthologies of the same era cover some of the same ground. John Callahan's *The Best of Callahan* has a similar irreverent approach to minority culture (in his case, the disabled).

> *Stonewall Riots.* Guttenburg, NJ: Venus Envy, 1990.
>
> *The Night Audrey's Vibrator Spoke.* San Francisco: Cleis Press, 1992.
>
> *Rubyfruit Mountain.* San Francisco: Cleis Press, 1993.

Ortleb, Charles, and Richard Fiala.

Christopher Street Cartoons. G L

Single-panel cartoons poke fun at gay stereotypes and political events and give glimpses into gay life prior to the AIDS epidemic.

Subjects: Humor • Politics

Read-Alikes: For the same ironic humor, readers may want to try *The New Yorker Book of True Love Cartoons*.

> *Relax!: This Book Is Only a Phase You're Going Through.* New York: St. Martin's Press, 1978.
>
> *Le Gay Ghetto: Gay cartoons from Christopher Street.* New York: St. Martin's Press, 1980.

Vellekoop, Maurice.

🎖 *Maurice Vellekoop's ABC Book: A Homoerotic Primer.* New York: Gates of Heck, 1998. **G**

This alphabet book shows gay men in a variety of sexual situations, each suggested by a word starting with a different letter. The art style is reminiscent of Tom Bouden.

Awards: Firecracker Alternative Press Award, 1999

Subjects: Erotica • Humor

Read-Alikes: This lusty look at gay men could be supplemented by the slightly tamer *Manga Boys*, by Kinu Sekigushi.

Short Story Anthologies (Multiple Authors)

Each anthology is the work of several artists, edited and pulled together into a single volume. The formats collected vary, from single-panel works to short fiction to excerpts from a continuing saga.

Kirby, Robert, and David Kelly, eds.

The Book of Boy Trouble: Gay Boy Comics with a New Attitude. San Francisco: Green Candy Press, 2006. **G**

The best comics from the first ten years of the alternative comic *Boy Trouble* join twenty-four pages of new material on the young gay male experience—from coming out to getting high, from creepy come-ons to the thrill of a crush.

Subjects: Anthologies • Coming out • Erotica • Humor

Read-Alikes: *Adventures of a Joe Boy*, by Joe Phillips, follows the theme of young gay life and love.

McClure, Regan, and Liz Fitting, eds.

Queer Sense of Humour: A Collection of Lesbian, Gay and Bisexual Cartoons. Toronto: Queer Press, 1993. **G** **L** **B**

This anthology includes several Canadian artists, including Alan Bell, Leanne Franson, and Rupert Kinnard.

Subjects: Anthologies • Canada and Canadians• Humor

Read-Alikes: Kevin Isom's *Tongue in Cheek & Other Places* and *It Only Hurts When I Polka* give another look into Canadian GLBT humor.

Robbins, Trina, Bill Sienkiewicz, and Robert Triptow, eds.

Strip AIDS USA: A Collection of Comic Art to Benefit People with AIDS. San Francisco: Last Gasp, 1988. **G** **L**

This collection of cartoons and comic strips, meant to raise awareness and money for the treatment of AIDS, presents observations on AIDS, safe sex, and love. Contributors include both straight and GLBT artists, such as Sergio Aragones, Alison Bechdel, Margaret Clark, Howard Cruse, Donelan, Will Eisner, Jules Feiffer, Nicole Hollander, and Harvey Pekar.

Subjects: AIDS • Anthologies • Humor

Read-Alikes: *Out, Loud, and Laughing*, edited by Charles Flowers, is a collection of stand-up and other humor pieces on GLBT life; proceeds from this book went to support Broadway Cares/Equity Fights AIDS.

Triptow, Robert, ed.

🏷 *Gay Comics.* New York: Plume, 1989. **G** **L**

Triptow introduces readers to the world of gay and lesbian cartooning with examples from across thirty years, interspersed with insights into its history. Among the mostly male contributors are Tim Barela, Howard Cruse, Donelan, Jeffrey A. Krell, Charles Ortleb, and Tom of Finland; some important women artists in the book are Alison Bechdel, Jennifer Camper, Roberta Gregory, and Mary Wings.

Awards: Lambda Literary Award, 1989

Subjects: Anthologies • Humor

Read-Alikes: *A Funny Time to Be Gay*, by Ed Karvoski Jr., gives the same historical treatment to GLBT stand-up comedy of the 1970s, 1980s, and 1990s; thoughtful interviews with the featured comedians accompany examples of their routines.

Warren, Roz, ed.

Dyke Strippers: Lesbian Cartoonists from A to Z. San Francisco: Cleis Press, 1995. **L**

Examples of the work of a diverse group of lesbian cartoonists, interspersed with artist interviews, introduce a broad range of lesbian comic art. This book includes work by cartoonists Alison Bechdel, Jennifer Camper, Diane DiMassa, Leanne Franson, Roberta Gregory, Andrea Natalie, and many others.

Subjects: Anthologies • Humor

Read-Alikes: Roz Warren also coedited (with Nicole Hollander) *When Cats Talk Back*, an anthology of cartoons by women about cats.

Graphic Novels

Long-running GLBT strips readily lend themselves to collection and publication in book format and can superficially resemble graphic novels. True graphic novels, though, are works of fiction or nonfiction conceived of and published in their entirety as a book, without having been first published serially. Because the author can present the entire work to the reader at once, complicated and serious subjects like love, racism, or death can be explored more deeply than in comic strips. Howard Cruse's *Stuck Rubber Baby*, first published in 1995, became an immediate classic, both of GLBT literature and of the graphic novel genre.

Graphic Fiction

Most graphic novels are fiction. The author is telling a story and uses illustration to take the place of textual descriptions. The author is then empowered to use his or her skills at language mainly on dialogue. Like written fiction, graphic fiction can have any setting, deal with any theme, and be of any genre.

Bouden, Tom.

Max & Sven. San Francisco: Green Candy Press, 2004. **G**

A remarkably trauma-free gay teen, Max, becomes fast friends with a new student, Sven. Max hopes for more than friendship, but Sven is straight; still, the bond of their friendship easily survives this, and Max's fumbling entry into gay life.

Subjects: Coming out • Erotica • Friendship

Camper, Jennifer.

SubGURLZ. San Francisco: Cleis Press, 1999. **L**

A trio of edgy lesbian superheroes looks for love and the meaning of life as they fight crime and corruption from their lair in the subway tunnels.

Subjects: Crime • Dating • Homeless • Homophobia • Superheroes

Read-Alikes: Read *The Amazing Adventures of Kavalier and Clay*, by Michael Chabon, for a GLBT-nuanced look at the creation of comic book superheroes in World War II America. Patrick Fillion's *Heroes* shows his illustrations of gay superheroes.

Cruse, Howard.

Stuck Rubber Baby. New York: DC Comics, 2000. **G** **B** **Teen**

Toland Polk, a gay white man in the Deep South, comes of age and comes out while the nation is embroiled in the civil rights movement of the 1960s.

Subjects: 1960s • Civil rights • Coming out • Death and dying • Race relations • Southern states

Read-Alikes: Nina Revoyr's *Southland* is driven by racial tensions during the 1965 Watts Riots.

Denson, Abby.

Tough Love: High School Confidential. San Francisco: Manic D Press, 2006. **G** **Teen**

High school freshman Brian finds a boyfriend in Chris, an older student he meets at their school's Martial Arts Club. They help their friend Julie find a boyfriend, too.

Subjects: Coming out • Friendship • Homophobia

Read-Alikes: A similar plot and tone are found in Francesca Lia Block's *Weetzie Bat*.

Parks, Ande. Illustrated by Chris Samnee.

Capote in Kansas: A Drawn Novel. Portland, OR: Oni Press, 2005. **G**

Truman Capote, looking for his next breakthrough, travels to Kansas with his friend Harper Lee to research his "nonfiction novel," *In Cold Blood*, about the horrific murder of the Clutter family by a couple of drifters. Initially, the townspeople are put off by Capote's cosmopolitan attitude but haunted by the tragedy; he perseveres and creates a classic.

Subjects: Capote, Truman • Ghosts • Murder

Read-Alikes: Kim Powers wrote another take on this period in the life of Harper Lee and Truman Capote, also titled *Capote in Kansas,* and involving a haunting.

Schimel, Lawrence. Illustrated by Sebas.

Vacation in Ibiza. New York: NBM Publishing, 2003. **G**

Best friends Berndt and Marek visit the gay resort Ibiza. As Berndt cuts a swath through the crowds of sexy gay men on holiday (while secretly wanting someone special), Marek makes a romantic connection with a local but longs to be more wanton.

Subjects: Dating • Erotica • Friendship • Sex • Spain • Travel

Read-Alikes: *Summer Share,* edited by Chris Kenry, contains stories with a similar approach to vacation romance.

Watasin, Elizabeth.

Charm School Book One: Magical Witch Girl Bunny. San Jose, CA: Slave Labor Graphics, 2002. **L** **Teen**

Bunny, lesbian teen witch, must choose between two rivals for her heart: girlfriend Dean, daughter of the vampire overlord, or Fairer Than, faerie princess with a hint of dragon blood.

Subjects: Dating • Humor • Supernatural

Read-Alikes: *Bending the Landscape: Fantasy,* edited by Nicola Griffith and Stephen Pagel, contains several romances. Patrons looking for humor as well as fantasy should check out *The Drag Queen of Elfland,* by Lawrence Schimel.

Wilde, Oscar, and Tom Bouden.

The Importance of Being Earnest. Hamburg, Germany: Männerschwarm, 2000. **G** **Teen**

Wilde's clever comedy of manners and mistaken identity is brought into the present day, illustrated, and recast with all of the principals gay men. Algernon is in love with Jack's ward, Cecil; Jack loves Glenn, Algernon's cousin. However, both Cecil and Glenn have determined that they can only love Ernest, Jack's invented brother.

Subjects: Couples • Friendship • Humor

Read-Alikes: Ethan Mordden, in his *Buddies Cycle,* has deftly captured the style of the comedy of manners pioneered by Oscar Wilde.

Graphic Memoirs and Nonfiction

A nonfiction variant of graphic novels is the memoir in graphic form. The groundbreaking mainstream graphic work, *Maus,* by Art Speigelman, is an early instance of a memoir told in graphic novel form. Judd Winick's *Pedro and Me* is a GLBT example found in many libraries, often shelved with the graphic novels.

Additional memoirs, in the more traditional text format, are annotated in chapter 16.

9

10

11

12

13

15

16

Bechdel, Alison.

🎗 *Fun Home: A Family Tragicomic.* Boston: Houghton Mifflin, 2006. **G** **L** **B** **Teen**

Cartoonist Bechdel returns to her childhood journals to construct this autobiographical work. Her father's life as a funeral home director and high school English teacher is contrasted with his life as a husband, father, and closeted gay man. Her father awakened her love of literature but remained emotionally distant, creating a relationship too complex for easy resolution.

Awards: Alice B. Award, 2007; Lambda Literary Award, 2007; Stonewall Book Award, 2007

Subjects: Authors • Autobiography • Bechdel, Alison • Comic strips • Graphic novels • Relationships, parent–child

Read-Alikes: *Running with Scissors,* by Augusten Burroughs, is another portrait of childhood in a dysfunctional family.

🎗 *The Indelible Alison Bechdel: Confessions, Comix, and Miscellaneous Dykes to Watch Out For.* Ithaca, NY: Firebrand Books, 1998. **L**

Alison Bechdel is the cartoonist who created the wildly popular comic strip, <u>Dykes to Watch Out For</u>. Fans will revel in this biography cum comic book packed with narrative insights and illustrations from Bechdel's early career. Many never before published strips, seven years of calendar art, story time lines, and plenty of background notes on character development round out this work.

Awards: Lambda Literary Award, 1998

Subjects: Authors • Autobiography • Bechdel, Alison • Comic strips • Graphic novels

Read-Alikes: F. Valentine Hooven's *Tom of Finland: His Life and Times* combines text with examples of the gay artist's work to tell Touko Laaksonen's life story.

Bouden, Tom.

In Bed with David & Jonathan. Berlin: Bruno Gmünder, 2006. **G**

Tom Bouden, cruising online, arranges a tryst with a gay couple. In post-coital bliss, one of the men reveals he is a fan of the artist and receives a free copy of Bouden's latest comic book, *David & Jonathan.* In that story within a story (told entirely without words), two men meet while cruising in a local park but lose contact. True love triumphs when, some weeks later, they again meet in the same park.

Subjects: Computers • Erotica • Relationships

Read-Alikes: Joe Phillips's *Adventures of a Joe Boy* takes the same amusing but frank look at gay sexual behavior. *Sticky,* by Dale Lazarov and Steve MacIsaac, is an erotic story told entirely in pictures, like the story-in-a-story *David & Jonathan.*

Delany, Samuel. Illustrated by Mia Wolff.

Bread and Wine: An Erotic Tale of New York. New York: Juno Books, 1999. **G**

Science fiction author Samuel Delany tells how he met Dennis, his lover and life partner, living filthy and homeless on the streets of New York. The two are initially wary but soon form a fast friendship; Delany invites Dennis to move in with him. Mia Wolff's black-and-white illustrations are spare but evocative.

Subjects: Couples • Delany, Samuel • Homeless • New York City

Read-Alikes: Readers who want to know more about the life of Samuel Delany will want to read his autobiographies, *The Motion of Light in Water* and *Times Square Red, Times Square Blue*. The theme of desire crossing class lines is repeated in several of Delany's books, most notably *Stars in My Pockets Like Grains of Sand*.

Winick, Judd.

Pedro and Me: Friendship, Loss and What I Learned. New York: Henry Holt, 2000. **G Teen**

AIDS educator Pedro Zamora became the public face of the HIV positive during MTV's *The Real World: San Francisco*. His friend and roommate from the show, cartoonist Judd Winick, tells the story of Pedro's life and eventual death from the complications of AIDS.

Subjects: AIDS • California • Death and dying • Friendship • Hispanics • Zamora, Pedro

Read-Alikes: Another nonfiction treatment of the loss of friends is Edmund White's *Loss Within Loss*. In Rebecca Brown's *The Gifts of the Body*, a caretaker learns from the people with AIDS that she assists.

9

10

11

12

13

15

16

Chapter 15

Drama

Definition

Drama encompasses literary works intended to be performed on stage, in a theater, or in other public spaces that contain a series of events or group of characters whose interactions create tensions, resolved through a major emotional or physical change.

Description and Characteristics

The deliberately created tensions of dramatic presentations offer authors a structure to explore opposing or controversial subjects. Characters can range from stereotypes to cutting-edge social rebels and mainstream personalities, serving as public voices of debate on issues from same-sex relationships to civil rights, to AIDS, to the search for love. Emotions can be explored in detail, providing both insight and confrontation. The possible outcomes for characters that the audience and readers come to care about (and even take sides with) engage and help focus attention, making drama both generically accessible and deeply personal.

History and Development

The history of gay and lesbian characters in dramatic works began in the early twentieth century, where they appeared as the problem that had to be eliminated by various means before the final curtain. Even these plays were often considered too risqué for production, an example being Mae West's depiction of gay life in the 1920s, *The Drag*, which was barred from New York City after its New Jersey opening in 1927.

During the 1930s, homosexuality gradually established a stage presence, through either coded representations or subtexts or, if openly admitted, through the suicide of the GLBT character. During the 1950s, the American attitude toward gays and lesbians was seen in *Tea and Sympathy* by Robert Anderson, in which heterosexuality is affirmed through corrective seduction, and in Lillian Hellman's famed *The Children's Hour*. The British and French theater world was open to realistic explorations beyond stereotyped effeminacy, in plays by Noel Coward, André Gide, and Joe Orton. American theater's contemporary tradition of visibly gay and lesbian drama began with Mart Crowley's hugely successful 1968 work *The Boys in the Band*, latest in a series of plays written and produced in New York's Off-Off-Broadway experimental theaters that also included Lanford Wilson's *The Madness of Lady Bright* (1964).

The Stonewall Riots of June 1969, commonly considered the beginning of the contemporary gay liberation and rights movements, also mark a dividing line between the older drama and a new approach born in the small experimental theaters catering to urban gay and women's communities. These experimental theaters cast gays and lesbians as open, whole, and complex characters in their own right. An example of this is the work of Jane Chambers, the first major openly lesbian playwright, who used dramatic realism to construct detailed, thought-provoking plays rich in emotional content, such as her widely performed *A Late Snow*, written in 1974.

Mainstream theaters also served as homes for this new theater, with gay male playwrights creating such arresting works as Martin Sherman's portrayal of the persecution of gay people in Nazi Germany, *Bent* (1979); Harvey Fierstein's award-winning *Torch Song Trilogy* (1981); and Terrence McNally's exploration of the fear of AIDS, *Lips Together, Teeth Apart* (1991). The AIDS pandemic was powerfully brought to the stage by activist playwright Larry Kramer, whose *The Normal Heart* (1985) and *The Destiny of Me* (1992) took audiences to the humanity of both infected persons and those who loved them. In 1992 the appearance of Tony Kushner's two-part epic *Angels in America* showed the maturation of this type of work through its exploration of conflict within the gay community, abandoning the older heterosexual/homosexual "us-versus-them" model. This trend has continued with the transformation of gay and lesbian plays into musical theater and even films, notably *Rent*.

Issues for the Readers' Advisor

Some readers, particularly those with an appreciation for theater, are eager to read dramatic works and often know exactly what they are seeking. However, this group represents only a small minority of the reading public. Drama as a type of literature has not always been considered "good writing," a legacy of the popular stage, and, later, radio and television "melodramas," with their highly charged emotional content and exaggerated conflicts and situations. Likewise, because plays are primarily intended to be performed, readers often overlook works in this format as possible reading material. Therefore, one task of the readers' advisor will be to assure patrons that these works are indeed legitimate in their own right and acceptable reading. An effective way of doing this is to learn what genre or theme the patron is most interested in, then consult reference works such as Ken Furtado's and Nancy Hellner's *Gay and Lesbian American Plays: An Annotated Bibliography* (Scarecrow Press, 1993) to identify specific authors. Searching the public online catalog of the Library of Congress http://www.loc.gov/ under the headings most applicable for this diverse genre, "Gay men-Drama" and "Lesbians, Drama," can serve as a way of keeping current with such works.

The chapter offers a wide variety of types of dramatic productions, beginning with the familiar genres of musicals, comedy (where the gay penchant for wit and dialogue shines), and tragedy. What may surprise both librarians and patrons is the use of contemporary history as the source of plot and setting, ranging from the concentration camps of Nazi Germany in *Bent* to the 1998 murder of Matthew Shepard in Wyoming in *The Laramie Project*. Patrons familiar with performance art from video sites will be pleased to find the work of troupes they may have heard of or seen before, while the massive publicity surrounding the groups of plays centered on AIDS in print since the 1980s will have resulted in some readers being very knowledgeable about individual works. If the patron is completely unfamiliar with any playwright or performer, the advisor should recommend one of the survey collections to allow the user to select the type of dramatic works he or she finds most appealing.

Chapter Organization

The chapter begins with looks at three standard subgenres of drama: comedy, tragedy, and historical. Two topics of particular importance to GLBT audiences, coming out and AIDS, are covered next, followed by musicals and performance art. Collected works by single authors or troupes are scattered throughout the chapter, but anthologies by multiple authors have their own section at the end.

Sources

Clum, John M. "Dramatic Literature: Contemporary Drama." In *Gay and Lesbian Literary Heritage*, edited by Claude J. Summers, 203–8.. New York: Holt, 1995.

Clum, John M. "Dramatic Literature: Modern Drama." In *Gay and Lesbian Literary Heritage*, edited by Claude J. Summers, 199–203. New York: Holt, 1995.

Curtin, Kaier. *We Can Always Call Them Bulgarians: the emergence of lesbians and gay men on the American stage*. Boston: Alyson Publications, 1987.

Furtado, Ken, and Nancy Hellner. *Gay and Lesbian American Plays: An Annotated Bibliography*. Metuchen, NJ: Scarecrow, 1993.

Sinfield, Alan. *Out on Stage: Lesbian and Gay Theatre in the Twentieth Century*. New Haven, CT: Yale University Press, 1999.

Comedy

The ability to laugh at one's own oppression and burlesque the limits on life imposed by an uncaring society is a hallmark of gay and lesbian humor, making it natural that one of the larger categories of GLBT drama would be flavored with laughter. For some eighty years, beginning with work such as Mae West's plays in the 1920s and *The Killing of Sister George* in 1965, the challenges and realities of being homosexual have been portrayed on stage with deliberately chosen jokes and exaggerations. These choices push the boundaries of what is acceptable and raise the question of whether they should remain in place.

Allen, Claudia.

She's Always Liked the Girls Best: Lesbian Plays. Chicago: Third Side Press, 1993. **L**
Claudia Allen set out to write plays featuring competent, compassionate lesbians. Three plays, *Roomers, Raincheck,* and *Hannah Free,* highlight the reality of lesbian life in small towns. *Movie Queens* takes us back to 1930s Hollywood and the restrictions on GLBT life present then.

Subjects: Humor • Relationships • Small towns

Read-Alikes: April Sinclair's <u>Stevie Stevenson Series</u> introduces Stevie, a capable and giving bisexual woman. *The Father of Frankenstein,* by Christopher Bram, is a novelization of the last days of director James Whale, who suffered from Hollywood's homophobia in the 1930s and 1940s.

Donaghy, Tom.

The Beginning of August. New York: Dramatists Play Service, 2001. **G B**
When Jackie's wife leaves him and their baby, their neighbors make it their business. Missing his wife, Jackie finds temporary solace in the arms of Ben.

Subjects: Humor • Parenting • Relationships

Read-Alikes: *Execution Texas: 1987,* by D. Travers Scott, captures the same anomie but with a younger cast of characters. Jay Quinn's *The Good Neighbor* also explores the intersection of gay and straight suburbia.

Fierstein, Harvey.

Torch Song Trilogy. New York: Villard, 1983. **G B**
Love is elusive for Arnold—sometimes his affairs end humorously, occasionally in tragedy. But he perseveres, in a heartwarming and uplifting story that shows the point of carrying a torch.

Subjects: AIDS • Books to film • Death and dying • Friendship • Humor • Love • New York City

Read-Alikes: Ethan Mordden's *I've a Feeling We're Not in Kansas Anymore* also looks at gay relationships in Manhattan during the 1970s and early 1980s. *Dancer from the Dance,* by Andrew Holleran, is set a few years earlier and takes place mostly on Fire Island.

Grimsley, Jim.

Mr. Universe: And Other Plays. Chapel Hill, NC: Algonquin Books of Chapel Hill, 1998. **G T**
Mr. Universe is the name given to a seemingly mute bodybuilder found covered in blood by two New Orleans drag queens, only one of whom is looking to help him. *The Lizard of Tarsus* has Paul interrogating his prisoner, J., for whom he has trouble admitting his love. *Math and Aftermath* tells the story of a gay porn film being shot on Bikini Atoll (just before it is used to test a nuclear weapon) and the jockeying for position of the various members of the cast.

Subjects: Humor • Louisiana • Murder • Pornography • Religion

Read-Alikes: Readers who enjoyed *Mr. Universe* should also like John Berendt's *Midnight in the Garden of Good and Evil*, in which the city of Savannah stands in for decadent New Orleans.

Kirkwood, James.

P.S. Your Cat Is Dead! A Comedy in Two Acts. New York: Samuel French, 1976. **B**

After a messy New Year's Eve breakup with his girlfriend, struggling writer Jimmy Zoole overpowers Vito, an attractive but inept cat burglar. Over the course of the evening, Jimmy and Vito argue, joke, and end up as pals. A madcap comedy with a hint of violence at its core, this play takes place entirely inside Jimmy's New York City loft apartment. This story was later written as a novel by the same author and was also made into a movie in 2002.

Subjects: Books to film • Crime • Humor • Relationships

Read-Alikes: The same crazed but black humor permeates *Holidays on Ice* (including the hilarious "Santaland Diaries") , by David Sedaris.

Marcus, Frank.

The Killing of Sister George: A Comedy. New York: Random House, 1965. **L**

BBC executives decide to boost the flagging ratings of their soap opera by killing off one of their characters, the much-beloved country nurse Sister George. June, the actress who plays Sister George, is grasping for work. The woman the studio sends to help her is poised to take advantage of June's foundering relationship with Childie, her submissive lover.

Subjects: Actors and actresses• Books to film • Humor • Jealousy • Relationships • Sadomasochism

McNally, Terrence.

Corpus Christi. New York: Grove Press, 1999. **G**

The story of Jesus is reset in a Texas high school. Judas comes to the aid of a troubled Jesus/Joshua and they become friends and lovers, before Joshua begins his public ministry.

Subjects: Humor • Relationships • Religion

Read-Alikes: Other messianic heroes are found in *The Song of the Earth*, by Hugh Nissenson. The rigors of secondary education in Texas for GLBT youth are touched on in D. Travers Scott's *Execution, Texas: 1987*.

Love! Valour! Compassion! New York: Plume, 1995. **G**

Eight men share a beach house over three summer holiday weekends: Gregory, the homeowner; his blind lover Bobby; Art and Perry, a couple celebrating fourteen years together; James, cheerful and friendly despite his advanced AIDS; John, who hates James, his twin; Ramon, John's lover for the summer; and Buzz, recently diagnosed as HIV positive. The shifting friendships and relationships overlay an ongoing affection that holds the group together. This work won a 1994 Tony Award.

Subjects: AIDS • Books to film • Friendship • Humor • Infidelity

Read-Alikes: Ethan Mordden's *Buddies Cycle* looks at the same themes of love and friendship against the emerging backdrop of AIDS.

Orton, Joe.

Entertaining Mr. Sloan. New York: Grove Press, 1976. **G** **B**

A gay man and his sex-starved sister use the opportunity of their father's death to blackmail a young ruffian into both their beds.

Subjects: Books to film • Crime • Humor

Read-Alikes: Oscar Wilde's *The Importance of Being Earnest* (particularly as adapted into a graphic novel by Tom Bouden) has the same arch humor.

Rudnick, Paul.

The Most Fabulous Story Ever Told and *Mr. Charles, Currently of Palm Beach.* Woodstock: Overlook Press, 2000. **G** **L**

Adam and Steve, not Adam and Eve, are the initial creation, causing confusion as they and their new friends Mabel and Jane try to live their lives by the Bible foisted on them by a member of the audience. In the second play, the flamboyant, self-assured Mr. Charles answers questions about homosexuality on his call-in radio show with hilarious quips that still contain trenchant truths.

Subjects: Humor • Radio • Relationships • Religion

Read-Alikes: This is ironic humor in the tradition of Oscar Wilde's *Lady Windermere's Fan* and Quentin Crisp's *The Naked Civil Servant*.

Turner, Guinevere, and Rose Troche.

🎖 *Go Fish.* Woodstock: Overlook Press, 1995. **L**

Ely uses the excuse of a long-distance relationship to avoid dating, while Max bemoans the lack of attractive lesbians available for dating. A group of friends urge Max to give Ely a chance, because one never knows where love may be hiding. Secondary characters deal with parental rejection, bisexuality, and interracial relationships. This play was made into a film in 1994.

Awards: Lambda Literary Award, 1995

Subjects: Books to film • Dating • Humor • Love

Read-Alikes: Alison Bechdel's <u>Dykes to Watch Out For</u> series looks at many aspects of lesbian political and social life, including romance, through the interactions of a wide group of friends.

West, Mae.

Three Plays. New York: Routledge, 1997. **G** **B** **T**

Two of Mae West's plays are known as her "gay plays": *The Drag* and *Pleasure Man*. In *The Drag*, a closeted young man has married and given up his gay lover to hide his secret, but still looks for a straight man to give him pleasure. A huge drag ball at the end of the play allowed West to cast many of her gay friends and associates. In *Pleasure Man*, the main character is a cad with an interest in both sexes. (*Sex*, the other play in this collection, has some important feminist points but no GLBT content.)

Subjects: Cross-dressing • Humor

Read-Alikes: The burlesque of West's plays is perhaps best approximated by Jerry Herman's *La Cage aux Folles*. Her fans would appreciate the recent biography *Mae West: An Icon in Black and White*, by Jill Watts.

Tragedy

Building on the traditional themes of mainstream dramatic works, this class of GLBT stage writings expands its focus to include same-gender relationships and their own unique pleasures and perils.

Asch, Solomon.

God of Vengeance. New York: Theatre Communications Group, 2004. **L**

A man and his wife make a show of piety and respectability to protect their daughter from the influences of the brothel they own—but the daughter runs away with one of the prostitutes and comes to a bad end. Originally performed in 1922, this play is also included in the anthology *Forbidden Acts*.

Subjects: Families • Religion • Sex workers

Read-Alikes: *Waking Beauty*, by Paul Whitcover, involves a society with a similarly negative view of women. Margaret Atwood's *The Handmaid's Tale* also has a rigid religious hierarchy enforcing male supremacy.

Greenberg, Richard.

Take Me Out: A Play. New York: Faber & Faber, 2003. **G**

Darren Lemming, center fielder for the New York Empires, roils his team, friends, and fans when he announces he is gay. A star player, he stays the leader of his team but unleashes the dark and twisted rage of relief pitcher Shane Mungitt—with fatal results.

Subjects: Baseball • Coming out • Homophobia • Race relations

Read-Alikes: As in Howard Cruse's graphic novel, *Stuck Rubber Baby*, racism and homophobia build quietly to an explosion. A less troubling but still powerful work on baseball and homophobia is Peter Lefcourt's *The Dreyfuss Affair*.

Hellman, Lillian.

The Children's Hour. New York: Dramatists Play Service, 1953. **L**

A boarding school for girls is forced to shut down over the unfounded accusation of an unnatural relationship between the two proprietors. One woman kills herself because she realizes she is a lesbian, and the other proprietor ends her engagement when her fiancé proves unsupportive.

Subjects: Books to film • Coming out • Homophobia • Students • Teachers

Read-Alikes: The true story on which *The Children's Hour* is based is detailed in Lillian Faderman's *Scotch Verdict: Miss Pirie and Miss Woods v. Dame Cumming Gordon*.

Historical

The limited number of plays depicting gays and lesbians in historical contexts is due in part to the fact that much of the history of this community is only now being gathered into coherent form. Prior to the creation of gay and lesbian studies as a distinct field of study, GLBT people only appeared in the historical record as scattered characters or as the subject of legal persecutions, as in Nazi Germany. That this genre is a living one is demonstrated by such works as *The Laramie Project*, based on the 1998 murder of Matthew Shepard, a young gay man in Wyoming.

Drader, Brian.

🎭 *Prok.* Winnipeg, MB: Scirocco Drama, 2003. **G** **B**

A dramatization of the life of famed sex research Professor Alfred Kinsey.

Awards: Lambda Literary Award, 2003

Subjects: Kinsey, Alfred • Sex

Read-Alikes: Kinsey's life is the subject of the motion picture *Kinsey*, an Academy Award and Golden Globe nominee. A good, if scholarly, biography is Jonathan Gathorne-Hardy's *Sex the Measure of All Things: A Life of Alfred C. Kinsey*.

Kaufman, Moises.

🎭 *Gross Indecency: The Three Trials of Oscar Wilde.* New York: Vintage, 1997. **G** **B**

At the end of three trials, Oscar Wilde was condemned to hard labor for the crime of loving other men. Kaufman brilliantly takes the transcripts from the trials, personal letters, interviews, newspaper accounts, and more to bring the three trials—and Oscar Wilde and his contemporaries—to life.

Awards: Lambda Literary Award, 1998.

Subjects: Trials • Wilde, Oscar

Read-Alikes: Merlin Holland's *The Real Trial of Oscar Wilde* provides the transcript and evaluation of Wilde's first trial, making the argument that Wilde was as ill-served by his lawyers as by his own flippancy. In *Oscar Wilde's Last Stand*, by Philip Hoare, the continued disdain for same-sex love manifests itself in slanders against the actress who portrayed Salome in a 1918 production of Wilde's work.

Kaufman, Moisés and the Tectonic Theatre Project.

🎭 *The Laramie Project.* New York: Vintage, 2001. **G**

The brutal murder of Matthew Shepard is explored through interviews with the people of Laramie, from the woman who found Shepard to his friends. The monologues trace the town's reaction to the murder and the media firestorm that followed. A creative, dramatic depiction of the consequences of homophobia, this work was made into a TV movie in 2002.

Awards: Stonewall Book Award, 2002.

Subjects: Books to film • Homophobia • Murder • Shepard, Matthew • Wyoming

Read-Alikes: Beth Loffreda's *Losing Matt Shepard* attempts to answer difficult questions about society and hatred through the eyes of Laramie's citizens.

Sherman, Martin.

Bent. New York: Avon, 1979. **G** **T**

9

Paragraph 175 of the German penal code outlawed homosexual acts. It was largely ignored during the heady days of the Weimar Republic, but Max and his partner Rudy get swept up (and Rudy killed) as the Nazis tighten their grip. Max learns to survive—and the price of doing so—from Horst, another concentration camp inmate. This play was made into a movie in 1997.

10

Subjects: Books to film • Friendship • Germany • Nazis • Relationships

Read-Alikes: A survivor's account of his arrest and conviction as a "degenerate" and being sent to a concentration camp under the Nazis can be found in Heinz Heger's *The Men with the Pink Triangle.* Readers should also see the documentary film *Paragraph 175.*

Stokes, Leslie, and Sewell Stokes.

11

Oscar Wilde. New York: Random House, 1938. **G** **B**

A sympathetic portrait of writer Oscar Wilde, this play covers his trials in England and his exile in France. First performed in 1938, this work is also available in the anthology *Forbidden Acts.*

Subjects: Relationships • Trials • Wilde, Oscar

12

Read-Alikes: Neil McKenna's *The Secret Life of Oscar Wilde* covers Wilde's sexual and literary history, providing background for this play.

Wright, Doug, and Charlotte von Mahlsdorf.

🏆 *I Am My Own Wife.* New York: Faber & Faber, 2004. **T**

13

Each act in this one-person play is like a snapshot, a moment in the life of Charlotte von Mahlsdorf. Taken together, the snapshots depict the life of an eccentric transvestite trapped in Nazi and then Communist Germany.

Awards: Lambda Literary Award, 2004

Subjects: Biography • Cross-dressing • Germany • Mahlsdorf, Charlotte von • Nazis

14

Read-Alikes: *The Men with the Pink Triangle,* by Heinz Heger, though nonfiction, is a moving description of life for gay men in Nazi Germany. Readers may appreciate von Mahlsdorf's biography, the similarly titled *I Am My Own Woman.*

AIDS

15

Although the representation of disease in literature is familiar in mainstream theater and film, the devastating impact of the AIDS pandemic on the gay community is uniquely reflected in the plays written by its members. Beginning with Larry Kramer's groundbreaking *The Normal Heart* in 1985, the next two decades saw the appearance of stage works addressing relationships upset by AIDS and depicting how relationships could survive with dignity and humor. Common threads in these dramas are love as a long-term duty, willingly chosen, and diverse angers at the government, medicine, and one's fellow man.

16

Crowley, Mart.

The Men from the Boys. New York: Samuel French, 2004. **G B T**

Michael, whose birthday was celebrated in Crowley's 1968 play *The Boys in the Band*, again hosts a gathering, nearly forty years later, to mourn the death of Larry. Older and wiser, the remaining guests from the birthday party reflect on personal and social changes with some younger gay men also touched by Larry.

Subjects: AIDS • Politics

Read-Alikes: This is a sequel to Crowley's *The Boys in the Band*. The two plays read together give a good sense of the emergence and development of gay life across the years. Readers who want more of the younger crowd's outlook should check out Jameson Currier's *Desire, Lust, Passion, Sex*.

Hoffman, William.

As Is. New York: Random House, 1985. **G**

Rich takes in his ex-lover Saul when Saul is diagnosed with AIDS. Through a personal and often humorous telling, the audience is slowly drawn into the dawning realization of the real love between the two men, amid the devastation wrought by the epidemic.

Subjects: AIDS • Books to film • Humor • Relationships

Read-Alikes: In Lisa Shamess's *Borrowed Light*, main character David grapples with his impending death and the repair of damaged relationships.

Kramer, Larry.

The Normal Heart. New York: New American Library, 1985. **G**

This is a thinly fictionalized account of the formation of the Gay Men's Health Crisis in response to New York City's refusal to acknowledge the AIDS crisis in the early 1980s, mixed with the personal tales of some of those first affected. Larry Kramer's anger, frustration, and determination virtually bleed through the pages.

Subjects: AIDS • New York City • Politics

Read-Alikes: A good nonfiction work that covers many of the same events and brings in a national perspective is *And the Band Played On*, by Randy Shilts.

Kushner, Tony.

🌿 *Angels in America. Part One: Millennium Approaches; Part Two: Perestroika.* New York: Dramatists Play Service, 1992. **G**

Prior is an AIDS patient abandoned by his lover, Louis, who falls for Joe, a Mormon with a mentally ill wife. Joe's mother attempts to rescue her family, but instead saves Prior. Set in the 1980s, the characters' lives intermingle to form a story simultaneously funny, tragic, and poignant that contrasts well with the final days of the closeted conservative crusader Roy Cohn.

Awards: Lambda Literary Award, 1993.

Subjects: AIDS • Books to film • Homophobia • Politics • Religion

Read-Alikes: *Citizen Cohn*, by Nicholas von Hoffman, tells the life of Roy Cohn, hatchetman for Joe McCarthy and J. Edgar Hoover, a deeply closeted man who died from

AIDS-related cancer in 1986. *Latter Days*, by C. Jay Cox and T. Fabris, finds a Mormon missionary in Los Angeles coming to terms with his attraction to men.

Lucas, Craig.

Longtime Companion. New York: William Morris Agency, 1988. **G**

Longtime Companion follows the lives of several gay friends as they deal with the impact of AIDS through the decade or so following its first mention in the papers. At the start, AIDS is a problem for other people, but as the play progresses, HIV touches all of their lives. *Longtime Companion* was made into a motion picture in 1990.

Subjects: AIDS • Books to film • Friendship • Grief

Read-Alikes: A good nonfiction companion to this is Randy Shilts's *And the Band Played On*. Armistead Maupin's Tales of the City ended in 1989 with Michael "Mouse" Tolliver learning he was HIV positive; in Maupin's latest novel, *Michael Tolliver Lives*, we find Michael happy and still alive, thanks to the development of protease inhibitors.

Rudnick, Paul.

Jeffrey. New York: Dramatists Play Service, 1998. **G**

Jeffrey is smitten, but the man of his dreams is HIV positive—and Jeffrey isn't sure he can handle it.

Subjects: AIDS • Books to film • Friendship • Love

Read-Alikes: In Joseph Caldwell's *The Uncle from Rome*, an American mourning the AIDS-related death of his partner is able to find love again. David Feinberg's *Eighty-Sixed* and *Spontaneous Combustion* are very humorous novels dealing with AIDS.

Coming Out

Personal stories of working toward acceptance of gay and lesbian identity are a stock genre of GLBT literature in all forms and provide a window into how this process has changed over time. Ranging in date from the McCarthy era of the 1950s to the early twenty-first century, these plays enable the audience to follow the gradual evolution of coming out, from a defiant act of rebellion to an action seen by many to be a different but not shocking life choice.

Anderson, Jane.

Looking for Normal. New York: Dramatists Play Service, 2002. **T**

Roy tells Irma, his wife of twenty-five years, that he is a woman in a man's body and wants sex-reassignment surgery. Initially unsupportive, Irma comes to realize the depth of the connection she shares with Roy, and they explore how they can continue their relationship and raise their children as Roy transitions into womanhood.

Subjects: Coming out • Families • Gender identity • Humor • Parenting • Sex change

Read-Alikes: Jackie Kay's novel, *Trumpet,* about the post-death revelation that jazz musician Joss Moody was actually a woman, shows love and family triumphing after the initial shock.

Crowley, Mart.

The Boys in the Band. New York: Farrar, Straus & Giroux, 1968. **G**

Eight gay men gather, pre-Stonewall, to celebrate a birthday, but the party breaks down into recriminations as each man deals with the tensions of being homosexual in a society that demands they hide their passions.

Subjects: Books to film • Coming out • Friendship • Parties

Read-Alikes: *The Boys in the Band* was made into a motion picture in 1970. Crowley wrote *The Men from the Boys* (annotated above, in the AIDS section) as a sequel to this play in 2004. Patrons may also enjoy *The Best Little Boy in the World*, by John Reid.

Goetz, Augustus, and Ruth Goetz.

The Immoralist: A Drama in Three Acts. New York: Dramatists Play Service, 1954. **G** **B**

In this drama of self-discovery Michel, a married homosexual (who has nonetheless managed to get his wife pregnant), allows himself to be seduced by Bachir, a Moroccan teen. In a touching end scene, the husband and wife reconcile and resolve to try to work together for the benefit of the child. Based on the book by André Gide, this play was James Dean's 1954 Broadway break.

Subjects: Coming out • Crime • Illness • Morocco

Read-Alikes: In the dusty Burgundian landscape of Elizabeth Knox's *The Vintner's Luck,* an angel caught between God and Satan helps a winemaker find himself. The combination of a languid North African setting and existential angst can also be found in Albert Camus's *The Stranger*.

Lucas, Craig.

🏶 *What I Meant Was: New Plays and Selected One-Acts.* New York: Theater Communications Group, 1999. **G** **L** **B**

Several of the pieces in this collection have gay or bisexual characters. *The Dying Gaul* tells of the struggle of a gay writer to control the unqueering of his magnum opus when it is optioned for a movie. In *God's Heart,* the other full-length play, same-sex marriage activist couple, Barbara and Eleanor, is caught up in a drug deal gone wrong.

Awards: Lambda Literary Award, 2000.

Subjects: Coming out • Crime • Film industry • Homophobia • Marriage

Read-Alikes: The hypocrisy of Hollywood in *The Dying Gaul* is mirrored in Christopher Bram's *The Father of Frankenstein,* a treatment of 1950s homophobia and the closet.

Musicals

This is one of the newer forms of GLBT drama, although it continues the legacy of energy expressed in the performances of bar drag performers both before and after

Stonewall. Plots are based on both literature and other more mainstream plays familiar to the audience.

Larson, Jonathan.

Rent. New York: Rob Weisbach Books, 1997. **G** **L** **B** **T**

Larson updated Puccini's *La Boheme,* creating a pop opera that chronicles a year in the lives of struggling anti-establishment East Village artists Roger and Mark. Roger, a recovering ex-junkie rock star, finds love and agony in Mimi; Mark lost his passion when his girlfriend Maureen left him for Jo-anne, but finds it again helping Maureen claim a performance space. Addicts, homeless, and sellouts drift through the wasteland and promise of mid-1990s New York. This play was made into a movie in 2005.

Subjects: AIDS • Books to film • New York City • Performance art • Substance abuse

Read-Alikes: The counterculture of an earlier generation is given musical voice in *Hair.* Sarah Schulman's *People in Trouble* contains many of the same themes, so much so that Schulman claimed, in her 1998 book *Stagestruck,* that Larson had stolen her work.

Mitchell, John Cameron, and Stephen Trask.

✿ *Hedwig and the Angry Inch.* Woodstock, NY: Overlook Press, 2002. **T**

An effeminate East German musician's love for an American GI leads to sexual reassignment surgery as a route to legal marriage and American immigration. The dual failure of love and musical career is told in lyrical flashbacks. This musical was made into a movie in 2001.

Awards: Lambda Literary Award, 2000

Subjects: Books to film • Love • Music • Sex change

Read-Alikes: Glam rock opera with gender-bending overtones was pioneered in 1973 by Richard O'Brian in the cult classic *The Rocky Horror Picture Show.*

Performance Art

This type of GLBT dramatic work draws on the legacies left by the drag tradition born in many bars across the country. Presentations by individual actors blend humor and social commentary on a variety of issues. Troupes such as Split Britches and The Five Lesbian Brothers can be seen as a fusion of the mainstream idea of a theater company with the defiantly challenging approach taken by many gay and lesbian writers to their subjects.

Ensler, Eva.

Vagina Monologues. New York: Dramatists Play Service, 2000. **L** **B**

Hundreds of women were interviewed and asked to discuss their vaginas. The resulting monologues will transport the reader from laughter to tears, while addressing a range of topics from sexual assault and discrimination to appearance. The play inspired V-day, a global movement to stop violence against women.

Subjects: Books to film • Feminism • Sexual abuse

Five Lesbian Brothers (Theater Troupe).

Five Lesbian Brothers: Four Plays. New York: Theatre Communications Group, 2000. **L**

The Five Lesbian Brothers, a small theater collective, humorously deconstructs modern life and its many indignities, pulling in bits from musical theater, film critiques, and science fiction in fast-paced farces. Includes *Voyage to Lesbos, Brave Smiles . . . Another Lesbian Tragedy, The Secretaries, and Brides of the Moon.*

Subjects: Film criticism • Humor • Mental health • Space flight

Read-Alikes: Lisa Kron, a member of the Five Lesbian Brothers, has released some individual performance pieces in *2.5 Minute Ride* and *101 Humiliating Stories.*

Margolin, Deb.

Of All the Nerve: Deb Margolin, Solo. New York: Cassell, 1999. **L** **B**

Seven edgy but entertaining performance scripts by Deb Margolin explore desire through the prisms of religion, race, culture, language, and gender. Margolin includes extensive stage directions, and each play is followed by the academic commentary of editor Lynda Hart. Includes *Of All the Nerve, 970-DEBB, Gestation, Of Mice, Bugs and Women, Carthieves! Joyrides!, O Wholly Night and Other Jewish Solecisms,* and *Critical Mass,* a dark and caustic comedy.

Subjects: Feminism • Humor • Jews • Performance art

Read-Alikes: Lisa Kron's performance pieces *2.5 Minute Ride* and *101 Humiliating Stories.* also investigate these themes from a Jewish perspective. *Three Seconds in the Key,* a 2005 Margolin play, deals not with desire but with her experience living with Hodgkin's disease.

Split Britches (Theater Troupe).

🎗 *Split Britches: Lesbian Practice/Feminist Performance.* New York: Routledge, 1996. **L**

Four plays explore lesbian/feminist issues through satire, schtick, and sexual radicalism.

Awards: Lambda Literary Award, 1997.

Subjects: Families • Feminism • Film criticism • Performance art

Read-Alikes: Two of this troupe's cofounders, Peggy Shaw and Lois Weaver, helped Isabel Miller develop her award-winning book, *Patience and Sarah,* into a play.

Troyano, Alina, and Ela Troyano and Uzi Parnes.

I, Carmelita Tropicana: Performing Between Cultures. Boston: Beacon Press, 2000. **L**

Social and political commentaries with a humorous edge are presented in this collection of plays, performance scripts, and prose showcasing Alina Troyano's alter ego: the multicultural, multilingual, multinational lesbian beauty queen Cuban emigré, Carmelita Tropicana.

Subjects: Hispanics • Humor • Immigrants • Performance art

Read-Alikes: Readers who enjoyed the Cuban American experience will find the collections *Don't Explain,* by Jewelle Gomez, and *We Came All the Way from Cuba So You Could Dress Like This?,* by Achy Obejas, worth exploring.

Anthologies

These collections offer a valuable introduction to GLBT drama for readers unfamiliar with a specific writer or work. Readers will find the introductions of particular value in deciding which playwright's creations to pursue.

Hodges, Ben, ed.

Forbidden Acts: Pioneering Gay & Lesbian Plays of the Twentieth Century. New York: Applause Theatre and Cinema Books, 2003. **G L B**

Most of these groundbreaking plays are readily available published (and annotated) separately, but Hodges did a great service by pulling them together in an inexpensive volume well-suited to most libraries. Also, the chronological arrangement, from Solomon Asch's *God of Vengeance* in 1922 to Terrence McNally's *Love! Valour! Compassion!* in 1995, allows the reader to trace the development of GLBT themes.

Subjects: Anthologies • Theater

Hughes, Holly, ed.

🏵 *O Solo Homo: The New Queer Performance.* New York: Grove Press, 1998. **G L B T**

An anthology of scripts and performance texts from several of the most important performance artists of the 1990s, including Holly Hughes, Tim Miller, and Ron Vawter, this work shows the burgeoning diversity of the field in the late twentieth century. Informative editor's notes preface each of the entries in this collection.

Awards: Lambda Literary Award, 1999

Subjects: Anthologies • Humor • Performance art • Politics

Osborn, M. Elizabeth, ed.

The Way We Live Now: American Plays and the AIDS Crisis. New York: Theatre Communications Group, 1990. **G**

This collection of excerpts and plays about AIDS covers well-known pieces such as *Angels in America* and *As Is,* as well as some that are relatively unknown. The plays date from the last half of the 1980s.

Subjects: AIDS • Anthologies • Theater

15

Senelick, Laurence, ed.

Lovesick: Modernist Plays of Same-Sex Love, 1894–1925. New York: Routledge, 1999. **G L B T**

Six early pieces of drama on gay and lesbian love provide important literary and historical background for readers. Contains *The Blackmailers,* a comedy by two associates of Oscar Wilde; *At Saint Judas',* in which unrequited love leads to a man's death, possibly at the hands of the object of his affection; *"Mistakes,"* in which a gay man agrees to marry but is brought low by a blackmailer; *The Dangerous Precaution,* a musical fable of cross-dressing; *The Gentleman of the Chrysanthemums,* a comedy of manners loosely based on the celebrity of Oscar Wilde; and *Ania and Esther,* a troubling romance set in a school for unrepentant children.

Subjects: Anthologies • Crime • Relationships • Theater

Chapter 16

Life Stories: Biography, Autobiography, and Memoirs

Definition

Biographical writing in all its forms tells the story of an individual whose life is considered to have been important because of his or her contributions to a specific cause or community. The voice of the narrator can be either that person, in an autobiography or memoir, or a historian or writer (possibly a fellow professional) sufficiently familiar with the contributions made by that person to place him or her in context, in a biography. Examples of these genres in this chapter are William J. Mann's *Wisecracker: The Life and Times of William Haines, Hollywood's First Openly Gay Star* (1988) and *Icebreaker: The Autobiography of Rudy Galindo* (1997), and Leslie Feinberg's *Transgender Warriors* (1996).

Description and Characteristics

Biographies of individuals whose sexual preference are (or were) for their own gender were rare before the gay liberation movements of the late nineteenth and early twentieth centuries. This was due in part to the cultural repression of past times and the resulting absence of documentary information about many people who later were associated with this group. Another factor was the reluctance of mainstream historians to include such aspects of their subjects even when they were known, unless the information was too obvious to ignore, as in the case of the Roman emperor Hadrian. Gay, lesbian, or bisexual characteristics were more often tolerated in biographies of people involved with the arts—literature, fine arts, or the theater—where such orientation was sometimes explained as simply part of the artistic temperament.

Even after movements for homosexual equality appeared in Germany in 1897, the early biographical essays in these movements' periodicals centered on the notable figures of classical times rather than contemporary persons, who might then have been subjected to various legal and police sanctions. The first openly gay activist for homosexual rights was Dr. Magnus Hirschfeld, who, despite giving numerous public lectures and founding the Institute for Sexual Science in Berlin, was not made the subject of a book-length biography until 1986. Although he left a serial autobiography in letters to his family, Karl Heinrich Ulrichs, the first jurist to openly advocate for homosexual rights, was not the subject of a biography until 1988.

Issues for the Readers' Advisor

Many of the GLBT figures about whom biographies have been written are not well known outside that community. This makes it necessary for the librarian to become familiar with the contents of such works to identify titles of interest to patrons by field of activity or time period. A second issue may be the availability of such works, because many books and anthologies were issued by small presses that no longer exist, and they may not have been collected by many libraries. The Library of Congress subject headings for this area are constructed on the model of "Gay men—United States—Biography" and "Lesbians—United States—Biography", with the country serving as a necessary part of the search term. These two categories—containing arguably the largest portion of the extant literature in this field—are useful places for the advisor wishing to begin searching in the Library of Congress online catalog, at http://www.loc.gov/. Recent headings have also been provided by cultural background, such as "African American gay men" and "Asian American lesbians". For older materials, it may be necessary to look under the heading for which the person is best known; for example, the Roman emperor Hadrian can be found under "Emperors —Rome—Biography".

Chapter Organization

The chapter is divided into sections reflecting the areas of activity/accomplishment of the subjects, arranged in alphabetical order. Biography, autobiography, and memoirs are integrated within those sections, and the terms *biography* and *autobiography* are used in the subject line. The final section covers anthologies. The range of subjects and professional fields reflects both those traditionally associated with and accepting of GLBT people—such as acting, music, comedy, literature, and art—and those in which claiming an alternative sexual identity comes with a higher price in courage and determination, examples being the military services and athletics. Categories that may be unexpected are teachers and students, travelers and explorers, healthcare workers, children and their families, and the ministry. Given the range of possible life paths, and that GLBT people are and have been part of virtually every profession, readers curious about a particular field should be advised to consult one of the excellent reference works on GLBT culture, such as *Lesbian Histories and Cultures* and *Gay Histories and Cultures*, both published in 2000, for background and the names of specific individuals to research.

Sources

Bergman, David. *Gaiety Transfigured: Gay Self-representation in American Literature.* Madison: University of Wisconsin Press, 1991.

Bronski, Michael. *Outstanding Lives: Profiles of Lesbians and Gay Men*. New York: Visible Ink, 1997.

Cohler, Bertram J. *Writing Desire: Sixty Years of Gay Autobiography*. Madison: University of Wisconsin Press, 2007.

De Cecco John P., Dawn M. Krisko, and Sonya L. Jones, eds. *A Sea of Stories: The Shaping Power of Narrative in Gay and Lesbian Cultures*. New York: Harrington Park Press, 2000.

Haggerty, George E. *Gay Histories and Cultures: An Encyclopedia*. New York: Garland, 2000.

Marcus, Eric. *Making History: The Struggle for Gay and Lesbian Equal Rights, 1945–1990: An Oral History*. New York: HarperCollins, 1992.

Tóibín, Colm. *Love in a Dark Time: And Other Explorations of Gay Lives and Literature*. New York: Scribner, 2001.

Tyrkus, Michael J., ed. *Gay & Lesbian Biography*. Detroit: St. James Press, 1997.

Zimmerman, Bonnie. *Lesbian Histories and Cultures: An Encyclopedia*. New York: Garland, 2000.

Activists and Politicians

Although much of the biographical writing on activists for GLBT rights has taken the form of articles and interviews, the late 1980s saw the beginning of book-length studies of individual lives. The books in this genre provide a degree of background useful for the general reader who wants to place a man or woman in the context of more familiar mainstream culture.

Martin Duberman

Duberman, Martin. **G**
A trio of books traces the life of historian Martin Duberman as he struggles to eradicate his homosexuality and other personal demons.

Subjects: Authors • Autobiography • Coming out • Duberman, Martin • Mental health • Politics • Teachers

Cures: A Gay Man's Odyssey. Boulder, CO: Westview Press, 2002 (1991).
Duberman shares the details of his twenty-year search to cure to his homosexuality through psychiatric consultations and alternative therapies, ultimately realizing that self-acceptance and coming out were the keys to peace.

Left Out: The Politics of Exclusion. Cambridge, MA: South End Press, 2002.
This lengthy, nuanced collection of essays summarizes Duberman's political views, but reveals little of his personal life.

9

10

11

12

13

14

15

16

Midlife Queer. New York: Scribner, 1996.

> Covering the period 1950–1970, Duberman recounts grudges, rants about professional injustices, and is generally unhappy, once again pursuing psychological therapy as a cure until forced to reexamine his life after a near-fatal heart attack.

Leslie Feinberg

Feinberg, Leslie.

🎗 *Transgender Warriors.* Boston: Beacon Press, 1996. **T**

> Feinberg's life is the backdrop for discussing transgendered history, the emerging political movement, and her beliefs about society's backlash against trans people. Packed with photographs, this work is easy to read.
>
> **Awards:** Firecracker Alternative Book Award, 1997
>
> **Subjects:** Autobiography • Feinberg, Leslie • Gender identity • Politics • Sexual identity
>
> **Read-Alikes:** For a fictionalized biography of Feinberg, readers should check out *Stone Butch Blues.*

Harry Hay

Timmons, Stuart.

The Trouble with Harry Hay: Founder of the Modern Gay Movement. Boston: Alyson Publications, 1990. **G B**

> Timmons utilizes historical documents and interviews with Hay and friends to produce a significant biography of the founder of the Mattachine Society.
>
> **Subjects:** Biography • Hay, Harry • Politics
>
> **Read-Alikes:** Read Hay's autobiography, *Radically Gay.*

Harvey Milk

Shilts, Randy.

The Mayor of Castro Street. New York: St. Martin's Griffin, 1988. **G**

> Milk moved to San Francisco in search of the freedom to live as an openly gay man and transformed himself into a populist politician, becoming the first gay elected official of a major American city. Milk's life and his eventual assassination lend context to a political climate charged with fear of homosexuality.
>
> **Subjects:** Biography • California • Milk, Harvey • Murder • Politics
>
> **Read-Alikes:** Milk paved the way for future gay politicians such as former Republican Congressman Steve Gunderson, who relates his story in *House and Home.*

Anchee Min

Min, Anchee.

🎗 *Red Azalea.* New York: Pantheon Books, 1994. **L B**

> Embracing the Chinese Communist ideal, Min subjugated herself to the Party and was rewarded with forced labor on a remote farm. Lonely and disillusioned, Min

engaged in a dangerous affair with her supervisor. A story of personal hardship and first love.

Awards: Publishing Triangle's 100 Best Lesbian and Gay Novels, Reader's Choice

Subjects: Asians • Autobiography • China • Min, Anchee • Politics

Read-Alikes: Lillian Lee's *Farewell My Concubine* uses Chinese history and opera as the setting for a love triangle; in David Henry Hwang's classic *M Butterfly*, a diplomat reflects on an affair with a woman subsequently revealed to be a male communist spy.

Eleanor Roosevelt

Streitmatter, Rodger.

Empty Without You: The Intimate Letters of Eleanor Roosevelt and Lorena Hickok. New York: Simon & Schuster, 1998. **L B**

Spanning thirty years, the letters between First Lady Eleanor Roosevelt and journalist Lorena Hickok demonstrate an intense friendship and imply a romantic relationship between the women. This astonishing collection sheds new light on Roosevelt's life and alters history's perceptions of the famous First Lady.

Subjects: Authors • Biography • Hickok, Lorena • Love letters • Politics • Roosevelt, Eleanor

Read-Alikes: Readers may want to try the love letters between May Sarton and Juliette Huxley in *Dear Juliette*, edited by Susan Sherman.

Bayard Rustin

D'Emilio, John.

🎖 *Lost Prophet: The Life and Times of Bayard Rustin.* New York: Free Press, 2003. **G**

Rustin, right-hand man to Dr. Martin Luther King Jr., is rescued from obscurity in this remarkable biography. D'Emilio follows the traditional chronological layout, flavoring the story with personal anecdotes and demonstrating how homophobia kept Rustin behind the scenes.

Awards: Stonewall Book Award, 2004; Publishing Triangle Award, 2004

Subjects: African Americans • Biography • Homophobia • Politics • Race relations • Rustin, Bayard

José Sarria

Gorman, Michael R.

🎖 *The Empress Is a Man.* New York: Haworth, 1998. **G T**

This semiautobiographical work outlines Sarria's extensive activism. Best known as a singer/performance artist, he ran for elected office, established human rights organizations, and founded the Imperial Court system, a nonprofit organization raising funds via drag shows.

Awards: Lambda Literary Award, 1998

Subjects: Biography • California • Cross-dressing • Music • Politics • Sarria, José

Riki Anne Wilchins

Wilchins, Riki Anne.

Read My Lips: Sexual Subversions and the End of Gender. Ithaca, NY: Firebrand Books, 1997. **T**

Part personal story, part theoretical discourse. Wilchins uses her life to challenge the concepts of sex, gender, and identity. Moments of humor provide temporary relief from the theory and the reality of the costs of self-acceptance.

Subjects: Autobiography • Gender identity • Politics • Wilchins, Riki Anne

Actors and Actresses

Given the relatively accepting environment of the theater for gays and lesbians, it is noteworthy that many actors and actresses remain closeted for fear of compromising their careers. As a result, biographical works generally fall into two categories: speculative or academic. The entries here represent the latter category or are autobiographies. Both film and television stars are represented, and the period covered is unusual for American gay cultural history, beginning with the silent film star William Haines and reaching to such contemporary figures as RuPaul and the late Divine.

Tallulah Bankhead

Lobenthal, Joel.

Tallulah! The Life and Times of a Leading Lady. New York: Regan, 2004. **L** **B**

The result of twenty-five years of research, this lengthy biography is culled from extensive interviews. Packed with juicy tidbits about Bankhead's alcoholism, drug use, and bisexual encounters.

Subjects: Actors and actresses • Bankhead, Tallulah • Biography • Substance abuse

Read-Alikes: Bankhead, Dietrich, Garbo, and many others are featured in Diana McLellan's *Girls: Sappho Goes to Hollywood*.

Richard Chamberlain

Chamberlain, Richard.

Shattered Love. New York: Regan, 2004. **G**

Stylistically unpretentious, Chamberlain, who starred in the popular television series *Dr. Kildare,* focuses on his acting career and spirituality. Considering sexual orientation only an aspect of life, he devotes to it only a chapter and passing references to his long-term partner, in this easy-to-read autobiography.

Subjects: Actors and actresses • Autobiography • Chamberlain, Richard • Spirituality

James Dean

Alexander, Paul.

Boulevard of Broken Dreams: The Life, Times, and Legend of James Dean. New York: Viking, 1994. **G** **B**

A controversial work asserting that the film icon suffered conflicting feelings about his sexuality and slept with men as a way to gain entrance to Hollywood stardom. Dean fans will find little about his short-lived career and considerable speculation about male lovers.

Subjects: Actors and actresses • Biography • Dean, James

Marlene Dietrich

Spoto, Donald.

*Blue Angel: The Life of Marlene Dietric*h. New York: Doubleday, 1992. **L** **B**

Frequent film scenes with lesbian overtones, such as the top hat and tuxedo scene and the same-sex kiss in *Morocco*, have caused much speculation about the gorgeous German's sexual preferences. Spoto's biography is an honest exploration of the star's lovers of both genders.

Subjects: Actors and actresses • Biography • Dietrich, Marlene

Read-Alikes: Steven Bach's *Marlene Dietrich: Life and Legend* is a stronger critique of Dietrich's career but also covers her same-sex love affairs.

Divine

Milstead, Frances, Kevin Heffernan, and Steve Yeager.

My Son Divine. Los Angeles: Alyson Books, 2001. **T**

Packed with pictures, this illustrated biography by Divine's mom and friends provides a frank and unabashed look at her son's career as a female impersonator and actor in independent filmmaker John Waters's films, such as *Pink Flamingos*. Includes interviews with filmmaker John Waters and concludes with a filmography and list of CDs.

Subjects: Actors and actresses • Biography • Cross-dressing • Divine

Read-Alikes: In *Not Simply Divine*, Bernard Jay, Divine's former manager, presents an unsympathetic view. Patrons should also see the award-winning documentary film *Divine Trash*.

Greta Garbo

Paris, Barry.

Garbo. New York: Knopf, 1995. **L** **B**

The sexuality of the svelte Swedish actress is much debated despite considerable evidence of same-sex attraction. This sweeping, thoroughly researched biography asserts that the starlet was "technically bisexual, predominantly lesbian."

Subjects: Actors and actresses • Biography • Garbo, Greta

16

330 16—Life Stories: Biography, Autobiography, and Memoirs

William Haines

Mann, William J.

🏵 *Wisecracker: The Life and Times of William Haines, Hollywood's First Openly Gay Star.* New York: Viking, 1998. **G**

Haines, a silent film star, battled Hollywood over his sex life, eventually sacrificing career in favor of personal principles. Now virtually forgotten, he maintained a successful career as an interior decorator and a fifty-year relationship with his partner. A gossipy portrait of Hollywood circa 1930.

Awards: Lambda Literary Award, 1998

Subjects: Actors and actresses • Biography • Couples • Haines, William

Read-Alikes: For a look at Haines's life as a decorator, readers should see *Class Act,* by Peter Schifando, and for a composite approach to Hollywood's closet, they should try *Open Secret,* by David Ehrenstein.

Rock Hudson

Hudson, Rock, and Sara Davidson.

Rock Hudson: His Story. New York: William Morrow, 1987. **G** **B**

During most of his acting career, Hudson's homosexuality was invisible to the larger population, who were shocked by his AIDS diagnosis in 1985. The duality of leading a secret life is Davison's emphasis, complete with attendant alcohol problems and tempestuous relationships.

Subjects: Actors and actresses • AIDS • Autobiography • Hudson, Rock • Substance abuse

Read-Alikes: In *Montgomery Clift,* Patricia Bosworth aptly renders Montgomery Clift's painful life, plagued by living the lie of heterosexuality.

Tab Hunter

Hunter, Tab, and Eddie Muller.

Tab Hunter Confidential. Chapel Hill, NC: Algonquin, 2005. **G**

A mid-twentieth-century heartthrob, movie star, and singer, Hunter's meteoric rise and fall inside Hollywood's closet are detailed. A rare look inside the techniques employed by Hollywood to create a star and to downplay homosexuality.

Subjects: Actors and actresses • Autobiography • Hunter, Tab

Paul Lynde

Wilson, Steve, and Joe Florenski.

Center Square: The Paul Lynde Story. Los Angeles: Advocate Books, 2005. **G**

For the first generation of TV viewers, comedian and actor Paul Lynde was the only on-air image of a gay person. He starred in such popular television shows as *Bewitched* and *Hollywood Squares.* Open about his sexual preference long before it was common, Lynde's external witticism covered up personal pain and struggles with alcohol.

Subjects: Actors and actresses • Biography • Comedians • Humor • Lynde, Paul • Substance abuse

Read-Alikes: For a gossipy, composite view of several gay actors, readers may want to try *Hollywood Gays,* by Boze Hadleigh.

Anthony Perkins

Winecoff, Charles.

Anthony Perkins: Split Image. New York: Advocate Books, 2006. **G** **B**

Like so many actors of Hollywood's golden age, Perkins lived a double life, secretly pursuing homosexual relationships while married for twenty years. This cradle-to-grave biography frequently mentions fellow actor Tab Hunter but stops short of calling the men lovers.

Subjects: Actors and actresses • Biography • Perkins, Anthony

RuPaul

RuPaul.

Lettin' It All Hang Out. New York: Hyperion, 1995. **T**

RuPaul, a 1990s cross-dressing entertainer, capitalizes here on his national notoriety with this lightweight, chatty autobiography. Much is learned about his likes, dislikes, and disputes with Hollywood's elites, but little about the psyche of the man.

Subjects: Actors and actresses • Autobiography • Cross-dressing • RuPaul

Read-Alikes: In *Hiding My Candy,* regional phenomenon The Lady Chablis presents a revealing look at her life.

Artists

Society's image of artists as inhabiting a world that is different because of their gifts, a world less restrictive and easier about same-sex orientations, is reflected in these titles. Subjects range from dancers and photographers to the more expected artists working in paint and various types of drawings, and include figures from contexts as varied as the Harlem Renaissance and the leather community.

Alvin Ailey

Ailey, Alvin, and A. Peter Bailey.

Revelations: The Autobiography of Alvin Ailey. Bridgewater, NJ: Replica Books, 1999. **G**

The title of dancer Ailey's famed ballet *Revelations* became that of this attempted autobiography, cut short by his untimely AIDS-related death. Tragic self-loathing and fear of family reactions caused Ailey to downplay his homosexuality, both in life and in this work.

Subjects: African Americans • Ailey, Alvin • Art and artists • Autobiography • Dancing • Mental health • Substance abuse

Read-Alikes: For a fuller biography with more extensive consideration of Ailey's sexuality, readers may want to see *Alvin Ailey: A Life in Dance,* by Jennifer Dunning.

Keith Haring

Haring, Keith, and Robert Farris Thompson.

Keith Haring: Journals. New York: Viking, 1996. **G**

Peek inside artist Keith Haring's mind with this collection of his personal diaries, arranged by year and illuminated with sketches. Readers will find a socially aware, sensitive talent and gain insight into the artist's creative thought processes and feelings about the purpose and business of art.

Subjects: Art and artists • Autobiography • Haring, Keith

Read-Alikes: John Gruen's *Keith Haring: The Authorized Biography* is a mixture of interviews and artwork.

Robert Mapplethorpe

Morrisroe, Patricia.

Mapplethorpe: A Biography. New York: Da Capo Press, 1997. **G**

Mapplethorpe caused a stir with his sensual, oversized, black-and-white male nude photographs. Morrisroe interviewed family, friends, and lovers to produce this sympathetic portrayal of the controversial photographer's life. Candid descriptions of Mapplethorpe's rigid religious upbringing stand alongside equally detailed summaries of his sex life. Thirty-two photographs are included.

Subjects: Art and artists • Biography • Mapplethorpe, Robert • Photography • Sadomasochism

Read-Alikes: Former lover Jack Fritscher's biography, *Mapplethorpe: Assault with a Deadly Camera,* is a less nuanced portrait.

Richard Bruce Nugent

Wirth, Thomas.

Gay Rebel of the Harlem Renaissance. Durham, NC: Duke University, 2002. **G**

Eclipsed by Zora Neale Hurston, Langston Hughes, and others, Richard Bruce Nugent was nearly forgotten as an actor, writer, and artist of the Harlem Renaissance. Nugent's life is chronicled and complemented by his excellent drawings and personal photographs. Highly recommended for rescuing Nugent from obscurity and gathering the artist's most significant works.

Subjects: African Americans • Art and artists • Authors • Biography • Harlem Renaissance • Nugent, Richard Bruce

Read-Alikes: *Amazing Grace: A Biography of Beauford Delaney,* by David Leeming, relates the sad tale of this brilliant African American artist who was plagued by mental illness and struggling with his sexuality. For a collective approach to this era, readers may want to try A. B. Christa Schwarz's *Gay Voices of the Harlem Renaissance.*

Tom of Finland

Hooven, F. Valentine.

Tom of Finland: His Life and Times. New York: St. Martin's Griffin, 1994. **G**

Tom of Finland, a pseudonym for Touko Laaksonen, worked in advertising and sketched hypermasculine, working-class men in his free time. The life story of the artist who launched the leather and chaps subculture is filled with quotations and richly illustrated with drawings and photographs.

Subjects: Art and artists • Biography • Erotica • Laaksonen, Touko • Leather • Stonewall Inn Editions (series)

Read-Alikes: Readers should try Justin Spring's heavily illustrated *Paul Cadmus: The Male Nude.*

David Wojnarowicz

Wojnarowicz, David.

🎗 *Memories That Smell Like Gasoline.* San Francisco: Artspace Books, 1992. **G**

Painter, performance artist, photographer, filmmaker, and gay rights activist Wojnarowcz's life is presented in this slim volume composed of black-and-white drawings, varying text sizes, and an intentionally chopped up style devoid of punctuation, lending a snapshotlike feel to the work.

Awards: Lambda Literary Award, 1992

Subjects: AIDS • Art and artists • Autobiography • Wojnarowicz, David

Athletes

The macho atmosphere of professional and amateur sports and athletics was long taken to be very heterosexual and to exclude lesbians and gay men, so the biographies of those who chose to come out had great impact. Sports represented are swimming, baseball, horse racing, track and field, sailing, powerboat racing, tennis, and football.

Billy Bean

Bean, Billy, and Chris Bull.

Going the Other Way. New York: Marlowe, 2003. **G B**

Not a typical jock, baseball star Billy Bean was living a lie, denying his attraction to men in the testosterone-soaked world of professional sports. Bean shares his journey from childhood to baseball success and his historic coming out story.

Subjects: Autobiography • Baseball • Bean, Billy • Coming out

Read-Alikes: Sports fans might enjoy Dan Woog's two books, *Jocks* and *Jocks 2*.

Marion Barbara "Joe" Carstairs

Summerscale, Kate.

Queen of Whale Cay. New York: Viking, 1998. **L**

> Marion Barbara "Joe" Carstairs was an eccentric, cross-dressing British heiress who gained notoriety as an early speedboat racer, particularly in the late 1920s and 1930s. Her colorful life as a war veteran, small business owner, autocratic island ruler, and relentless womanizer has been rescued from obscurity.
>
> **Subjects:** Biography • Boating • Butches • Caribbean • Carstairs, Marion Barbara • Cross-dressing

Rudy Galindo

Galindo, Rudy, and Eric Marcus.

Icebreaker: The Autobiography of Rudy Galindo. New York: Simon & Schuster, 1997. **G**

> In 1996, a Mexican American kid from the wrong side of the tracks became the first professional skater to admit homosexuality. Galindo recalls a painful childhood and gushes thanks to all the family and friends who supported his dreams.
>
> **Subjects:** Autobiography • Coming out • Galindo, Rudy • Hispanics • Skating

Michael Klein

Klein, Michael.

Track Conditions. New York: Persea, 1997. **G**

> Alcohol and memories of an abusive childhood haunt Klein's personal relationships until Swale, a former Kentucky Derby winner, provides solace and salvation. A behind-the-scenes look at professional horse racing, recounted in poignant prose.
>
> **Subjects:** Autobiography • Horse racing • Klein, Michael • Substance abuse

David Kopay

Kopay, David, and Perry Deane Young.

The David Kopay Story. Los Angeles: Advocate Books, 2001 (1977). **G**

> In the macho world of professional football, Kopay did the unthinkable when, in 1975, he publicly admitted his homosexuality. His courageous decision is recalled in this stereotype-shattering biography.
>
> **Subjects:** Autobiography • Coming out • Football • Kopay, David
>
> **Read-Alikes:** Autobiographies of other out football players include Esera Tuaolo's *Alone in the Trenches* and *Out of Bounds,* by Roy Simmons.

Greg Louganis

Louganis, Greg, and Eric Marcus.

Breaking the Surface. New York: Random House, 2002. **G**

> Overcoming personal obstacles to go from being a lonely, adopted child to a world-class athlete, four-time Olympic gold medalist Louganis struggles with the trappings of success and the pain of hiding his sexuality and HIV status.
>
> **Subjects:** AIDS • Autobiography • Books to film • Coming out • Louganis, Greg • Swimming
>
> **Read-Alikes:** Canadian Olympic gold medal swimmer Mark Tewksbury comes out in *Inside Out*.

Martina Navratilova

Navratilova, Martina, and George Vecsey.

Martina. New York: Ballantine, 1986. **L**

> Tennis star Navratilova describes her family, life under communism, and her determination to win at Wimbledon. The successful realization of her dreams is detailed through tennis matches, scores, and press reports. Although her official coming out occurred much later, she frankly discusses her sexuality and the costs of being an openly lesbian sports star.
>
> **Subjects:** Autobiography • Navratilova, Martina • Tennis
>
> **Read-Alikes:** *Martina: The Lives and Times of Martina Navratilova,* by Adrianne Blue, updates the tennis star's life story through 1994. Also, readers may want to read Selena Roberts's biography of Billie Jean King, *Necessary Spectacle*.

William Storandt

Storandt, William.

Outbound. Madison: University of Wisconsin Press, 2000. **G**

> His story unfurling like a slowly rising tide, the author contrasts his coming out and finding love with the concept of leaving port on a sailing trip. Details of sailing the Caribbean with his partner and a later voyage to Scotland are passionately, introspectively retold.
>
> **Subjects:** Autobiography • Boating • Caribbean • <u>Living Out: Gay and Lesbian Autobiographies</u> (series) • Scotland • Storandt, William • Travel

Authors, Writers, Playwrights, Poets, Columnists, and Journalists

Literature provides the earliest documented evidence of same-sex attraction. The written word, in all its myriad forms, whether for private consumption in the form of diaries and letters or intended for public consumption in the form of books and plays, is the dominant vehicle for self-expression. The works in this section include biography, autobiography, and personal letters and represent authors working in a variety of genres, including poetry, fiction, drama, and humor.

Dorothy Allison

Allison, Dorothy. L

Allison's rough Southern childhood provides the inspiration for these stories.

Subjects: Allison, Dorothy • Authors • Autobiography • Families • Feminism • Sexual abuse • South Carolina

🏵 *Skin: Talking About Sex, Class & Literature.* Ithaca, NY: Firebrand Books, 1994.

Allison's previous writings focused on her horrific childhood, but here she goes a step further, extrapolating from those experiences to find personal meaning in and motivation for her work. Her characteristically clear, pull-no-punches style shines in this often-overlooked collection.

Awards: Lambda Literary Award, 1994; Stonewall Book Award, 1995

Two or Three Things I Know for Sure. New York: Plume, 1996.

Acclaimed author Dorothy Allison tells brutal tales of lust, rape, loss, and poverty without ever succumbing to meanness. Intended as performance pieces, these stories demand to be read aloud repeatedly.

Reinaldo Arenas

Arenas, Reinaldo.

Before Night Falls. New York: Penguin, 1994. G

Through intense poverty, an indifferent family, and torturous imprisonment, the Cuban poet, playwright, and author Arenas's powerful memoir demonstrates the power of art in the face of oppression. Condemned for his writing and homosexuality, exile in the United States brought a partial but brief relief before AIDS provided the final blow to his career.

Subjects: Arenas, Reinaldo • Authors • Autobiography • Books to film • Cuba • Hispanics • Politics

Read-Alikes: Arenas's *Singing from the Well*, *Palace of White Skunks*, *Farewell to the Sea*, *Assault* and *Color of Summer* form a "pentagonia" of semiautobiographical novels, but vary widely in style. Readers who enjoy Arenas's style should also try Manuel Puig's novel, *Kiss of the Spider Woman*.

Elizabeth Bishop and Lota de Macedo Soares

Oliveria, Carmen L. Translated by Neil K. Besner.

Rare and Commonplace Flowers: The Story of Elizabeth Bishop and Lota de Macedo Soares. New Brunswick, NJ: Rutgers University Press, 2002. L

Oliveira humanizes two brilliant women in this Brazilian best seller: the renowned poet Elizabeth Bishop and her Brazilian architect partner, Lota de Macedo Soares. Relationship difficulties caused by cultural differences, illnesses, and career stresses bring greater intensity to the story. Originally published in Brazil in 1995.

Subjects: Architects • Authors • Biography • Bishop, Elizabeth • Brazil • Soares, Lota De Macedo

Rita Mae Brown

Brown, Rita Mae.

Rita Will: Memoir of a Literary Rabble-Rouser. New York: Bantam Doubleday Dell, 1999. **L**

This funny memoir of author Rita Mae Brown's life emphasizes her Southern upbringing and family life and is punctuated by frequent acknowledgments of her lovers, friends, and cats.

Subjects: Authors • Autobiography • Brown, Rita Mae

William S. Burroughs

Caveney, Graham.

Gentleman Junkie: The Life and Legacy of William S. Burroughs. Boston: Little, Brown, 1998. **G** **B**

This biography weaves pop culture material, color, image, and text into an art book cum biography of the acerbic and controversial beat writer, William S. Burroughs. A brief introduction to Burroughs's life that works more for its stunning visual layout than for its narrative content.

Subjects: Authors • Biography • Burroughs, William S. • Substance abuse

Read-Alikes: For a well-researched account of Burroughs's life, readers should try Ted Morgan's *Literary Outlaw*.

Quentin Crisp

Crisp, Quentin.

🎗 *The Naked Civil Servant.* New York: Penguin, 1997. **G**

A feminine child, Crisp minced around his home claiming to be a beautiful princess, and as an adult suffered the violence often perpetrated on effeminate men. Crisp, a writer and flamboyant figure who refused to hide his homosexuality, vividly recounts his life in pre–gay liberation Britain. Crisp, born Denis Charles Pratt, originally published this work in England in 1968.

Awards: Publishing Triangle's 100 Best Lesbian and Gay Novels, Reader's Choice

Subjects: Actors and actresses • Authors • Books to film • Crisp, Quentin • England • Homophobia

Mercedes De Acosta

Schanke, Robert A.

🎗 *That Furious Lesbian.* Carbondale: Southern Illinois University Press, 2004. **L** **B**

De Acosta, a minor playwright of Hispanic descent, is best known for the company she kept. Lover to starlets of the early twentieth century, including Marlene Dietrich and Greta Garbo, her story is pieced together in a lyrical style, punctuated by poetry.

Awards: *ForeWord Magazine* Book of the Year Award, 2003

Subjects: Actors and actresses • Authors • Biography • De Acosta, Mercedes • Hispanics • <u>Theater in the Americas</u> (series)

Read-Alikes: In 1960 Mercedes De Acosta penned her autobiography, *Here Lies the Heart*.

Samuel Delany

Delany, Samuel.

The Motion of Light in Water. Minneapolis: University of Minnesota Press, 2004 (1988). **G** **B**

Acclaimed science fiction writer Samuel Delaney traces his development as a gay black writer living inside a heterosexual, interracial, open marriage. The unique elements of his life and character unfold against the backdrop of New York City during the political and sexual revolutions of the 1960s. A candid and descriptive account.

Subjects: African Americans • Authors • Autobiography • Delany, Samuel • Interracial relationships

Mark Doty

Doty, Mark. **G**

Noted for his poetry, Doty's first narrative works draw upon painful personal experiences yet manage to communicate hope.

Subjects: AIDS • Authors • Autobiography • Coming out • Couples • Death and dying •Doty, Mark • Families • Love • Roberts, Wally

Read-Alikes: Author Bernard Cooper penned his memoir, *Truth Serum*. D. A. Powell produced the poetic trilogy *Tea, Lunch,* and *Cocktails,* about growing up in the age of AIDS and contracting the virus. Englishman Thom Gunn won critical acclaim for his AIDS-related poems in *Man with Night Sweats*.

Firebird. New York: HarperCollins, 1999. **G**

In this wry account of growing up in mid-twentieth-century America, poet Mark Doty relates his dysfunctional family's history and discovering his sexuality.

Heaven's Coast. New York: HarperCollins, 1996. **G**

The touching story of caring for his AIDS-infected partner of twelve years, Wally. Doty's poetic manipulation of language evokes a place where even death cannot separate loved ones.

Coleman Dowell

Dowell, Coleman.

🎖 *A Star-Bright Lie.* New York: Penguin Group, 1993. **G**
This slim volume evolves from autobiographical chapters found upon the suicide of minor songwriter-novelist Coleman Dowell. Insights into Dowell's life and book characters share the page with skewering rants against luminaries such as David Merrick and Carl Van Vechten.

Awards: Lambda Literary Award, 1993

Subjects: Authors • Autobiography • Dowell, Coleman • Music

Janet Flanner

See Natalia Danesi Murray and Janet Flanner.

Michael Thomas Ford

Ford, Michael Thomas. **G**
Thomas's crazy, pop culture–infused life stories will make readers laugh out loud.

Subjects: Authors • Autobiography • Ford, Michael Thomas • Humor

🎖 *Alec Baldwin Doesn't Love Me and Other Trials of My Queer Life.* Los Angeles: Alyson Books, 1998.
Writer and journalist Michael Thomas Ford's obsessions and neuroses, like his attraction to Alec Baldwin's chest, make for funny reading. Everything from Ford's love life to Martha Stewart is offered up for laughs, demonstrating the disappointing reality that movies and television are not nearly as funny as everyday life.

Awards: Lambda Literary Award, 1998

It's Not Mean If It's True: More Trials from My Queer Life. New York: Penguin Group, 2000.
Ford's riffs on contemporary culture and media continue as he turns his queer eye on *MTV's Real World*, Teletubby Tinky Winky, and RuPaul.

The Little Book of Neuroses: Ongoing Trials from My Queer Life. Los Angeles: Alyson Books, 2001.
Ford effortlessly exploits and explains his neuroses and why they are good for him—and good for a few laughs. Silly quizzes help readers determine their potential success as a drag performer and porn star and provide useful tips on how to annoy people.

My Big Fat Queer Life. New York: Penguin Group, 2003.
A collection of previously published essays by the humorous writer and journalist Michael Thomas Ford joined by seven new pieces.

🔥 *That's Mr. Faggot to You.* New York: Penguin Group, 1999.

In his second collection of essays, Ford pokes fun at religious fundamentalists by proposing a line of Christian action figure toys, sings the praises of his dog, and bemoans his love life.

Awards: Lambda Literary Award, 1999

Doris Grumbach

Grumbach, Doris.

🔥 *Life in a Day.* Boston: Beacon, 1996. **L**

A day in the life of author Grumbach is a quiet trip down memory lane, an introspective look at the author's daily life, making coffee and willing her self to write. Writers will easily identify with the gentle person portrayed in this slim volume.

Awards: Lambda Literary Award, 1996

Subjects: Authors • Autobiography • Grumbach, Doris • Maine

Read-Alikes: Grumbach's other memoirs include *Coming into the End Zone,* an examination of life as she approaches age seventy, and *Extra Innings,* a thoughtful musing on living in the face of mortality.

E. Lynn Harris

Harris, E. Lynn.

What Becomes of the Brokenhearted? New York: Doubleday, 2003. **G**

Growing up with an abusive father is difficult, but add the pain of being poor, black, and gay—and living in the South—and the author's depression is not surprising. Seeking solace in writing, Harris discovered himself and the voice that propelled him onto best-seller lists. An inspiring story.

Subjects: African Americans • Authors • Autobiography • Harris, E. Lynn • Mental health

Patricia Highsmith

Meaker, Marijane.

Highsmith: A Romance of the 1950's. San Francisco: Cleis, 2003. **L**

Patricia Highsmith is a highly acclaimed novelist and short story writer. Many of her crime stories have been made into movies, including *Strangers on a Train* and *The Talented Mr. Ripley*. Meaker's confessional style provides glimpses into Highsmith's enigmatic personality and seems to be an attempt to excise the ghost of their turbulent relationship. A well-painted portrait of lesbian life circa the 1950s.

Subjects: Authors • Biography • Highsmith, Patricia • Meaker, Marijane

Read-Alikes: *Beautiful Shadow,* by Andrew Wilson, is the first scholarly biography of Highsmith.

Florence King

King, Florence.

 Confessions of a Failed Southern Lady. New York: St. Martin's Press, 1990 (1984). **L B**

Shaped by her grandmother like a piece of clay from her native Virginia, King was raised to be a perfect Southern lady. However, things did not turn out the way grandmother planned. The resultant atheist, gun-totting, lesbian columnist for the *National Review* infuses her comedic bio with a drawl and dry humor.

Awards: Publishing Triangle's 100 Best Lesbian and Gay Novels, Reader's Choice

Subjects: Authors • Autobiography • Humor • King, Florence • Virginia

Paul Lisicky

Lisicky, Paul.

Famous Builder. St. Paul, MN: Graywolf, 2002. **G**

Growing up working class, Lisicky dreamed of being a famous builder but eventually abandoned the idea in favor of a musical and writing career. This is a personal history tracing one family's rise to the middle class and the son's journey toward self-awareness and acceptance.

Subjects: Authors • Autobiography • Families • Lisicky, Paul • New Jersey

Audre Lorde

De Veaux, Alexis.

 Warrior Poet: A Biography of Audre Lorde. New York: W.W. Norton, 2004. **L**

Although a bit on the academic side, this lengthy biography breaks new ground, humanizing American poet Audre Lorde through an examination of her childhood, adult life, and emergence as a lesbian, activist, and poet.

Awards: Lambda Literary Award, 2004

Subjects: African Americans • Authors • Biography • Lorde, Audre

Read-Alikes: More accessible and personal are Lorde's *Zami*, a fictionalized version of her life, and *Cancer Journals*.

Armistead Maupin

Gale, Patrick.

Armistead Maupin. Bath, England: Absolute Press, 1999. **G**

Maupin's fans will not want to miss this short, readable biography based on a series of interviews between Gale and Maupin. The interview approach results in a nonliner account of the author's life, revealing connections between persona and plots.

Subjects: Authors • Biography • Maupin, Armistead • <u>Outlines</u> (series)

9

10

11

12

13

14

15

16

Read-Alikes: Other books about authors in the <u>Outlines</u> series include Peter Burton's biography *Somerset Maugham*.

Paul Monette

Monette, Paul. G

Widely considered one of the earliest AIDS memoirs. Monette introduces readers to his life from childhood through adulthood. His suffering, as well as that of his long-term partner, are heartbreakingly rendered in these award-winning pieces.

Subjects: AIDS • Authors • Autobiography • Coming-of-age • Coming out • Couples • Death and dying • Homophobia, self directed • Horwitz, Roger • Love • Monette, Paul

Read-Alikes: Monette's memoir concludes in *Last Watch of the Night*, a series of essays about politics, religion, and AIDS, and he is featured in an autobiographical 1996 film, *Paul Monette: The Brink of Summer's End*. Monette eulogized Roger in *Love Alone: 18 Elegies for Rog*.

Becoming a Man: Half a Life Story. San Diego: Harcourt, Brace, Jovanovich, 1992.

Author, poet, and gay rights activist Paul Monette takes the reader through his family life, school years, and early adulthood, poignantly demonstrating the pain caused by hiding his sexuality and repressing emotions. In the end, he realizes that changing the past would deny him the present's happiness.

Awards: Lambda Literary Award, 1992

🏅 ***Borrowed Time.*** San Diego: Harcourt, 1988.

As the AIDS crisis begins, writer Paul Monette and his partner Roger hope they are virus free, but a nagging cough leads to the dreaded diagnosis. Paul recounts the battle to keep Roger alive, running the gamut from homophobic healthcare providers to government indifference and delay. A touching story, considered the first personal AIDS memoir.

Awards: Lambda Literary Award, 1988

Cherríe Moraga

Moraga, Cherríe.

Loving in the War Years. Cambridge, MA: South End Press, 2000 (1983). **L**

Moraga employs poetry, prose, and personal stories to express the pain of being a lesbian in a Chicano community and of being a Chicano in the lesbian community. Some Spanish text marks this personal-political discourse.

Subjects: Authors • Autobiography • Feminism • Hispanics • Moraga, Cherrie

Read-Alikes: Gloria Anzaldúa's employs a similar technique in *La frontera/Borderlands*.

Joyce Murdoch

See Deb Price and Joyce Murdoch.

Natalia Danesi Murray and Janet Flanner

Murray, William.

Janet, My Mother, and Me: A Memoir of Growing Up with Janet Flanner and Natalia Danesi Murray. New York: Simon & Schuster, 2000. **L**

> Surrounded by strong, loving women, Murray was raised by same-sex parents during the 1940–1950s. His mother's thirty-eight-year relationship with famed essayist Janet Flanner is interwoven with his personal life story, and recounted with warmth and self-deprecating wit.
>
> **Subjects:** Authors • Biography • Couples • Flanner, Janet • Murray, Natalia Danesi
>
> **Read-Alikes:** *Darlinghissima*, by Flanner and Murray, presents the couple's love letters.

Felice Picano

Picano, Felice.

A House on the Ocean, a House on the Bay. New York: Penguin Group, 2003. **G**

> Claiming this work is a "folio of four unwritten books," author Picano captures the golden era of life on Fire Island and a writer's personal development, the choice between making art and living artfully.
>
> **Subjects:** Authors • Autobiography • Picano, Felice
>
> **Read-Alikes:** Picano's two previous memoirs are *Ambidextrous* and *Men Who Loved Me*.

Minnie Bruce Pratt

Pratt, Minnie Bruce.

S/HE. Los Angeles: Alyson Books, 2004. **L T**

> Short vignettes illustrate poet-activist Minnie Bruce Pratt's political awakening as a feminist and her attraction to butch lesbians. Although told in the first person, the stories omit all names, lending detachment to the events. An exploration of the politics of gender through personal experience.
>
> **Subjects:** Autobiography • Authors • Butches • Coming out • Feminism • Femmes • Gender identity • Pratt, Minnie Bruce

Deb Price and Joyce Murdoch

Price, Deb, and Joyce Murdoch.

And Say Hi to Joyce: America's First Gay Column Comes Out. New York: Doubleday, 1995. **L**

> A collection of newspaper columns by Deb Price, America's first openly gay, nationally syndicated columnist. By relating personal stories in the

columns, Price and partner Murdoch put a real face on the issues facing GLBT persons.

Subjects: Authors • Autobiography • Couples • Murdoch, Joyce • Price, Deb

Dan Savage

Savage, Dan.

🏵 *Skipping Towards Gomorrah.* New York: Dutton, 2002. **G**

In this combination of memoir, travelogue, and political commentary, journalist Dan Savage embarks on a cross-country tour, intentionally indulging in the seven deadly sins. The result is a sometimes serious, sometimes funny exposure to American culture and the hypocritical views of neoconservatives.

Awards: Lambda Literary Award, 2002

Subjects: Authors • Autobiography • Humor • Politics • Savage, Dan

Gertrude Stein and Alice B.Toklas

Turner, Kay.

Baby Precious Always Shines. New York: St. Martin's Press, 1999. **L**

After an academic introduction, these never-before-published love notes are presented in their original form. The notes, typical of Stein's disjointed and repetitive style, are not always poetic, but are evidence of a deep and loving relationship.

Subjects: Authors • Biography • Love letters • Poetry • Stein, Gertrude • Toklas, Alice B.

Alice B. Toklas

See Gertrude Stein and Alice B.Toklas.

Gore Vidal

Vidal, Gore.

Palimpsest. New York: Random House, 1995. **G**

A blunt, narrative, unchronological account of the first forty years of author Gore Vidal's life. His life becomes an object reflecting history, filled with biting accounts of relationships with political and literary luminaries: Kennedys and Roosevelts share space with Ginsberg, Kerouac, and Anaïs Nin in this gossipy biography.

Subjects: Authors • Autobiography • Vidal, Gore

Read-Alikes: Vidal's *Point to Point Navigation* updates his life and includes reflections on the death of his partner of over fifty years. Fred Kaplan takes a linear and scholarly approach to Vidal's life in *Gore Vidal: A Biography.*

Alice Walker

White, Evelyn C.

Alice Walker: A Life. New York: W. W. Norton, 2004. **L** **B**

Most chapters in this pioneering biography are short and manageable, despite the book's nearly 500 pages. The chronological arrangement follows Walker from her Southern childhood through her marriage to a Caucasian, to her success as a novelist. Not in the least bit academic, White's work is marked by a conversational tone.

Subjects: African Americans • Authors • Biography • Walker, Alice

Edmund White.

Fleming, Keith and David Leavitt.

Original Youth. New York: Penguin Group, 2004. **G**

Fleming reveals an intimate family perspective on author Edmund White, but the story works best when he quotes the acclaimed author. The uneven treatment may leave the reader feeling Fleming is riding his uncle's famous coattails.

Subjects: Authors • Biography • White, Edmund

Read-Alikes: As a prequel to this book, Fleming wrote *Boy with the Thorn in His Side,* which explores White's rescue and nurturing of Fleming.

White, Edmund.

My Lives. New York: Ecco, 2005. **G**

Author Edmund White arranges his autobiography by subject, addressing topics such as "My Mother" and "My Father," and then moves on to chapters about his shrinks, hustlers, friends, and life in Europe. An open, honest, and sometimes funny book.

Subjects: Authors • Autobiography • White, Edmund

Tennessee Williams

Williams, Tennessee.

Memoirs. New York: New Directions, 2006 (1975). **G**

Williams, taken to task by his contemporaries for not admitting his homosexuality, responded with this frank autobiography. Written eight years before his accidental death, this confessional work concentrates on Williams's personal life, revealing sexual dalliances, drug abuse, and a stay in a psychiatric ward, and causing critics to wish Williams had stayed quiet.

Subjects: Authors • Autobiography • Substance abuse • Williams, Tennessee

Read-Alikes: For a concise biographical treatment of Williams's life, readers may want to try Donald Spoto's *Kindness of Strangers: The Life of Tennessee Williams.*

9

10

11

12

13

14

15

Clergy; Religious and Spiritual Figures

Perhaps no other professions have influenced the perception and reception of GLBT persons, on both personal and social levels, as those associated with religion. The contentious relationship between formal religions and homosexuals is illustrated in these autobiographies of GLBT persons struggling to reconcile faith and sexuality.

Marc Adams

Adams, Marc.

The Preacher's Son. West Hollywood, CA: Window Books, 1996. **G**

A rigidly religious home life led to self-isolation, until a same-sex relationship in college set Adams on the path to self-acceptance. An accurate picture of fundamentalism's role in the struggle to resolve faith and sexuality.

Subjects: Adams, Marc • Autobiography • Coming out • Homophobia, self-directed • Religion

Read Alikes: The life of the first openly gay Episcopal bishop, Gene Robinson, is highlighted in Elizabeth Adams's *Going to Heaven*.

Fenton Johnson

Johnson, Fenton.

🌳 *Keeping Faith.* Boston: Houghton Mifflin, 2003. **G**

Johnson's Catholic upbringing resonated in a desire to become a monk, a calling ultimately rejected because of the Church's policies about and treatment of homosexuals. Angry for decades, he embarked on a spiritual quest through Buddhism and back to Catholicism. One man's journey of faith.

Awards: Lambda Literary Award, 2003

Subjects: Authors • Autobiography • Johnson, Fenton • Religion • Spirituality

Mark Thompson

Thompson, Mark.

Gay Body: A Journey Through Shadow to Self. New York: St. Martin's Griffin, 1999. **G**

Thompson mixes elements of autobiography with psycho-spiritual observation and theory in a dense exploration of the relationship between body and being.

Subjects: Autobiography • Mental health • Spirituality • Thompson, Mark

Mel White

White, Mel.

Stranger at the Gate: To Be Gay and Christian in America. New York: Plume Penguin, 1995. **G B**

> Raised in a strict religious home, White prayed earnestly for God to remove the curse of homosexuality. Throwing himself into work, marriage, and curative attempts, he was unable to find peace until he recognized homosexuality as God's gift.
>
> **Subjects:** Autobiography • Clergy • Coming out • Religion • White, Mel
>
> **Read-Alikes:** Troy Perry, founder of the only church exclusively serving the GLBT community, relates his story in *The Lord Is My Shepherd and He Knows I'm Gay* and *Don't Be Afraid Anymore.*

Barbara Wilson

Wilson, Barbara.

🎗 *Blue Windows: A Christian Science Childhood.* New York: Picador, 1998. **L**

> Wilson's faith is challenged by her mother's illnesses, leading to a period of disillusionment and soul searching. Only a little GLBT content.
>
> **Awards:** Lambda Literary Award, 1997
>
> **Subjects:** Autobiography •Families • Illness • Religion • Sexual abuse • Wilson, Barbara
>
> **Read-Alikes:** Wilson covered the same topic in her novel *If You Had a Family.*

Comedians

The connection between comedy and the GLBT community is often a double-edged sword. Stereotypical homosexual characters, such as the limp-wristed sissy or the butch lesbian truck driver, are often parodied in the name of comedy. In the 1980s, the growing popularity of stand-up comedy produced a new generation of comedian—the openly gay/lesbian comedian. Included here are the autobiographies of several prominent GLBT performers.

Margaret Cho

Cho, Margaret.

🎗 *I'm the One That I Want.* New York: Riverhead Books, 2005. **L B**

> Humorist Cho gives readers a glimpse of her life as a Korean American caught between two cultures. Based on her comedic monologues, she relates substance abuse and weight control problems in a brassy style that dares the reader to deal with her reality.

Awards: Lambda Literary Award, 2001

Subjects: Asians • Autobiography • Books to film • Cho, Margaret • Comedians • Humor

Kate Clinton

Clinton, Kate.

Don't Get Me Started. New York: Ballantine, 1998. **L**

Stand-up comedian Clinton has been performing since the 1980s, and this first attempt at biography is as humorous as one of her shows. In this part stand-up routine, part essay, Clinton pokes fun at herself, picks on politicians, and never has to prod to produce laughter.

Subjects: Autobiography • Clinton, Kate • Comedians • Humor • Politics

Read-Alikes: Readers should try Clinton's *What the L?*

David Rakoff

Rakoff, David.

🎗 *Fraud.* New York: Broadway Books, 2002. **G**

Spare autobiographical details and GLBT content mark this collection of essays from public radio personality David Rakoff. His status as gay, Jewish, and Canadian provides a unique perspective for droll views on American urban life.

Awards: Lambda Literary Award, 2001

Subjects: Autobiography • Canada and Canadians • Comedians • Humor • Jews • Radio • Rakoff, David

Read-Alikes: Rakoff followed up with *Don't Get Too Comfortable.*

David Sedaris

Sedaris, David. **G**

Greek American, expatriate Sedaris pokes fun at himself and his family for some side-splitting laughs.

Subjects: Autobiography • Comedians • Families • France • Humor • North Carolina • Sedaris, David

Read-Alikes: Readers who liked Sedaris may want to try Augusten Burroughs's *Magical Thinking.*

Barrel Fever. Boston: Little, Brown, 1994.

The first half of the book contains short stories, while the second half features autobiographical essays. Included is "SantaLand Diaries," the story that original brought Sedaris national recognition.

🎗 *Naked.* Boston: Little, Brown, 1997.

Sedaris's laugh-out-loud personal stories finds him licking light switches, spying on neighbors, suffering the humiliations of youth camp, and taking his first job—in a mental institution.

Awards: Publishing Triangle Award, 1998

🎗 *Me Talk Pretty One Day.* Boston: Little, Brown, 2000.

Sedaris's autobiographical essays are a humorous cultural exploration, with every topic fair game. Weird family behaviors and the paranoia of American tourists are satirized alongside rants about the death of the typewriter. In what might be the funniest piece, Sedaris contrasts his childhood speech lessons with later attempts to learn French.

Awards: Lambda Literary Award, 2000

🎗 *Dress Your Family in Corduroy and Denim.* Boston: Little, Brown, 2004.

Humorist and writer David Sedaris is at it again, poking fun at himself and his family. The wedding of Sedaris's brother featured feces-eating dogs; his mother's fawning over a rich relative and more experiences from his life in France round out this installment.

Awards: Lambda Literary Award, 2004

Bob Smith

Smith, Bob. 🄶

Family foibles and love lives are the fodder for Smith's funny, personal stories.

Subjects: Autobiography • Comedians • Couples • Families • Humor • Smith, Bob

🎗 *Openly Bob.* New York: William Morrow, 1999.

Family relations, dating, politics, and the perils and joys of a long-term relationship are fodder for Smith's humorous observations. Smith pokes fun at others in a gentle way, but not nearly as often as he pokes fun at himself.

Awards: Lambda Literary Award, 1997; Publishing Triangle's 100 Best Lesbian and Gay Novels, Reader's Choice

Way to Go Smith. New York: HarperCollins, 2000.

The break-up of Smith's long-term relationship and his attempts to start dating form the crux of these essays.

Healthcare Workers

The healthcare professions regarded homosexuality as a mental illness until it was declassified as such in 1973 by the American Psychological Association. Prior to declassification, GLBT persons in the medical professions were forced to remain closeted or be rejected by the very professions they served. As a result, the contributions of GLBT persons to the medical fields are not well documented. The life of Dr. Howard Brown (1924–1975) is a prime example of this situation. Dr. Brown sought psychiatric help for his same-sex attraction and was reassured that he was not gay, because homosexuals did not become doctors. He remained closeted, subsequently becoming a successful, high-ranking New York City health official, but when someone threatened to reveal his sexual orientation, he resigned. In 1973, when Dr. Brown publicly admitted his sexual orientation, it was front-page news in the *New York Times*. The various reactions to Dr. Brown's life and the fact that no biography about his life exists is testament to "the limited presence [of GLBT] persons in the standard histories of science, medicine, and public health."[1]

Betty Berzon

Berzon, Betty.

🎗 *Surviving Madness.* Madison: University of Wisconsin Press, 2002. **L**
Pressured to conform to society's heterosexual standards, the despondent Berzon was institutionalized for attempted suicide. Recovered but in deep denial about her sexuality she pursued a career in psychotherapy, eventually shifting her career emphasis to gay and lesbian patients and causes.

Awards: Lambda Literary Award, 2002

Subjects: Autobiography • Berzon, Betty • Healthcare workers • Homophobia, self-directed • Living Out: Gay and Lesbian Autobiographies (series) • Mental health

Rafael Campo

Campo, Rafael.

🎗 *Poetry of Healing.* New York: Norton, 1997. **G**
Campo explores the many facets of his personality, attempting to connect his life as a Hispanic, physician, gay man, and poet.

Awards: Lambda Literary Award, 1997

Subjects: AIDS • Autobiography • Campo, Rafael • Healthcare workers • Hispanics

Read-Alikes: Readers wishing to learn more about this author should investigate Campo's many volumes of poetry. An alternate title for this work is *Desire to Heal*.

Military Figures

The affiliation between gays and lesbians and the U.S. military represents a tenuous duality. Although the military has officially barred homosexuals from service, history demonstrates the persistent presence and contribution of gay and lesbian soldiers. The duality of the situation obtained national recognition in 1993 with the passage of Public Law 103-160, popularly referred to as "Don't Ask, Don't Tell." Technically, this law permits gays and lesbians to serve in the military but requires soldiers keep their personal lives secret, in effect causing military personnel to lie and by extension violate the military's code of conduct. The books in this section concern soldiers who have challenged this controversial policy.

Magarethe Cammermeyer

Cammermeyer, Margarethe, and Chris Fisher.

Serving in Silence. New York: Viking, 1994. **L B**
Cammermeyer, a Vietnam veteran and Bronze Star recipient, shares her personal story of military service and family life before and after she was discharged from the military for admitting homosexuality.

Subjects: Autobiography • Books to film • Cammermeyer, Margarethe • Coming out • Soldiers and sailors

Read-Alikes: Air Force Sergeant Leonard Matlovich, the first openly gay person to challenge the military's antigay policies, is remembered in Mike Hippler's *Matlovich: The Good Soldier*. For a historical approach to the issue of gays and lesbians in the military, readers should try Randy Shilts's *Conduct Unbecoming* and Mary Ann Humphrey's *My Country, My Right to Serve*.

Jose Zuniga

Zuniga, Jose.

Soldier of the Year. New York: Pocket Books, 1994. **G**

Award-winning journalist, Gulf War Veteran, and the Army's 1992 Soldier of the Year gives an account of his life. Written at the height of the "don't ask, don't tell" controversy, Zuniga personalizes life in the military's closet.

Subjects: Autobiography • Coming out • Hispanics • Soldiers and sailors • Zuniga, Jose

Read-Alikes: Joe Steffan's *Honor Bound* is the account of a gay sailor at the Naval Academy.

Musicians

The arts have long been a haven for gay and lesbian persons, and music may provide a mode of expression not permitted in the larger society; for example, lyricists may code same-sex emotions behind acceptable wording. The contributions of GLBT persons to this genre span the centuries, from liturgical music composed in same-sex monastic environments, to today's mega-stars of the rock and rap world. The following selection reflects artists of various racial and sexual identities working across genres during contemporary times.

Aaron Copeland

Pollack, Howard.

Aaron Copeland: The Life and Work of an Uncommon Man. New York: Henry Holt, 1999. **G**

The book's 702 pages contain a meticulously researched yet highly readable account of the talented Copeland's life and career. Analysis of the openly gay composer-conductor's work predominates, but is informed by frank acknowledgment of Copeland's homosexuality.

Subjects: Biography • Copeland, Aaron • Jews • McCarthyism • Music

Read-Alikes: The famed conductor Leonard Bernstein, a friend of Copeland, found his bisexuality burdensome, as described in Humphrey Burton's *Leonard Bernstein*.

Melissa Etheridge

Etheridge, Melissa, and Laura Morton.

Truth Is: My Life in Love and Music. New York: Villard, 2001. **L**

Etheridge recounts her childhood, the dream of becoming a rock and roll star, and her path to success. The personal stories behind the lyrics are revealed in frank explanations of various adult relationships, the birth of her children, and the break-up of her long-term relationship.

Subjects: Autobiography • Etheridge, Melissa • Music

Elton John

Norman, Philip.

Sir Elton: The Definitive Biography. New York: Carroll & Graf, 2001. **G**

The first authoritative biography of the flamboyant singer covers all the bases of career and personal life, including John's coming out. Each chapter is entitled with a quote from the singer. The book rings so true that Sir Elton said, "He's got me spot on."

Subjects: Biography • Coming out • John, Elton • Music • Substance abuse

Read-Alikes: The equally flamboyant musician Boy George shares his life in the tell-all *Take It Like a Man*.

k. d. lang

Starr, Victoria

k.d. lang: All You Get Is Me. New York: St. Martin's Press, 1995. **L**

A readable although at times impersonal account of Canadian singer and ingénue k. d. lang. Lang's individualism is clearly delineated by her refusal to conform to musical styles and her admission of lesbianism, which made her the first openly homosexual pop singer.

Subjects: Biography • Canada and Canadians • Coming out • lang, k. d. • Music

Read-Alikes: William Robertson draws much of his information for *k.d. lang: Carrying the Torch* from magazine articles. Readers may also want to try *k.d. lang*, by Rose Collis.

Cole Porter

McBrien, William.

Cole Porter: A Biography. New York: Knopf, 1998. **G B**

Composer-songwriter Cole Porter was devoted to his wife Linda, but McBrien's exhaustively researched work asserts it was a marriage of convenience because Porter was exclusively homosexual. Through Porter's correspondence, the reader will learn of the musician's relationships with prominent architects, choreographers, dancers, and directors.

Subjects: Biography • Music • Porter, Cole

Read-Alikes: Porter's frequent collaborations with fellow homosexual musician Noel Coward are the topic of *Noel and Cole—The Sophisticates,* by Stephen Citron.

Billy Strayhorn

Hajdu, David.

Lush Life: A Biography of Billy Strayhorn. New York: Farrar, Straus & Giroux, 1996. **G**

> This biography brings composer Billy Strayhorn out of the shadows of his better-known collaborator, Duke Ellington. Relying on interviews, Hadju examines whether Strayhorn opted to play second fiddle in order to live openly as a gay man or if Ellington forced Strayhorn into the background. The truth is unclear, but either way Hadju has rescued Strayhorn from obscurity in this first biographical book-length treatment.
>
> **Subjects:** African Americans • Biography • Harlem Renaissance • Music • Strayhorn, Billy
>
> **Read-Alikes:** *Something to Live For,* by Walter van de Leur, is a critical examination of Strayhorn's contribution to the musical world.

Billy Tipton

Middlebrook, Diane Wood.

Suits Me: The Double Life of Billy Tipton. Boston: Houghton Mifflin, 1998. **L T**

> Nightclubs were the stomping ground of Billy Tipton, a jazz musician of regional renown in the 1930s and 1940s. The husband and father resisted fame to hide a secret that was not revealed until his death. A fascinating picture of risking everything to be true to one's self.
>
> **Subjects:** Biography • Cross-dressing • Music • Tipton, Billy

Parents, Children, Families, Couples, and Friends

The multifaceted bonds intrinsic to human nature are exceptionally complex for gay and lesbian persons. Condemned in many cultures and religions, these bonds may be damaged or severed, leaving gay and lesbian persons to forge new relationships and family structures outside society's traditionally accepted views. The following stories explore the relationships between parent and child, siblings, and lovers.

Barrie Jean Borich

Borich, Barrie Jean.

🎖 *My Lesbian Husband: Landscape of a Marriage.* St.Paul, MN: Graywolf Press, 2000. **L**

> Alternating between present and past, everyday slices of life are seen within the context of a long-term lesbian relationship. Attending a wedding prompts the author to ponder what she should call her partner; is a

ceremony necessary to recognize and legitimize her relationship? A touching story of love and devotion.

Awards: Stonewall Book Award, 2000

Subjects: Autobiography • Authors • Borich, Barrie Jean • Couples • Love • Substance abuse

Phyllis Burke

Burke, Phyllis.

🎗 *Family Values: A Lesbian Mother's Fight for Her Son.* New York: Vintage, 1994. **L**
No longer able to pass for straight after the birth of her partner's son, Burke's attempts to adopt the boy push her into political activism. The story mingles the political with the personal and sometimes overshadows the familial aspects.

Awards: Stonewall Book Award, 1994

Subjects: Adoption • Autobiography • Burke, Phyllis • California • Parenting

Ellen DeGeneres

DeGeneres, Betty.

🎗 *Love, Ellen.* New York: William Morrow, 1999. **L**
Betty DeGeneres, the mom most gay people wish for, explains why she was not always an accepting parent. For twenty years, DeGeneres denied and hid daughter Ellen's sexuality lest it affect Ellen's success. Ellen's coming out is also mom's, as Betty is propelled from average mom to Hollywood mother and activist.

Awards: Lambda Literary Award, 2002

Subjects: Autobiography • Comedians • Coming out • De Generes, Betty • DeGeneres, Ellen • Parenting • Relationships, parent–child

Read-Alikes: DeGeneres expands her memoir in *Just A Mom*. For a neutral perspective on Ellen's life and career, readers may want to see Kathleen Tracy's *Ellen: The Real Story of Ellen DeGeneres.*

Jon Galluccio and Michael Galluccio

Galluccio, Jon, and Michael Galluccio.

American Family. New York: St. Martin's Press, 2001. **G**
Jon and Michael Galluccio's big hearts are open to society's unwanted children, yet they cannot adopt because they are gay. This is the story of the Galluccios' fight to end homophobic-based adoption laws and to keep their children.

Subjects: Adoption • Autobiography • Galluccio, Jon • Galluccio, Michael • Parenting

Jesse Green

Green, Jesse.

🎗 *Velveteen Father.* New York: Ballantine, 2000. **G**

The trials and tribulations of adoption, the joys and pain of child rearing form the locus of this novel-like story. Journalist Green finds unexpected enjoyment in instant parenthood.

Awards: Lambda Literary Award, 1999

Subjects: Adoption • Autobiography • Families • Green, Jesse • Parenting

Noelle Howey

Howey, Noelle.

🎗 *Dress Codes: Of Three Girlhoods—My Mother's, My Father's and Mine.* New York: Picador, 2002. **T**

Howey contrasts her budding adolescence with her father's struggle as a transgendered individual. The author's graceful, witty style lends readers an honest perspective on what it is like to deal with personal and societal ideas of the transgendered.

Awards: Lambda Literary Award, 2002

Subjects: Autobiography • Cross-dressing • Families • Gender identity • Howey, Noelle

Mark Matousek

Matousek, Mark.

🎗 *Boy He Left Behind.* New York: Riverhead Books, 2000. **G**

Matousek's search for inner peace leads him to find his father, who disappeared thirty years earlier. Conflicted about the entire process, fretting about possible results, Matousek finds peace through an unexpected parental connection. An intensely personal story.

Awards: Publishing Triangle Award, 2001

Subjects: Autobiography • Divorce • Families • Matousek, Mark • Missing persons • Relationships, parent–child

Jay Quinn

Quinn, Jay.

The Mentor. New York: Penguin Group, 2000. **G**

Quinn develops a platonic friendship with an older gay male who shares a similar personal history. Focused primarily on Quinn's hedonistic story, the importance of developing relationships with older members of the GLBT community and creating an extended, supportive family is illustrated.

Subjects: Autobiography • Coming-out • Friendship • Quinn, Jay • Substance abuse

Felice Schragenheim

See Elisabeth Wust and Felice Schragenheim.

Alison Smith

Smith, Alison.

🎗 *Name All the Animals.* New York: Scribner, 2004. **L**

Grieving after the premature death of her brother, Alison stumbles into a lesbian relationship and develops an eating disorder. The grief mixes with guilt over the relationship and grows to include survivor's guilt. A portrait of a family suffering.

Awards: Lambda Literary Award, 2004

Subjects: Autobiography • Death and dying • Families • Religion • Smith, Alison

B. D. Wong

Wong, B. D.

Following Foo: (The Electronic Adventures of the Chestnut Man). New York: HarperEntertainment, 2003. **G**

The premature arrival of twins catapults Wong into conflicting emotions; joy is overshadowed by the death of one boy and the precarious health situation of the surviving twin. A touching, funny story of parenthood told through e-mail correspondence with family and friends.

Subjects: Autobiography • Computers • Illness • Parenting • Wong, B. D.

Elisabeth Wust and Felice Schragenheim

Fischer, Erica.

🎗 *Aimee and Jaguar.* New York: HarperCollins, 1995. **L**

Model mother and wife of a Nazi officer, Lilly Wust fell in love with Jewish resistance fighter Felice. Against all odds, the women pursued a passionate relationship until the Gestapo caught up with Felice. A tragic, true love affair.

Awards: Lambda Literary Award, 1995

Subjects: Biography • Books to film • Germany • Nazis • Schragenheim, Felice • Wust, Elisabeth

Read-Alikes: Lutz Van Dijk's *Damned Strong Love* is the true story of love between a Nazi solider and a Polish teenager. *I, Pierre Seel, Deported Homosexual,* by Pierre Seel is a personal memoir, and *Bent,* by Martin Sherman, is the story of love between two men in a concentration camp.

Sex Workers

Prostitution, frequently described as the world's oldest profession, is generally perceived as the only form of sex work. In recent years, the concept of sex work has expanded to include any person receiving financial benefit from sexually motivated consumers. A wide range of professions are represented in the industry—exotic dancers, phone sex operators, escorts, publishers, and nightclub owners—as well as in the following entries, which include actors, photographers, and performance artists.

Gavin Geoffrey Dillard

Dillard, Gavin Geoffrey.

In the Flesh. New York: Barricade Books, 1998. **G**
A minion in the gay porn business, Dillard cashes in on his cachet with a gossipy story of Hollywood lovers, substance abuse, and sexploits.

Subjects: Actors and actresses • Autobiography • California • Dillard, Gavin Geoffrey • Pornography • Sex workers • Substance abuse

Read-Alikes: Former porn star Scott O'Hara regales readers with his stories in *Rarely Pure and Never Simple* and *Autopornography.*

Amber Hollibaugh

Hollibaugh, Amber.

🏵 *My Dangerous Desires.* Durham, NC: Duke University, 2000. **L**
A collection of essays and personal photos recounts the author's life as a "lesbian sex radical ex-hooker incest survivor rural gypsy working-class poor white trash high femme dyke"

Awards: Publishing Triangle Award, 2001

Subjects: Autobiobraphy • Feminism • Hollibaugh, Amber • Pornography • Sex workers

Bruce LaBruce

LaBruce, Bruce.

Reluctant Pornographer. New York: Penguin Group, 1999. **G**
Pornographic filmmaker LaBruce deposits assorted columns he authored for a music magazine in this oddly formatted book, complemented by photographs. The columns cover everything from drag queens to frustrations of shooting porn films in this tour of underground gay life.

Subjects: Autobiography • Canada and Canadians • LaBruce, Bruce • Pornography • Sex workers

Annie Sprinkle

Sprinkle, Annie.

🏵 *Hardcore from the Heart.* New York: Continuum, 2001. **L** **B**
Sprinkle, a former sex worker, recounts her introduction to pornography and her gradual subversion of the genre into performance art packing powerful political statements. Includes photos and interviews.

Awards: Firecracker Alternative Book Award, 2002

Subjects: Autobiography • Performance art • Pornography • Sex workers • Sprinkle, Annie

Teachers and Students

The potential for a sexually charged relationship between teacher and student has resulted in vociferous public attempts to ban anything related to homosexuality from the educational system. In 1978 California's Proposition 6, also known as the Briggs Initiative, attempted to ban gays and lesbians from teaching. The educational system continues to be a battleground about homosexuality; textbooks are challenged for "promoting" homosexuality, same-sex couples fight to attend proms, and GLBT literature is routinely challenged in school libraries. The following stories reveal the harsh stereotyping, bullying, and discrimination faced by teachers and students, while simultaneously demonstrating the significant contributions of this group.

Newton Arvin

Werth, Barry.

🏃 *Scarlet Professor: Newton Arvin, a Literary Life Shattered by Scandal.* New York: Anchor, 2002. **G**

Newton Arvin, a Smith College professor and nationally recognized author, is forgotten today because of one event. A victim of McCarthyism, Newton lost his job and died in obscurity. In Werth's hands, this otherwise sad tale leaves the reader angry about society's persecution of homosexuals.

Awards: Lambda Literary Award, 2001; Stonewall Book Award, 2002

Subjects: Arvin, Newton • Biography • Homophobia • McCarthyism • Teachers

Louise Blum

Blum, Louise.

You're Not from Around Here, Are You? A Lesbian in Small-Town America. Madison: University of Wisconsin Press, 2001. **L**

In small towns, there are few secrets, and the town of Wellsboro knows the local college professor is a lesbian. Using a witty tone, Professor Blum describes the town's reaction to their lesbian neighbors, particularly when Blum and her partner decide to have a child.

Subjects: Autobiography • Blum, Louise • Living Out: Gay and Lesbian Autobiographies (series) • Parenting • Pennsylvania • Small towns • Teachers

Jennifer Finney Boylan

Boylan, Jennifer Finney.

🏃 *She's Not There.* New York: Broadway Books, 2003. **T**

Boyle was married and a successful professor, harboring a secret feeling that he should have been born female. James's transition to Jennifer is a bittersweet, episodic tale.

Awards: Lambda Literary Award, 2003

Subjects: Autobiography • Boylan, Jennifer Finney • Gender identity • Sex change • Teachers

Read-Alikes: Christine Jorgensen's self-titled autobiography *Christine Jorgensen* was the first of its kind.

Frank DeCaro

DeCaro, Frank.

A Boy Named Phyllis. New York: Viking, 1996. **G**

DeCaro forges a short, sweetly sardonic story about growing up gay in New Jersey. Typical parental problems and school bullying are mixed with pop cultural references in a lighthearted memoir in which youthful angst does not leave lifelong scars.

Subjects: Autobiography • Coming out • DeCaro, Frank • Families • New Jersey • Students

Lillian Faderman

Faderman, Lillian.

🏵 *Naked in the Promised Land.* Boston: Houghton Mifflin, 2003. **L**

Raised by a single mother and her aunt, Faderman is the last generation of a family destroyed in the Holocaust. Determined to rescue her mother from poverty, she strives to become an actress but stumbles into Hollywood's underbelly. Realizing she can only save herself, she pursues an education and becomes the best hope for her family's future.

Awards: Publishing Triangle Award, 2004

Subjects: Autobiography • Faderman, Lillian • Jews • Teachers

Aaron Fricke

Fricke, Aaron.

Reflections of a Rock Lobster: A Story About Growing Up Gay. Boston: Alyson Publications, 1981. **G**

Acknowledging his homosexuality led to school bullying and an emotional isolation that made Aaron feel like a shell at the bottom of the ocean, but by his senior year in 1979 Aaron was out, proud, and suing his high school for the right to bring a boyfriend to the prom.

Subjects: Autobiography • Coming out • Fricke, Aaron • Rhode Island • Students, high school

Karla Jay

Jay, Karla.

Tales of the Lavender Menace. New York: Basic Books, 1999. **L**
In this autobiography the personal is political, as the pioneering Jay weaves personal recollections with the history of the gay liberation movement.
Subjects: Autobiography • Feminism • Jay, Karla • Politics • Teachers

June Jordan

Jordan, June.

Soldier: A Poet's Childhood. New York: Basic Civitas Books, 2001. **L** **B**
Professor-author Jordan recalls adolescence in a staccato style laced with language reflecting her parent's Jamaican accent. The fine line between parental respect and fear is contrasted with a parental love so fierce it does anything to better the child.
Subjects: African Americans • Families • Jordan, June • Race relations • Teachers
Read-Alikes: Audre Lorde fictionalized her childhood in *Zami*.

Deirdre McCloskey

McCloskey, Deirdre.

Crossing. Chicago: University of Chicago Press, 1999. **T**
After four decades as husband, father, and renowned economist, Donald's transition to Deirdre results in acceptance and rejection in her personal and professional life. Divided into three parts—Donald, Dee, Deirdre—to show life prior to, during, and after the transition. Occasional political observations interrupt an otherwise interesting story.
Subjects: Autobiography • Gender identity • McCloskey, Deirdre • Sex change • Teachers
Read-Alikes: Readers may want to try Jan Morris's *Conundrum*.

Joan Nestle

Nestle, Joan.

Fragile Union: New and Selected Writings. New York: Penguin Group, 2001. **L**
Pioneering activist and prolific writer Joan Nestle provides a collection of essays, both political and personal. When not exploring the cultural politics of the butch-femme dynamic, the personal essays explore life's tenuous connections and sexual desire.
Subjects: Autobiography • Authors • Illness • Nestle, Joan • Relationships • Teachers

Kirk Read

Read, Kirk.

How I Learned to Snap: A Small-Town Coming-Out and Coming-of-Age Story. Athens, GA: Hill Street Press, 2001. **G**

Chanting "I am not afraid" and punctuating it with finger snapping as a way to scare people, the author uses snapping to change the scenes in this witty 1980s-infused account of growing up openly gay and Southern.

Subjects: Autobiography • Coming out • Read, Kirk • Students • Virginia

---

Travelers, Explorers, and Heroes

Evidence of GLBT travelers, explorers, and heroes stretches from ancient times to the present and includes both the notorious and the unknown. In a larger sense, any person who lived openly as GLBT prior to the late twentieth century may be considered a hero for defying society's constraints. Here are the stories of four average persons pushing the limits for either personal enrichment or the benefit of society.

Mark Bingham

Barrett, Jon.

Hero of Flight 93. Los Angeles: Alyson Books, 2002. **G**

Mark Bingham was an ordinary person when he boarded United Airlines flight 93 on September 11, 2001, but he proved to be an exemplary man, sacrificing his life to save others. Here is the real Bingham as remembered by family and friends.

Subjects: Bingham, Mark • Biography • Terrorism

Read-Alikes: Openly gay priest Father Mychal Judge was killed while administering last rites during the 9/11 attacks. Michael Ford chronicles the priest's life in *Father Mychal Judge: An Authentic American Hero.*

Judith Barrington

Barrington, Judith.

🏵 *Lifesaving.* Portland, OR: Eighth Mountain Press, 2000. **L B**

The death of Barrington's parents left her "alone in the world before [she] realized such a thing could happen" (p.113). *Lifesaving* recounts Barrington's three years in Spain spent denying her grief through alcohol, and her shutting out feelings for women through sex with men.

Awards: Lambda Literary Award, 2000

Subjects: Autobiography • Barrington, Judith • Death and dying • Grief • Spain • Travel

Read-Alikes: The juxtaposition of parental lives and lesbian self-identity are the subject of *After Long Silence,* by Helen Fremont, the child of Holocaust survivors.

Robert Tewdwr Moss

Moss, Robert Tewdwr.

Cleopatra's Wedding Present. Madison: University of Wisconsin Press, 2004 (1997). **G**

British journalist Moss mixes odd, interesting facts with tales of his sexual adventures in Syria.

Subjects: Autobiography • Living Out: Gay and Lesbian Autobiographies (series) • Moss, Robert Tewdwr • Syria • Travel

Read-Alikes: For lighthearted travel writing readers may want to try Lindsy Van Gelder's *Are You Two Together?* For a collective approach, they may want to read *Wonderlands,* edited by Raphael Kadushin.

Tobias Schneebaum

Schneebaum, Tobias.

🎖 *Wild Man.* Madison: University of Wisconsin Press, 2003 (1979). **G**

Schneebaum combines elements of biography, travel writing, and sociocultural history to explore relationships between men, connecting his youthful fascination with the concept of the "wild man" to his personal lusts and humankind's primitive desires.

Awards: Lambda Literary Award, 2004

Subjects: Art and artists • Autobiography • Living Out: Gay and Lesbian Autobiographies (series) • Schneebaum, Tobias • Travel

Other Life Stories

Gad Beck

Beck, Gad, and Frank Heibert.

Underground Life. Madison: University of Wisconsin Press, 1999. **G**

Beck, the child of a Protestant-Jewish marriage, provides a chatty, humorous look at life before the Nazis and a chilling look at his life in hiding as a gay, Jewish resistance fighter.

Subjects: Autobiography • Beck, Gad • Germany • Living Out: Gay and Lesbian Autobiographies (series) • Nazis

Read-Alikes: For another memoir about persecution of homosexuals under the Nazis, readers should see *Days of Masquerade,* by Claudia Schoppman.

Kevin Bentley

Bentley, Kevin.

Wild Animals I Have Known: Polk Street Diaries and After. San Francisco: Green Candy, 2002. **G**

> Entries from the author's diary are gathered together to form this look at gay San Francisco circa the 1970s. Bentley gives the reader ample detail about his sexual conquests, while providing a glimpse of gay lifestyle prior to the AIDS onslaught.
>
> **Subjects:** Autobiography • Bentley, Kevin • California • Lust • Sex
>
> **Read-Alikes:** Unlike Bentley, Vincent succumbed to AIDS before writing an autobiographical account of his free-loving ways. Instead, Vincent bequeathed his diaries to a former teacher, Elizabeth Stone, who recounts his story in *A Boy I Once Knew.*

Augusten Burroughs

Burroughs, Augusten. G

> Burroughs's satirical exploration of a childhood so unusual it is almost unbelievable catapulted him to national attention and is followed up by books exploring his adult problems.
>
> **Subjects:** Autobiography • Books to film • Burroughs, Augusten • Families • Humor • Relationships, parent–child • Substance abuse

Running with Scissors. New York: St. Martin's Press, 2002.

> Being placed by your mother in the custody of her psychoanalyst is strange enough, but when the analyst suffers from scatological obsessions, talks openly of his sex life, freely dispenses narcotics, and permits his patients to live with his family, the result is a recipe for dysfunction. Burroughs's sardonic humor shines in this account of his bizarre childhood.
>
> **Read-Alikes:** J. T. LeRoy's *The Heart Is Deceitful Above All Things* is a shocking fictional story about one boy's bizarre childhood.

Dry. New York: St. Martin's Press, 2003.

> Blaming his career in advertising and believing that he just needs to cut back a bit on his drinking, Burroughs delivers a brilliantly parched, tongue-in-cheek account of his struggle with alcohol and the often crooked path to recovery.
>
> **Read-Alikes:** John Moriarty's struggle with alcoholism is as outrageous as Burroughs's, but written in a more serious manner, in *Liquid Lover.*

Magical Thinking: True Stories. New York: St. Martin's Press, 2004.

> Covering much of the same ground as in his previous volumes, Burroughs still manages to evoke laughter with a few new stories observing the latest gay trends in New York City and his dating-mating attempts.
>
> **Read-Alikes:** *I Am Not Myself These Days* explores the over-the-top life of gay male escort and drag queen Josh Kilmer-Purcell.

9

10

11

12

13

14

15

16

Possible Side Effects. New York: St. Martin's Press, 2006.

> Rehashing his childhood and expanding on the addiction theme to cover cigarettes, Burroughs also includes work, pets, and partners in these stories, but by now the satire is running thin.

Kim Chernin

Chernin, Kim.

My Life as a Boy. Chapel Hill, NC: Algonquin, 1997. **L** **B**

> Suffering from empty nest syndrome, Chernin reclaims her lost youth by exploring her masculine side in response to an intense attraction to another woman. A meditative search for gender and sexual identity.

> **Subjects:** Autobiography • Chernin, Kim • Gender identity • Sexual identity

David Reimer

Colapinto, John.

As Nature Made Him. New York: HarperCollins, 2000. **T**

> Following a tragic medical error, doctors, firmly believing gender identity is learned, convinced Bruce's family to raise him as Brenda. Dresses, dolls, and all things feminine, including hormone treatments, failed to persuade Brenda she was a girl. Eventually, Brenda declared she was David and reclaimed her male identity. David's torment continued until his suicide in 2004.

> **Subjects:** Biography • Families • Gender identity • Reimer, David • Sex change

Daphne Scholinski

Scholinski, Daphne, and Jane Meredith Adams.

Last Time I Wore a Dress. New York: Riverhead Books, 1997. **L**

> Daphne, a rebellious teen, was sent to various institutions for behavioral problems and a gender identity disorder. Recounted in reflections and doctor's notations, Daphne details attempts to correct her masculine ways by requiring feminizing behavior. A modern tale indicting society's failure to accept gender diversity.

> **Subjects:** Autobiography • Coming out • Gender identity • Mental health • Scholinski, Daphne

> **Read-Alikes:** Susanna Kaysen's psychiatric incarceration is told with thin lesbian overtones in *Girl, Interrupted.*

Michelle Tea

Tea, Michelle.

Chelsea Whistle. New York: Seal, 2002. **L** **B**

> Tea's stream of consciousness style is manifest in this candid examination of her adolescent life and family dysfunctions. Alcohol, drugs, sex, and class and racial prejudice figure prominently in this typical teenage rebellion story.

Subjects: Autobiography • Families • <u>Live Girl Series</u> • Massachusetts • Tea, Michelle

Andrew Tobias

Tobias, Andrew, and John Reid. **G**

A study in hiding one's sexuality by presenting a perfect public persona while secretly loathing one's self.

Subjects: Autobiography • Coming out • Homophobia • Homophobia, self-directed • Tobias, Andrew

Best Little Boy in the World. New York: Penguin Group, 1993 (1973).

Considered a classic for its early, guilt-free portrayal of growing up gay, *Best* may seem dated in some respects, yet anyone who has come out will easily relate. A model child and responsible adult, the author's emergence from the closet demonstrated that gay people are normal, everyday people. When this was first published, Tobias was a successful financial writer and used John Reid as his pseudonym.

Best Little Boy in the World Grows Up. New York: Ballantine Books, 1999.

Personal history and the political progress of the gay rights movement. At times sarcastic, humorous, and self-deprecating, the personal story is the more interesting one.

Anthologies

Bentley, Kevin, ed.

Boyfriends from Hell: True Tales of Tainted Lovers, Disastrous Dates, and Love Gone Wrong. New York: Penguin Group, 2003. **G**

A collection of dating tales almost too funny to be true.

Subjects: Anthologies • Autobiography • Dating • Humor • Sex

Cameron, Loren.

🎗 *Body Alchemy: Transexual Portraits.* San Francisco: Pittsburgh, PA: Cleis Press, 1996. **T**

Cameron's beautiful black-and-white photographs of himself, his partner, and other female to male transsexuals are accompanied by sparse narration about what it means to be transsexual.

Awards: Lambda Literary Award, 1996

Subjects: Autobiography • Cameron, Loren • Gender identity • Photography • Sex change

Read-Alikes: *Phallus Palace,* by Dean Kotula, is a photographic look at female to male transsexuals; Mariette Pathy Allen's *Gender Frontier* examines a broader spectrum of the transsexual experience.

Donnelly, Nisa, ed.

🏵 *Mom: Candid Memoirs by Lesbians About the First Woman in Their Life.* Los Angeles: Alyson Books, 1998. **L**

A diverse group of authors explores the sometimes comforting, sometimes complicated mother–daughter relationship.

Awards: Lambda Literary Award, 1999

Subjects: Anthologies • Autobiography • Relationships, parent–child

Read-Alikes: Lori L. Lake collected daughters' recollections of their mothers in *Milk of Human Kindness*. For the mom's perspective, readers should try the <u>Different Daughter</u> series, by Louise Rafkin.

Ford, Michael Thomas.

Outspoken: Role Models from the Lesbian and Gay Community. New York: Morrow/Avon, 1998. **G L B T**

Intended to provide role models for GLBT youth; an actor, police officer, rabbi, writer, editor, boxer, doctor, and teacher are asked a series of questions. Their stories of coming out and family life dispel stereotypes and demonstrate the diversity within the community. Resource lists conclude each interview.

Subjects: Anthologies • Biography

Read-Alikes: Ann Heron pioneered this technique with *One Teenager in Ten* and *Two Teenagers in Twenty*.

Mastoon, Adam.

🏵 *Shared Heart: Portraits and Stories Celebrating Lesbian, Gay, and Bisexual Young People.* New York: William Morrow, 1997. **G L B T Teen**

Beautiful black-and-white portraits of GLBT youths illustrate first-person accounts about growing up gay. The young people come from a diverse range of racial, economic, and family backgrounds. Sons, daughters, athletes, class presidents, and students reveal the courage it takes to live honestly and openly. The portraits form the basis for a traveling exhibition with the same title.

Awards: Stonewall Book Award, 1998

Subjects: Biography • Coming out • Photography • Students, high school

Mixner, David.

Brave Journeys: Profiles in Gay and Lesbian Courage. New York: Bantam Books, 2001. **G L**

Seven average people are profiled. The collection includes Del Martin, Phyllis Lyon, Sir Ian McKellen, Elaine Noble, Roberta Actenberg, Lt. Tracy Thorne, and Dianne Hardy-Garcia.

Subjects: Anthologies • Biography • Coming-of-age • Coming out

Nestle, Joan, and John Preston, eds.

🎗 *Sister and Brother: Lesbians and Gay Men Write about Their Lives To-gether.* London: Cassell, 1995. **G** **L** **B** **T**

Thirty original essays celebrate the similarities and differences in the GLBT community and the friendships, relationships, and familial support systems between gay men and lesbians.

Awards: Lambda Literary Award, 1994

Subjects: Anthologies • Autobiography • Friendship

Preston, John, ed.

🎗 *Member of the Family: Gay Men Write About Their Families.* New York: Penguin, 1992. **G**

The profound influence of family, both positive and negative, is examined by a group of ethnically and religiously diverse writers in this down-to-earth collection commissioned by editor Preston. Features Michael Nava and Andrew Holleran.

Awards: Lambda Literary Award, 1993

Subjects: Anthologies • Autobiography • Families

Read-Alikes: Dan Woog's *Friends & Family* contains true stories about heterosexual family and friends who support GLBT persons and causes.

White, Edmund, ed.

Loss Within Loss: Artists in the Age of AIDS. Madison,: University of Wisconsin Press, 2001. **G**

Contemporary writers memorialize twenty gay artists who succumbed to AIDS. Profiled are writers, filmmakers, painters, sculptors, choreographers, puppeteers, playwrights, and architects. A touching collection that demonstrates the devastating effect of AIDS on the art community.

Subjects: AIDS • Art and artists • Authors • Biography • Living Out: Gay and Lesbian Autobiographies (series)

Read-Alikes: Andrea R. Vaucher interviewed many of the same artists in *Muses from Chaos and Ash: AIDS, Artists, and Art.*

Notes

1. Bert Hansen, "Public Careers and Private Sexuality: Some Gay and Lesbian Lives in the History of Medicine and Public Health," *American Journal of Public Health* 92, no. 1 (January 2002): 36–44.

Bibliography

Books

Adams, Stephen. *The Homosexual as Hero in Contemporary Fiction*. New York: Barnes & Noble, 1980.

Austen, Roger. *Playing the Game: The Homosexual Novel in America*. Indianapolis: Bobbs-Merrill, 1977.

Bergman, David. *Gaiety Transfigured: Gay Self-representation in American Literature*. MadisonI: University of Wisconsin Press, 1991.

Betz, Phyllis M. *Lesbian Detective Fiction: Woman as Author, Subject, and Reader*. Jefferson, NC: McFarland, 2006.

Bronski, Michael, ed. *Outstanding Lives: Profiles of Lesbians and Gay Men*. New York: Visible Ink, 1997.

Cart, Michael. *From Romance to Realism: 50 Years of Growth and Change in Young Adult Literature*. New York: HarperCollins, 1996.

Cart, Michael, and Christine A. Jenkins. *The Heart Has Its Reasons: Young Adult Literature with Gay/Lesbian/Queer Content, 1969–2004*. Lanham, MD: Scarecrow, 2006.

Castle, Terry. *The Apparitional Lesbian: Female Homosexuality and Modern Culture*. New York: Columbia University Press, 1993.

———. *The Literature of Lesbianism*. New York: Columbia University, 2005.

Clute, John, and Peter Nichols, ed. *Encyclopedia of Science Fiction*. New York: St. Martin's Griffin, 1993.

Clyde, Laurel. *Out of the Closet and Into the Classroom: Homosexuality in Books for Young People*. 2nd ed. Port Melbourne, Victoria, Australia: ALIA Press, 1996

Cohler, Bertram J. *Writing Desire: Sixty Years of Gay Autobiography*. Madison: University of Wisconsin Press, 2007.

Curtin, Kaier. *We Can Always Call Them Bulgarians: The Emergence of Lesbians and Gay Men on the American Stage*. Boston: Alyson Publications, 1987.

Cuseo, Allan. *Homosexual Characters in Young Adult Novels, a Literary Analysis, 1969–1982*. Metuchen, NJ: Scarecrow Press, 1992.

Day, Frances Ann. *Lesbian and Gay Voices: An Annotated Bibliography and Guide to Literature for Children and Young Adults*. Westport, CT: Greenwood Press, 2000.

De Cecco, John P., Dawn M. Krisko, and Sonya L. Jones, eds. *A Sea of Stories: The Shaping Power of Narrative in Gay and Lesbian Cultures*. New York: Harrington Park Press, 2000.

Forrest, Katherine V. *Lesbian Pulp Fiction: The Sexually Intrepid World of Lesbian Paperback Novels, 1950–1965*. San Francisco: Cleis Press, 2005.

Foster, David William, ed. *Latin American Writers on Gay and Lesbian Themes: A Bio-critical Sourcebook*. Westport, CT: Greenwood, 1994.

Foster, Jeanette H. *Sex Variant Women in Literature: A Historical and Quantitative Survey*. New York: Vantage Press, 1956.

Friedler, Anna B. *Guide to the 400 Best Children's and Adult's Multicultural Books about Lesbian and Gay People*. Centre, MA: Lift Every Voice, 1997.

Furtado, Ken, et al. *Gay and Lesbian American Plays: An Annotated Bibliography*. Lanham, MD: Scarecrow Press, 1993.

Garber, Eric, and Lyn Paleo. *Uranian Worlds: A Guide to Alternative Sexuality in Science Fiction, Fantasy and Horror*. 2nd ed. Boston: G. K. Hall, 1990.

Garde, Noel I. *The Homosexual in Literature: A Chronological Bibliography, circa 700 B.C.–1958*. New York: Village Press, 1959.

Gifford, James. *Dayneford's Library: American Homosexual Writing, 1900–1913*. Amherst: University of Massachusetts Press, 1995.

Gosselin, Adrienne Johnson, ed. *Multicultural Detective Fiction: Murder from the "Other" Side*. New York: Garland, 1999.

Gough, Cal, and Ellen Greenblatt. *Gay and Lesbian Library Service*. Jefferson, NC: McFarland, 1990.

Grier, Barbara, ed. *The Lesbian in Literature*. 3rd ed. Tallahassee, FL: Naiad Press, 1981.

Griffin, Gabriele. *Who's Who in Lesbian and Gay Writing*. New York: Routledge, 2002.

Gunn, Drewey Wayne. *The Gay Male Sleuth in Print and Film: A History and Annotated Bibliography*. Lanham, MD: Scarecrow Press, 2005.

Haggerty, George E. *Gay Histories and Cultures: An Encyclopedia*. New York: Garland, 2000.

Hobby, Elaine, and Chris White. *What Lesbians Do in Books: Lesbians as Writers, Readers and Characters in Literature*. London: Women's Press, 1991.

Hogan, Steve, and Lee Hudson, eds. *Completely Queer: The Gay and Lesbian Encyclopedia*. New York: Henry Holt, 1998.

James, Edward, and Farah Mendlesohn. *Cambridge Companion to Science Fiction*. New York: Cambridge University Press, 2003.

Jenkins, Christine. *A Look at Gayness: An Annotated Bibliography of Gay Materials for Young People*. Ann Arbor, MI: Kindred Spirit Press, 1982.

Kruger, Steven F. *AIDS Narratives: Gender and Sexuality, Fiction and Science*. New York: Garland, 1996.

Leavitt, David, and Mark Mitchell. *Pages Passed from Hand to Hand: The Hidden Tradition of Homosexual Literature in English from 1748 to 1914*. Boston: Houghton Mifflin, 1998.

Leonard, Kathy S. *Bibliographic Guide to Chicana and Latina Narrative*. New York: Praeger, 2003.

Levin, James. *The Gay Novel in America*. New York: Garland, 1991.

Marcus, Eric. *Making History: The Struggle for Gay and Lesbian Equal Rights, 1945–1990: An Oral History*. New York: HarperCollins, 1992.

Markowitz, Judith A. *The Gay Detective Novel: Lesbian and Gay Main Characters and Themes in Mystery*. Jefferson, NC: McFarland, 2004.

Nelson, Emmanuel S., ed. *AIDS: The Literary Response*. New York: Twayne Publishers, 1992.

————. *Contemporary Gay American Novelists: A Bio-bibliographical Critical Sourcebook*. Westport, CT: Greenwood, 1992.

————. *Critical Essays: Gay and Lesbian Writers of Color*. New York: Haworth Press, 1993.

Pastore, Judith. *Confronting AIDS through Literature: The Responsibilities of Representation*. Urbana: University of Illinois Press, 1993.

Pearl, Nancy, et al. *Now Read This: A Guide to Mainstream Fiction, 1978–1998*. Englewood, CO: Libraries Unlimited, 1999.

Pollack, Sandra, and Denise D. Knight. *Contemporary Lesbian Writers of the United States: A Bio-bibliographical Critical Sourcebook*. Westport, CT: Greenwood, 1993.

Ramos, Juanita, ed. *Compañeras: Latina Lesbians: An Anthology*. New York: Latina Lesbian History Project, 1987.

Rowse, A. L. *Homosexuals in History: A Study of Ambivalence in Society, Literature, and the Arts*. New York: Macmillan, 1977.

Rule, Jane. *Lesbian Images*. New York: Doubleday, 1975.

Sarotte, Georges-Michel. *Like a Brother, Like a Lover: Male Homosexuality in the American Novel and Theatre from Herman Melville to James Baldwin*. Garden City, NY: Anchor/Doubleday, 1978.

Schlager, Neil, ed. *St. James Press Gay and Lesbian Almanac*. Detroit: St. James Press, 1998.

Schrader, Alvin, and Kris Wells. *Challenging Silence, Challenging Censorship: Inclusive Resources, Strategies and Policy Directives for Addressing Bisexual, Gay, Lesbian, Trans-identified and Two-spirited Realities in School and Public Libraries*. Ottawa, ON: Canadian Teachers' Federation, 2007

Sinfield, Alan. *Out on Stage: Lesbian and Gay Theatre in the Twentieth Century.* New Haven, CT: Yale University Press, 1999.

Slide, Anthony. *Lost Gay Novels: A Reference Guide to Fifty Works from the First Half of the Twentieth Century.* New York: Harrington Park Press, 2003.

Smith, Raymond A. *Encyclopedia of AIDS: A Social, Political, Cultural, and Scientific Record of the HIV Epidemic.* Chicago: Fitzroy Dearborn, 1998.

Streitmatter, Roger. *Unspeakable: The Rise of the Gay and Lesbian Press in America.* Boston: Faber and Faber, 1995.

Summers, Claude J. *The Gay and Lesbian Literary Heritage: A Reader's Companion to the Writers and Their Works, from Antiquity to the Present.* New York: Routledge, 2002.

———. *Gay Fictions: Wilde to Stonewall: Studies in a Male Homosexual Literary Tradition.* New York: Continuum, 1990.

Tóibín, Colm. *Love in a Dark Time: And Other Explorations of Gay Lives and Literature.* New York: Scribner, 2001.

Turjillo, Carla. *Chicana Lesbians: The Girls Our Mothers Warned us About.* Berkeley, CA: 3rd Woman Press, 1991.

Tyrkus, Michael J., ed. *Gay & Lesbian Biography.* Detroit: St. James Press, 1997.

Zimmerman, Bonnie. *Lesbian Histories and Cultures: An Encyclopedia.* New York: Garland, 2000.

———. *The Safe Sea of Women: Lesbian Fiction, 1969–1989.* Boston: Beacon Press, 1990

Journals

Blithe House Quarterly: http://www.blithe.com/
A forum for new fiction.

Bloom Magazine: http://www.bloommagazine.org/
Supported by an impressive advisory board of established GLBT authors, *Bloom* premiered in 2004 as an outgrowth of the nonprofit Arts in Bloom Project, Inc. Includes original fiction, essays, and poetry, although only the poetry section is available online.

The Gay & Lesbian Review Worldwide: http://glreview.com/index.html
Originally entitled the *Harvard Gay & Lesbian Review* (1994–1999), this publication offers articles about the arts and thought-provoking, signed book reviews of both fiction and nonfiction.

GLQ: A Journal of Lesbian and Gay Studies: http://glq.dukejournals.org/
Founded in 1993 as a scholarly journal with queer perspectives on diverse subject matter. Features lengthy critical book reviews.

Harrington Gay Men's Literary Quarterly
A quarterly publication of Haworth Press (www.haworthpress.com), established in 1999 and focusing on gay male literature by leading authors. Includes book reviews, translations of non-English-language fiction, critical commentary on classic fiction, and special thematic issues.

International Gay & Lesbian Review: http://gaybookreviews.info
Reviews and abstracts GLBT publications, including theses and dissertations. Founded in 1997, its editorial guidelines emphasize substantive and constructive reviews. Visitors may access the reviews by author, title, or searching the site.

Journal of Homosexuality: http://www.haworthpress.com
Established in 1974, the journal features scholarly research from all disciplines, including law, medicine, history, the social sciences, and the humanities. Divided into three sections containing articles, book reviews, and an annotated bibliography.

Lambda Book Report: http://www.lambdaliterary.org/lambda_book_report/lbr.html
Devoted to book reviewing and published quarterly. Expect to find high-quality, signed book reviews of fiction, nonfiction, and poetry. Also includes commentary and author interviews.

Women's Review of Books: http://www.wcwonline.org/womensreview
Published since 1983, this periodical includes writing and critical book reviews of works by and about women.

Databases

Books in Print
The online version of the venerable print resource is offered by a variety of vendors.

Fiction Catalog
Delivers information on adult works of fiction, either written in or translated into English. Entries provide complete bibliographic data, price, a descriptive annotation, notes about related works, and evaluative quotations from a review when available.

GLBT Life
Provides indexing and abstracts from more than eighty gay/lesbian periodicals dating back to the 1960s.

NoveList
A searchable database of fiction for all ages. Search by author, title, or keyword to find other authors or titles of interest. Includes more than 1,200 booklists, arranged thematically, and 200 award lists, with links to thousands of author-related articles and Web sites.

Readers' Advisor Online
Based on the popular Genreflecting series from Libraries Unlimited, this database allows users to search by "reading interests" (of which GLBT is one), in

conjunction with genres, subgenres, subjects, awards, and more, as well as author and title.

What Do I Read Next?
    Based on the popular print series. The 115,000 titles are either award winners or appeared on best-seller lists. More than half the entries contain plot summaries. Notation of award status, geographic area, and time period complement the bibliographic information Search by genre, subject, author, title, and more.

Internet Resources

Annotated Bibliography of Canadian Literature with Lesbian Content: http://www.canadianLesbianLiterature.ca/images/Annocanbiblio.pdf
    A forty-nine-page bibliography with lengthy critical annotations.

Big Gay Read: http://www.biggayread.com/
    A UK-based effort to identify the nation's favorite GLBT novels, the Web site includes a recommended reading list.

Books to Watch Out For: http://www.btwof.com
    Available via subscription, this trio of online newsletters is devoted to reviewing gay, lesbian, and women's books. Signed reviews average fifty to seventy-five words and include cover art, purchasing, and bibliographic data. The "community links" section contains useful, although not comprehensive, links to bookstores, clubs, and distributors, organizations, and writers.

Fiction_L: http://www.webrary.org/flmenu.html
    This subscriber-based listserv, founded in 1995, is "devoted to reader's advisory topics . . . and a wide variety of other topics of interest to librarians, book discussion leaders, and others. Fiction_L was developed for and by librarians dealing with fiction collections and requests; however fiction lovers worldwide are welcome to join the discussion." The purpose of Fiction_L is discussion and communication, so visitors should not expect to find book reviews, but rather reading suggestions. Check out the *Booklist* section to find books arranged by genre, character, setting, subject, author, audience, "best-of," and miscellaneous. Each *Booklist* section includes a "last updated" notation. Alternatively, search the archives by keyword.

Gay Asian Literature: http://www.geocities.com/westhollywood/3821/
    A listing of books with Asian content. Last updated in 2004.

Gay League: http://www.gayleague.com/home.php
    Online community for GLBT comic fans, collectors, and creators worldwide. Read about, discuss, review, discover, trade, buy, sell, and acquire information about comics. Includes a list of GLBT comic characters.

Gaylactic Network: http://www.gaylacticnetwork.org/
    An international organization with chapters in Boston, San Francisco, Washington, DC, Niagara Falls, NY, Minneapolis, Los Angeles, Toronto, Atlanta, and San Diego, devoted to science fiction, fantasy, and horror. Sponsors a message board, periodic conferences, and fan-related parties.

GLBT Fantasy Fiction Resources: http://www.glbtfantasy.com/
Fantasy and science fiction books with GLBT characters are reviewed and complemented by essays, reading lists, news, and author interviews.

GLBT Literature—Gay and Lesbian Reading Group: http://jclarkmedia.com/ Gaybooks/index.html
This New York City based reading club began in 1982 and acquired a Web presence in 1997. The recommended reading list is arranged by period and genre and contains author, title, and a one-sentence summary.

In and Out of the Closet: Fiction and Nonfiction for Gay and Lesbian Teens. http://www.epl.org
From the Evanston (IL) Public Library, this reading list provides short book summaries. Last updated in 2004.

Independent Gay Writer: http://www.rldbooks.com
This online book review magazine began in 2003 as a venue for independent GLBT writers to submit information about books, Web sites, and reviews of independently published GLBT-themed novels. Content is updated approximately once a month.

InsightOut Book Club: http://www.insightoutbooks.com
Backed by the power of the Book of the Month Club™, InsightOut is a commercial Web site primarily interested in selling books. Membership results in discounted purchases, receipt of the Club's book review magazine, and access to author interviews. As at other online bookstores, readers may browse by subject; conduct author, title or keyword searches; rate their enjoyment of items; and post personal reviews. The Club, open only to U.S. citizens age eighteen and older, donates a portion of the membership fees to GLBT causes and sponsors the Violet Quill award to recognize emerging writers.

Lambda Sci-Fi: http://www.lambdasf.org
A Washington, D.C.–based club devoted to GLBT science fiction in various media. The book section includes reviews, literary links, and recommended reading lists. The archive of book discussions dates back to 1999 and contains reading and discussion guides.

Lavender Salon Reader Online: http://www.focol.org/lsr/
Search for book reviews pre-1999, locate a book club, or find information about starting a club. Includes links to selected publishers and authors.

Marionberry Salon Book Group: http://members.aol.com/marionberrysalon/ myhomepage/
Contains an interesting article entitled "The Joy of Collecting Gay Books," by Jesse Monteagudo. This Oregon-based book club, which has met since 1998, has a simple Web site listing the books they have read each year. Prior to reading an item, a member posts a short summary.

Our Own Voices: A Directory of Lesbian and Gay Periodicals, 1890s–2000s. Compiled by Alan V. Miller: http://www.clga.ca/Material/PeriodicalsLGBT/inven/ oov/oovint.htm
A continuation of a 1981 project by the Canadian Lesbian and Gay Archives, the site offers a history of GLBT periodicals and extensive information about peri-

odicals published in North America and the United Kingdom. Entries indicate year of publication and provide Web links if available.

Prism Comics: http://www.prismcomics.org
This colorful site is devoted to reviewing GLBT-themed comics and characters and providing news and links. Publishes *Prism Comics: Your LGBT Guide to Comics*.

Queer Horror: http://www.queerhorror.com/
Dedicated to exploring the connections between GLBT literature and the horror genre, this site is arranged by types of characters (i.e., vampires, ghosts, etc.) and by medium (i.e., film, books, etc.) Includes original stories, articles, interviews, and chat and searching features.

Worth the Trip: Queer Books for Kids and Teens: http://worththetrip.wordpress.com/
Established in 2007 and maintained by Kathleen T. Horning, the librarian-director of the Cooperative Children's Book Center, this blog contains book reviews, GLBT author and literature links, and the opportunity to interact with other visitors to the site.

Publishers

Absolute Press: http://www.absolutepress.co.uk/
Alyson: http://www.alyson.com
AttaGirl: http://attagirlpress.com/index.html
Bella Books: http://www.bellabooks.com/
Cleis Press: http://www.cleispress.com/
Crossing Press: http://www.tenspeed.com/aboutus/crossing.htm
Feminist Press: http://www.feministpress.org/
Firebrand: http://www.firebrandbooks.com/
GLB Publishers: http://www.glbpubs.com/
Haworth Press: http://www.haworthpress.com
Kensington Books: http://www.kensingtonbooks.com/
Millivres Prowler Press: http://www.millivres.co.uk/mpg/
New Victoria Publishers: http://www.newvictoria.com
New York University Press: http://www.nyupress.org/
Redbone: http://www.redbonepress.com/
Romentics: http://www.romentics.com
Soft Skull: http://www.softskull.com/
Spinster's Ink: http://www.spinsters-ink.com/
St. Martin's Press: http://www.stmartins.com/
Suspect Thoughts Press: http://www.suspectthoughts.com
University of Chicago Press, Worlds of Desire Series: http://www.press.uchicago.edu/Complete/Series/WD-CSSGC.html
University of Wisconsin Press, Living Out Series: http://www.wisc.edu/wisconsinpress/books/livingout.htm
Wayward Books: http://waywardbooks.com
Wildcat International: http://wildcatintl.com/

Articles

Alexander, Linda, and Sarah Miselis. "Hear the Silent Pleas of Our Gay Youth." *Knowledge Quest* 34, no. 5 (May–June 2006): np.

American Library Association. Social Responsibilities Round Table. Gay Task Force. "What to Do Until Utopia Arrives." *Wilson Library Bulletin* 50, no. 7 (March 1976): 532–33. Available online at http://isd.usc.edu/~trimmer/glbtrt/bibthemeslit.htm.

Cart, Michael. "Honoring Their Stories, Too: Literature for Gay and Lesbian Teens." *The ALAN Review* 25, no. 1 (Fall 1997). Available online at http://scholar.lib.vt.edu/ejournals/ALAN/fall97/cart.html.

Cart, M. "Lives Are at Stake." *Young Adult Library Services: The Journal of the Young Adult Library Services Association* 1, no. 1 (Fall 2002): 22–23.

Clyde, Laurel, and Marjorie Lobban. "A Door Half Open: Young People's Access to Fiction Related to Homosexuality." *School Libraries Worldwide* 7, no. 2 (July 2001): 17–30.

Creelman, Janet A. E.. and Roma M. Harris. "Coming Out: The Information Needs of Lesbians." *Collection Building* 10, nos. 3–4 (1989): 37–41.

Curry, Ann. "If I Ask, Will They Answer?: Evaluating Public Library Reference Service to Gay/Lesbian Youth." *Reference & User Services Quarterly* 45, no. 1 (Fall 2005): 65–75. Available online at http://www.slais.ubc.ca/RESEARCH/current-research/curry/GLBT_2005_06_22.pdf.

Downey, Jennifer. "Public Library Collection Development Issues Regarding the Information Needs of GLBT Patrons." *Progressive Librarian* 25 (Summer 2005): 86–95.

Franklin, Morris E. "Coming Out in Comic Books: Letter Columns, Readers, and Gay and Lesbian Characters." In *Comics and Ideology*, edited by Matthew P. McAllister, Edward H. Sewell Jr., and Ian Gordon, 221–50. New York: Peter Lang, 2001.

Gardner, C. A. "Welcoming Our GLBT Patrons." *Virginia Libraries* 52, no. 2 (April/May/June 2006). Available online at http://scholar.lib.vt.edu/ejournals/VALib/v52_n2/gardner3.html.

"Gay and Lesbian Literature since World War II: History and Memory: Special Issue." *Journal of Homosexuality* 34, nos. 3–4 (1998): 1–235.

Greenblatt, Ellen. "Barriers to GLBT Library Service in the Electronic Age." *Information for Social Change* 12 (Winter 2001). Available at http://libr.org/isc/articles/12-Greenblatt.html (accessed February 11, 2008).

Hanckel, F., and J. Cunningham. "Can Young Gays Find Happiness in YA Books?" *Wilson Library Bulletin* 50, no. 7 (March 1976):528–34.

Hughes-Hassell, Sandra, and Alissa Hinckley. "Reaching Out to Lesbian, Gay, Bisexual, and Transgender Youth." *Journal of Youth Services in Libraries* 15, no. 1 (2001): 39–41.

Jenkins, Christine. "Heartthrobs and Heartbreaks: A Guide to Young Adult Books with Gay Themes." *Out/Look: National Lesbian and Gay Quarterly* (Fall 1988): 82–92.

———. "Young Adult Novels with Gay/Lesbian Characters & Themes 1969–1992: A Historical Reading of Content Gender and Narrative Distance," *Journal of Youth Services in Libraries* (Fall 1993): 743–55.

Joyce, Steven L. "Lesbian, Gay, and Bisexual Library Service: A Review of the Literature." *Public Libraries* 39, no. 5 (2002): 270–79.

Lafky, Sue A., and Bonnie Brennen. "For Better or for Worse: Coming Out in the Funny Pages." *Studies in Popular Culture* 18, no. 1 (October 1995): 24–47.

Loverich, Patricia, and Darrah Degnan. "Out on the Shelves? Not Really: Gay, Lesbian, Bisexual Books in Short Supply." *Library Journal* 124, no. 11 (1999): 55.

Martin, Hillias J. "A Library Outing: Serving Queer and Questioning Teens." *Young Adult Library Services: The Journal of the Young Adult Library Services Association*. 4, no. 4 (Summer 2006): 38–39.

McDowell, Sara. "Library Instruction for Lesbian, Gay, Bisexual, Students." In *Teaching the New Library to Today's Users: Reaching International, Minority, Senior Citizens, Gay/Lesbian, First Generation, At-risk, Graduate and Returning Students, and Distance Learners*, edited by Trudi E. Jacobson and Helene C. Williams, 71–86. New York: Neal-Schuman, 2000.

Norman, Mark. "Out on Loan: A Survey of the Information Needs of Users of the Lesbian, Gay and Bisexual Collection of the Brighton and Hove Libraries." *Journal of Librarianship and Information Science* 31, no. 4 (December 1999): 188–96.

Plummer, Kenneth. "The Modernisation of Gay and Lesbian Stories." *In Telling Sexual Stories*, 81–96, New York: Routledge, 1995.

Sánchez, Alberto Sandoval. "Breaking the Silence, Dismantling Taboos: Latino Novels on AIDS." *Journal of Homosexuality* 34, nos. 3–4 (1998): 155–75.

Seborg, Liesl. "Sharing the Stories of Gay, Lesbian, Bisexual and Transgendered Community: Providing Library Service to the GLBT Patron." *PNLA Quarterly* 69, no. 4 (Summer 2005): 15–17.

Spence, Alex. "Gay Young Adult Fiction in the Public Library: A Comparative Survey." *Public Libraries* 38, no. 4 (1999): 224–29.

St. Clair, Nancy. "Outside Looking In: Representations of Gay and Lesbian Experiences in the Young Adult Novel." *The ALAN Review* 23, no. 1 (Fall 1995): 38–43. Available online at http://scholar.lib.vt.edu/ejournals/ALAN/fall95/Clair.html.

Sun, H. "The Evolution of Pre-and Post-Stonewall Gay Literature in America." *Foreign Literature Studies* 28, no. 2 (April 2006): 122–28.

Sweetland, James, and Peter Christensen. "Gay, Lesbian and Bisexual Titles: Their Treatment in the Review Media and Their Selection by Libraries." *Collection Building* 14, no. 2 (1995): 32–41.

Taylor, Jami. "The Library Collection and Transgender Individuals." *Versed: Bulletin of the Office for Diversity* [American Library Association] (January 2006). Available at http://www.ala.org/ala/diversity/versed/versedbackissues/ january2006abc/transgendercollection.cfm (accessed February 11, 2008).

———. "Information Seeking and Information Use in the Transgender Community." *Current Studies in Librarianship* 26, nos. 1 & 2 (2002): 85–109.

Teasley, Alan B. "YA Literature about AIDS: Encountering the Unimaginable." *ALAN Review* 20, no. 3 (Spring 1993): 18–23.

Vare, Jonatha W., and Terry L. Norton. "Bibliotherapy for Gay and Lesbian Youth Overcoming the Structure of Silence." *The Clearing House* 77, no. 5 (May–June 2004): 190–94.

Webunder, Dave, and Sarah Woodard. "Homosexuality in Young Adult Fiction and Nonfiction: An Annotated Bibliography." *ALAN Review* 23, no. 2 (Winter 1996): 40–48.

Whelan, Debra Lau. "Out and Ignored: Why Are So Many School Libraries Reluctant to Embrace Gay Teens?" *School Library Journal* 52, no. 1 (2006): 46–50.

Whitt, Alisa. "The Information Needs of Lesbians." *Library & Information Science Research* 15 (1993): 275–88.

Wilson, Anna. "Death and the Mainstream: Lesbian Detective Fiction and the Killing of the Coming-out Story." *Feminist Studies* 22, no. 2 (Summer 1996): 251–78.

Wilson, D. "The Open Library: YA Books for Gay Teens." *English Journal* 73 (1984): 60–63.

Author/Title Index

Subject Index

PlanetOut, 288
Playwrights. *See* Authors
Poetry, 62, 344
Poets. *See* Authors
Police procedurals, 241–249
Police. *See* Law enforcement personnel
Politicians, 325–328
Politics, 46, 52, 65, 81, 92, 112, 117, 128, 152,
    155, 158, 164, 190, 200, 202, 208, 211,
    213, 218, 227, 232, 234, 242, 248, 259,
    264–265, 279, 285, 291–292, 294, 296,
    299, 315–316, 321, 325–328, 336, 344,
    348, 360. *See also* Feminism;
    McCarthyism
Pompey, 260
Pornography, 247, 258, 280, 311, 357–358
Porter, Cole, 352
Possession, 180, 190, 206, 230–232
Powell, D. A. 338
Pratt, Denis Charles. *See* Crisp, Quentin
Pratt, Minnie Bruce, 343
Pregnancy, 126. *See also* Healthcare workers;
    Medicine
Pre-nineteenth-century GLBT literature, 45
Price, Deb, 343
Prism Comics, 288
Prisoners of war. *See* War
Prisons, 215, 280. *See also* Convicts
Private investigators, 249–263
Professional organizations, 17–18
Prostitution. *See* Sex workers
Proust, Marcel, 191
Psychics, 162, 168, 188, 206, 208–210, 212, 214,
    220, 237
Psychologists. *See* Healthcare workers
Psychology. *See* Mental health
Publishers, 14–16, 24
Publishing Triangle, 18
Publishing Triangle Awards. *See* Book awards
Pulitzer Prize. *See* Book awards

Quinn, Jay, 355

Race relations, 50, 55, 57, 59, 76, 79, 93, 96, 99,
    106–107, 117–118, 121, 123, 131, 142,
    148, 150, 155, 201, 218, 234, 245, 280,
    294, 296, 302, 313, 327, 360. *See also*
    Interracial relationships
Radio, 161, 312, 348
Rakoff, David, 348
Rape. *See* Sexual abuse
Read, Kirk, 361
Reader's advisory, 27–39
Reading clubs, 16
Real World: San Francisco, 305
Redbone Press, 15, 19
Reimer, David, 364
Reincarnation, 191–192

Relationships, 50, 55, 59, 79, 100, 105, 114–115,
    124, 127, 138, 156–157, 179, 204, 211,
    220, 221, 242, 245, 250, 255, 261,
    266–267, 272, 276–278, 281–282, 294,
    296, 304, 310–312, 315–316, 322, 360. *See
    also* Couples; Families; Friendship;
    Interracial relationships; Siblings
Relationships, parent-child, 45, 52, 68–70, 75,
    77, 81, 84–86, 88, 93, 95, 99, 113,
    117–118, 120, 125–126, 128–129, 139,
    141–142, 144, 163, 258, 279, 304,
    354–355, 363, 366. *See also* Parenting
Religion, 20, 33, 49, 53, 56, 62, 82, 85–86, 91, 95,
    97, 100, 113, 116, 118, 123, 128–130, 143,
    162, 165–166, 170, 180, 183–184, 187,
    190–194, 200–201, 203, 206, 210,
    218–219, 227, 229, 233–234, 244, 269,
    280, 282, 311–313, 316, 320, 342,
    346–347, 353, 356. *See also* Spirituality
Renaissance, 186–189
Reporters. *See* Authors
Resolution on Threats to Library Materials, 31
Revelations, 331
Revenge, 47, 62, 226–227, 229, 294
Rhode Island, 359
Riegle, Mike, 140
Rising Tide Press, 15, 23
Ritual, 187, 211
Roberts, Wally, 338
Robinson, Gene, 346
Rodeo, 114
Rodwell, Craig, 16–17
Romance. *See* Love
Roommates, 295
Roosevelt Eleanor, 327
Rose, Larry, 140
Rosenblum, Barbara, 143
Rugby, 127
Running, 113, 167
RuPaul, 328, 331, 339
Rustin, Bayard, 327
Ruth Benedict Prize. *See* Book awards

Sadomasochism, 53, 62, 71, 74, 77, 84, 86, 92,
    169, 172, 184, 194, 215, 227, 229–230, 332
Sagarin, Edward, 16
Saints and Sinners Literary Festival, 19
Sarria, José, 327
Sarton, May, 327
Savage, Dan, 344
Schneebaum, Tobias, 362
Scholinski, Daphne, 364
Schools. *See* Students; Teachers
Schragenheim, Felice, 356
Science fiction, 58, 174, 176, 197–221
Scotland, 83, 115, 280, 335
Sculptors. *See* Art and artists
SeaHorse Press, 15

About the Authors and Editor

ELLEN BOSMAN is an associate professor and head of Technical Services, New Mexico State University Library, Las Cruces, and a member of ALA's Gay, Lesbian, Bisexual, and Transgendered Round Table. She is a former chair of the Stonewall Book Awards Committee and a Lambda Literary Awards judge.

JOHN P. BRADFORD, head of Automation & Technical Services at the Villa Park Public Library, has been a member of the GLBT Round Table of the American Library Association since the early 1990s. He served from 1998 to 2002 as a member of its Stonewall Book Award Committee (Chair 2001–2002). He is editor of the *GLBTRT Newsletter*, an important continuing source of GLBT book reviews, and volunteers weekends as librarian at the Leather Archives & Museum.

ROBERT B. RIDINGER (MA, MLS), is a full professor in the Northern Illinois University Libraries and has been active for over twenty-five years in researching and restoring the gay and lesbian history of the United States. Among his writings are contributions to *Gay and Lesbian Literary Heritage* and the *Gay and Lesbian Almanac* and the compilation of the groundbreaking anthology *Speaking for Our Lives: Speeches and Rhetoric of Gay and Lesbian Rights* (1992–2000).